THE SOUTHERN FELLS

WALKERS EDITIONS

Published 2015		*First published*	*First revision*
Book One:	The Eastern Fells	1955	2005
Book Two:	The Far Eastern Fells	1957	2005

Published 2016		*First published*	*First revision*
Book Three:	The Central Fells	1958	2006

Published 2017		*First published*	*First revision*
Book Four:	The Southern Fells	1960	2007

Published 2018		*First published*	*First revision*
Book Five:	The Northern Fells	1962	2008

Published 2019		*First published*	*First revision*
Book Six:	The North-Western Fells	1964	2008

Published 2020		*First published*	*First revision*
Book Seven:	The Western Fells	1966	2009

PUBLISHER'S NOTE

Fellwalking can be dangerous, especially in wet, windy, foggy or icy conditions. Please be sure to take sensible precautions when out on the fells. As A. Wainwright himself frequently wrote: use your common sense and watch where you are putting your feet.

A PICTORIAL GUIDE
TO THE
LAKELAND FELLS

WALKERS EDITION

REVISED BY CLIVE HUTCHBY

being an illustrated account of a study and exploration of the mountains in the English Lake District

by

AWainwright

BOOK FOUR

THE SOUTHERN FELLS

Frances Lincoln Publishing
74–77 White Lion Street
London N1 9PF
www.QuartoKnows.com

First published by Henry Marshall, Kentmere, 1960
First published by Frances Lincoln 2003
Second (revised) edition published by Frances Lincoln, 2007
Reprinted with minor corrections 2007, 2008
Walkers (revised) edition published by Frances Lincoln, 2017

Printed and bound in the United Kingdom

A CIP catalogue record is available for this book from the British Library

ISBN 978 0 7112 3657 8

2 4 6 8 9 7 5 3 1

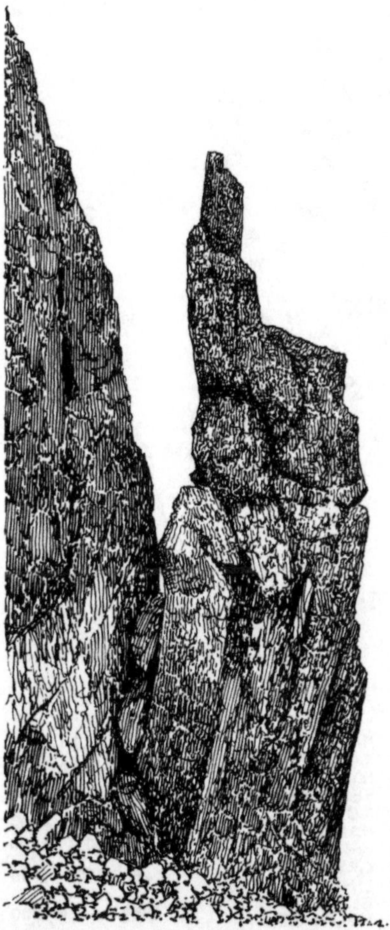

Gladstone's Finger,
Gladstone Knott,
Crinkle Crags

THIS REVISED AND
UPDATED EDITION
FOR WALKERS
PUBLISHED BY
FRANCES LINCOLN,
LONDON

THE SOUTHERN FELLS

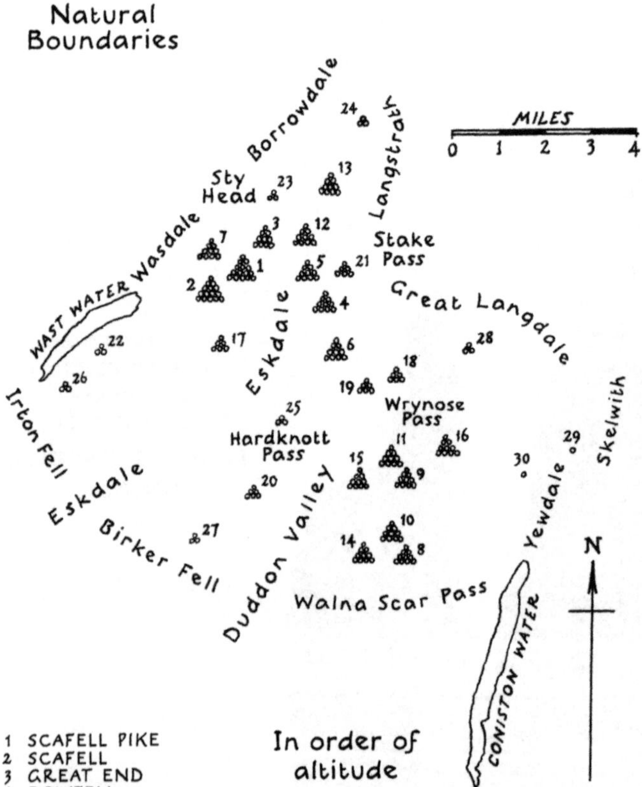

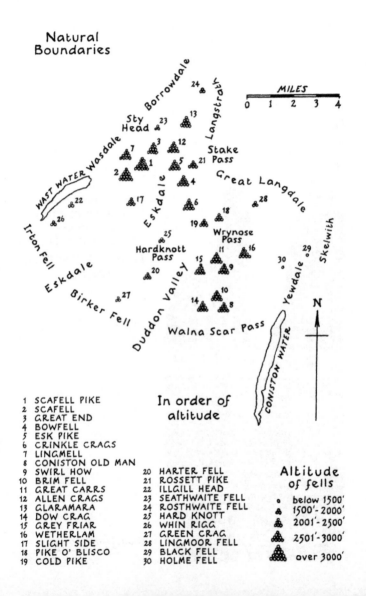

Natural Boundaries
Borrowdale
Langstrath
MILES
0 1 2 3 4
Sty Head
Wasdale
Stake Pass
WAST WATER
Great Langdale
Eskdale
Irton Fell
Hardknott Pass
Wrynose Pass
Skelwith
Eskdale
Duddon Valley
Yewdale
Birker Fell
Walna Scar Pass
CONISTON WATER
N

In order of altitude

1 SCAFELL PIKE
2 SCAFELL
3 GREAT END
4 BOWFELL
5 ESK PIKE
6 CRINKLE CRAGS
7 LINGMELL
8 CONISTON OLD MAN
9 SWIRL HOW
10 BRIM FELL
11 GREAT CARRS
12 ALLEN CRAGS
13 GLARAMARA
14 DOW CRAG
15 GREY FRIAR
16 WETHERLAM
17 SLIGHT SIDE
18 PIKE O' BLISCO
19 COLD PIKE
20 HARTER FELL
21 ROSSETT PIKE
22 ILLGILL HEAD
23 SEATHWAITE FELL
24 ROSTHWAITE FELL
25 HARD KNOTT
26 WHIN RIGG
27 GREEN CRAG
28 LINGMOOR FELL
29 BLACK FELL
30 HOLME FELL

Altitude of fells

- below 1500'
- 1500'-2000'
- 2001'-2500'
- 2501'-3000'
- over 3000'

THE SOUTHERN FELLS

in the order of
their appearance
in this book

Reference to map opposite: over 3000'	2501'-3000'	2001'-2500'	1500'-2000'	below 1500'		Altitude in feet
	12				ALLEN CRAGS	2572
				29	BLACK FELL	1056
	4				BOWFELL	2960
	10				BRIM FELL	2611
		19			COLD PIKE	2300
	8				CONISTON OLD MAN	2633
	6				CRINKLE CRAGS	2816
	14				DOW CRAG	2555
	5				ESK PIKE	2903
	13				GLARAMARA	2569
	11				GREAT CARRS	2575
	3				GREAT END	2984
			27		GREEN CRAG	1602
	15				GREY FRIAR	2536
			25		HARD KNOTT	1803
		20			HARTER FELL	2140
				30	HOLME FELL	1040
			22		ILLGILL HEAD	1983
	7				LINGMELL	2649
			28		LINGMOOR FELL	1539
		18			PIKE O' BLISCO	2313
		21			ROSSETT PIKE	2106
			24		ROSTHWAITE FELL	1807
2					SCAFELL	3162
1					SCAFELL PIKE	3210
			23		SEATHWAITE FELL	1970
		17			SLIGHT SIDE	2499
	9				SWIRL HOW	2630
	16				WETHERLAM	2502
			26		WHIN RIGG	1755
2	14	5	7	2		

30

Each fell is the subject
of a separate chapter

INTRODUCTION TO THE WALKERS EDITION

BY CLIVE HUTCHBY

INTRODUCTION TO THE WALKERS EDITION

When I finished work on *The Wainwright Companion* in April 2012 I never expected that, less than two years later, I would be following literally in the footsteps of AW on his beloved Lakeland fells. And those of Chris Jesty, as well, whose Second Edition revision of the guidebooks spurred me, at the end of 2010, to purchase the complete set for the umpteenth time – oh, how must the publishers have loved me down the years.

The full extent of Chris Jesty's revisions might surprise many people, but to revise books that were half a century old really was a monumental task. A lot had happened in the previous fifty years, and almost as much has followed in the ten years since. Typical changes in that period have been stiles being replaced by gates, new footbridges, paths being repaired – and even re-aligned – by Fix the Fells, the construction of fences and planting of trees, as well as all the usual things that happen when thousands of people tramp the fells: some paths fall out of fashion others spring up from nowhere.

I have largely succeeded in checking all the recommended routes with and without paths in the Southern Fells, despite an awful winter that restricted time outdoors following the devastating floods of December 2015 and a painful knee injury sustained in Staveley, of all places, while I was jumping down off a wall! I *was* watching where I was putting my feet but obviously not keenly enough.

Between these mishaps, of course, were dozens of walks on wonderful fells. Naturally, I was never on my own while climbing well used routes on favourites such as Scafell Pike, Bowfell, Crinkle Crags, Pike o' Blisco, Glaramara, Coniston Old Man, Dow Crag, Wetherlam and Lingmoor Fell, which is what I expected. What I didn't expect, however, were the number of times I never saw a soul while on fells such as Harter Fell (beautiful), Seathwaite Fell (the 'blue pool' fell with all those summit-plateau tarns), Lingmell and Cold Pike (both underrated) and the low-level 'twins' of Holme Fell and Black Fell – absolutely charming places that have both gatecrashed my personal top twenty following frequent visits to their delightful slopes. I'm certainly not complaining; who doesn't like solitude at times (or all the time in the case of some fellwakers)? But, putting personal gratification aside, it's sad to see so many walkers on so few routes on such a limited number of fells.

This was brought home to me while while walking the ridge between Whin Rigg and Illgill Head one sunny day. Far below, Wast Water was as blue as the Aegean Sea. AW recommends following the path that hugs the edge of 'The Screes', which offers the best selection of ever-changing downhill views in Lakeland bar none, a non-stop succession of plunging rocky arêtes falling to the most dramatic lake in the district. Yet during the two hours I spent on the route (it really is *that* good) I saw a dozen walkers scurrying between the two fells on the dull grassy path away from the edge, none of whom had the truly memorable walk I experienced that day.

To reiterate my advice from Book Three: once you have built up some experience on the fells I would urge you to get off the beaten track if you want to see the best of Lakeland! This is perfectly possible even on the popular fells I mentioned earlier. Two examples of this are included in this revision: *Scafell Pike 22* – if you climbed England's highest mountain a hundred times *via* Little Narrowcove and Pen I doubt if you would meet more than a handful of fellow walkers on this very fine route; *Crinkle Crags 5* – the new way up shown on this page visiting Gladstone's Finger is exhilarating, and it's one which discerning walkers must have been using for some time: eighteen months before I set foot on this route I spotted the path from high up on Loft Crag way across Great Langdale and marked it for future exploration.

AW said that he hoped people would use his guidebooks as a basis for their own notes; that is what I have tried to achieve with the changes made in this revision, plus, where space has allowed, I have added information that might be of interest, much as Chris did. As in the Second Edition, paths remain in red, but this time a brighter tone and with bolder lines to make them stand out more. Also, I have used three criteria for the paths (formerly they were just *'clear'* and *'intermittent'*); now they are *'clear'*, *'intermittent or thin'* and *'sketchy'*. Of course, if you would like to use AW's original guidebooks as the basis for your own notes, you can still do so so long as the original hardback editions remain in print. I'll always have a set in my bookcase.

I would like to thank the following for their help and support in revising Book Four: Maggie Allan (who very kindly researched a number of paths on Allen Crags, Rosthwaite Fell, Glaramara and various locations in Eskdale), Sean McMahon (who researched walks from the Duddon Valley aided by Dougal and Fletcher), Margy Ogg, Chris Jesty, Andy Beck, Don Dawber and Derek Cockell, plus Jane King and Annie Sellar (from the Wainwright Estate), and (from publishers Frances Lincoln) John Nicoll, Andrew Dunn and Michael Brunström.

Clive Hutchby
February 2017

BOOK FOUR

is dedicated to

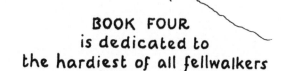

the hardiest of all fellwalkers

THE SHEEP OF LAKELAND

the truest lovers of the mountains,

their natural homes

and providers of their food and shelter

INTRODUCTION
BY
A. Wainwright

INTRODUCTION

Surely there is no other place in this whole wonderful world quite like Lakeland ... no other so exquisitely lovely, no other so charming, no other that calls so insistently across a gulf of distance. All who truly love Lakeland are exiles when away from it.

Here, in small space, is the wonderland of childhood's dreams, lingering far beyond childhood through the span of a man's life: its enchantment grows with passing years and quiet eventide is enriched by the haunting sweetness of dear memories, memories that remain evergreen through the flight of time, that refresh and sustain in the darker days. How many, these memories .... *the moment of wakening, and the sudden joyful realisation that this is to be another day of freedom on the hills ...... the dawn chorus of bird song ...... the delicate lacework of birches against the sky .... morning sun drawing aside the veils of mist; black-stockinged lambs, in springtime, amongst the daffodils .... silver cascades dancing and leaping down bracken steeps ..... autumn colours .... a red fox running over snow .... the silence of lonely hills ...... storm and tempest in the high places, and the unexpected glimpses of valleys dappled in sunlight far beneath the swirling clouds .... rain, and the intimate shelter of lichened walls ....fierce winds on the heights and soft breezes that are no more than gentle caresses .... a sheepdog watching its master ...... the snow and ice and freezing stillnesses of*

midwinter: a white world, rosy-pink as the sun goes down ...... the supreme moment when the top cairn comes into sight at last, only minutes away, after the long climb .... the small ragged sheep that brave the blizzards ...... the symphonies of murmuring streams, unending, with never a discord .... curling smoke from the chimneys of the farm down below amongst the trees, where the day shall end ...... oil lamps in flagged kitchens, huge fires in huge fireplaces, huge suppers .... glittering moonlight on placid waters ...... stars above dark peaks ..... the tranquillity that comes before sleep, when thoughts are of the day that is gone and the day that is to come ....
All these memories, and so many more, breathing anew the rare quality and magical atmosphere of Lakeland .... memories that belong to Lakeland, and could not belong in the same way to any other place .... memories that enslave the mind forever.

Many are they who have fallen under the spell of Lakeland, and many are they who have been moved to tell of their affection, in story and verse and picture and song.

This book is one man's way of expressing his devotion to Lakeland's friendly hills. It was conceived, and is born, after many years of inarticulate worshipping at their shrines.

It is, in very truth, a love letter.

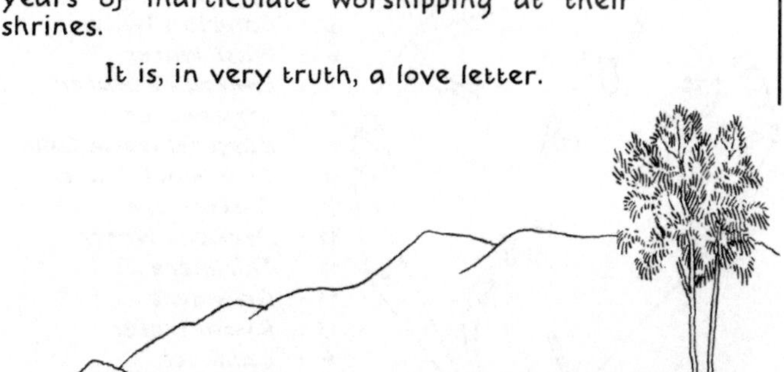

Classification and Definition

Any division of the Lakeland fells into geographical districts must necessarily be arbitrary, just as the location of the outer boundaries of Lakeland must always be a matter of opinion. Any attempt to define internal or external boundaries is certain to invite criticism, and he who takes it upon himself to say where Lakeland starts and finishes, or, for example, where the Central Fells merge into the Southern Fells and *which* fells *are* the Central Fells and which the Southern and *why* they need be so classified, must not expect his pronouncements to be generally accepted.

Yet for present purposes some plan of classification and definition must be used. County and parochial boundaries are no help, nor is the recently defined area of the Lakeland National Park, for this book is concerned only with the high ground.

First, the external boundaries. Straight lines linking the extremities of the outlying lakes enclose all the higher fells very conveniently. There are a few fells of lesser height to the north and east, however, that are typically Lakeland in character and cannot properly be omitted: these are brought in, somewhat untidily, by extending the lines in those areas. Thus:

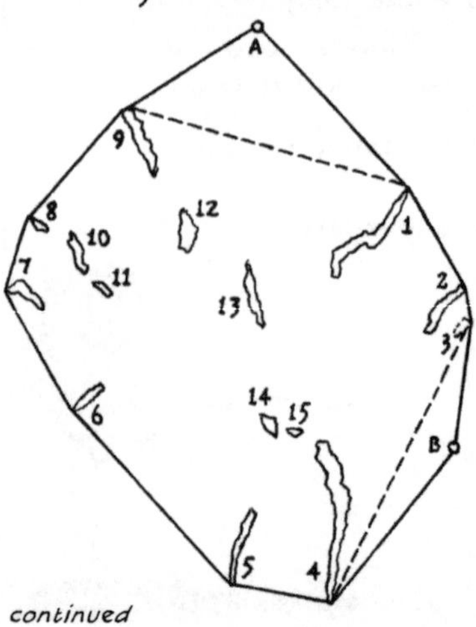
A
B
1
2
3
4
5
6
7
8
9
10
11
12
13
14
15

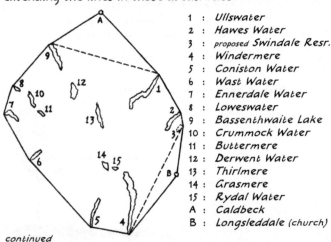

1 : *Ullswater*
2 : *Hawes Water*
3 : *proposed Swindale Resr.*
4 : *Windermere*
5 : *Coniston Water*
6 : *Wast Water*
7 : *Ennerdale Water*
8 : *Loweswater*
9 : *Bassenthwaite Lake*
10 : *Crummock Water*
11 : *Buttermere*
12 : *Derwent Water*
13 : *Thirlmere*
14 : *Grasmere*
15 : *Rydal Water*
A : *Caldbeck*
B : *Longsleddale (church)*

continued

Classification and Definition

continued

The complete Guide includes all the fells in the area enclosed by the straight lines of the diagram. This is an undertaking quite beyond the compass of a single volume, and it is necessary, therefore, to divide the area into convenient sections, making the fullest use of natural boundaries (lakes, valleys and low passes) so that each district is, as far as possible, self-contained and independent of the rest.

This division gives seven areas, each with a well defined group of fells, and each area is the subject of a separate volume

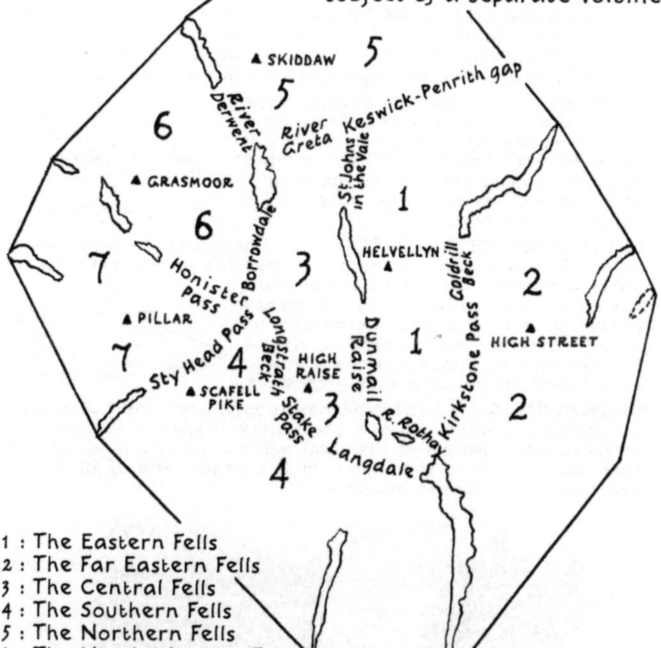
SKIDDAW
5
5
Keswick-Penrith gap
River Derwent
River Greta
6
St Johns in the Vale
1
GRASMOOR
6
Borrowdale
3
HELVELLYN
Goldrill Beck
2
7
Honister Pass
PILLAR
Sty Head Pass
Longstrath Beck
Dunmail Raise
1
HIGH STREET
Kirkstone Pass
7
4
HIGH RAISE
SCAFELL PIKE
Stake Pass
3
R. Rothay
2
Langdale
4

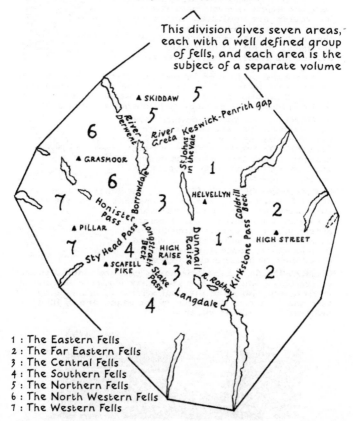

1 : The Eastern Fells
2 : The Far Eastern Fells
3 : The Central Fells
4 : The Southern Fells
5 : The Northern Fells
6 : The North Western Fells
7 : The Western Fells

INTRODUCTION

Notes on the Illustrations

THE MAPS................Many excellent books have been written about Lakeland, but the best literature of all for the walker is that published by the Director General of Ordnance Survey, the 1" map for companionship and guidance on expeditions, the 2½" map for exploration both on the fells and by the fireside. These admirable maps are remarkably accurate topographically but there is a crying need for a revision of the paths on the hills: several walkers' tracks that have come into use during the past few decades, some of them now broad highways, are not shown at all; other paths still shown on the maps have fallen into neglect and can no longer be traced on the ground.

The popular Bartholomew 1" map is a beautiful picture, fit for a frame, but this too is unreliable for paths; indeed here the defect is much more serious, for routes are indicated where no paths ever existed, nor ever could — the cartographer has preferred to take precipices in his stride rather than deflect his graceful curves over easy ground.

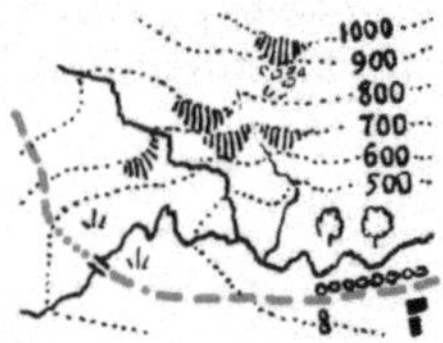
1000
900
800
700
600
500
8

Hence the justification for the maps in this book: they have the one merit (of importance to walkers) of being dependable as regards delineation of *paths*. They are intended as supplements to the Ordnance Survey maps, certainly not as substitutes.

THE VIEWS..................Various devices have been used to illustrate the views from the summits of the fells. The full panorama in the form of an outline drawing is most satisfactory generally, and this method has been adopted for the main viewpoints.

BOWFELL
ESK PIKE
SCAFELL
SCAFELL PIKE

THE DIAGRAMS OF ASCENTS ....The routes of ascent of the higher fells are depicted by diagrams that do not pretend to strict accuracy: they are neither plans nor elevations; in fact there is deliberate distortion in order to show detail clearly: usually they are represented as viewed from imaginary 'space stations'. But it is hoped they will be useful and interesting.

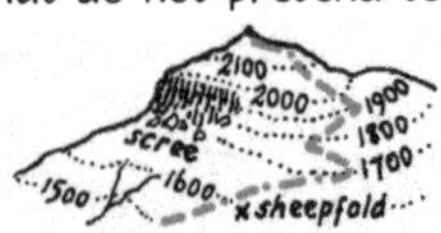
2100
2000
1900
1800
1700
scree
1500
1600
x sheepfold

THE DRAWINGS............The drawings at least are honest attempts to reproduce what the eye sees: they illustrate features of interest and also serve the dual purpose of breaking up the text and balancing the layout of the pages, and of filling up awkward blank spaces, like this:

Thirlmere

THE SOUTHERN FELLS

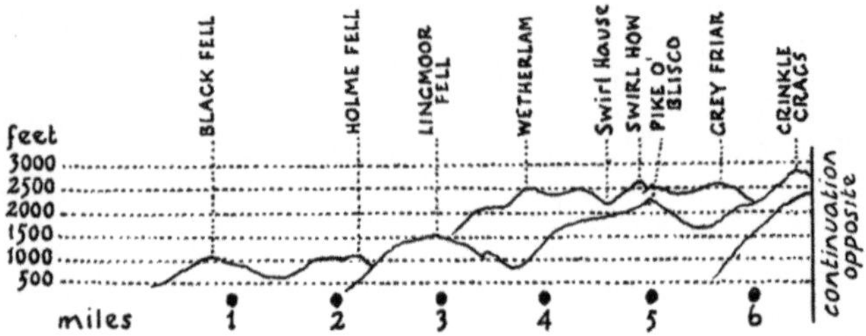
BLACK FELL
HOLME FELL
LINGMOOR FELL
WETHERLAM
Swirl Hause
SWIRL HOW
PIKE O' BLISCO
GREY FRIAR
CRINKLE CRAGS
feet
3000
2500
2000
1500
1000
500
miles
1
2
3
4
5
6
continuation opposite

The Southern Fells comprise two well-defined mountain systems.

The larger is the Scafell - Bowfell massif, which forms a great arc around the head of Eskdale; it is bounded by Wasdale in the west, and eastwards by the headwaters of the Duddon and the Brathay, while to the north the high ground descends into Borrowdale and Great Langdale. Within this area the fells are the highest, the roughest and the grandest in Lakeland: they are of volcanic origin and the naked rock is much in evidence in the form of towering crags and wildernesses of boulders and scree. Progress on foot across these arid wastes is slow and often laborious, but there is an exhilarating feeling of freedom and sense of achievement on the airy ridges poised high above deep valleys. This is magnificent territory for the fellwalker. There is nothing better than this.

The smaller group, the Coniston fells, rises east of the Duddon and west of Yewdale; the Brathay is the northern boundary. Compact, distinctive, with several summits of uniform height just above 2500' the slaty Coniston fells bear many industrial scars which detract little from the general excellence of the scenery and, indeed, provide an added interest. The dry turfy ridges are a joy to tread.

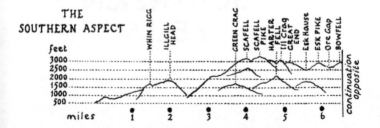

THE SOUTHERN ASPECT

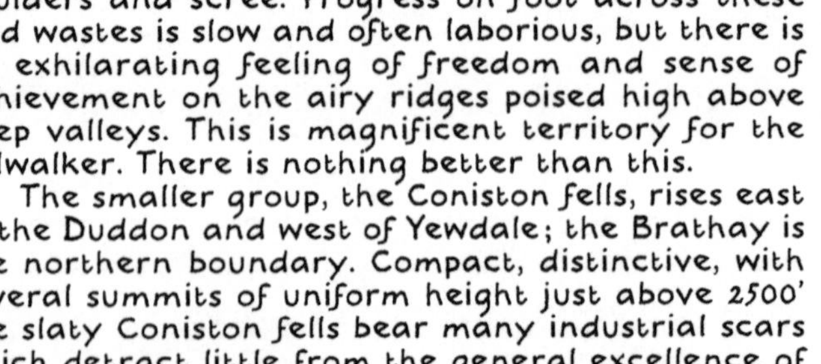
WHIN RIGG
ILLGILL HEAD
GREEN CRAG
SCAFELL
SCAFELL PIKE
HARTER FELL
Ill Crag
GREAT END
Esk Hause
ESK PIKE
Ore Gap
BOWFELL
feet
3000
2500
2000
1500
1000
500
miles
1
2
3
4
5
6
continuation opposite

THE NORTHERN ASPECT

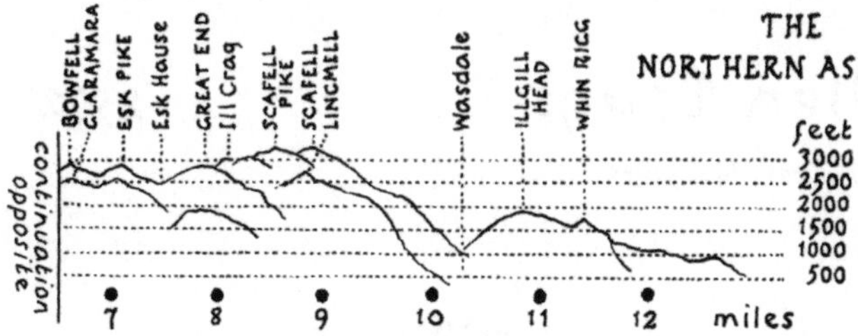

BOWFELL
GLARAMARA
ESK PIKE
Esk Hause
GREAT END
Ill Crag
SCAFELL PIKE
SCAFELL
LINGMELL
Wasdale
ILLGILL HEAD
WHIN RIGG
feet
3000
2500
2000
1500
1000
500
continuation opposite
7
8
9
10
11
12
miles

The rugged heights of the Southern Fells are set off to perfection by the lovely valleys leading into them, and much of the pleasure of mountain days spent in this region is contributed by the delightful approaches. The valleys have strongly individual characteristics — Great Langdale has glorious curves and a simple grandeur; Wasdale is primitive and unspoiled, an emerald amongst sombre hills; Borrowdale has enchanting recesses and side valleys; the Duddon has pockets of afforestation — yet all are alike in their sparkling radiance, in their verdant freshness. But precedence must be granted to Eskdale, the one valley that gives full allegiance to the Southern Fells and in some ways the most delectable of all. This is a valley where walkers really come into their own, a sanctuary of peace and solitude, a very special preserve for those who travel on foot.

The provision of accommodation is a major industry in Borrowdale and Great Langdale, and at Coniston, but is strictly limited in the remote, less accessible and sparsely populated southern valleys. In summertime, in all the valleys serving the area, the available accommodation is fully taxed, and seekers after beds and breakfasts are advised to arrange each night's lodging in advance.

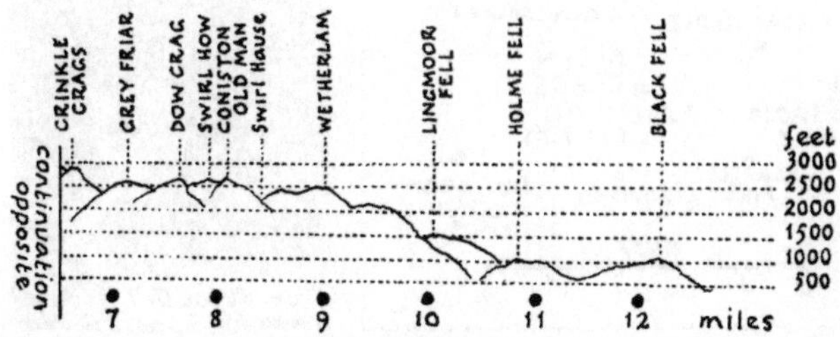

CRINKLE CRAGS
GREY FRIAR
DOW CRAG
SWIRL HOW
CONISTON OLD MAN
Swirl Hause
WETHERLAM
LINGMOOR FELL
HOLME FELL
BLACK FELL
feet
3000
2500
2000
1500
1000
500
continuation opposite
7
8
9
10
11
12
miles

Allen Crags 2572'

OS grid ref: NY237085

from Sprinkling Tarn

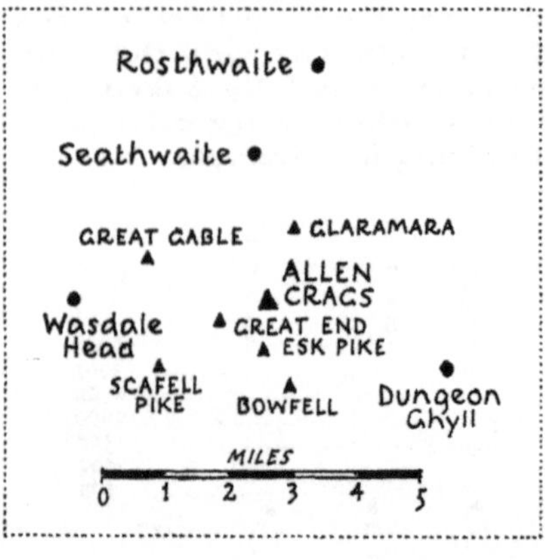

Rosthwaite
Seathwaite
GREAT GABLE
GLARAMARA
ALLEN CRAGS
Wasdale Head
GREAT END
ESK PIKE
SCAFELL PIKE
BOWFELL
Dungeon Ghyll
MILES
0
1
2
3
4
5

from Ruddy Gill

NATURAL FEATURES

Some fells there are, of respectable height, of distinct merit as viewpoints, and often in fine situations, which never seem to attract or challenge walkers and have no place in fireside memories of Lakeland: they are 'left for another day', habitually passed by, and rarely find mention in print or conversation. Such a one is Allen Crags, grandly positioned overlooking Esk Hause; it is really in the heart of things and on intimate terms with Bowfell, the Scafells and Great Gable — old favourites, glorious objectives for a day's walk and climbed many thousands of times every year. But did anyone, apart from an odd guidebook writer or other eccentric, ever set forth from Wasdale or Borrowdale or Langdale with the sole unswerving purpose of climbing Allen Crags?

It is true that the summit is frequently traversed, but only because it lies athwart the fine ridge between Esk Hause and Glaramara and so cannot well be avoided on this journey. The ridge must properly be regarded as the most northerly extremity of the Scafell structure for the Esk Hause–Sty Head path, which is often thought to mark its furthest extension, merely runs along a high shelf, geographically insignificant, across the gradual fall to valley level. The Scafell *massif* has its northern roots in Borrowdale.

The two principal summits on the ridge are Allen Crags and Glaramara. The former is slightly the higher, but Glaramara has the greater appeal and is a popular ascent. A low depression between them, occupied by a cluster of miniature tarns, is a convenient common boundary. On the crest of Allen Crags walking is simple, but rocky outcrops occur everywhere. To east and west the fell is clearly defined, with a rough declivity to Allencrags Gill on the east flank and an easier slope, characterised by grey slabs, descending to Grains Gill westwards.

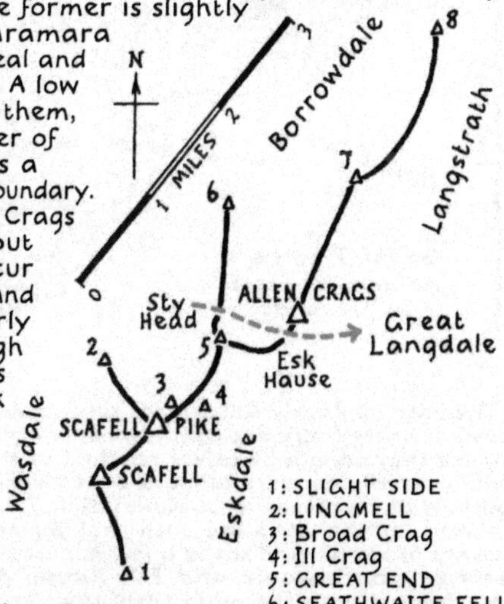
N
MILES
0
1
2
3
Borrowdale
Langstrath
Wasdale
Eskdale
ALLEN CRAGS
Sty Head
Great Langdale
Esk Hause
SCAFELL PIKE
SCAFELL
1
2
3
4
5
6
7
8

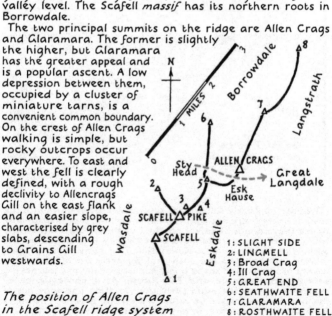

The position of Allen Crags in the Scafell ridge system

1: SLIGHT SIDE
2: LINGMELL
3: Broad Crag
4: Ill Crag
5: GREAT END
6: SEATHWAITE FELL
7: GLARAMARA
8: ROSTHWAITE FELL

MAP

Walkers proceeding between Esk Hause and Glaramara may, if desired, avoid the short rise and fall to and from the top of Allen Crags by the expedient of contouring around the western slope on a broad grassy shelf containing many small and attractive tarns: this bypass is not at all clear at the Esk Hause end (go left below the scree and look for a faint track). But the summit is too good to be sacrificed for such a trivial saving in effort.

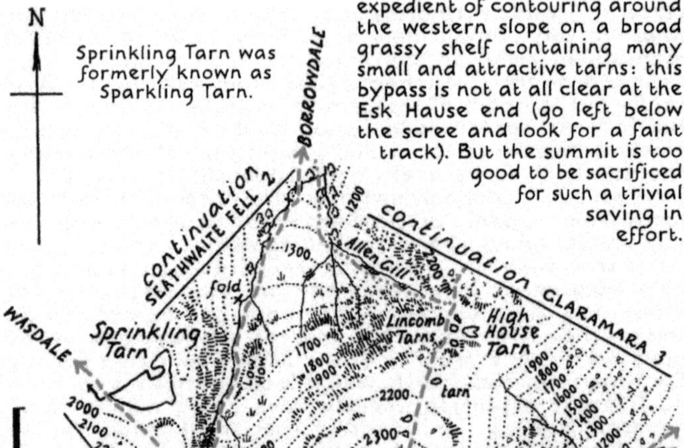
N
Sprinkling Tarn was formerly known as Sparkling Tarn.
BORROWDALE
continuation SEATHWAITE FELL 2
continuation GLARAMARA 3
WASDALE
Sprinkling Tarn
fold
Allen Gill
Lincomb Tarns
High House Tarn
Low How
tarn
Ruddy Gill
ALLEN CRAGS 2572'
LANGSTRATH
continuation GREAT END 4
ONE MILE
shelter
Esk Hause
SCAFELL PIKE
Allencrags Gill
Tongue Head
tarn
Angle Tarn
Angletarn Gill
continuation ROSSETT PIKE 2
ESK PIKE
continuation ESK PIKE 5
GREAT LANGDALE
See Esk Pike 3 & 4 for detailed notes on Esk Hause

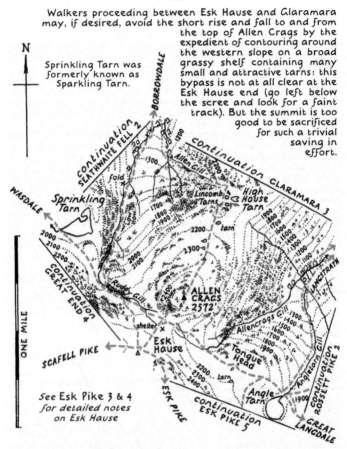

The path up Ruddy Gill affords spectacular views down into the ravine, where there are rowan trees and plants that flourish only where they cannot be safely reached by sheep. Above the ravine the stream meanders along a green valley overlooked by the path. Walkers returning to Ruddy Gill after many years will look in vain for the variation path that formerly cut off the sharp corner of the gill and saved a few minutes for anyone journeying between Borrowdale and Esk Hause. As a consequence of improvements to the main path, the variation has gone out of use and can no longer be discerned on the ground. The views from the main path are, in any case, much to be preferred.

ASCENT FROM BORROWDALE

2250 feet of ascent : 4½ miles from Seatoller
(4 miles via Allen Gill)

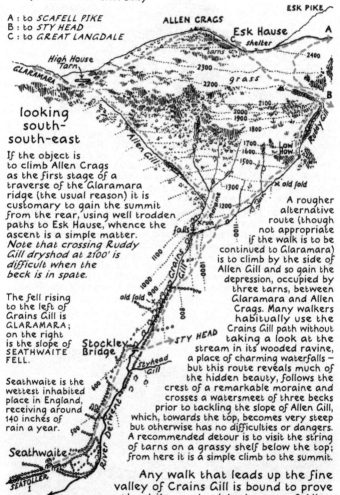

A : to *SCAFELL PIKE*
B : to *STY HEAD*
C : to *GREAT LANGDALE*

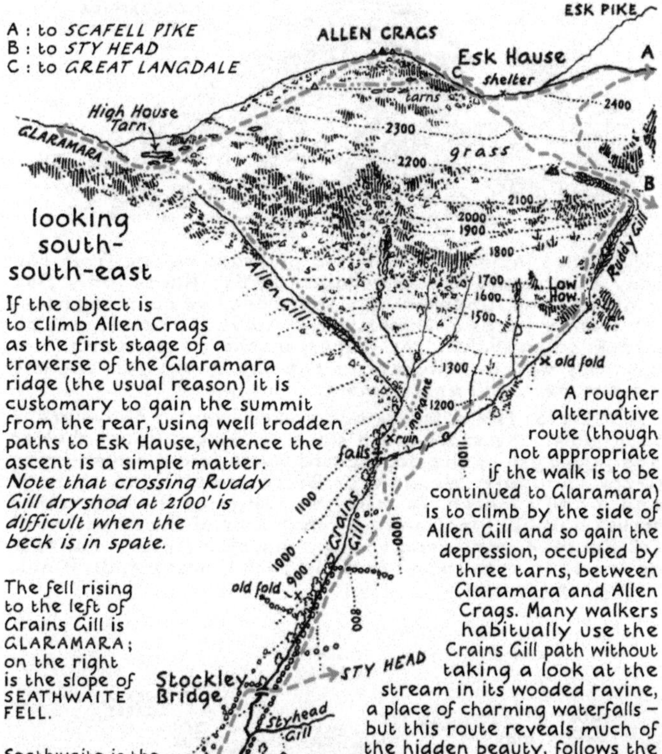
ESK PIKE
ALLEN CRAGS
Esk Hause
A
C
shelter
tarns
2400
High House Tarn
GLARAMARA
2300
grass
2200
B
2100
2000
1900
1800
Ruddy Gill
Allen Gill
1700
1600
Low How
1500
old fold
1300
moraine
1200
ruin
falls
1100
Crains Gill
1000
900
old fold
800
STY HEAD
Stockley Bridge
Styhead Gill
600
River Derwent
500
Seathwaite
SEATOLLER
1

looking south-south-east

If the object is to climb Allen Crags as the first stage of a traverse of the Glaramara ridge (the usual reason) it is customary to gain the summit from the rear, using well trodden paths to Esk Hause, whence the ascent is a simple matter. *Note that crossing Ruddy Gill dryshod at 2100' is difficult when the beck is in spate.*

The fell rising to the left of Crains Gill is GLARAMARA; on the right is the slope of SEATHWAITE FELL.

Seathwaite is the wettest inhabited place in England, receiving around 140 inches of rain a year.

A rougher alternative route (though not appropriate if the walk is to be continued to Glaramara) is to climb by the side of Allen Gill and so gain the depression, occupied by three tarns, between Glaramara and Allen Crags. Many walkers habitually use the Crains Gill path without taking a look at the stream in its wooded ravine, a place of charming waterfalls — but this route reveals much of the hidden beauty, follows the crest of a remarkable moraine and crosses a watersmeet of three becks prior to tackling the slope of Allen Gill, which, towards the top, becomes very steep but otherwise has no difficulties or dangers. A recommended detour is to visit the string of tarns on a grassy shelf below the top; from here it is a simple climb to the summit.

Any walk that leads up the fine valley of Crains Gill is bound to prove worth while, and, with the top of Allen Crags as the objective, a good expedition of moderate length is assured, especially if combined with the ridge to Glaramara.

THE SUMMIT

GLARAMARA
(main summit)

This quiet, attractive top is a pleasant refuge from the busy thoroughfares converging on Esk Hause, only five minutes away. Unexpectedly there are two good cairns on the twenty yards of level summit, that to the south, set on a rock, being slightly the higher. Patches of stones and low outcrops add an interest to the top of the fell but the distant views will appeal more.

DESCENTS: The quickest and easiest way to anywhere is to go down the short south slope to the Esk Hause shelter and make use of the good paths there found, which bring Great Langdale, Wasdale or Borrowdale within an hour and a half's march. *In mist*, the higher of the two cairns serves a useful function as an indicator of the direction of Esk Hause. A small crag to the right of the route makes it desirable to keep to the sketchy path if possible, or, if not, to proceed warily.

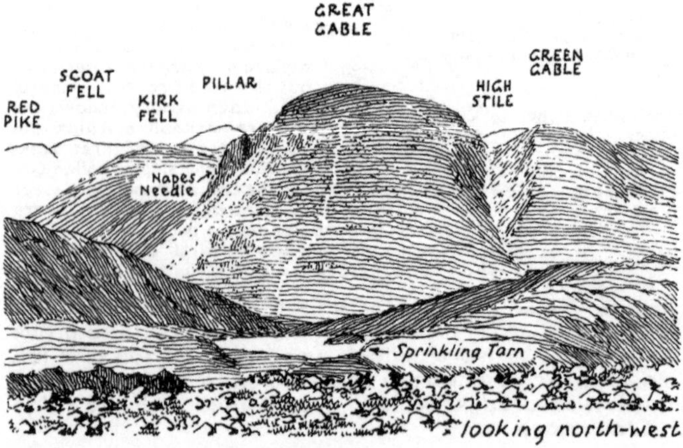
GREAT
GABLE
GREEN
GABLE
SCOAT
FELL
PILLAR
HIGH
STILE
RED
PIKE
KIRK
FELL
Napes
Needle
Sprinkling Tarn
looking north-west

THE VIEW

The high shadowed walls of the Bowfell and Scafell groups effectively close the southern horizon at close quarters (although there is a distant view to Black Combe over Esk Hause) and from this viewpoint appear sombre, gloomy and unattractive.

Interest lies mainly in the northern arc, where there is a wealth of detail, all of it pleasant to behold, Borrowdale and its environs making a beautiful picture. It may be noted that from this summit (and no other) the two High Raises are seen, one beyond the other, in a direct line, but this is hardly worth writing home about.

The furrowed precipice of Great End holds the attention, but the finest mountain scene is provided by Great Gable, and keen eyes may detect the black silhouette of Napes Needle on its steep southern slope.

Principal Fells

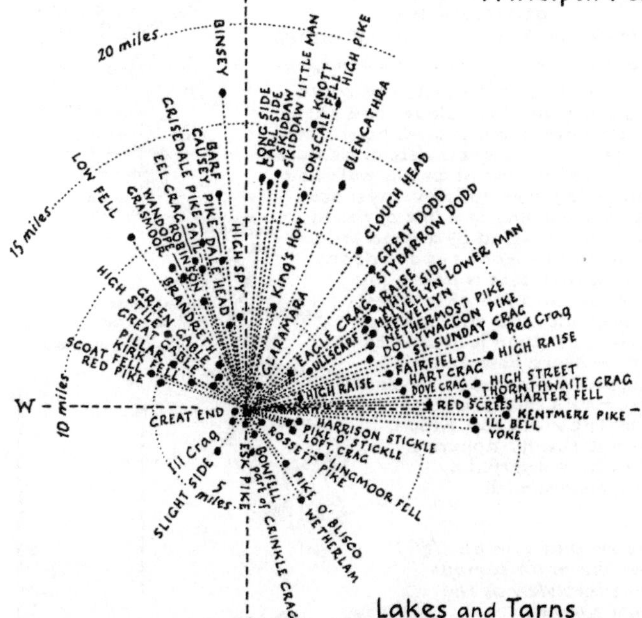
N
S
E
W
20 miles
15 miles
10 miles
5 miles
BINSEY
LONG SIDE
CARL SIDE
SKIDDAW
SKIDDAW LITTLE MAN
LONSCALE FELL
KNOTT
HIGH PIKE
BLENCATHRA
CLOUGH HEAD
GREAT DODD
STYBARROW DODD
RAISE
WHITE SIDE
HELVELLYN LOWER MAN
HELVELLYN
NETHERMOST PIKE
DOLLYWAGGON PIKE
ST. SUNDAY CRAG
Red Crag
HIGH RAISE
FAIRFIELD
HART CRAG
DOVE CRAG
HIGH STREET
THORNTHWAITE CRAG
HARTER FELL
RED SCREES
KENTMERE PIKE
ILL BELL
YOKE
HIGH RAISE
EAGLE CRAG
ULLSCARF
CLARAMARA
King's How
HIGH SPY
BARF
CAUSEY PIKE
DALE HEAD
GRISEDALE PIKE
SAIL
EEL CRAG
ROBINSON
WANDOPE
CRASMOOR
LOW FELL
BRANDRETH
GREEN GABLE
GREAT GABLE
HIGH STILE
PILLAR
KIRK FELL
SCOAT FELL
RED PIKE
GREAT END
Ill Crag
SLIGHT SIDE
ESK PIKE
BOWFELL
part of CRINKLE CRAGS
ROSSETT PIKE
PIKE O' BLISCO
WETHERLAM
LINGMOOR FELL
LOFT CRAG
PIKE O' STICKLE
HARRISON STICKLE

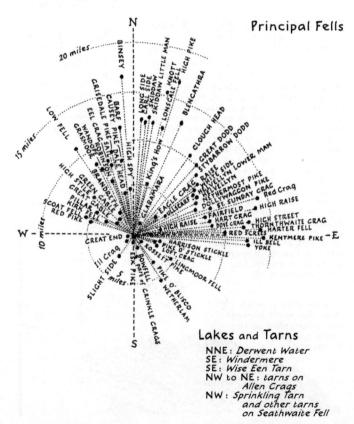

Lakes and Tarns

NNE: *Derwent Water*
SE: *Windermere*
SE: *Wise Een Tarn*
NW to NE: *tarns on Allen Crags*
NW: *Sprinkling Tarn and other tarns on Seathwaite Fell*

RIDGE ROUTE

A perfect mountain tarn (see diagram below) – a splendid subject for an artist's canvas.

Only the very brave will attempt the full circuit of this tarn at the waterline.

To GLARAMARA, 2569′ : 1¾ miles : generally NNE

Five depressions : 500 feet of ascent

A delightful walk along a fascinating path.

For the first 300 yards the route goes down an easy slope. The path is intermittent, but it gives no trouble; in fact, it gives a great deal of pleasure. There was a time when this walk had little help from trodden ways, but then the building of a line of cairns led to the blazing of a good trail, which, with its many ups and downs and ins and outs is now a joy to follow and full of interest besides making the passage much easier than it used to be. Tired walkers, however, will be disappointed by the succession of summits that prove not to be the main top, which, when it finally appears in view, is dwarfed by the second summit.

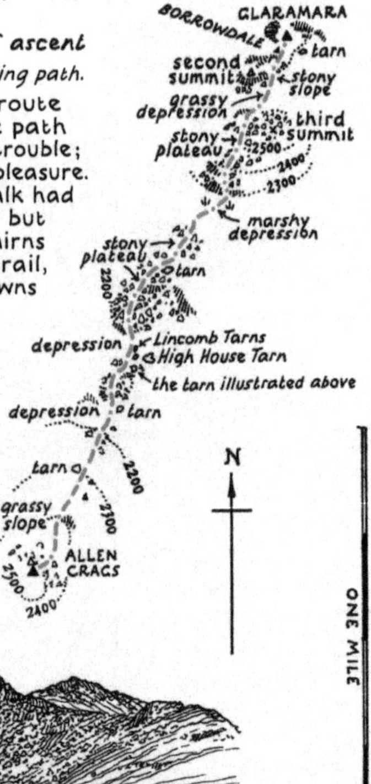
BORROWDALE
GLARAMARA
tarn
second summit
stony slope
grassy depression
third summit
stony plateau
2500
2400
2300
marshy depression
stony plateau
tarn
2200
depression
Lincomb Tarns
High House Tarn
the tarn illustrated above
depression
tarn
tarn
2200
grassy slope
2300
ALLEN CRAGS
2500
2400
N
ONE MILE

The second summit (left) and the main summit come into view as the third summit is passed.

Great End from Allen Crags

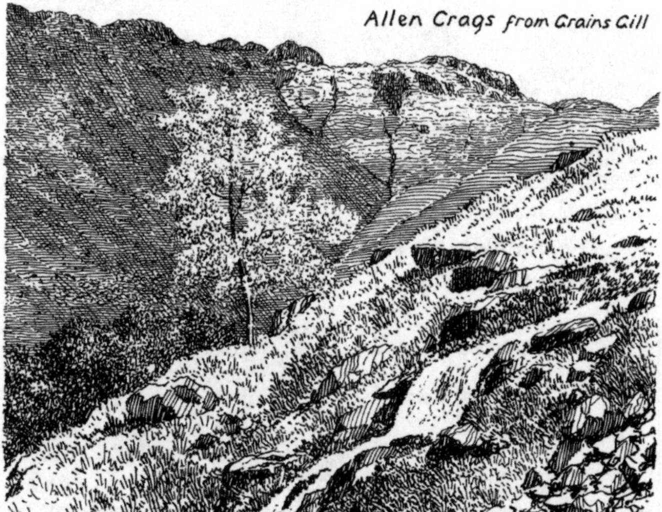

Allen Crags from Grains Gill

Black Fell 1056′

OS grid ref: NY340016

Ambleside
Skelwith Bridge
BLACK FELL
Hawkshead
Coniston
MILES
0 1 2 3 4

from Tarn Hows

MAP

The bridleway between the A593 near Park Fell and the Oxen Fell–Borwick Lodge lane is a good alternative to road-walking for persons bound for Tarn Hows from the Skelwith area.

The viewpoint west of the top of Park Fell is identified by a cluster of rocks and a holly bush; it provides a suitably photogenic foreground for images of the Langdale Pikes.

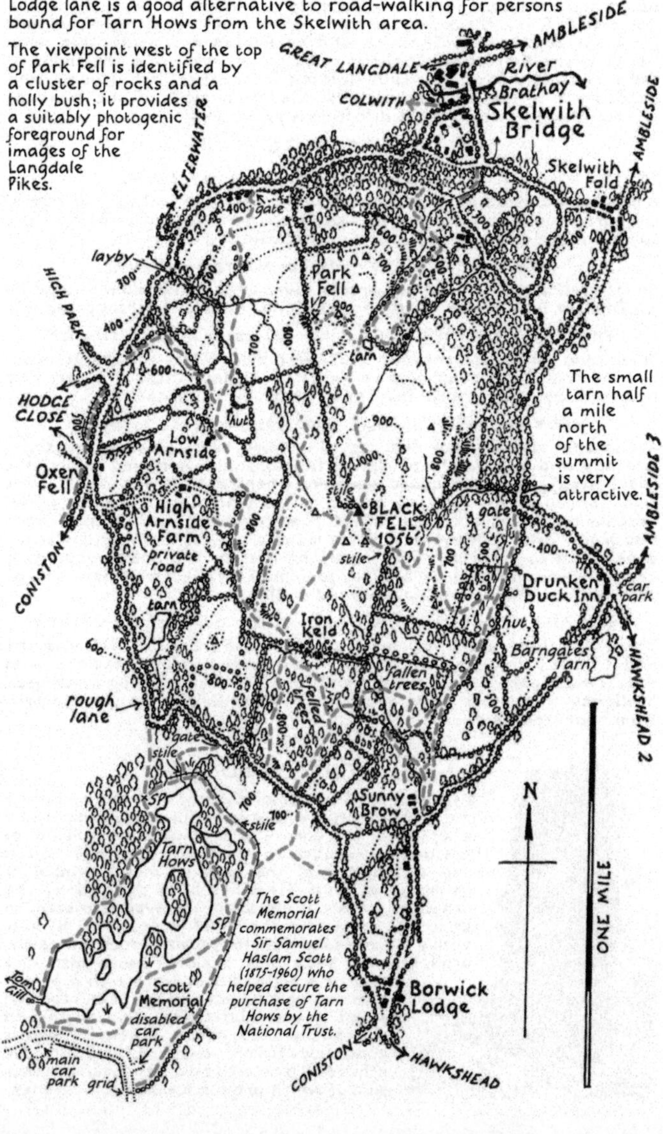
AMBLESIDE
GREAT LANGDALE
River Brathay
COLWITH
Skelwith Bridge
ELTERWATER
AMBLESIDE
Skelwith Fold
gate
400
300
600
700
Park Fell
VP
900
tarn
layby
HIGH PARK
HODGE CLOSE
hut
Low Arnside
Oxen Fell
1000
stile
BLACK FELL 1056
gate
500
AMBLESIDE 3
High Arnside Farm
private road
CONISTON
stile
Drunken Duck Inn
car park
tarn
Iron Keld
hut
Barngates Tarn
HAWKSHEAD 2
800
fallen trees
felled trees
SP
rough lane
gate
stile
SP
stile
Sunny Brow
N
Tarn Hows
ONE MILE
SP
Tom Gill
Scott Memorial
disabled car park
main car park
grid
Borwick Lodge
CONISTON
HAWKSHEAD

The small tarn half a mile north of the summit is very attractive.

The Scott Memorial commemorates Sir Samuel Haslam Scott (1875-1960) who helped secure the purchase of Tarn Hows by the National Trust.

NATURAL FEATURES

Everybody knows Tarn Hows, but few the summit of the fell rising behind, above scattered conifers and slopes richly clothed in bracken, to the north-east. This is Black Fell, springing rather steeply in dense woodlands from the Brathay at Skelwith and occupying a considerable area between the Ambleside–Coniston road on the west and the fields of Outgate to the east. It is thus isolated from other high ground, and because it is the first substantial elevation west of the head of Windermere the view in that direction is particularly good.

ASCENTS

FROM TARN HOWS – *900 feet of ascent : 2 miles*

A popular and beautiful ascent route with a choice of paths either side of the tarn which join near to Iron Keld; from here the grassy path to the summit is the easiest way up, and is delightful.

FROM SUNNY BROW – *800 feet of ascent : 1½ miles*

An interesting route through an area of fallen trees. Combined with that *via* the Drunken Duck Inn and a little road walking, this is an excellent round trip.

FROM THE DRUNKEN DUCK INN – *900 feet of ascent : 1½ miles*

Some road walking on the lane to Skelwith Bridge does not detract from this increasingly popular way up, which takes advantage of a new stile near the south-east cairn. It is the quickest line of ascent.

FROM SKELWITH BRIDGE – *1100 feet of ascent : 1¾ miles*

A beautiful way up, but one requiring some route finding. Cross the Brathay and go straight on up the lane opposite, following a footpath (signposted) beside the village community centre. At a narrow road turn right for 100 yards, then left onto a rutted track through woods which reaches a gate at the open fellside. A path rises through bracken to a flat grassy area (rowan trees) where it splits, although the sketchy track snaking up to the right may easily be missed. The paths meet at a charming tarn below the subsidiary summit of Park Fell. From here a clear path leads to the summit, just beyond a stile.

FROM A593 (CONISTON ROAD) – *650-800 feet of ascent : 2–2½ miles*

There are three ways up from the A593: those from Park Fell and the Hodge Close turn-off meet near Low Arnside, a picturesque Lakeland farm that is much photographed; the route from Oxen Fell utilises a much-used bridleway. The latter stage of all these routes follows the popular path from near Iron Keld.

THE SUMMIT

BLACK CRAG

The highest point is a small outcrop with the ambitious name of Black Crag, and is given further distinction by the erection thereon of a triangulation column of the standard pattern to which has been affixed the extra adornment of the familiar metal symbol of the National Trust. (This has been defaced by the scratched initials of visitors of the type who seem to see in this practice a chance of immortality. It must readily be conceded that, for people of such mentality, probably it is their only chance.) South-east, and lower, is a big well-built cairn with a plinth-seat: a noble edifice . It has been repaired since it was illustrated, and is now in an excellent condition. A nearby wall is continuous from one end of the fell to the other and is crossed by a step-stile, the other side of which are some windswept larches.

THE VIEW

The lovely countryside around the head of Windermere is delightfully pictured, this being the best viewpoint for the sylvan charms of the area between Ambleside, Wray Castle and Hawkshead. Southwards, Coniston Water is seen above the indented and wooded shores of Tarn Hows, which appears as beautiful as ever but a trifle foreign to the district. The mountain scene, although restricted, is good, the Langdale Pikes being especially well displayed. There is a peep of Scafell Pike, just overtopping the north ridge of the Crinkles. North, the various tops of the Helvellyn range are not seen distinctively, the mass appearing as a single mountain.

The south-east cairn

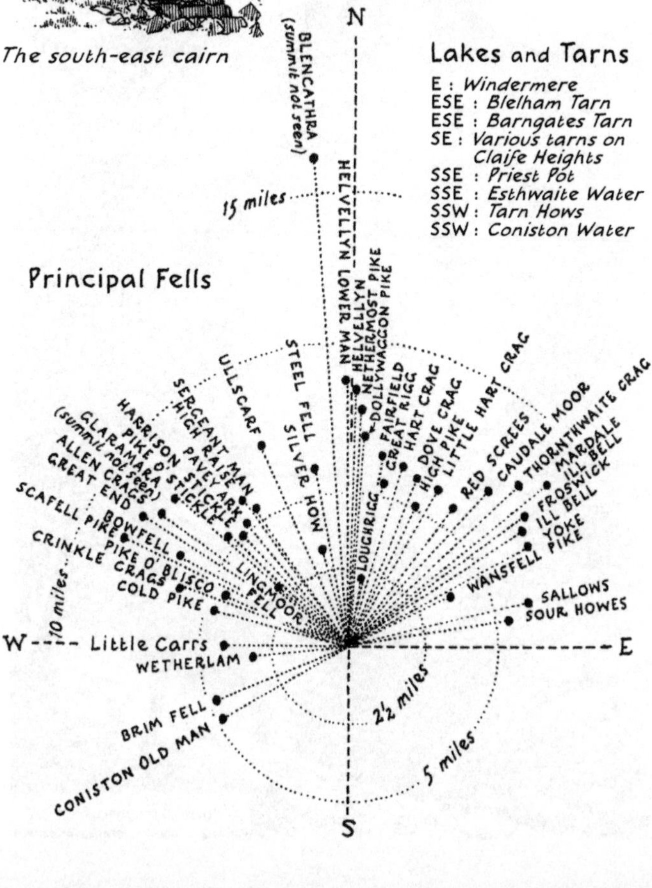
N
S
E
W
BLENCATHRA (summit not seen)
15 miles
HELVELLYN LOWER MAN
HELVELLYN
NETHERMOST PIKE
DOLLYWAGGON PIKE
FAIRFIELD
GREAT RIGG
HART CRAG
DOVE CRAG
HIGH PIKE
LITTLE HART CRAG
RED SCREES
CAUDALE MOOR
THORNTHWAITE CRAG
MARDALE ILL BELL
FROSWICK
ILL BELL
YOKE
PIKE
WANSFELL PIKE
SALLOWS
SOUR HOWES
LOUGHRIGG
STEEL FELL
SILVER HOW
ULLSCARF
SERGEANT MAN
HIGH RAISE
HARRISON STICKLE
PAVEY ARK
PIKE O' STICKLE
GLARAMARA (summit not seen)
ALLEN CRAGS
GREAT END
SCAFELL PIKE
BOWFELL
CRINKLE CRAGS
PIKE O' BLISCO
LINGMOOR FELL
COLD PIKE
10 miles
Little Carrs
WETHERLAM
BRIM FELL
CONISTON OLD MAN
2½ miles
5 miles

Principal Fells

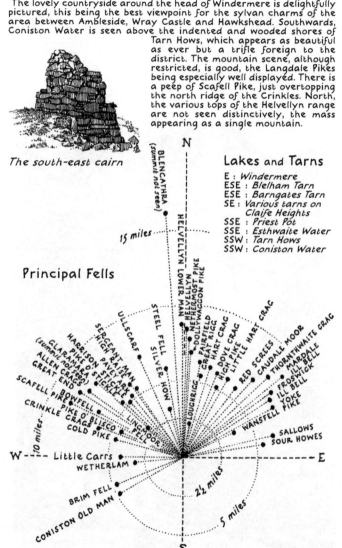

Lakes and Tarns

E : *Windermere*
ESE : *Blelham Tarn*
ESE : *Barngates Tarn*
SE : *Various tarns on Claife Heights*
SSE : *Priest Pot*
SSE : *Esthwaite Water*
SSW : *Tarn Hows*
SSW : *Coniston Water*

Bowfell 2960'

OS grid ref: NY245064

'Bow Fell' (two words)
on Ordnance Survey maps

from Lingmoor Fell

NATURAL FEATURES

A favourite of all fellwalkers, Bowfell is a mountain that commands attention whenever it appears in a view. And more than attention respect and admiration, too; for it has the rare characteristic of displaying a graceful outline and a sturdy shapeliness on all sides. The fell occupies a splendid position at the hub of three well known valleys, Great Langdale, Langstrath and Eskdale, rising as a massive pyramid at the head of each, and it is along these valleys that its waters drain, soon assuming the size of rivers. The higher the slopes rise the rougher they become, finally rearing up steeply as a broken rim of rock around the peaked summit and stony top. These crags are of diverse and unusual form, natural curiosities that add an exceptional interest and help to identify Bowfell in the memory. Under the terraced northern precipices, in a dark hollow, is Angle Tarn.

As much as any other mountain, the noble Bowfell may be regarded as affording an entirely typical Lakeland climb, with easy walking over grass giving place to rough scrambling on scree, and a summit deserving of detailed exploration and rewarding visitors with very beautiful views.

Rank Bowfell among the best half-dozen! *

* The author is not prepared to say, at this stage, which he considers to be the other five. This opinion will be given in the last pages of Book Seven.

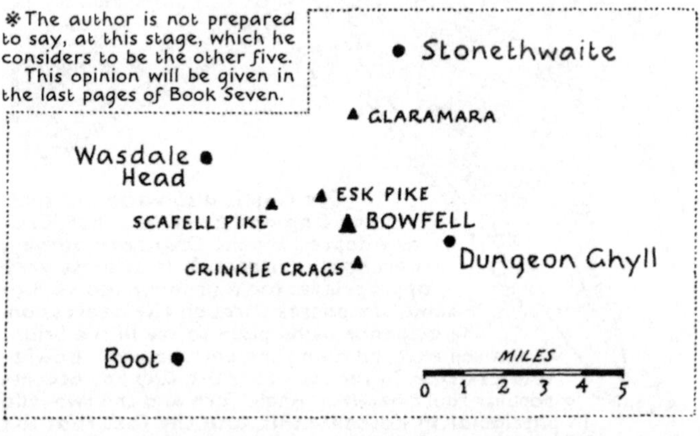
Stonethwaite
GLARAMARA
Wasdale Head
ESK PIKE
SCAFELL PIKE
BOWFELL
Dungeon Ghyll
CRINKLE CRAGS
Boot
MILES
0 1 2 3 4 5

A rarely visited subsidiary summit – Bowfell North Top, 2840' – is situated half a mile north of the summit and is marked by a small cairn. Its OS grid reference is NY244070.

MAP

Clear weather is essential if the route shown on this map from Rossett Pass south to Bowfell Buttress is followed. It crosses rocky ground on the eastern flank of Hanging Knotts and good visibility is needed for route finding.

N
ESK HAUSE ½
continuation ESK PIKE 5
continuation ESK PIKE 5
Angletarn Gill
Angle Tarn
continuation ROSSETT PIKE 2
Rossett Gill
ESK PIKE
Ore Gap
Hanging Knotts
cairns
North Top
ONE MILE
continuation ESK PIKE 5 and 6
Yeastyrigg Gill
Slate Crag
BOWFELL 2960
Green Tongue
continuation on opposite page
Hart How
Three Tarns
Buscoe Sike
Green Hole
Rest Gill
Churn How
CRINKLE CRAGS
continuation CRINKLE CRAGS 3
Hell Gill
continuation CRINKLE CRAGS 3
Lingcove Beck
ESKDALE

Ore Gap is also variously spelt Ure Gap and Ewer Gap, but 'Ore', as adopted by the Ordnance Survey, is probably correct. It is at least very appropriate, for a pronounced vein of haematite passes through the depression, the evidence being plain to see in the bright red soil exposed along the path between Bowfell and Esk Pike. In recent years Ore Gap has become a popular route between Angle Tarn and the two fells, in particular in descent; this, and the fact that the Rossett Gill path to Great Langdale has been extensively improved, has made this route an attractive option for walkers contemplating an ascent of Bowfell from Great Langdale.

MAP

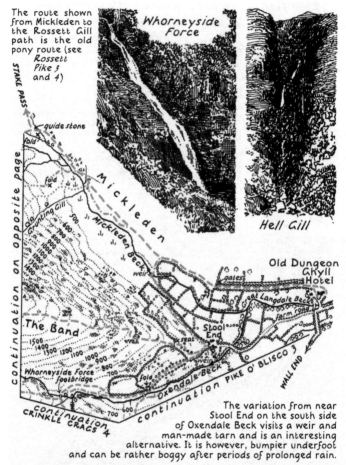

The route shown from Mickleden to the Rossett Gill path is the old pony route (see *Rossett Pike 3* and *4*)

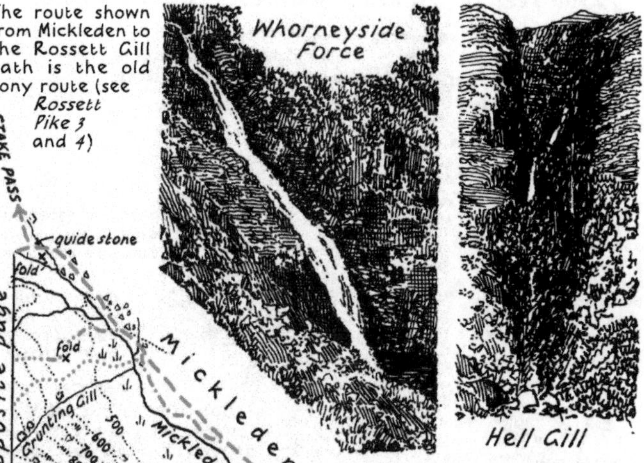
Whorneyside Force
Hell Gill
STAKE PASS
guide stone
fold
fold
Mickleden
Mickleden Beck
Grunting Gill
weir
Old Dungeon Ghyll Hotel
gates
Great Langdale Beck
farm road
Stool End
seat
The Band
weir
fold
Whorneyside Force footbridge
Oxendale Beck
continuation on opposite page
continuation CRINKLE CRAGS 4
continuation PIKE O' BLISCO 3
WALL END
500
600
700
800
900
1000
1100
1200
1300
1400
1500

The variation from near Stool End on the south side of Oxendale Beck visits a weir and man-made tarn and is an interesting alternative. It is however, bumpier underfoot and can be rather boggy after periods of prolonged rain.

Before local government reorganisation in 1974 the county boundary between Cumberland and Westmorland passed over the top of Bowfell, coming up from Wrynose Pass *via* Crinkle Crags and Three Tarns. From the summit it followed the height of land to Hanging Knotts, where the main ridge was left in favour of the lesser watershed of Rossett Pass, whence it continued the circuit of Mickleden. Thus, Great Langdale and all the waters thereof were wholly within Westmorland.

ASCENT FROM DUNGEON GHYLL

2700 feet of ascent : 3 miles (3¼ via Three Tarns)

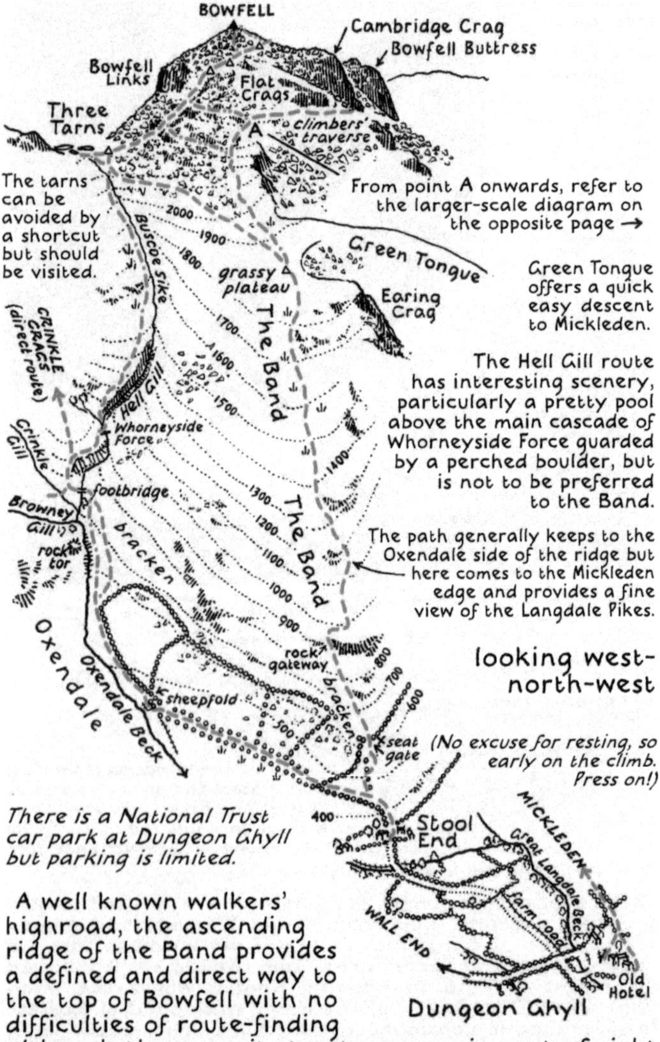
BOWFELL
Cambridge Crag
Bowfell Buttress
Bowfell Links
Flat Crags
Three Tarns
A
climbers' traverse
2000
1900
1800
1700
1600
1500
1400
1300
1200
1100
1000
900
800
700
600
500
400
Buscoe Sike
grassy plateau
The Band
Green Tongue
Earing Crag
CRINKLE CRAGS (direct route)
Hell Gill
Whorneyside Force
Crinkle Gill
footbridge
Browney Gill
rock tor
bracken
Oxendale
Oxendale Beck
rock gateway
sheepfold
seat
gate
Stool End
MICKLEDEN
Great Langdale Beck
farm road
WALL END
Old Hotel
Dungeon Ghyll

The tarns can be avoided by a shortcut but should be visited.

From point A onwards, refer to the larger-scale diagram on the opposite page →

Green Tongue offers a quick easy descent to Mickleden.

The Hell Gill route has interesting scenery, particularly a pretty pool above the main cascade of Whorneyside Force guarded by a perched boulder, but is not to be preferred to the Band.

The path generally keeps to the Oxendale side of the ridge but here comes to the Mickleden edge and provides a fine view of the Langdale Pikes.

looking west-north-west

(No excuse for resting, so early on the climb. Press on!)

There is a National Trust car park at Dungeon Ghyll but parking is limited.

A well known walkers' highroad, the ascending ridge of the Band provides a defined and direct way to the top of Bowfell with no difficulties of route-finding although the summit structure remains out of sight until the height of 1750' is reached.

ASCENT FROM DUNGEON GHYLL

The upper section, looking west

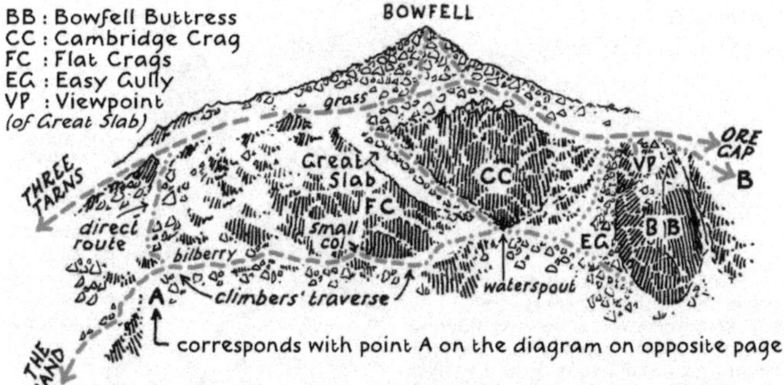
BB : Bowfell Buttress
CC : Cambridge Crag
FC : Flat Crags
EG : Easy Gully
VP : Viewpoint
(of Great Slab)
BOWFELL
grass
ORE GAP
B
THREE TARNS
Great Slab
CC
VP
FC
BB
direct route
small col
EG
bilberry
A
climbers' traverse
waterspout
THE BAND
corresponds with point A on the diagram on opposite page

The stony path coming up the ridge from the Band leads to, and is continued as, the climbers' traverse. At the exact point where the horizontal traverse commences the direct route wiggles away up to the left where there is a patch of light-coloured scree and may be passed unnoticed.

The climbers' traverse is a very enjoyable high-level route leading to excellent rock scenery. The path is quite distinct and perfectly easy, with a little very mild scrambling, hardly worth mentioning. The traverse is a series of little ups and downs, but generally keeps to a horizontal course. Except at the small col the ground falls away steeply on the valley side of the path.

The best way off the traverse to the summit lies up the fringe of a 'river' of boulders along the south side of Cambridge Crag where there is a clear path all the way to the plateau below the summit, or, more tediously, the wide scree gully between Cambridge Crag and Bowfell Buttress may be ascended. (Cambridge Crag is identifiable, beyond all doubt, by the waterspout gushing from the base or the cliff — and nothing better ever came out of a barrel or a bottle.)

The climbers' traverse

The striations of Flat Crags are of particular interest, even to non-geologists. Note how the angle of tilt is repeated in the slope of the Great Slab.

ASCENT FROM WASDALE

Although Bowfell is well hidden from Wasdale Head it is not too distant to be climbed from there in comfortable time, but the walk has the disadvantage (for those who object to retracing footsteps) that very little variation of route is possible on the return journey to Wasdale Head. Esk Pike stands in the way and must be climbed first (and traversed later).

For a diagram of the ascent of Esk Pike from Wasdale Head see Esk Pike 8.

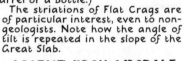

ASCENT FROM MICKLEDEN

2500 feet of ascent : 1¾ miles from the sheepfold

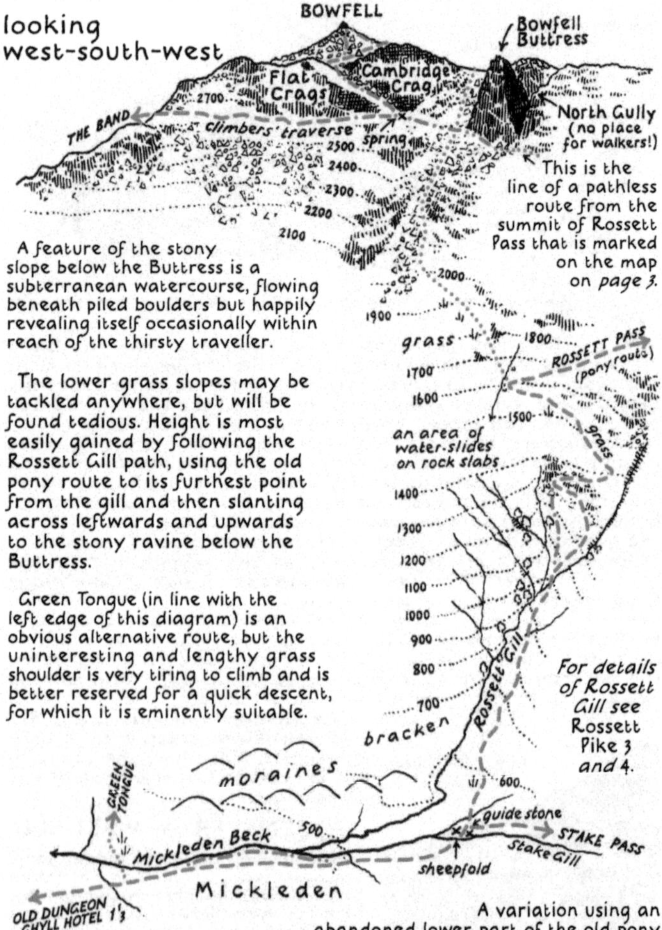

looking west-south-west
BOWFELL
Bowfell Buttress
Flat Crags
Cambridge Crag
2700
THE BAND
climbers' traverse
spring
North Gully (no place for walkers!)
2500
2400
2300
2200
2100
This is the line of a pathless route from the summit of Rossett Pass that is marked on the map on page 3.
2000
1900
grass
1800
ROSSETT PASS (pony route)
1700
1600
1500
grass
an area of water-slides on rock slabs
1400
1300
1200
1100
1000
900
800
700
Rossett Gill
For details of Rossett Gill see Rossett Pike 3 and 4.
bracken
moraines
600
GREEN TONGUE
500
guide stone
STAKE PASS
Mickleden Beck
Stake Gill
sheepfold
Mickleden
OLD DUNGEON GHYLL HOTEL 1⅓

A feature of the stony slope below the Buttress is a subterranean watercourse, flowing beneath piled boulders but happily revealing itself occasionally within reach of the thirsty traveller.

The lower grass slopes may be tackled anywhere, but will be found tedious. Height is most easily gained by following the Rossett Gill path, using the old pony route to its furthest point from the gill and then slanting across leftwards and upwards to the stony ravine below the Buttress.

Green Tongue (in line with the left edge of this diagram) is an obvious alternative route, but the uninteresting and lengthy grass shoulder is very tiring to climb and is better reserved for a quick descent, for which it is eminently suitable.

A variation using an abandoned lower part of the old pony route to the second zig-zag is shown on *Rossett Pike 3*.

The Mickleden face, 2500 feet of continuous ascent, is a route for scramblers rather than walkers. The rock scenery becomes imposing as height is gained, Bowfell Buttress in particular being an impressive object when seen at close quarters.

ASCENT FROM ESKDALE

2900 feet of ascent : $7\frac{1}{2}$ miles from Boot

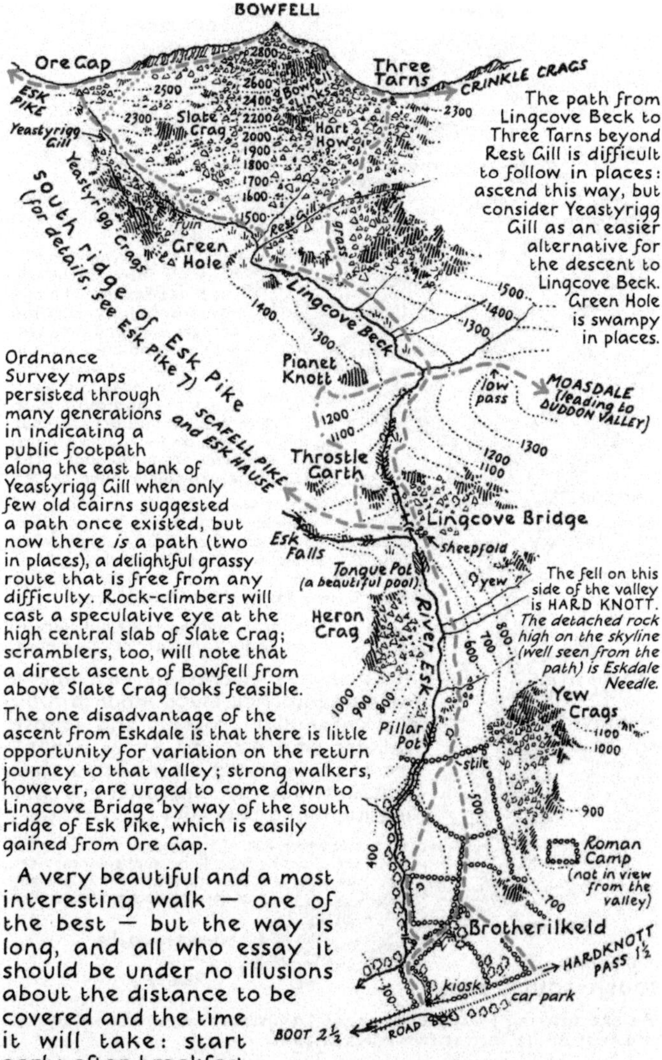
BOWFELL
Ore Gap
ESK PIKE
Three Tarns
CRINKLE CRAGS
Bowfell Links
Slate Crag
Hart How
Yeastyrigg Gill
Yeastyrigg Crags
ruin
Green Hole
Rest Gill
grass
south ridge of Esk Pike
(for details, see Esk Pike 7)
Lingcove Beck
Pianet Knott
low pass
MOASDALE (leading to DUDDON VALLEY)
SCAFELL PIKE and ESK HAUSE
Throstle Garth
Lingcove Bridge
sheepfold
Esk Falls
Tongue Pot (a beautiful pool)
yew
Heron Crag
River Esk
Yew Crags
Pillar Pot
stile
Roman Camp
(not in view from the valley)
Brotherilkeld
HARDKNOTT PASS $1\frac{1}{2}$
kiosk
car park
BOOT $2\frac{1}{2}$
ROAD

The path from Lingcove Beck to Three Tarns beyond Rest Gill is difficult to follow in places: ascend this way, but consider Yeastyrigg Gill as an easier alternative for the descent to Lingcove Beck. Green Hole is swampy in places.

Ordnance Survey maps persisted through many generations in indicating a public footpath along the east bank of Yeastyrigg Gill when only few old cairns suggested a path once existed, but now there *is* a path (two in places), a delightful grassy route that is free from any difficulty. Rock-climbers will cast a speculative eye at the high central slab of Slate Crag; scramblers, too, will note that a direct ascent of Bowfell from above Slate Crag looks feasible.

The fell on this side of the valley is HARD KNOTT. *The detached rock high on the skyline (well seen from the path) is Eskdale Needle.*

The one disadvantage of the ascent from Eskdale is that there is little opportunity for variation on the return journey to that valley; strong walkers, however, are urged to come down to Lingcove Bridge by way of the south ridge of Esk Pike, which is easily gained from Ore Gap.

A very beautiful and a most interesting walk — one of the best — but the way is long, and all who essay it should be under no illusions about the distance to be covered and the time it will take: start early after breakfast or be late for supper.

looking north-north-east

ASCENT FROM STONETHWAITE

2650 feet of ascent : 6½ miles

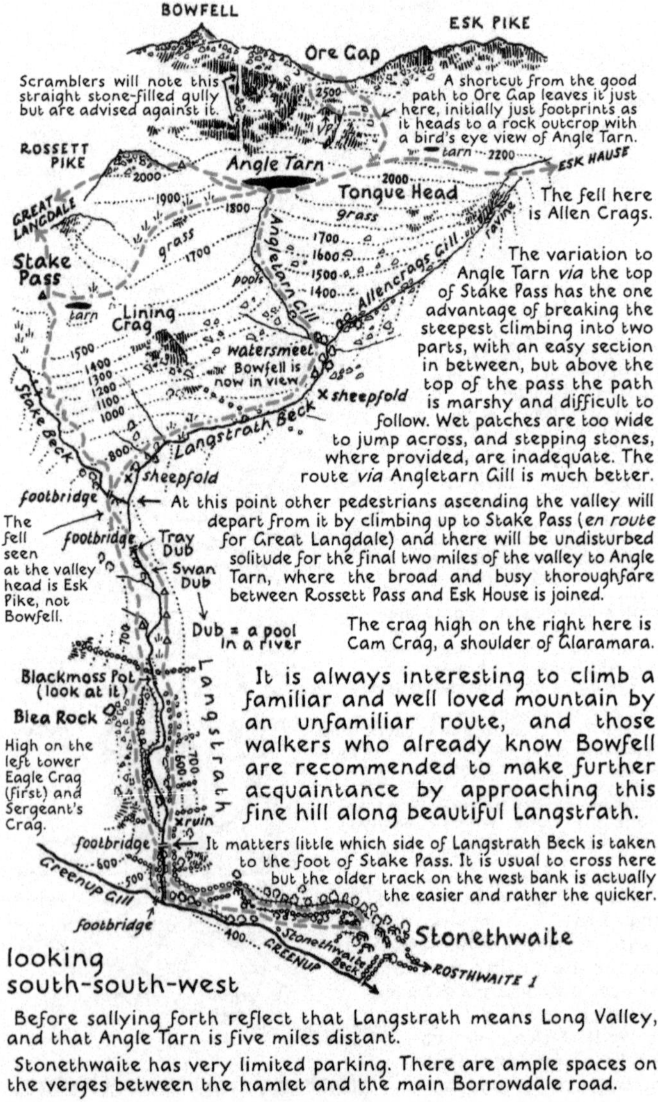
BOWFELL
ESK PIKE
Ore Gap
Scramblers will note this straight stone-filled gully but are advised against it.
2500
A shortcut from the good path to Ore Gap leaves it just here, initially just footprints as it heads to a rock outcrop with a bird's eye view of Angle Tarn.
ROSSETT PIKE
tarn
2200
ESK HAUSE
Angle Tarn
2000
2000
Tongue Head
The fell here is Allen Crags.
GREAT LANGDALE
1900
1800
grass
grass
1700
ravine
Angletarn Gill
1700
1600
1500
1400
Allencrags Gill
Stake Pass
pools
The variation to Angle Tarn *via* the top of Stake Pass has the one advantage of breaking the steepest climbing into two parts, with an easy section in between, but above the top of the pass the path is marshy and difficult to follow. Wet patches are too wide to jump across, and stepping stones, where provided, are inadequate. The route *via* Angletarn Gill is much better.
tarn
Lining Crag
watersmeet
Bowfell is now in view
1500
1400
1300
1200
1100
1000
x sheepfold
Stake Beck
Langstrath Beck
800
x sheepfold
footbridge
At this point other pedestrians ascending the valley will depart from it by climbing up to Stake Pass (*en route* for Great Langdale) and there will be undisturbed solitude for the final two miles of the valley to Angle Tarn, where the broad and busy thoroughfare between Rossett Pass and Esk House is joined.
The fell seen at the valley head is Esk Pike, not Bowfell.
footbridge
Tray Dub
Swan Dub
Dub = a pool in a river
The crag high on the right here is Cam Crag, a shoulder of Glaramara.
700
Blackmoss Pot (look at it)
Blea Rock
Langstrath
High on the left tower Eagle Crag (first) and Sergeant's Crag.
700
600
x ruin
footbridge
It matters little which side of Langstrath Beck is taken to the foot of Stake Pass. It is usual to cross here but the older track on the west bank is actually the easier and rather the quicker.
600
500
Greenup Gill
footbridge
400
Stonethwaite Beck
GREENUP
Stonethwaite
ROSTHWAITE 1
looking south-south-west

It is always interesting to climb a familiar and well loved mountain by an unfamiliar route, and those walkers who already know Bowfell are recommended to make further acquaintance by approaching this fine hill along beautiful Langstrath.

Before sallying forth reflect that Langstrath means Long Valley, and that Angle Tarn is five miles distant.

Stonethwaite has very limited parking. There are ample spaces on the verges between the hamlet and the main Borrowdale road.

Cambridge Crag and Bowfell Buttress from the top of the Great Slab

THE SUMMIT

Bowfell's top is a shattered pyramid, a great heap of stones and boulders and naked rock, a giant cairn in itself.

The rugged summit provides poor picking for the Bowfell sheep, who draw the line at mosses and lichens and look elsewhere for their mountain greenery, and reserves its best rewards for the walkers who climb the natural rocky stairway to its upper limit for here, spread before them for their delectation, is a glorious panorama, which, moreover, may be surveyed and appreciated from positions of repose on the comfortable flat seats of stone (comfortable in the sense that everybody arriving here says how nice it is to sit down) with which the summit is liberally equipped. The leisurely contemplation of the scene will not be assailed by doubts as to whether the highest point has in fact been gained for rough slopes tumble away steeply on all sides.

The top pyramid stands on a sloping plinth which, to the east, extends beyond the base of the pyramid and forms a shelf or terrace where stones are less in evidence. It is from this shelf that Bowfell's main crags fall away, and from which, with care, they may be viewed; care is necessary because the boulders to be negotiated in carrying out this inspection are in a state of balance, in places, and liable to heel over and trap a leg.

It is possible, and does happen, that walkers ascend Bowfell and traverse its top quite unaware of the imposing line of crags overlooking Mickleden: from the summit and the shelf track there is little to indicate the presence of steep cliffs. But to miss seeing the crags is to miss seeing half the glory of Bowfell.

THE SUMMIT

continued

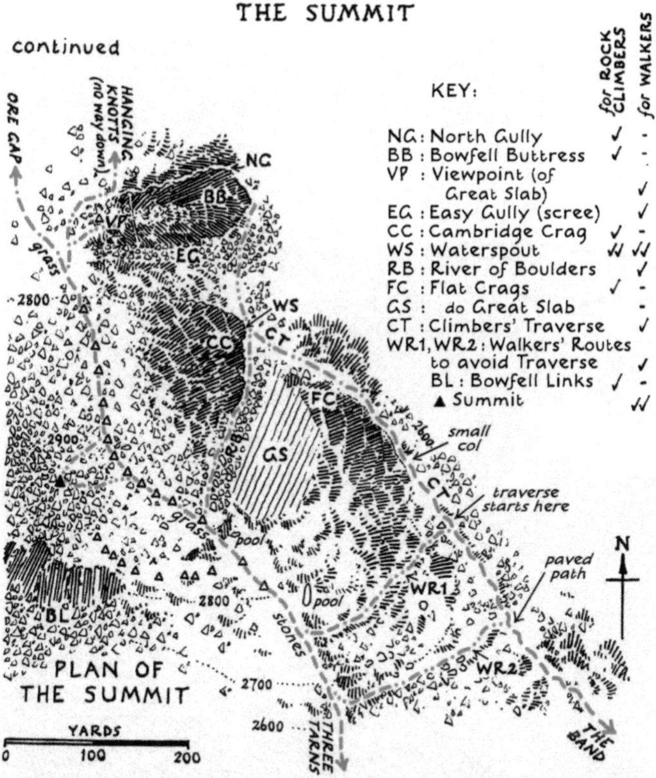
KEY:
for ROCK CLIMBERS
for WALKERS
NG : North Gully ✓ -
BB : Bowfell Buttress ✓ -
VP : Viewpoint (of Great Slab) ✓
EG : Easy Gully (scree) ✓
CC : Cambridge Crag ✓ -
WS : Waterspout ✓✓ ✓✓
RB : River of Boulders ✓
FC : Flat Crags ✓ -
GS : do Great Slab -
CT : Climbers' Traverse ✓
WR1, WR2 : Walkers' Routes to avoid Traverse ✓
BL : Bowfell Links ✓ -
▲ Summit ✓✓
ORE GAP
HANGING KNOTTS (no way down)
NG
BB
VP
EG
grass
2800
WS
CT
CC
FC
2600
small col
GS
RB
2900
traverse starts here
grass
pool
N
paved path
WR1
2800
pool
BL
stones
WR2
PLAN OF THE SUMMIT
2700
2600
THREE TARNS
THE BAND
YARDS
0
100
200

DESCENTS : The sloping grass shelf, east of the actual summit, carries the only cairned route across the top. It links the path to Ore Gap with that to Three Tarns, and each cairn is visible from the last. There is a further line of cairns to the south of the summit, but this cannot be seen from the summit or from the path from Three Tarns. For Langdale the steep lower section of the Three Tarns path may be avoided by using a terrace on the left at a gap in the wall of rocks (WR1 on the plan above), which leads to the start of the Climbers' Traverse. A similar gap lower down (WR2) also has a sketchy path but this is not so good underfoot as WR1 and is hardly any quicker than descending to Three Tarns. Neither of these routes is difficult to locate in good visibility. Direct descents to Eskdale over the steepening boulder slopes are not feasible.

In mist, the only safe objectives are Ore Gap (for Wasdale, Borrowdale or Eskdale) and Three Tarns (for Langdale *via* the Band, or Eskdale) avoiding Bowfell Links on the way thereto.

The Great Slab of Flat Crags

RIDGE ROUTES

To CRINKLE CRAGS, 2816′ : 1½ miles
SE, E, SE and then generally S
Main depression (Three Tarns) at 2320′
600 feet of ascent

BOWFELL
Flat Crags
2600
2500
2400
Bowfell Links
Three Tarns
2300
2400
2500
2600
tarn
Shelter Crags
2600
2700
CRINKLE CRAGS

A rough ridge-walk of high quality.

A beeline for Three Tarns runs foul of Bowfell Links, and the summit notes should be consulted for getting down to the gap. From there onwards the gradual climb to Crinkle Crags, with its many turns and twists and ups and downs is entirely delightful, *but not in mist.* (See *Crinkle Crags 13.*)

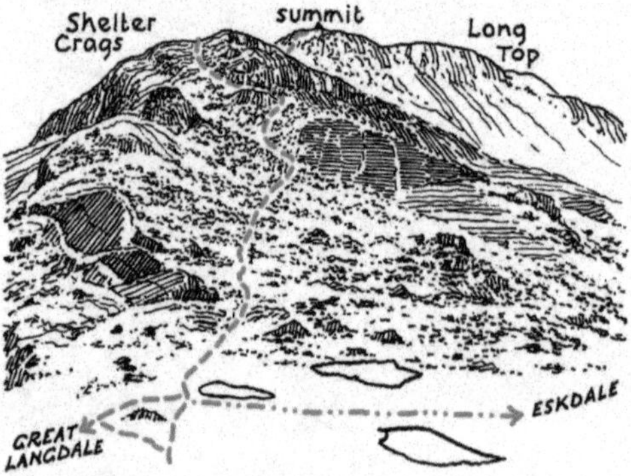
Shelter Crags
summit
Long Top
GREAT LANGDALE
ESKDALE

Crinkle Crags, as seen on the descent to Three Tarns from the summit of Bowfell. The path is indicated. The first three Crinkles are hidden behind Shelter Crags.

N
ONE MILE
ESK PIKE
2600
2700
Hanging Knotts
Ore Gap
2600
2500
top of North Gully
top of Easy Gully
BOWFELL

To ESK PIKE, 2903′ : 1 mile
NW, W and NW
Depression (Ore Gap) at 2575′
340 feet of ascent

A straightforward, rather rough, walk.

The path going up Esk Pike from Ore Gap is visible from afar, but the way thereto across Bowfell's stony top is less clearly marked but well indicated by cairns. Turn aside to look down the wide gully (*Easy Gully*) south of *Bowfell Buttress*; the more impressive *North Gully* may also be reached by a short and easy detour.

Three views from the Band

Right:
Browney Gill and Cold Pike

Bottom Right:
Pike o' Blisco

Below:
Pike o' Stickle

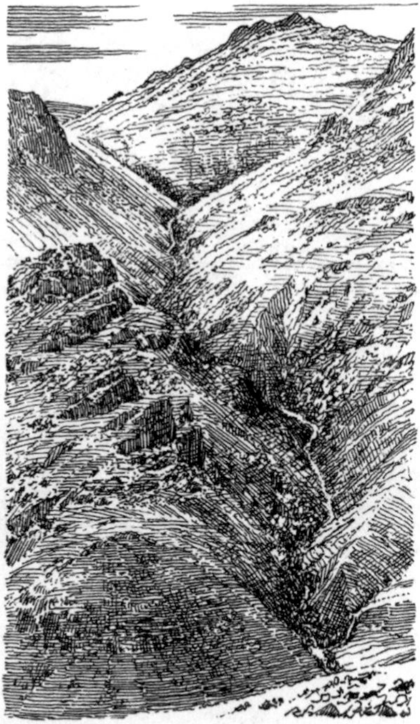

THE VIEW

(with distances in miles)

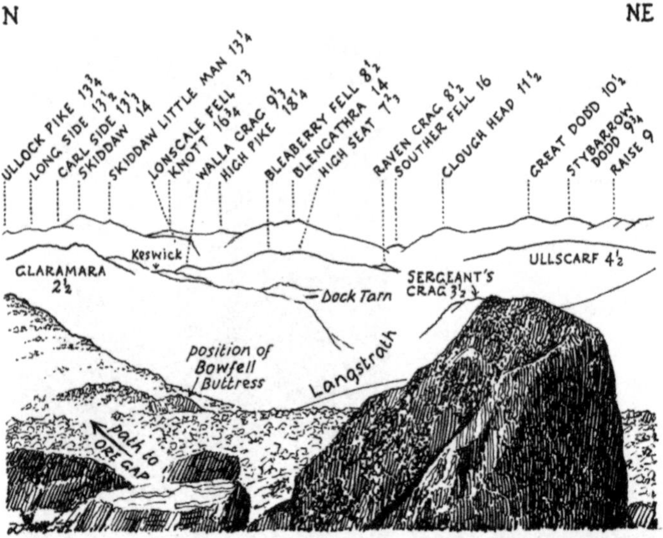
N
NE
ULLOCK PIKE 13¾
LONG SIDE 13½
CARL SIDE 13⅓
SKIDDAW 14
SKIDDAW LITTLE MAN 13¼
LONSCALE FELL 13
KNOTT 16¾
WALLA CRAG 9⅓
HIGH PIKE 18¼
BLEABERRY FELL 8½
BLENCATHRA 14
HIGH SEAT 7⅔
RAVEN CRAG 8½
SOUTHER FELL 16
CLOUGH HEAD 11½
GREAT DODD 10½
STYBARROW DODD 9¾
RAISE 9
Keswick
GLARAMARA 2½
ULLSCARF 4½
SERGEANT'S CRAG 3½
Dock Tarn
position of Bowfell Buttress
Langstrath
path to ORE GAP

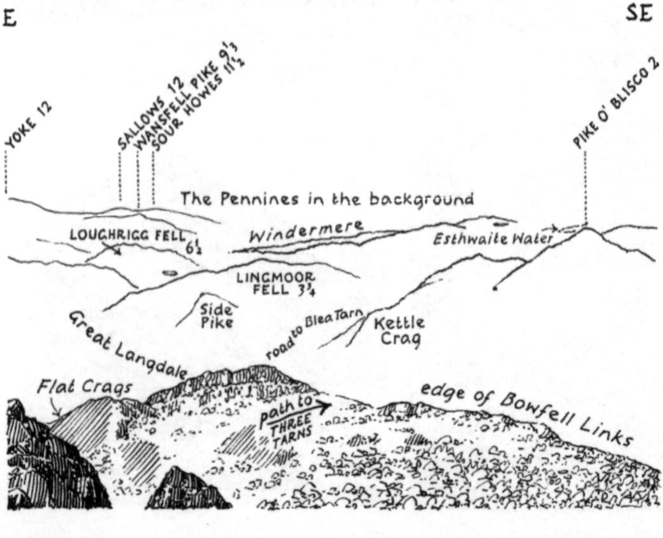
E
SE
YOKE 12
SALLOWS 12
WANSFELL PIKE 9⅓
SOUR HOWES 11½
PIKE O' BLISCO 2
The Pennines in the background
LOUGHRIGG FELL 6½
Windermere
Esthwaite Water
LINGMOOR FELL 3¾
Side Pike
road to Blea Tarn
Kettle Crag
Great Langdale
Flat Crags
path to THREE TARNS
edge of Bowfell Links

THE VIEW

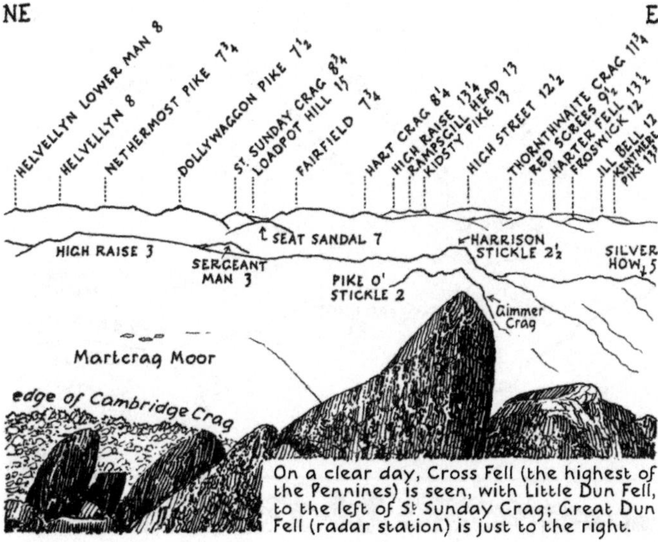
NE
E
HELVELLYN LOWER MAN 8
HELVELLYN 8
NETHERMOST PIKE 7¾
DOLLYWAGGON PIKE 7½
St SUNDAY CRAG 8¾
LOADPOT HILL 15
FAIRFIELD 7¾
HART CRAG 8¼
HIGH RAISE 13¾
RAMPSGILL HEAD 13
KIDSTY PIKE 13
HIGH STREET 12½
THORNTHWAITE CRAG 11¾
RED SCREES 9½
HARTER FELL 13½
FROSWICK 12
ILL BELL 12
KENTMERE PIKE 13¾
SEAT SANDAL 7
HIGH RAISE 3
SERGEANT MAN 3
HARRISON STICKLE 2½
SILVER HOW 5
PIKE O' STICKLE 2
Gimmer Crag
Martcrag Moor
edge of Cambridge Crag

On a clear day, Cross Fell (the highest of the Pennines) is seen, with Little Dun Fell, to the left of St Sunday Crag; Great Dun Fell (radar station) is just to the right.

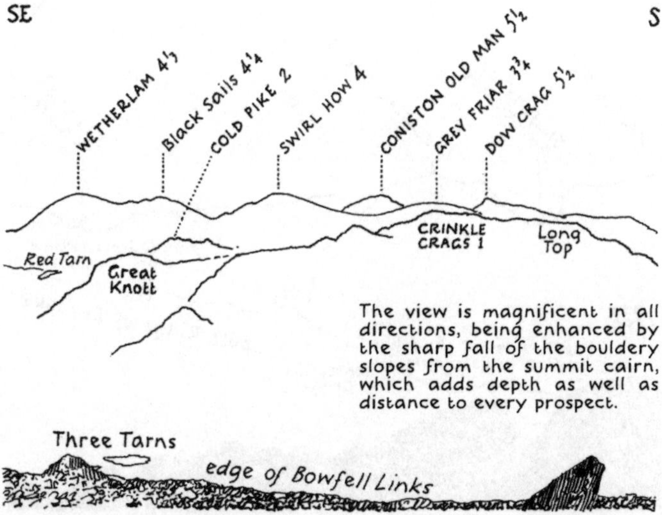
SE
S
WETHERLAM 4⅓
Black Sails 4¼
COLD PIKE 2
SWIRL HOW 4
CONISTON OLD MAN 5½
GREY FRIAR 3¾
DOW CRAG 5½
CRINKLE CRAGS 1
Long Top
Red Tarn
Great Knott
Three Tarns
edge of Bowfell Links

The view is magnificent in all directions, being enhanced by the sharp fall of the bouldery slopes from the summit cairn, which adds depth as well as distance to every prospect.

THE VIEW

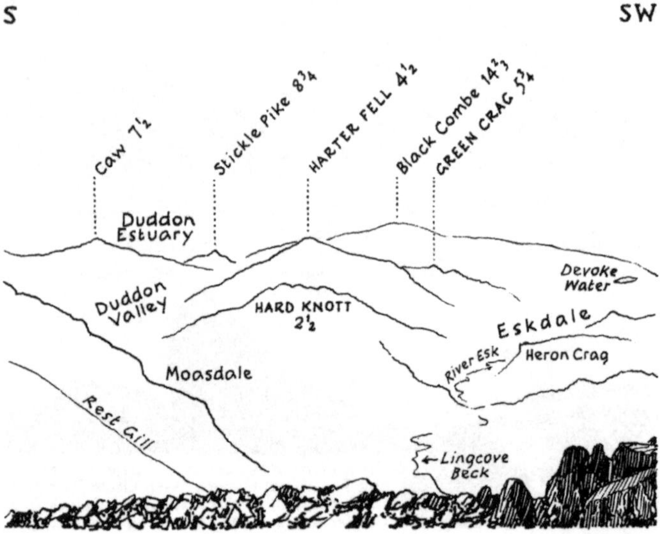
S
SW
Caw 7½
Stickle Pike 8¾
HARTER FELL 4½
Black Combe 14⅔
GREEN CRAG 5¾
Duddon Estuary
Duddon Valley
HARD KNOTT 2½
Devoke Water
Eskdale
River Esk
Heron Crag
Moasdale
Rest Gill
Lingcove Beck

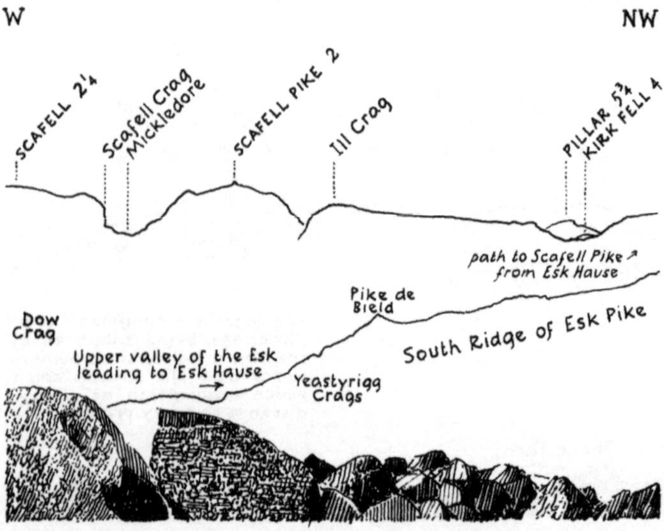
W
NW
SCAFELL 2¼
Scafell Crag
Mickledore
SCAFELL PIKE 2
Ill Crag
PILLAR 5¾
KIRK FELL 4
path to Scafell Pike from Esk Hause
Pike de Bield
Dow Crag
South Ridge of Esk Pike
Upper valley of the Esk leading to Esk Hause
Yeastyrigg Crags

THE VIEW

SW W

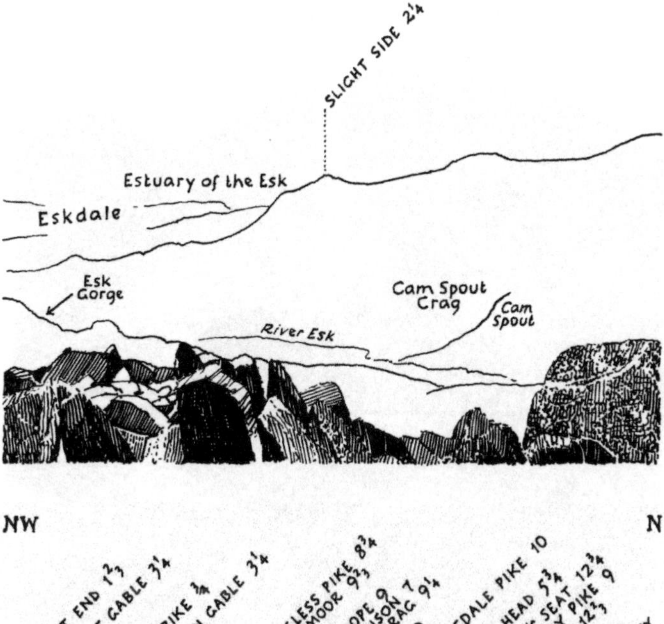
SLIGHT SIDE 2¼
Estuary of the Esk
Eskdale
Esk Gorge
Cam Spout Crag
Cam Spout
River Esk

NW N

GREAT END 1⅔
GREAT GABLE 3¼
ESK PIKE ¾
GREEN GABLE 3¼
WHITELESS PIKE 8¾
GRASMOOR 9⅔
WANDOPE 9
ROBINSON 7
EEL CRAG 9¼
SAIL 9
GRISEDALE PIKE 10
DALE HEAD 5¾
LORD'S SEAT 12¾
CAUSEY PIKE 9
BARF 12⅔
BINSEY 18
Solway Firth
Solway Firth
BRANDRETH 3¾
ALLEN CRAGS 1⅓
path to Esk Pike and Esk Hause
←path to Esk Hause from Angle Tarn
Ore Gap
top of Hanging Knotts
Yeastyrigg Gill

Brim Fell 2611'

OS grid ref: SD271986

from Little How Crags

WETHERLAM
GREY FRIAR
SWIRL HOW
BRIM FELL
CONISTON OLD MAN
DOW CRAG
Coniston
MILES
0
1
2
3

1
2
3
Swirl Hawse
1: Great Carrs
2: Swirl How
3: Great How Crags

The north-east cairn

NATURAL FEATURES

Brim Fell is the mile-long, whalebacked ridge linking Coniston Old Man with Swirl How, the latter fell being joined at the narrow depression of Levers Hawse, a high pass across the main watershed. Throughout its length the ridge is furnished with a most excellent turf, firm and dry and a pleasure to tread, but the featureless top, where a few stones intrude, is without interest. The western slope going steeply and roughly down amongst crags to Seathwaite Tarn is likewise dull, but the east face, craggy everywhere and narrowing quickly to the confluence of Low Water Beck and Levers Water Beck, is full of interesting detail, the best feature being the prominent buttress of Raven Tor thrusting out between the two attractive tarns of Low Water and Levers Water and the most fearsome a group of dangerous coppermine shafts in the vicinity of the sinister gash of Simon's Nick.

MAP

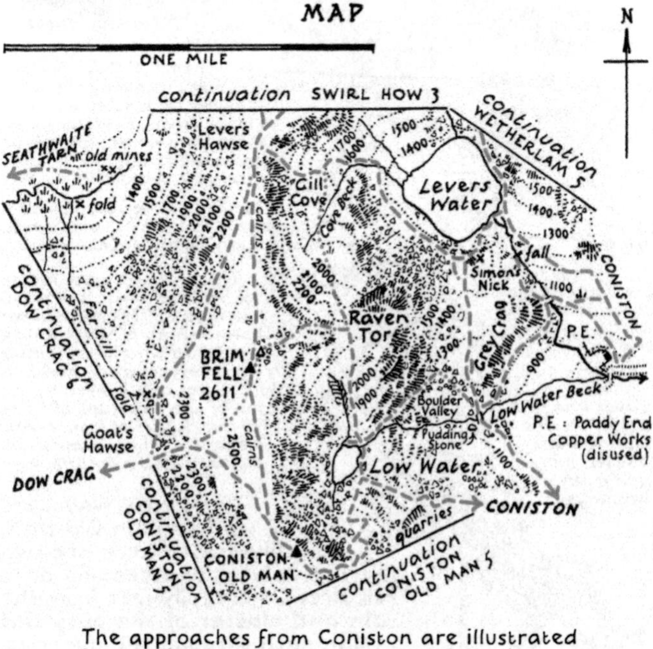
ONE MILE
N
continuation SWIRL HOW 3
continuation WETHERLAM 5
SEATHWAITE TARN
old mines
fold
Levers Hawse
Gill Cove
Cove Beck
Levers Water
fall
Simon's Nick
CONISTON
Raven Tor
Grey Crag
P.E.
BRIM FELL 2611'
cairns
Far Gill
continuation DOW CRAG 6
fold
Goat's Hawse
DOW CRAG
Boulder Valley
Low Water Beck
Pudding Stone
Low Water
P.E : Paddy End Copper Works (disused)
CONISTON
quarries
continuation CONISTON OLD MAN 5
CONISTON OLD MAN
continuation CONISTON OLD MAN 5

The approaches from Coniston are illustrated in the diagram on the next page following. →
For a map, see *Coniston Old Man 6*.

ASCENT FROM CONISTON

2450 feet of ascent : 3 miles (3½ via Gill Cove)

Brim Fell is the next summit northwards along the ridge from the Old Man, and is invariably attained (if at all) after first climbing the Old Man, the intervening ridge being a simple stroll on grass.

looking west

CONISTON OLD MAN
BRIM FELL
Levers Hawse
2600
2500
2400
2300
2200
2100
2000
1900
1800
1700
1600
1500
1400
1300
1200
1100
1000
900
800
700
600
400
spoil
cave (shelter)
Low Water
col
Raven Tor
Gill Cove
grass
quarries
tunnel
remains of water pipe
cave
Cove Beck
ruins
Colt Crag
Boulder Valley
Pudding Stone
shaft
shafts (dangerous)
Levers Water
Low Water Beck
WALNA SCAR ROAD
grass path
bracken
Coppermines Valley
juniper
Levers Water Beck
YOUTH HOSTEL
ROAD
gate
Miners Bridge
falls
Church Beck
CONISTON
Sun Hotel

The route above Boulder Valley is known as Brim Fell Rake; it is steep but easy to trace. From Low Water follow a grassy path which turns left at a *col* beside Raven Tor; it peters out near the summit plateau.

The Gill Cove approach offers a choice of routes in its latter stages, both of which join the path from Low Water.

Thus far the route is the same as that for Coniston Old Man.

Turn off to the quiet recess of Boulder Valley, and there follow one of the two routes shown — both of these entail some scrambling *and neither is recommended for descent.* Both routes give a much better idea of the structure of Brim Fell than is gained from a visit along the ridge. *In mist, the Old Man path is safer both ways.*

Caves and shafts on this diagram are disused mine and quarry workings.

The easy way up is *via* Coniston Old Man, but illustrated here are two alternative ways of ascending Brim Fell direct, mercifully free from the din and clatter of the busy Old Man path through the quarries.

Coniston (turn to the right behind the Sun Hotel)

THE SUMMIT

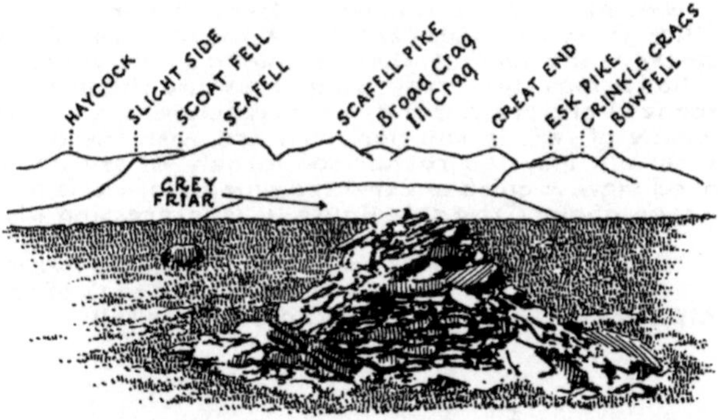
HAYCOCK
SLIGHT SIDE
SCOAT FELL
SCAFELL
SCAFELL PIKE
Broad Crag
Ill Crag
GREAT END
ESK PIKE
CRINKLE CRAGS
BOWFELL
GREY FRIAR

A very fine cairn, similar to the one on Coniston Old Man, marks the highest part of the broad grassy plateau on top of the fell; in fact, the cairn is somewhat more substantial than shown in the illustration. 100 yards north-east is a second big cairn in an eruption of grey stones. There is nothing else to mention.

DESCENTS: The summit is usually left along the ridge, but it is useful to know that the north-east cairn stands at the head of a simple direct descent for Coniston (the only easy breach in the eastern escarpment): on this route aim for the *col* linking Raven Tor to the fell and here turn right down a grass slope to Low Water. But *in mist* go first to the Old Man and descend from there.

RIDGE ROUTES

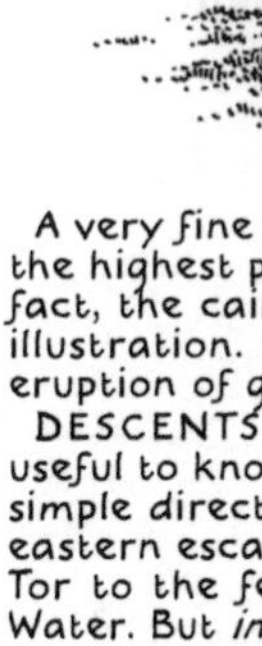
BRIM FELL
2500
2400
line of cairns
2500
DOW CRAG
CONISTON OLD MAN
N

To CONISTON OLD MAN, 2633′
½ mile : S
Depression at 2545′: 100 feet of ascent

An easy stroll

The path is well cairned, but the cairns are unnecessary, as the route is never in doubt. *In mist*, if steep ground is encountered keep on to the right, skirting it.

ONE MILE

To SWIRL HOW, 2630′
1½ miles : N, NE and N
Depression (Levers Hawse) at 2240′
400 feet of ascent

A long easy slope leads down to Levers Hawse, beyond which an improving path climbs to the right above Little How Crags to the top of Great How Crags, the most prominent feature on the journey; from here onwards only an easy promenade amidst outcrops remains to be done. This walk is safe *in mist* provided that all steep ground is kept on the right.

SWIRL HOW
2600
2500
2400
Great How Crags
2300
Little How Crags
Levers Hawse
2200
2300
2400
2500
BRIM FELL
N

THE VIEW

The view, although extensive, suffers in comparison with that from the adjacent Old Man because of the broadness of the summit, there being no single vantage point that brings the surrounding tarns into the picture. The scene therefore depends for attractiveness on the far skyline of fells in the northern arc, with the other Coniston hills looming rather too largely to present a balanced view. A quite unexpected glimpse of Little Mell Fell is seen above Grisedale Hause; it is interesting also to see the atomic power plants on the coast neatly bisected by the peak of the Eskdale Harter Fell.

Principal Fells

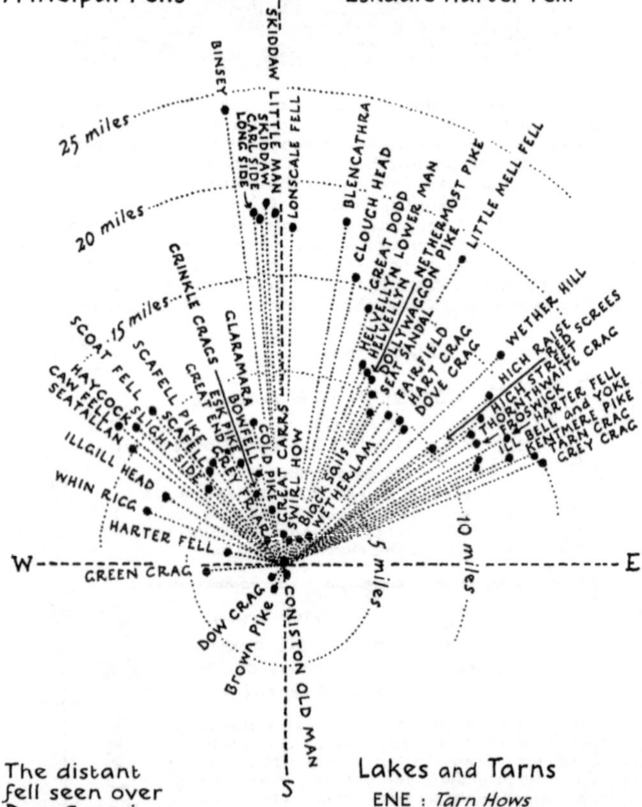
N
S
E
W
25 miles
20 miles
15 miles
10 miles
5 miles
BINSEY
SKIDDAW
LITTLE MAN
SKIDDAW
CARL SIDE
LONG SIDE
LONSCALE FELL
BLENCATHRA
CLOUGH HEAD
GREAT DODD
LOWER MAN
HELVELLYN
HELVELLYN
NETHERMOST PIKE
DOLLYWAGGON PIKE
SEAT SANDAL
LITTLE MELL FELL
FAIRFIELD
HART CRAG
DOVE CRAG
WETHER HILL
HIGH RAISE
RED SCREES
HIGH STREET
THORNTHWAITE CRAG
FROSWICK
HARTER FELL
ILL BELL and YOKE
KENTMERE PIKE
TARN CRAG
GREY CRAG
WETHERLAM
Black Sails
SWIRL HOW
GREAT CARRS
COLD PIKE
GREY FRIAR
BOWFELL
ESK PIKE
GREAT END
GLARAMARA
CRINKLE CRAGS
SCAFELL PIKE
SCAFELL
SLIGHT SIDE
SCOAT FELL
HAYCOCK
CAW FELL
SEATALLAN
ILLGILL HEAD
WHIN RIGG
HARTER FELL
GREEN CRAG
DOW CRAG
Brown Pike
CONISTON OLD MAN

The distant fell seen over Dow Crag is Black Combe.

Lakes and Tarns

ENE : *Tarn Hows*
E : *Windermere (2 sections)*
W : *Devoke Water*

Simon's Nick (top left) and the upper valley of Levers Water Beck from one of the old levels, Paddy End Copper Works.

Raven Tor, the east buttress of Brim Fell, from the dam at Levers Water

Cold Pike 2300′

OS grid ref: NY263036

from Pike o' Blisco

The true south ridge of Crinkle Crags follows the compass bearing to end in a long steep descent to Cockley Beck, but a spur running off south-east is more usually considered to continue the main spine of the mountain. This spur rises to the three rocky summits of Cold Pike before dropping down Wrynose Breast to the pass below; a concave eastern slope descends to the desolate upland hollow containing Red Tarn, so named from the rich colour of the shaly subsoil.

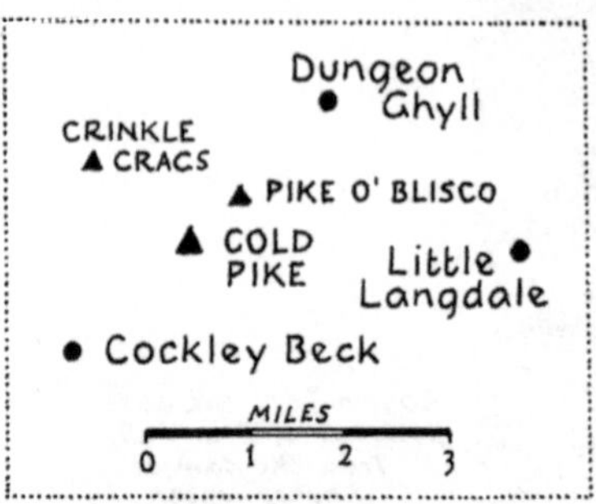

Dungeon Ghyll
CRINKLE CRAGS
PIKE O' BLISCO
COLD PIKE
Little Langdale
Cockley Beck
MILES
0
1
2
3

Although not of great significance, Cold Pike is prominent when seen from the north and east, and it has lovely views in those directions. All around, nearby, are higher fells, and they may be studied profitably from the triple peaks of this lowly one in their midst. Cold Pike is a Crinkle Crags in miniature.

MAP

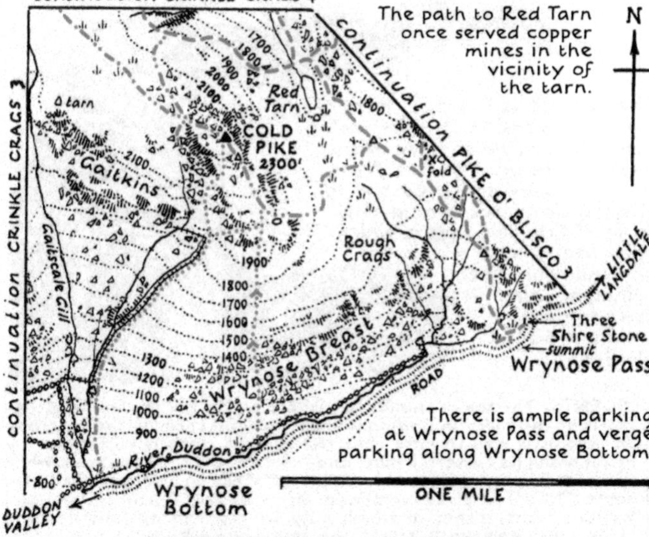
continuation CRINKLE CRAGS 4
continuation PIKE O' BLISCO 3
continuation CRINKLE CRAGS 3
N
The path to Red Tarn once served copper mines in the vicinity of the tarn.
Red Tarn
COLD PIKE 2300'
tarn
Gaitkins
Gaitscale Gill
fold
Rough Crags
LITTLE LANGDALE
Three Shire Stone
summit
Wrynose Pass
Wrynose Breast
ROAD
River Duddon
Wrynose Bottom
DUDDON VALLEY
ONE MILE
1700
1800
1900
2000
2100
1300
1200
1100
1000
900
800

There is ample parking at Wrynose Pass and verge parking along Wrynose Bottom.

ASCENT FROM WRYNOSE

1500 feet of ascent
(from Wrynose Bottom)
1000 feet of ascent
(from Wrynose Pass)
1¼ miles

Below the crag west of the summit are many mammoth boulders and one grotesque 12-foot fanged splinter

An appropriate name for it would be Cold Pike Tooth
Try to locate it!

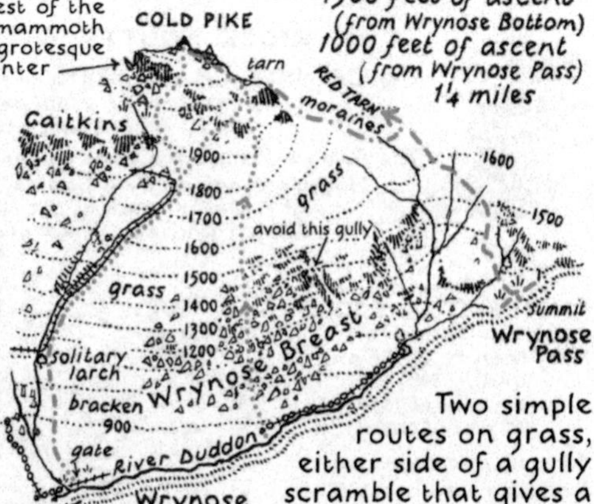
COLD PIKE
tarn
RED TARN
moraines
Gaitkins
grass
avoid this gully
solitary larch
bracken
gate
River Duddon
Wrynose Breast
summit
Wrynose Pass
Wrynose Bottom
DUDDON VALLEY
1900
1800
1700
1600
1500
1400
1300
1200
900

Two simple routes on grass, either side of a gully scramble that gives a touch of adventure.

looking north

An initial problem on the westerly Wrynose Bottom route is to get across the river (no bridge, no ford). Crossing is easier to reach the start of the gully route. *In mist*, none of these approaches are recommended.

THE SUMMIT

CRINKLE CRAGS
BOWFELL

The summit is the best part of the fell. It consists of three rocky humps (two of which have cairns), descending in altitude from north-west to south-east, and strongly reminiscent, on a small scale, of Crinkle Crags, of which they are strictly a continuation. The principal cairn stands on a pleasant rock platform.

DESCENTS: The top of the fell is without paths, but in clear weather there is no difficulty in finding an easy way off through the outcrops. *In mist*, it is well to note that the summit ridge is buttressed by crags along its eastern fringe, and more distantly on the west, while Wrynose Breast is much too rough and steep to be considered as a route. The safest places to aim for are Red Tarn (for Oxendale) and Wrynose Pass, either of which may be reached by following the ridge south-east (in line with the three humps) until a small tarn, with rising ground beyond: here go down grass to the left and continue eastwards to join the path linking Red Tarn and Wrynose Pass.

RIDGE ROUTES

CRINKLE CRAGS
2500
1800
1700
2100
2000
1900
OXENDALE
PIKE O' BLISCO
Red Tarn
COLD PIKE
WRYNOSE
N
HALF A MILE

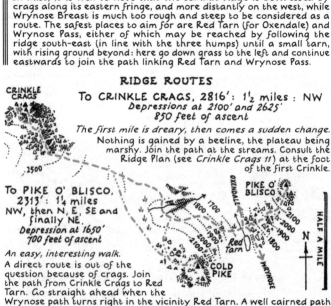

To CRINKLE CRAGS, 2816′: 1½ miles : NW

Depressions at 2100′ and 2625′
850 feet of ascent

The first mile is dreary, then comes a sudden change.
Nothing is gained by a beeline, the plateau being marshy. Join the path at the streams. Consult the Ridge Plan (see *Crinkle Crags 11*) at the foot of the first Crinkle.

To PIKE O' BLISCO, 2313′: 1¼ miles NW, then N, E, SE and finally NE.

Depression at 1650′
700 feet of ascent

An easy, interesting walk.
A direct route is out of the question because of crags. Join the path from Crinkle Crags to Red Tarn. Go straight ahead when the Wrynose path turns right in the vicinity Red Tarn. A well cairned path leads to a depression between Pike o' Blisco's twin tops; turn left and pick your way over attractive rocks to the well made summit cairn.

THE VIEW

The view between north and east is very extensive, but on the west side is severely restricted by the lofty south ridge coming down from Crinkle Crags. Perhaps the best features are the two splendid lowland prospects (1) over Little Langdale to Windermere and the distant Pennines, and (2) down the Duddon Valley to the estuary and the sea beyond.

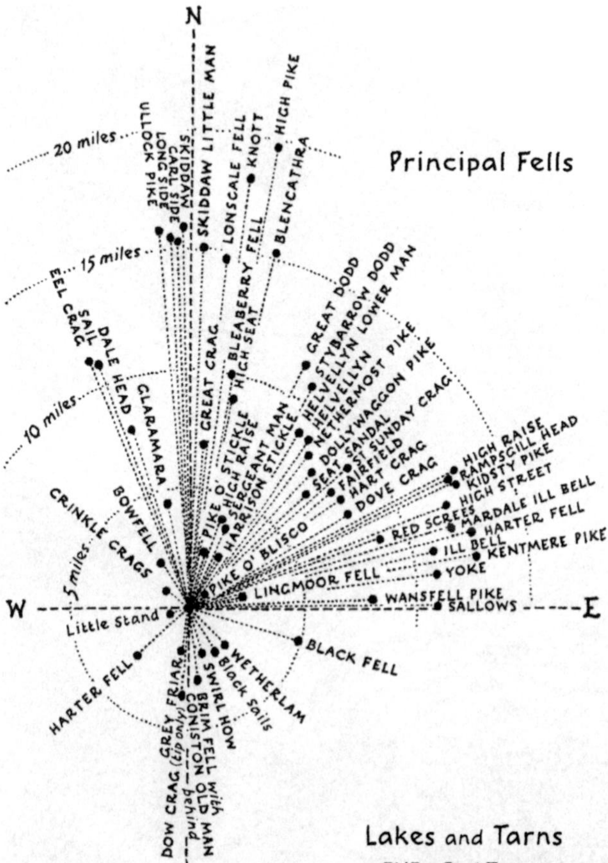

N
E
S
W
Principal Fells
20 miles
15 miles
10 miles
5 miles
ULLOCK PIKE
LONG SIDE
CARL SIDE
SKIDDAW
SKIDDAW LITTLE MAN
LONSCALE FELL
KNOTT
HIGH PIKE
BLENCATHRA
BLEABERRY FELL
HIGH SEAT
GREAT CRAG
EEL CRAG
SAIL
DALE HEAD
GLARAMARA
GREAT DODD
STYBARROW DODD
HELVELLYN LOWER MAN
HELVELLYN
NETHERMOST PIKE
DOLLYWAGGON PIKE
ST SUNDAY CRAG
SEAT SANDAL
FAIRFIELD
HART CRAG
DOVE CRAG
PIKE O' STICKLE
HIGH RAISE
SERGEANT MAN
HARRISON STICKLE
PIKE O' BLISCO
HIGH RAISE
RAMPSGILL HEAD
KIDSTY PIKE
HIGH STREET
MARDALE ILL BELL
HARTER FELL
RED SCREES
ILL BELL
KENTMERE PIKE
YOKE
LINGMOOR FELL
WANSFELL PIKE
SALLOWS
BOWFELL
CRINKLE CRAGS
Little Stand
HARTER FELL
BLACK FELL
WETHERLAM
Black Sails
SWIRL HOW
BRIM FELL with
CONISTON OLD MAN behind
GREY FRIAR
DOW CRAG (tip only)

Lakes and Tarns

ENE : *Red Tarn*
ESE : *Windermere* (two sections: Black Fell between)
SW : *Devoke Water*

Coniston Old Man 2633'

properly
The Old Man of Coniston

OS grid ref: SD272978

from Red Dell Head

NATURAL FEATURES

The Coniston fells form a separate geographical unit. They are almost entirely severed from the adjacent mountainous parts of Lakeland by the Duddon and Brathay valleys, with the watershed between the two, Wrynose Pass, 1270', providing the only link with other fells. Before 1974 all the Coniston fells were within Lancashire, the two valleys mentioned containing the boundaries of Cumberland (Duddon) and Westmorland (Brathay). Now the whole of the Lake District is in Cumbria.

Whilst the characteristics of the Coniston fells are predominantly Lakeland, with lofty ridges, steep and craggy declivities, lovely waterfalls and lonely tarns and the general scenic charm so typical of the district, there has been a great deal of industrial exploitation here, principally in copper mining (now abandoned) and quarrying (still active), resulting in much disfigurement. So strongly sculptured are these fine hills, however, and so pronounced is their appeal that the scars detract but little from the attractiveness of the picture: many people, indeed, will find that the decayed skeletons of the mine-workings add an unusual, and if explored an absorbing, interest to their walks.

The western slopes are comparatively dull, and the appeal of these hills lies in their aspect to the east, where the village of Coniston, in an Alpine setting, is the natural base for explorations. The ridgewalking, on soft turf, is excellent, but all slopes are very rough down to valley level. As viewpoints, the summits have the advantage of isolation between the main mass of Lakeland and the fine indented coastline of Morecambe Bay, the prospects in all directions being of a high quality.

Waterfalls, Church Beck

continued

NATURAL FEATURES

continued

The pattern of the Coniston Fells

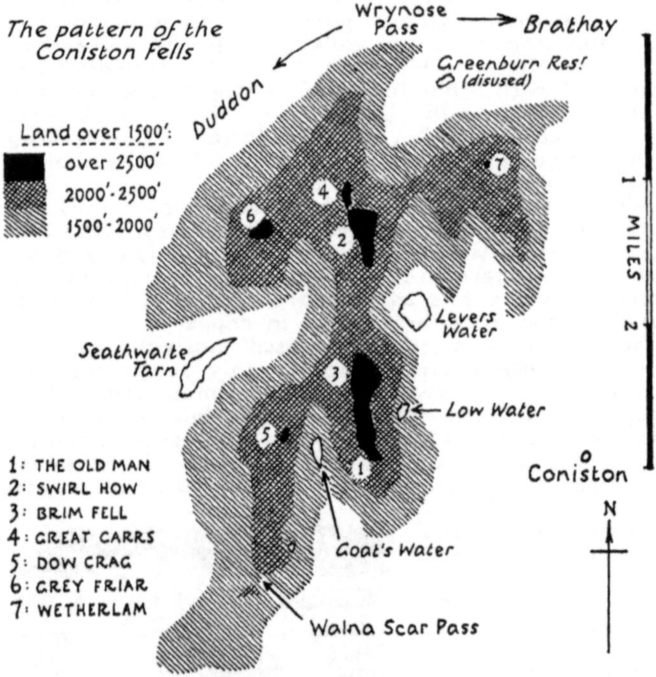
Wrynose Pass
Brathay
Duddon
Greenburn Res! (disused)
Land over 1500':
over 2500'
2000'-2500'
1500'-2000'
Levers Water
Seathwaite Tarn
Low Water
Goat's Water
Walna Scar Pass
Coniston
MILES
1
2
N
1: THE OLD MAN
2: SWIRL HOW
3: BRIM FELL
4: GREAT CARRS
5: DOW CRAG
6: GREY FRIAR
7: WETHERLAM

The northern Coniston Fells from Little Langdale

7
2
4
Wrynose Pass

NATURAL FEATURES

The highest (by a few feet) and best-known of the Coniston fells is the Old Man, a benevolent giant revered by generations of walkers and of particular esteem in the eyes of the inhabitants of the village he shelters, for he has contributed much to their prosperity. The Old Man is no Matterhorn, nor is Coniston a Zermatt, but an affinity is there in the same close links between mountain and village, and the history of the one is the history of the other. Coniston without its Old Man is unthinkable.

Yet the Old Man has little significance in the geographical arrangements hereabouts, the true hub of this group of hills being Swirl How, a summit of slightly lower elevation northwards. The Old Man is merely the termination of Swirl How's main ridge and ends high Lakeland in the south: the last outpost, looking far over the sea.

Although cruelly scarred and mutilated by quarries the Old Man has retained a dignified bearing, and still raises his proud and venerable head to the sky. His tears are shed quietly, into Low Water and Goat's Water, two splendid tarns, whence, in due course, and after further service to the community in the matter of supplies of electricity and water, they ultimately find their way into Coniston's lake, and there bathe his ancient feet.

Yet even during these peaceful ablutions the Old Man continues to be harassed. On the day this page was first prepared (November 10th, 1958) the world's water speed record was broken on Coniston Water, by Donald Campbell. Thus, from tip to toe, the mountain serves man.

POSTSCRIPT: In 1967 Donald Campbell died on Coniston Water attempting to break the record again.

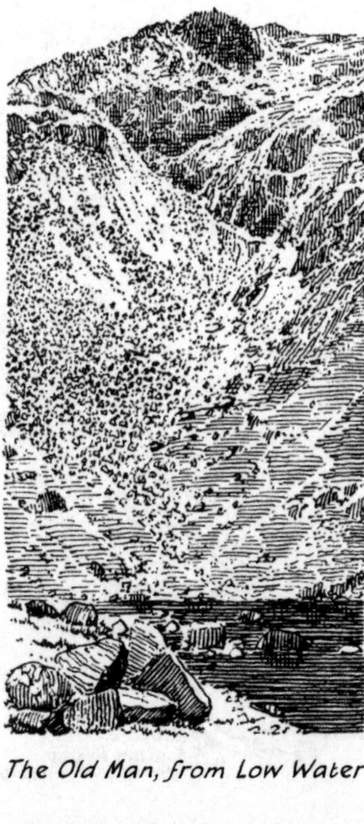

The Old Man, from Low Water

MAP

continuation BRIM FELL 2
continuation DOW CRAG 6
continuation opposite
BRIM FELL
Goat's Hawse
Boulder Valley
Low Water
working quarry
The Bell
CONISTON OLD MAN 2633'
Goat's Water
old quarries
old quarry road
Bursting Stone Quarry
Cove Quarries (disused)
pool
spoil heap
climbing hut
The Cove
ruins of Cove Hut
Little Arrow Moor
Boo Tarn
Walna Scar Road
SP
Torver Beck
Stone Circle (not easily discerned One prominent standing stone only; the rest are embedded. Circle 15 paces in diameter.)
Well in Crag (spring at base of small crag by side of path)
WALNA SCAR and DUDDON VALLEY
Cove Bridge
Ancient Enclosure (traces only)
large pool in bottom of quarry
Banishead Quarry (disused)
FB
sheepfold
Tranearth (climbing hostel)
lane
old quarry
barn
continuation alongside
N
ONE MILE
Crook (farm)
CONISTON 2¼ (car park)
Torver
Church
Inn
Station House (former railway station)
BROUGHTON 6½

MAP

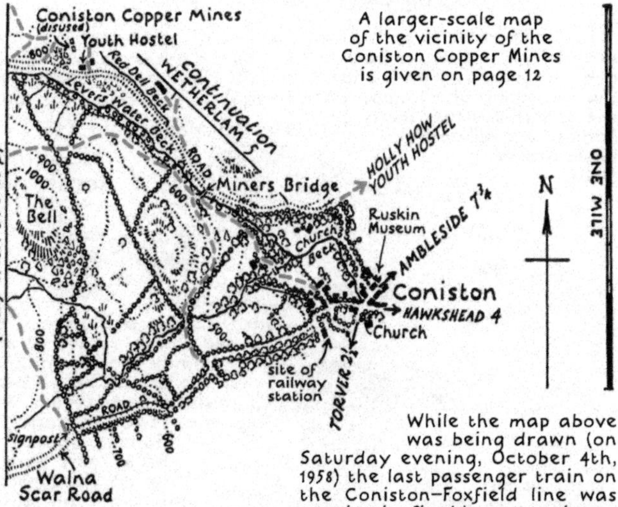
Coniston Copper Mines
(disused)
Youth Hostel
Red Dell Beck
Levers Water Beck
continuation WETHERLAM 5
continuation opposite
(half-inch overlap)
The Bell
ROAD
Miners Bridge
HOLLY HOW YOUTH HOSTEL
AMBLESIDE 7¾
Ruskin Museum
Church Beck
Coniston
HAWKSHEAD 4
Church
site of railway station
TORVER 2½
signpost
Walna Scar Road
N
ONE MILE

A larger-scale map of the vicinity of the Coniston Copper Mines is given on page 12

While the map above was being drawn (on Saturday evening, October 4th, 1958) the last passenger train on the Coniston–Foxfield line was running its final journey prior to the withdrawal of the service.

Detail is not given of the territory south of the Walna Scar Road except in the vicinity of the approach from Torver. Here is little to tempt the fellwalker, for a broad and dreary moor declines to the cultivated shores of Coniston Water, but this rather desolate expanse nevertheless is fruitful ground for the antiquary, there being many evidences of a civilisation long past. Ancient cairns, walled enclosures and stone circles are all revealed to the eager and learned searcher amongst the bracken, and excavators have unearthed a Bronze Age cemetery. How odd that the scene of these mouldering relics should be also the place where an ultra-modern flying saucer was first photographed!

Somewhere in the area covered by the map on the opposite page, *but not indicated*, is a small upright memorial stone roughly inscribed 'CHARMER 1911'. Charmer was a foxhound killed in a fall on Dow Crag, and it is rather nice to know that the memory of a faithful dog was revered in this way. But some visitors have seen nothing sacred in the stone and it has been uprooted and cast aside on occasion. For this reason it has been thought best not to disclose its exact location. Rest in peace, Charmer. They were happy days............

Charmer's Grave

ASCENT FROM CONISTON (via BOO TARN)
2400 feet of ascent: 3 miles

The south ridge is such a natural line of approach it is rather surprising it appears to be used by so few walkers (as evidenced by the narrow grassy path underfoot). The ridge is not reached until the 1700′ contour; the approach from Boo Tarn is initially across the grassy south-eastern flank of the fell above Little Arrow Moor.

CONISTON OLD MAN
looking north-west
south ridge
2100
old quarries
grass
2000
1900
grass
1800
1700
pool
Bursting Stone Quarry
1600
1500
1400
1300
spoil heap
quarry road
1200
Timley Knott
1100
1000
900
WALNA SCAR 2
SP
Boo Tarn (a small reedy pool)
Braidy Beck
dried-up tarn
bracken
800
car park
SP
old quarry road
gate
CONISTON

The route *via* Bursting Stone Quarry takes advantage of a disused quarry road that leads to a small pool. Beyond this, strike up the hill following a single-strand fence. When the fence reaches its highest point look for a faint path on the left. This eventually joins the main path to the Old Man from Low Water *(see facing page)*.

The long way round is *via* the Walna Scar path, then Goat's Water and Goat's Hawse. *See page 9.*

Starting from the car park at the beginning of the Walna Scar road cuts a mile off the ascent and saves 450′ of climbing.

At Boo Tarn a signposted path turns off the main Walna Scar track beside the rough road to Bursting Stone Quarry (which is still open after being recommissioned in 1960); this is the start of two little-frequented approaches to the Old Man that offer contrasting scenery as well as something in common: seclusion. These are the quietest ways to ascend a familiar fell. The south ridge route gives superb views of the impressive rock architecture of near neighbour Dow Crag.

An old cave at Bursting Stone Quarry (now gone)

ASCENT FROM CONISTON (DIRECT)
2450 feet of ascent : 3 miles (2½ via Church Beck)

looking west

This is the way the crowds go: the day trippers, the courting couples, troops of earnest Boy Scouts, babies and grandmothers, the lot. On this stony parade fancy handbags and painted toenails are as likely to be seen as rucksacks and boots. In its favour, it can be said that the route is absolutely safe in the worst weather — the densest mist cannot obscure the spiralling ribbon of stones. But let's be fair — the scenery of Low Water is very good.

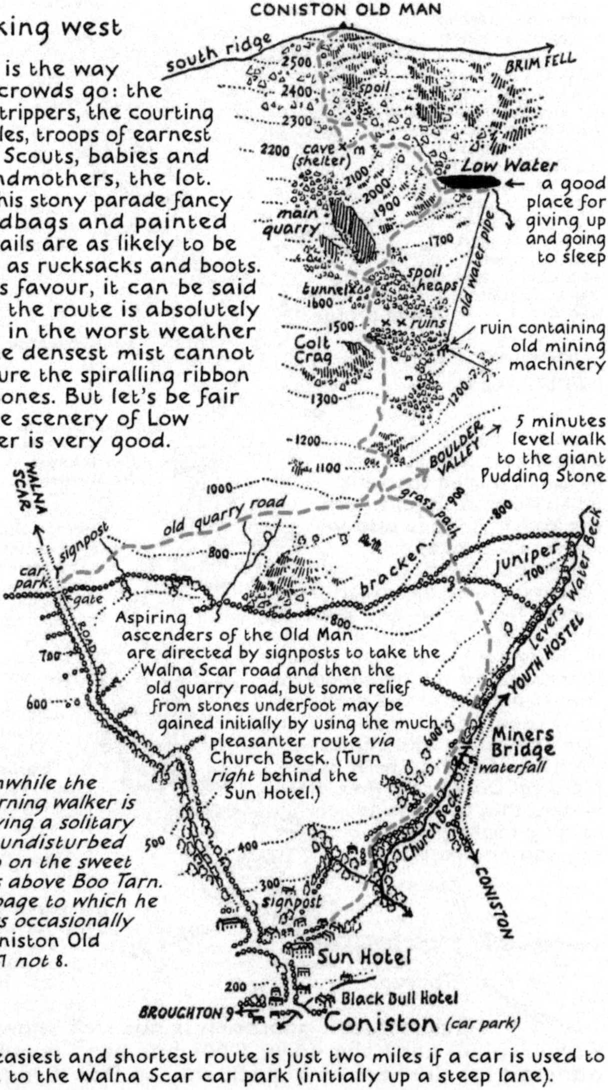

CONISTON OLD MAN
south ridge
BRIM FELL
2500
2400
2300
2200
spoil
cave (shelter)
Low Water
a good place for giving up and going to sleep
2100
2000
1900
main quarry
1700
old water pipe
spoil heaps
tunnel
1600
1500
ruins
ruin containing old mining machinery
Colt Crag
1300
1200
1200
5 minutes level walk to the giant Pudding Stone
1100
BOULDER VALLEY
1000
grass path
900
800
WALNA SCAR
old quarry road
signpost
800
car park
gate
bracken
juniper
700
Levers Water Beck
800
ROAD
700
YOUTH HOSTEL
600
Aspiring ascenders of the Old Man are directed by signposts to take the Walna Scar road and then the old quarry road, but some relief from stones underfoot may be gained initially by using the much pleasanter route *via* Church Beck. (Turn *right* behind the Sun Hotel.)
600
Miners Bridge
waterfall
Church Beck
500
400
CONISTON
300
signpost
Sun Hotel
200
Black Bull Hotel
BROUGHTON 9
Coniston (car park)

Meanwhile the discerning walker is enjoying a solitary and undisturbed climb on the sweet grass above Boo Tarn. The page to which he refers occasionally is Coniston Old Man 7 *not* 8.

The easiest and shortest route is just two miles if a car is used to drive to the Walna Scar car park (initially up a steep lane).

ASCENT FROM TORVER

2350 feet of ascent : 3¼ miles (3¾ via Goat's Hawse)

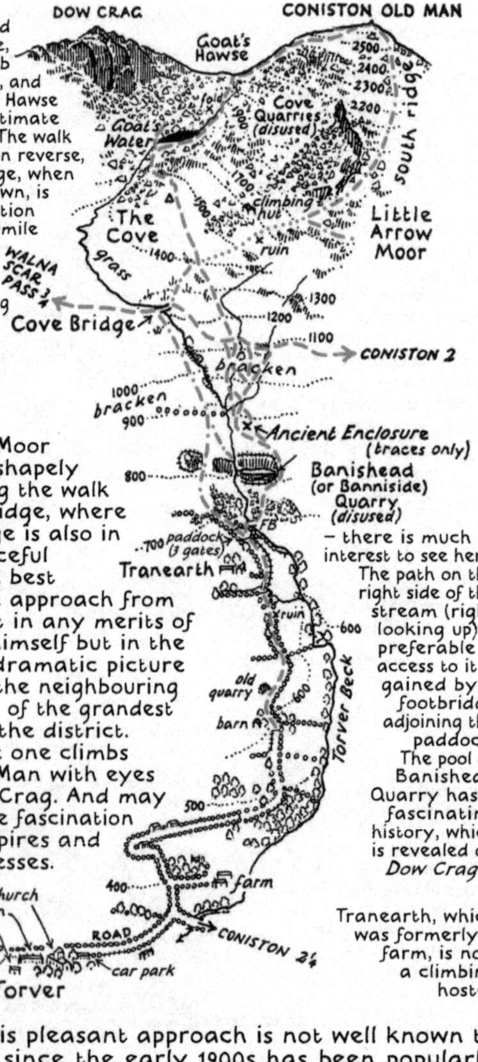
DOW CRAG
CONISTON OLD MAN
Goat's Hawse
2500
2400
2300
2200
south ridge
fold
Cove Quarries (disused)
1900
Goat's Water
1700
1500
climbing hut
The Cove
Little Arrow Moor
ruin
1400
grass
WALNA SCAR PASS 3/4
1300
1200
Cove Bridge
1100
CONISTON 2
bracken
1000
bracken
900
Ancient Enclosure (traces only)
800
Banishead (or Banniside) Quarry (disused)
FB
700
paddock (3 gates)
Tranearth
ruin
600
old quarry
600
Torver Beck
barn
500
farm
400
Church Inn
Station House
ROAD
CONISTON 2¼
BROUGHTON 6½
car park
Torver
ULVERSTON 12½

Preferably, ascend by the south ridge, which gives superb views of Dow Crag, and descend *via* Goat's Hawse for even more intimate views of the Crag. The walk is actually easier in reverse, but the south ridge, when used as a way down, is open to the objection that the quarter-mile precipice of Cove Quarries could be a dangerous trap in deteriorating weather.

looking north-west

Little Arrow Moor appears as a shapely pyramid during the walk up to Cove Bridge, where the south ridge is also in view as a graceful curve, but the best feature of the approach from Torver lies not in any merits of the Old Man himself but in the increasingly dramatic picture presented by the neighbouring Dow Crag, one of the grandest rock faces in the district.

On this route one climbs Coniston Old Man with eyes fixed on Dow Crag. And may understand the fascination of airy rock spires and soaring buttresses.

— there is much of interest to see here. The path on the right side of the stream (right looking up) is preferable — access to it is gained by a footbridge adjoining the paddock. The pool at Banishead Quarry has a fascinating history, which is revealed on *Dow Crag 6*.

Tranearth, which was formerly a farm, is now a climbing hostel.

This pleasant approach is not well known to walkers, but since the early 1900s has been popularly adopted by climbers as a quick way to Dow Crag.

Boulder Valley

Low Water Beck falls in steep cascades from its tarn to a level shelf 600 feet below and there meanders uncertainly before resuming its hurried journey to join Levers Water Beck.

This shelf is littered with boulders tumbled from the craggy slopes above, a scene common enough among the mountains, but in this particular instance several of the boulders are of quite uncommon size, big enough indeed to provide some entertainment and practice for rock climbers, who name the area Boulder Valley.

The most massive and most prominent of the boulders is the Pudding Stone, 25 feet high and as big as a house, which has a dozen climbing routes, one of them being considered easy, but not by everybody, and the others, by walkers' standards, ranging between various grades of impossibility. The Pudding Stone may not have the overall dimensions of the Bowder Stone in Borrowdale, but certainly gives the impression of a greater bulk and weight.

The Pudding Stone
(the easy side)

It is perhaps unnecessary to add that the figure up aloft is not the author.

Coppermines Valley

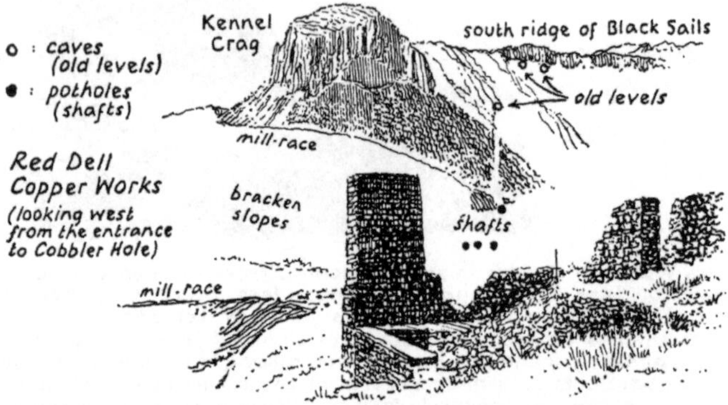
Kennel Crag
south ridge of Black Sails
o : caves (old levels)
• : potholes (shafts)
old levels
mill-race
Red Dell Copper Works
(looking west from the entrance to Cobbler Hole)
bracken slopes
shafts
mill-race

Fellwalkers based on Coniston need not sit moping in their lodgings if a wet day puts the high tops out of bounds for it is possible to occupy the mind and keep the body reasonably dry by dodging from one to another of the many caves, levels and tunnels of the Coppermines Valley, one mile distant.

This hollow among the hills presents a surprising scene of squalid desolation, typical of the dreary outskirts of many coalmining towns but utterly foreign to the Lake District, and it says much for the quality of the encircling mountains that they can triumph over the serious disfigurement of ugly spoil heaps and gaping wounds, and still look majestic. Here, in this strange amphitheatre, where flowers once grew, one sees the hopeless debris of the ruins of workings long abandoned, where flowers will never grow again, and, as always in the presence of death, is saddened — but a raising of the eyes discloses a surround of noble heights, and then the heart is uplifted too.

There is good fun and absorbing interest in locating all the tunnels and shafts of the former quarries and mines. The shafts, hideous potholes falling sheer into black depths, have now been provided with protective fences, and most of the hazardous passages are no longer accessible, but there are exceptions, and passages should be entered only with great caution: we can't afford to lose any readers here, not with a further three volumes of the Walkers Edition still to be sold.

A more detailed description of this area will be found in *Coniston Copper Mines: A Field Guide* by Eric G. Holland, published by the Cicerone Press in 1981 and reprinted with amendments in 2000. This includes details of passages that may be safely entered and eight-figure grid references for all entrances.

The accompanying map indicates the various holes of one sort and another in the Coppermines Valley area. There are others elsewhere on the Coniston fells, notably on Wetherlam. See *Wetherlam's Hundred Holes*, on Wetherlam 7.

continuing *Coppermines Valley*

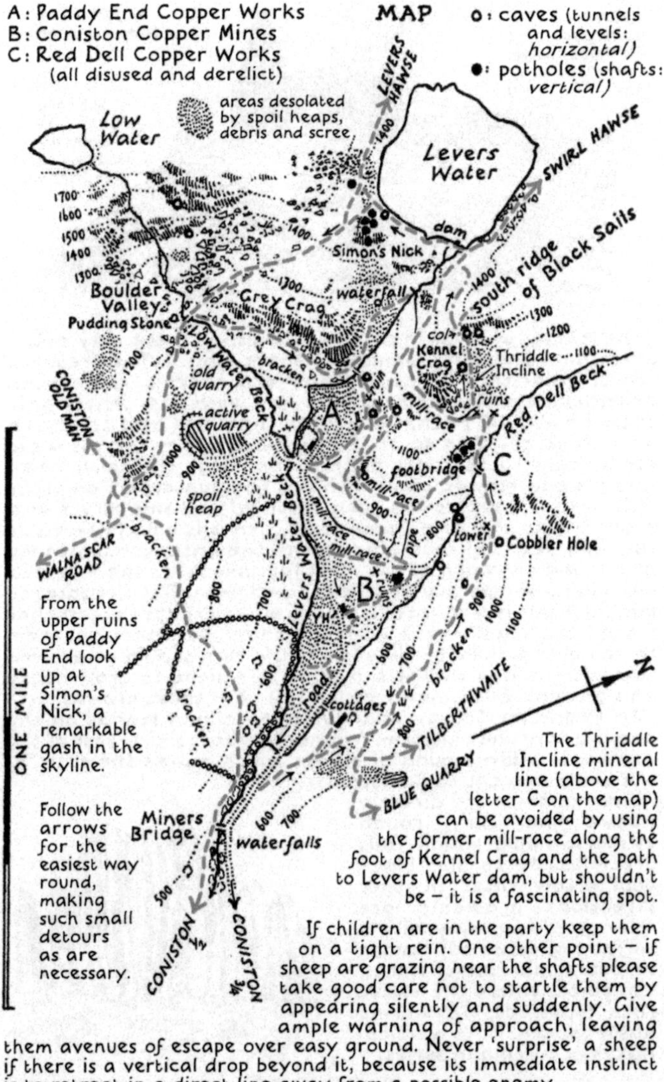

A: Paddy End Copper Works
B: Coniston Copper Mines
C: Red Dell Copper Works
(all disused and derelict)
MAP
o: caves (tunnels and levels: horizontal)
●: potholes (shafts: vertical)
areas desolated by spoil heaps, debris and scree
Low Water
Levers Water
LEVERS HAWSE
SWIRL HAWSE
south ridge of Black Sails
dam
Simon's Nick
waterfall
Grey Crag
Boulder Valley
Pudding Stone
Low Water Beck
old quarry
active quarry
bracken
Kennel Crag
Thriddle Incline
ruins
mill-race
Red Dell Beck
footbridge
CONISTON OLD MAN
spoil heap
Levers Water Beck
pipe
tower
Cobbler Hole
WALNA SCAR ROAD
YH
road
cottages
TILBERTHWAITE
BLUE QUARRY
Miners Bridge
waterfalls
CONISTON ½
CONISTON ¾
ONE MILE
N

From the upper ruins of Paddy End look up at Simon's Nick, a remarkable gash in the skyline.

Follow the arrows for the easiest way round, making such small detours as are necessary.

The Thriddle Incline mineral line (above the letter C on the map) can be avoided by using the former mill-race along the foot of Kennel Crag and the path to Levers Water dam, but shouldn't be – it is a fascinating spot.

If children are in the party keep them on a tight rein. One other point – if sheep are grazing near the shafts please take good care not to startle them by appearing silently and suddenly. Give ample warning of approach, leaving them avenues of escape over easy ground. Never 'surprise' a sheep if there is a vertical drop beyond it, because its immediate instinct is to retreat in a direct line away from a possible enemy.

THE SUMMIT

Tourists
looking for
Blackpool Tower
Boy Scouts
Typical
summit scene
Solitary
fellwalker,
bless him,
looking north
to the hills

There may be a cairn on the summit, or there may not..... Sometimes there is, sometimes there isn't..... The frequent visitor gains the impression that feud rages here between cairn-builders and cairn-destroyers, with the contestants evenly matched, so that one week there will be a cairn, the next week not, and so on. Indestructible, however, is a big solidly constructed slate platform on which the cairn, when there is one, stands, and which has no counterpart on other fells; into it a recess has been provided and this serves as a shallow wind shelter on occasions when it is not cluttered up with the debris of shattered cairns, the latter circumstance depending on which of the rival factions is, at the moment, enjoying a temporary and fleeting triumph. One hesitates to join in, if this is a private fight, but may perhaps suggest that if the word 'man' means 'a summit cairn', as authorities seem to be agreed, then, of all fells, the Old Man should be allowed to have one and that it should be left alone to grow hoary and ancient. But it never could. Not with those crowds.

An Ordnance Survey triangulation column stands on the north side of the platform. A hundred yards south-east of the summit is a low mound of stones which marks the start of the steep descent to Coniston.

The summit is directly above the very rough eastern slope, which falls precipitously to the black pool of Low Water; in other directions gradients are easy, predominantly with a surface of grass but having an occasional rash of stones.

In places where the native rock crops out, weathering has reduced it to vertical flakes occurring in series.

Typical rock formations on the summit

THE SUMMIT

DESCENTS:

TO CONISTON:

Although the start of the usual quarries path is indistinct for a few yards as it leaves the summit there should be no difficulty in finding and following it, even in the thickest mist: the path is one of the safest and surest (and stoniest) in the district.

The Boo Tarn route leaves the quarries path indistinctly after two hundred yards and is marked by cairns. This route is difficult to follow up or down, *and is confusing in mist.* When you come to a single-strand fence follow it down to the right to a disused road that bends left and leads to Bursting Stone Quarry.

The alternative route of descent to Boo Tarn is by way of the south ridge, with a decent path initially, but further down *it also is confusing in mist.*

TO TORVER:

Follow the south ridge (no path) to hit the Walna Scar Road anywhere, after which it is easy going; but the lower slopes of the ridge are rough and thick with bracken and are best avoided by inclining to the right *after Cove Quarries are passed* to join the good path from Goat's Water near the ruins of Cove Hut. *The quarries are an ugly trap in mist.*

When the Walna Scar Road is reached carry straight on through a maze of paths to Banishead Quarry, passing it on the left. At the foot of the slag heaps cross over the footbridge, and join the lane that links the climbing hut at Tranearth with the village of Torver.

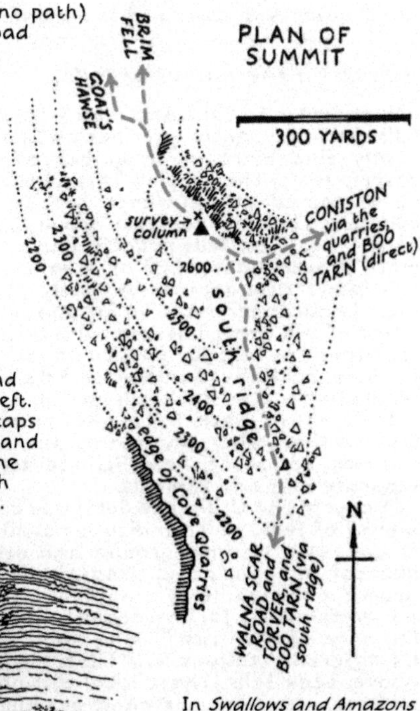
PLAN OF SUMMIT
BRIM FELL
GOAT'S HAWSE
300 YARDS
survey column
CONISTON via the quarries, and BOO TARN (direct)
2600
2500
2400
2300
2200
SOUTH ridge
edge of Cove Quarries
WALNA SCAR ROAD and TORVER, and BOO TARN (via south ridge)
N

In *Swallows and Amazons* by Arthur Ransome, Coniston Old Man is called 'Kanchenjunga'.

The summit from the north

The Coniston Fells: looking north along the ridge from the Old Man

A note on the names of fells:

Newcomers to Lakeland may wonder why many names of fells are prominently inscribed on Ordnance Survey maps yet rarely find mention, in guidebooks and other literature descriptive of the district. This neglect of official names can be explained by reference to the Coniston area as an example. Thus the compact group of hills known to walkers as the Coniston Fells is according to the Ordnance Survey, more properly described as a part of the Furness Fells, and this latter title appears in widely spaced capital letters on their Landranger maps. So far all right, but then this general name of the whole has several sub-titles in smaller but quite prominent letters for particular (but ill-defined) sections — Cockley Beck Fell, Seathwaite Fells, Tilberthwaite High Fells Troutal Fell, Coniston Fells (an area east of the principal ridge), Above Beck Fells, and so on. These names mean little to the walker, who soon trains his eye, when looking at the map, to ignore them. His interest is in the names of the separate hills and summits.

Of course the Ordnance Survey is correct in using the local names of fells, which indicate not hills but indefinite areas of uncultivated high ground and other rough pastures: in general, sheep-grazing areas. Walkers are quite wrong in applying the name of a summit to the whole fell as they do. Wetherlam, for instance, is the name of the top of a fell only, the fell itself being named variously according to its different sections, *e.g.* Tilberthwaite High Fells, Low Fell, Above Beck Fells. These local distinctions are of no use to walkers, who want one name per hill, although, on occasion, in the absence of a name for a summit, one of them may be adopted, *e.g.* Brim Fell.

The ideal map for fellwalkers would omit detail of purely local interest (and parish and other boundaries), and name all summits distinctively. *Do one for us, O.S., please.*

RIDGE ROUTES

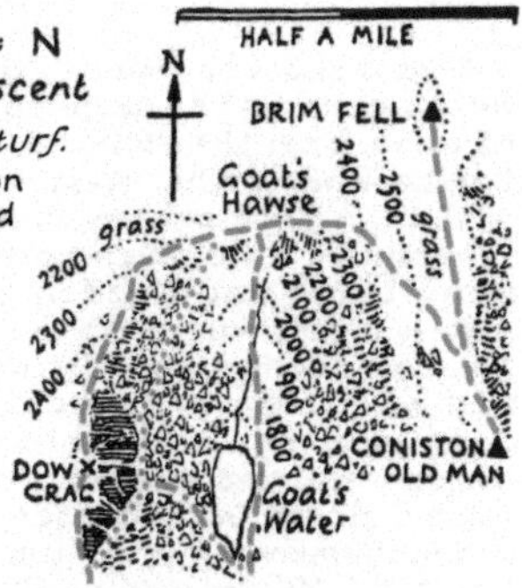
HALF A MILE
N
BRIM FELL
Goat's Hawse
grass
2200
2300
2400
2500
2100
2000
1900
1800
DOW CRAG
CONISTON OLD MAN
Goat's Water

To BRIM FELL, 2611′ : ½ mile : N
Depression at 2545′ : 80 feet of ascent

A ten minutes' stroll on excellent turf.

Brim Fell is the rounded top next on the ridge northwards. In mist it would be easy to take the Goat's Hawse path by mistake, but not if it is remembered that the route keeps to the ridge all the way.

To DOW CRAG, 2555′ : 1 mile : NW, W, SW and S
Depression (Goat's Hawse) at 2130′
425 feet of ascent

A walk of increasing interest.

An expert rockclimber who is also a good swimmer might attempt a straight course between the two summits, but ordinary mortals are forced to make a considerable detour *via* Goat's Hawse. A good path starts at the top of the Old Man and follows the ridge to the north. Turn left at the first junction and follow the path down to Goat's Hawse. After crossing the Hawse, a simple horizontal traverse may be made to the base of the great crag for a close view of the rock buttresses, but there is no trace of a path and the ground is extremely stony. However, there *is* a way up from here, *via* the South Rake. See *Dow Crag 3*.

Dow Crag from the Old Man

THE VIEW

A vast seascape makes a glorious sweep across the southern horizon, ranging from the Pennines to Black Combe, and, further west, to the Isle of Man. A rare beauty is added to the scene by the silver waters of the Kent, Leven and Duddon estuaries.

Most people who climb the Old Man, not being fellwalkers, fix their eyes in this direction, and squeals of joy announce the sighting of Sellafield nuclear reprocessing plant, Blackpool Tower, Morecambe Battery, the monument on Ulverston's Hoad Hill, Millom and sundry other man-made monstrosities. This book does not deign to cater for such tastes.

The fellwalker will prefer to gaze across the gulf of Eskdale to the natural and unmarred grandeur of the Scafell group, but, this scene apart, the mountain panorama, although very extensive, is a little disappointing due to the intervening bulk of the other Coniston fells.

The peep over the edge at the path zig-zagging upwards from Low Water, the tarn directly below, is, however, striking — the best bird's-eye view of an ascent route in Lakeland.

Swirl How is a much better viewpoint for the man who would rather look at hills than at Millom, and moreover, the peace will not be disturbed by squealing women and children and by knowledgeable males who noisily identify wrongly every hill in sight. Before fleeing to this sanctuary, however, wander a little way down the western slope until out of earshot of the congregation on the summit and so come face to face with the magnificent front of Dow Crag — and agree that nature fashions the finest architecture whatever the folk on the top may say.

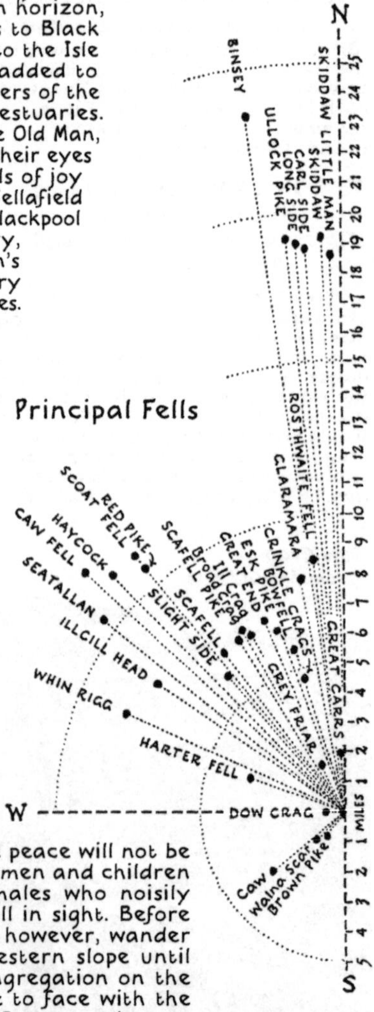
Principal Fells
N
S
W
MILES
BINSEY
SKIDDAW LITTLE MAN
SKIDDAW
CARL SIDE
LONG SIDE
ULLOCK PIKE
ROSTHWAITE FELL
GLARAMARA
CRINKLE CRAGS
BOWFELL
ESK PIKE
GREAT END
Ill Crag
Broad Crag
SCAFELL PIKE
RED PIKE
SCOAT FELL
HAYCOCK
CAW FELL
SEATALLAN
SLIGHT SIDE
SCAFELL
ILLCILL HEAD
WHIN RIGG
GREY FRIAR
GREAT CARRS
HARTER FELL
DOW CRAG
Caw
Walna Scar
Brown Pike

THE VIEW

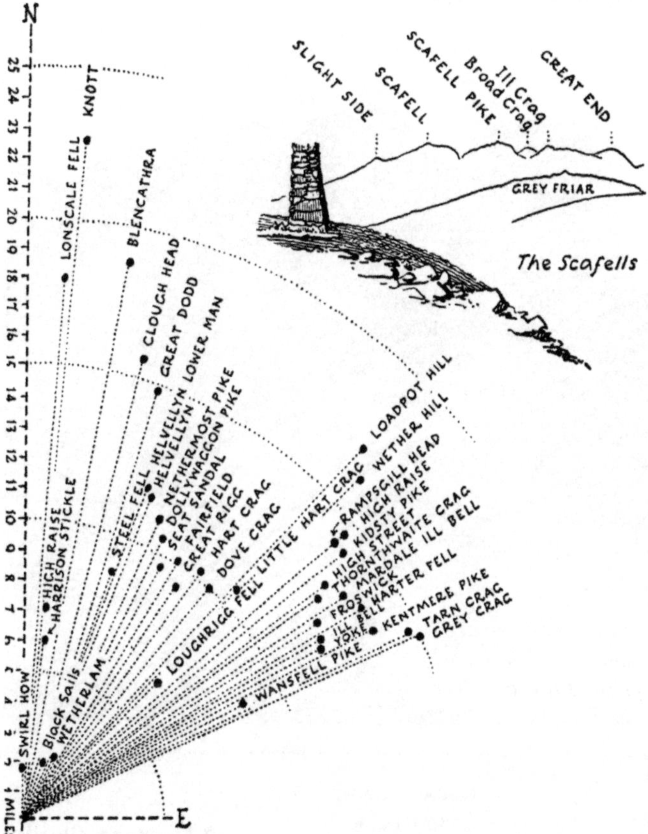
N
E
S
MILES
1
2
3
4
5
6
7
8
9
10
11
12
13
14
15
16
17
18
19
20
21
22
23
24
25
KNOTT
LONSCALE FELL
BLENCATHRA
CLOUGH HEAD
GREAT DODD
LOWER MAN
HELVELLYN LOWER MAN
HELVELLYN
NETHERMOST PIKE
DOLLYWAGGON PIKE
SEAT SANDAL
FAIRFIELD
GREAT RIGG
HART CRAG
DOVE CRAG
LITTLE HART CRAG
LOUGHRIGG FELL
STEEL FELL
HIGH RAISE
HARRISON STICKLE
SWIRL HOW
Black Sails
WETHERLAM
LOADPOT HILL
WETHER HILL
RAMPSGILL HEAD
HIGH RAISE
KIDSTY PIKE
HIGH STREET
THORNTHWAITE CRAG
MARDALE ILL BELL
FROSWICK
HARTER FELL
ILL BELL
YOKE
KENTMERE PIKE
TARN CRAG
GREY CRAG
WANSFELL PIKE
SLIGHT SIDE
SCAFELL
SCAFELL PIKE
Ill Crag
Broad Crag
GREAT END
GREY FRIAR
The Scafells

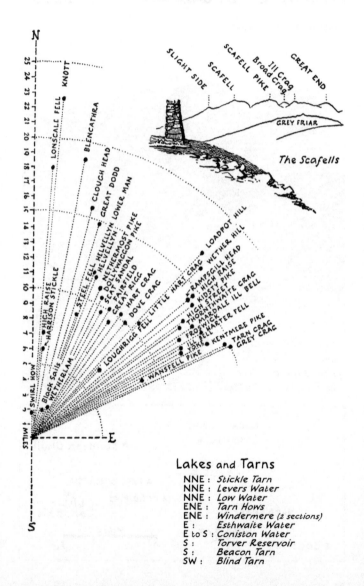

Lakes and Tarns

NNE : *Stickle Tarn*
NNE : *Levers Water*
NNE : *Low Water*
ENE : *Tarn Hows*
ENE : *Windermere (2 sections)*
E : *Esthwaite Water*
E to S : *Coniston Water*
S : *Torver Reservoir*
S : *Beacon Tarn*
SW : *Blind Tarn*

Crinkle Crags 2816'

OS grid ref: NY249049

from Pike o' Blisco

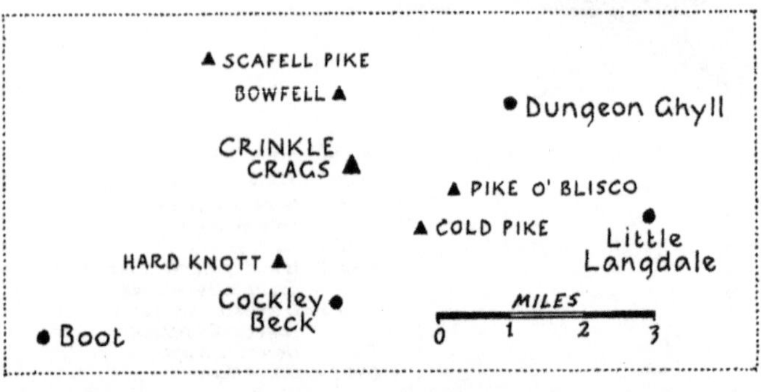
SCAFELL PIKE
BOWFELL
Dungeon Ghyll
CRINKLE CRAGS
PIKE O' BLISCO
COLD PIKE
Little Langdale
HARD KNOTT
Cockley Beck
MILES
0
1
2
3
Boot

NATURAL FEATURES

Some mountains are obviously named by reference to their physical characteristics. Crinkle Crags is one of these, and it was probably first so called by the dalesfolk of the valleys to the east and around the head of Windermere, whence its lofty serrated ridge, a succession of knobs and depressions, is aptly described by the name. These undulations, seeming trivial from a distance, are revealed at close range as steep buttresses and gullies above wild declivities, a scene of desolation and rugged grandeur equalled by few others in the district. Nor is the Eskdale flank any gentler, for here too are gaunt shattered crags rising from incredibly rough slopes. The high pass of Three Tarns links the ridge with Bowfell to the north while southwards Wrynose Bottom is the boundary.

Crinkle Crags is much too good to be missed. For the mountaineer who prefers his mountains rough, who likes to see steep craggy slopes towering before him into the sky, who enjoys an up-and-down ridge walk full of interesting nooks and corners, who has an appreciative eye for magnificent views, this is a climb deserving of high priority. But it is not a place to visit in bad weather for the top is confusing, with ins and outs as well as ups and downs and a sketchy path that cannot be relied on. Crinkle Crags merits respect, and should be treated with respect; then it will yield the climber a mountain walk long to be remembered with pleasure.

Is it 'Crinkle Crags IS...' or 'Crinkle Crags ARE...'?
Is it 'Three Tarns IS...' or 'Three Tarns ARE...'?
IS sounds right but looks wrong!

The outline of Crinkle Crags from Great Langdale

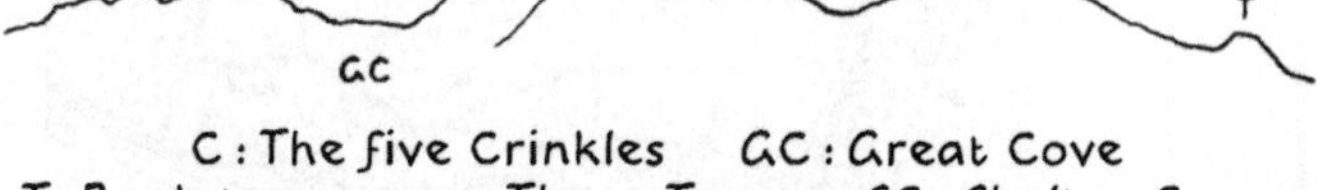
C
C
C
C
C
SC
T
GC

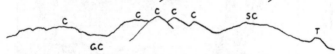

C : The five Crinkles   GC : Great Cove
T : Rock tower near Three Tarns   SC : Shelter Crags

The highest Crinkle (2816') is second from the left on the diagram. When seen from the valley it does not appear to be the highest, as it is set back a little from the line of the others.

MAP

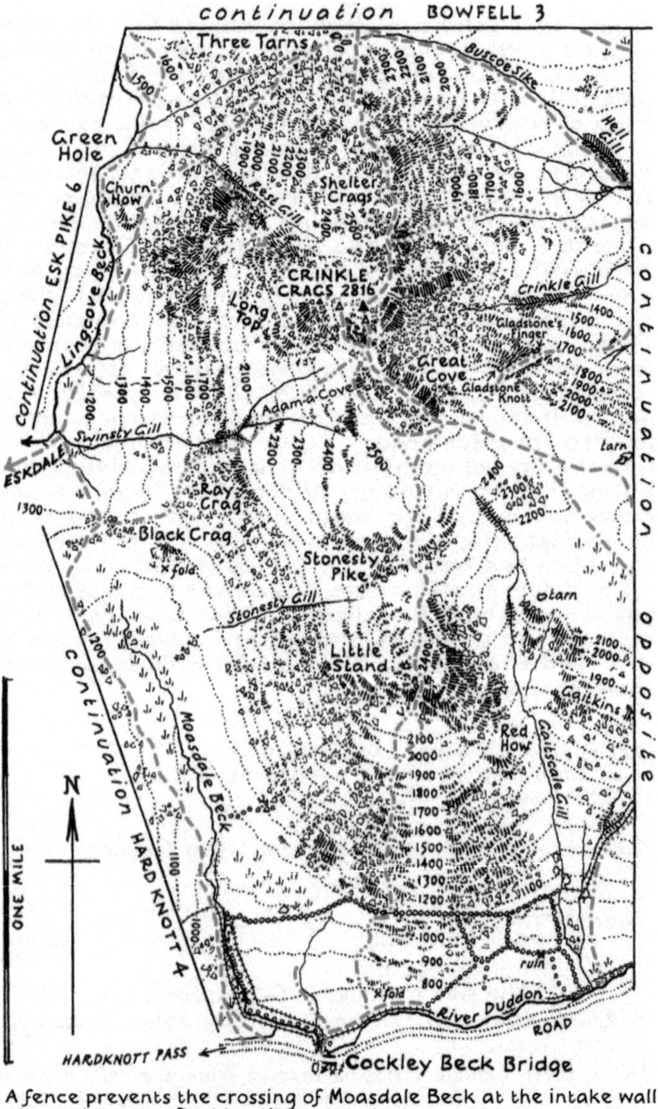
continuation BOWFELL 3
Three Tarns
Buscoe Sike
Hell Gill
Green Hole
Churn How
Rest Gill
Shelter Crags
continuation ESK PIKE 6
Lingcove Beck
CRINKLE CRAGS 2816
Long Top
Crinkle Gill
Gladstone's Finger
Great Cove
Gladstone Knott
Adam-a-Cove
Swinsty Gill
ESKDALE
tarn
continuation opposite
Ray Crag
Black Crag
fold
Stonesty Pike
Stonesty Gill
tarn
Little Stand
Gaitkins
Red How
continuation HARD KNOTT 4
Moasdale Beck
Gaitscale Gill
N
ONE MILE
ruin
fold
River Duddon
ROAD
HARDKNOTT PASS
Cockley Beck Bridge

A fence prevents the crossing of Moasdale Beck at the intake wall above the upper Duddon Valley.

MAP

continuation BOWFELL 4
The Band
Dry Gill
1400
1300
1200
1100
1000
900
800
700
seat
Stool End
DUNGEON GHYLL ½
Whorneyside Force
fold
Oxendale Beck
footbridge
500
600
700
800
900
1000
1100
1200
1300
1400
1500
continuation PIKE O' BLISCO 3
Isaac Gill
Brown Howe
Browney Gill
Great Knott
continuation opposite
1800
1900
2000
2100
1700
Red Tarn
COLD PIKE
1800
fold
continuation PIKE O' BLISCO 3
Rough Crags
LITTLE LANGDALE
1900
1800
1700
1600
1500
1400
1300
1200
1100
1000
900
Wrynose Breast
Three Shire Stone
summit
Wrynose Pass
ROAD
River Duddon
Wrynose Bottom

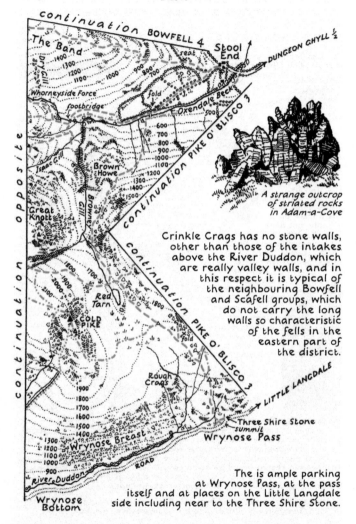

A strange outcrop of striated rocks in Adam-a-Cove

Crinkle Crags has no stone walls, other than those of the intakes above the River Duddon, which are really valley walls, and in this respect it is typical of the neighbouring Bowfell and Scafell groups, which do not carry the long walls so characteristic of the fells in the eastern part of the district.

The is ample parking at Wrynose Pass, at the pass itself and at places on the Little Langdale side including near to the Three Shire Stone.

The direct path between Cold Pike and Crinkle Crags crosses a grassy depression and is best avoided during periods of wet weather, and the shorter route to the Red Tarn–Crinkle Crags 'highway' be used instead.

Crinkle Crags 5

ASCENT FROM DUNGEON GHYLL (*via* RED TARN)
2600 feet of ascent : 4 miles

CRINKLE CRAGS
Consult the Ridge Plan here (page 11)
COLD PIKE
2500
2400
flat boulder
tarn
Gladstone Knott
looking west-south west
2100
2000
1900
2000
Gladstone's Finger
1900
1800
Red Tarn
1800
Great Knott
1700
WRYNOSE
1600
Grassy gully between crags
fall
1500
1400
grass
CRINKLE CRAGS (direct) and BOWFELL (via Hell Gill)
Browney Gill
Isaac Gill
Crinkle Gill
1600
footbridge
Brown Howe
1500
1400
tor
1300
1200
800
1100
Oxendale Beck
1000
700
600
900
800
700
sheepfold
600
dam
500
BOWFELL
500
Stool End
gate
bridge
gate
DUNGEON GHYLL ½

The route *via* Gladstone's Finger, being far more direct than that *via* Red Tarn, is nearly a mile shorter. The effort expended, however, is considerably more

The shapely spur between Issac and Crinkle Gills has a clear path initially, but once past the first rock band it becomes very sketchy. Consequently, *this route should be avoided in mist.*

The higher path is better underfoot

Rising high on the right is The Band, a spur of Bowfell

The final gully beside the imposing 25' high pinnacle of Gladstone's Finger is steep and desperately stony, but the view across the imposing eastern flank of the Crinkles backed by the Langdale Pikes is very impressive.

Gladstone's Finger

As far as Red Tarn, the route is that used for the ascent of Pike o' Blisco (the craggy slopes of which tower up on the left throughout) and for the high-level walk to Wrynose Pass. The path is one of many in the district that have been improved in recent years by being paved.

A route on the south side of Great Knott, reached from the west bank of Browney Gill, is not recommended.

The wide, bouldery course of Oxendale Beck testifies to its power in flood. The valley is outstanding for its impressive ravines.

The scenery throughout is excellent on this popular walk. Descend *via* Three Tarns in order to make the complete traverse of the summit ridge. An adventurous alternative visiting Gladstone's Finger needs clear weather.

ASCENT FROM DUNGEON GHYLL (*via* THREE TARNS)
2650 feet of ascent : 4 miles

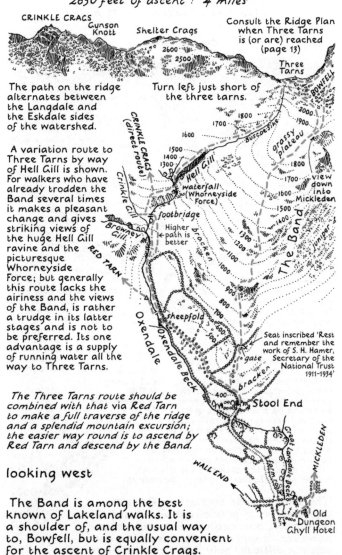

CRINKLE CRAGS
Gunson Knott
Shelter Crags
Consult the Ridge Plan when Three Tarns is (or are) reached (page 13)
2600
2500
Three Tarns

The path on the ridge alternates between the Langdale and the Eskdale sides of the watershed.

A variation route to Three Tarns by way of Hell Gill is shown. For walkers who have already trodden the Band several times it makes a pleasant change and gives striking views of the huge Hell Gill ravine and the picturesque Whorneyside Force; but generally this route lacks the airiness and the views of the Band, is rather a trudge in its latter stages and is not to be preferred. Its one advantage is a supply of running water all the way to Three Tarns.

The Three Tarns route should be combined with that via Red Tarn to make a full traverse of the ridge and a splendid mountain excursion; the easier way round is to ascend by Red Tarn and descend by the Band.

looking west

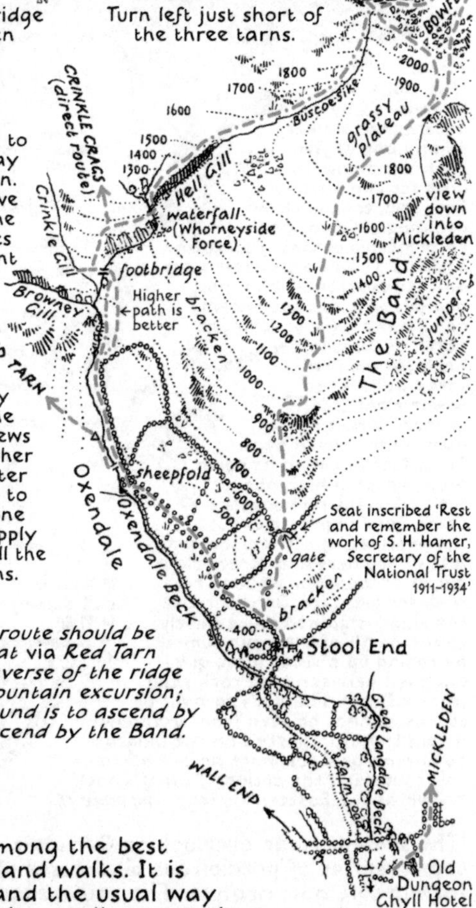
Turn left just short of the three tarns.
BOWFELL
2000
1900
1800
1700
1600
1500
1400
1300
Buscoe Sike
grassy plateau
CRINKLE CRAGS (direct route)
Hell Gill
waterfall (Whorneyside Force)
view down into Mickleden
Crinkle Gill
footbridge
Browney Gill
Higher path is better
bracken
The Band
juniper
RED TARN
1200
1100
1000
900
800
700
600
500
sheepfold
Oxendale
Oxendale Beck
Seat inscribed 'Rest and remember the work of S. H. Hamer, Secretary of the National Trust 1911–1934'
gate
bracken
400
Stool End
Great Langdale Beck
farm road
WALL END
MICKLEDEN
Old Dungeon Ghyll Hotel

The Band is among the best known of Lakeland walks. It is a shoulder of, and the usual way to, Bowfell, but is equally convenient for the ascent of Crinkle Crags.

ASCENT FROM DUNGEON GHYLL
(DIRECT CLIMB FROM OXENDALE)
2550 feet of ascent : 3½ miles

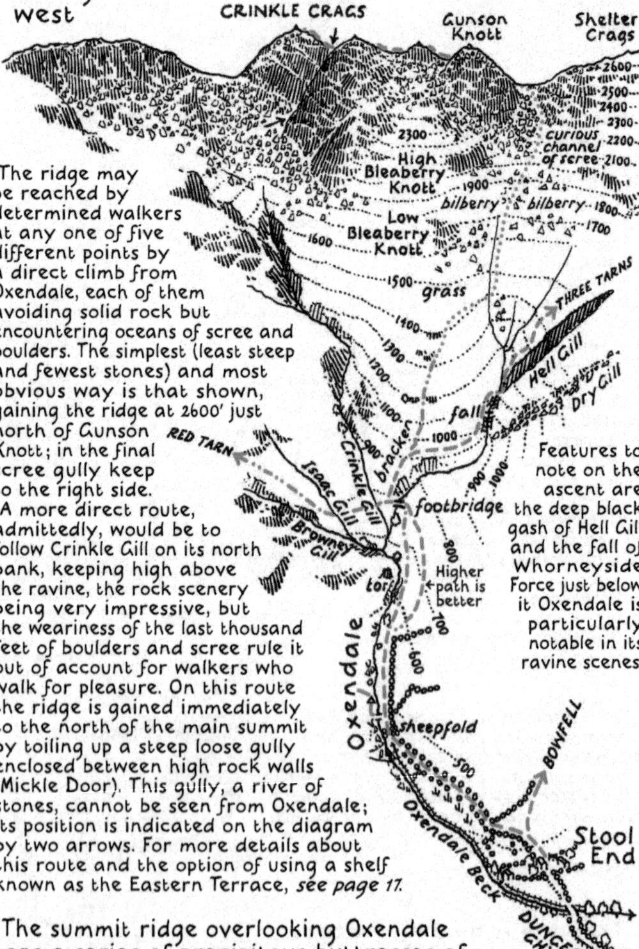
looking west
CRINKLE CRAGS
Gunson Knott
Shelter Crags
2600
2500
2400
2300
curious channel of scree
2200
2100
2300
High Bleaberry Knott
1900
bilberry
bilberry
1800
1700
Low Bleaberry Knott
1600
1500
grass
THREE TARNS
1400
1300
1200
Hell Gill
Dry Gill
1100
fall
1000
bracken
900
RED TARN
Crinkle Gill
Isaac Gill
footbridge
900
1000
Browney Gill
800
tor
Higher path is better
700
600
Oxendale
sheepfold
500
BOWFELL
Stool End
Oxendale Beck
DUNGEON GHYLL

The ridge may be reached by determined walkers at any one of five different points by a direct climb from Oxendale, each of them avoiding solid rock but encountering oceans of scree and boulders. The simplest (least steep and fewest stones) and most obvious way is that shown, gaining the ridge at 2600′ just north of Gunson Knott; in the final scree gully keep to the right side.

A more direct route, admittedly, would be to follow Crinkle Gill on its north bank, keeping high above the ravine, the rock scenery being very impressive, but the weariness of the last thousand feet of boulders and scree rule it out of account for walkers who walk for pleasure. On this route the ridge is gained immediately to the north of the main summit by toiling up a steep loose gully enclosed between high rock walls (Mickle Door). This gully, a river of stones, cannot be seen from Oxendale; its position is indicated on the diagram by two arrows. For more details about this route and the option of using a shelf known as the Eastern Terrace, *see page 17*.

Features to note on the ascent are the deep black gash of Hell Gill and the fall of Whorneyside Force just below it. Oxendale is particularly notable in its ravine scenes.

The summit ridge overlooking Oxendale tops a series of precipitous buttresses of formidable appearance. The route shown, however, is quite simple, becoming rough (but not difficult) only in the concluding stages.

ASCENT FROM ESKDALE

2650 feet of ascent : 7½ miles from Boot
(8 miles via Three Tarns)

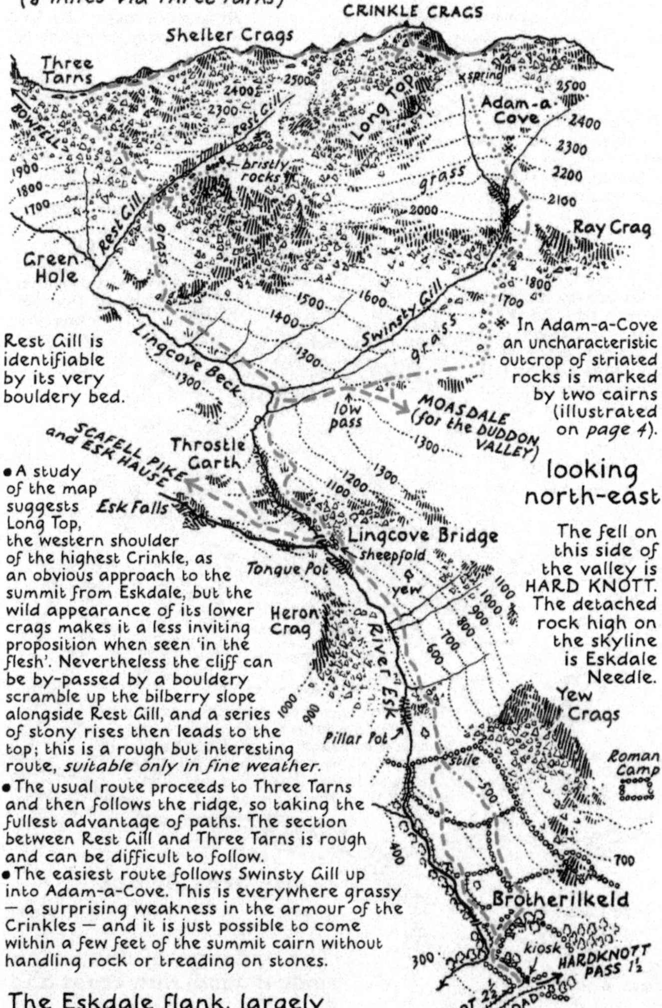
CRINKLE CRAGS
Shelter Crags
Three Tarns
BOWFELL
2500
2400
2300
2500
2400
2300
2200
2100
2000
1900
1800
1700
1800
1700
1600
1500
1400
1300
1300
1300
1200
1100
1100
1000
900
800
700
600
1000
900
500
400
300
700
Rest Gill
Rest Gill
Long Top
spring
Adam-a-Cove
bristly rocks
grass
grass
grass
Ray Crag
Green Hole
Swinsty Gill
Lingcove Beck
low pass
MOASDALE (for the DUDDON VALLEY)
SCAFELL PIKE and ESK HAUSE
Throstle Garth
Esk Falls
Lingcove Bridge
sheepfold
Tongue Pot
yew
Heron Crag
River Esk
Yew Crags
Pillar Pot
stile
Roman Camp
Brotherilkeld
kiosk
HARDKNOTT PASS 1½
BOOT 2½
ROAD

Rest Gill is identifiable by its very bouldery bed.

* In Adam-a-Cove an uncharacteristic outcrop of striated rocks is marked by two cairns (illustrated on *page 4*).

looking north-east

The fell on this side of the valley is HARD KNOTT. The detached rock high on the skyline is Eskdale Needle.

- A study of the map suggests Long Top, the western shoulder of the highest Crinkle, as an obvious approach to the summit from Eskdale, but the wild appearance of its lower crags makes it a less inviting proposition when seen 'in the flesh'. Nevertheless the cliff can be by-passed by a bouldery scramble up the bilberry slope alongside Rest Gill, and a series of stony rises then leads to the top; this is a rough but interesting route, *suitable only in fine weather.*
- The usual route proceeds to Three Tarns and then follows the ridge, so taking the fullest advantage of paths. The section between Rest Gill and Three Tarns is rough and can be difficult to follow.
- The easiest route follows Swinsty Gill up into Adam-a-Cove. This is everywhere grassy — a surprising weakness in the armour of the Crinkles — and it is just possible to come within a few feet of the summit cairn without handling rock or treading on stones.

The Eskdale flank, largely infrequented, offers walkers a choice of routes: safe (Three Tarns), adventurous (Rest Gill and Long Top) and secluded (Adam-a-Cove).

ASCENT FROM COCKLEY BECK BRIDGE
2350 feet of ascent : 3 miles

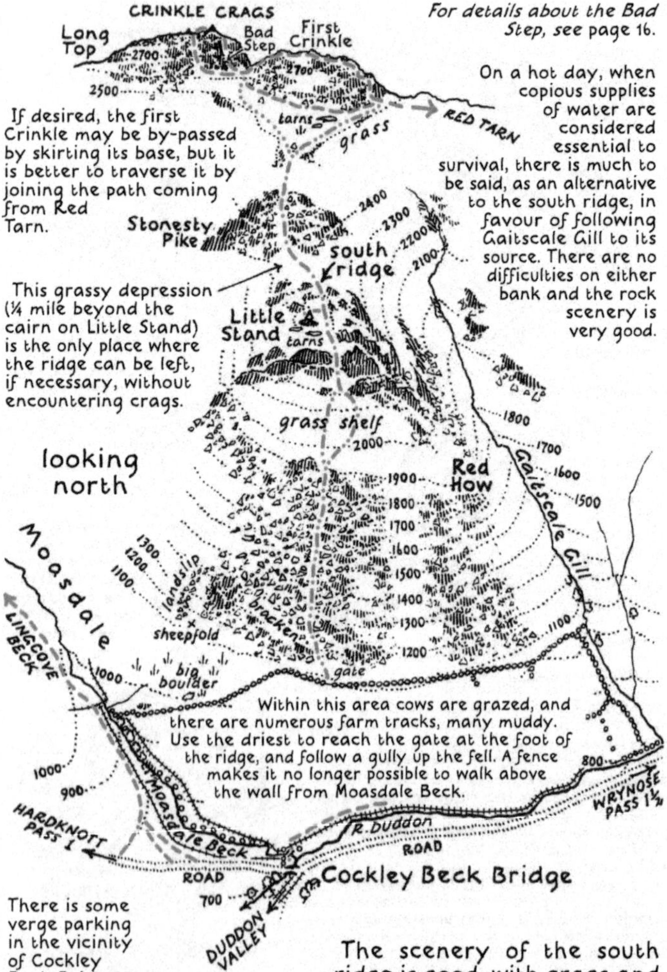
CRINKLE CRAGS
Long Top
Bad Step
First Crinkle
2700
2700
2500
tarns
grass
RED TARN
Stonesty Pike
2400
2300
2200
2100
South ridge
Little Stand
tarns
grass shelf
2000
1800
1700
1600
1500
Red How
Gaitscale Gill
1900
1800
1700
1600
1500
1400
1300
1200
1100
looking north
Moasdale
LINGCOVE BECK
1300
1200
1100
landslip
bracken
sheepfold
big boulder
gate
1000
800
WRYNOSE PASS 1½
R. Duddon
ROAD
Moasdale Beck
1000
900
HARDKNOTT PASS 1
ROAD
Cockley Beck Bridge
700
DUDDON VALLEY

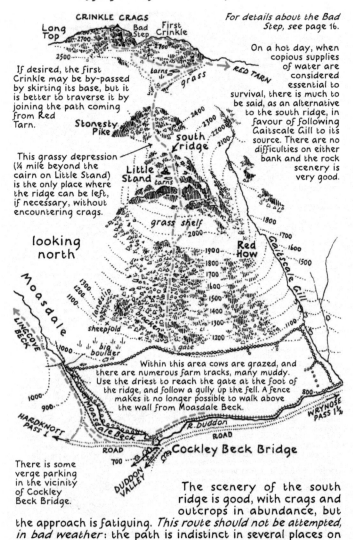

For details about the Bad Step, see page 16.

On a hot day, when copious supplies of water are considered essential to survival, there is much to be said, as an alternative to the south ridge, in favour of following Gaitscale Gill to its source. There are no difficulties on either bank and the rock scenery is very good.

If desired, the first Crinkle may be by-passed by skirting its base, but it is better to traverse it by joining the path coming from Red Tarn.

This grassy depression (¼ mile beyond the cairn on Little Stand) is the only place where the ridge can be left, if necessary, without encountering crags.

Within this area cows are grazed, and there are numerous farm tracks, many muddy. Use the driest to reach the gate at the foot of the ridge, and follow a gully up the fell. A fence makes it no longer possible to walk above the wall from Moasdale Beck.

There is some verge parking in the vicinity of Cockley Beck Bridge.

The scenery of the south ridge is good, with crags and outcrops in abundance, but the approach is fatiguing. *This route should not be attempted, in bad weather*: the path is indistinct in several places on the ridge, which has escarpments on both flanks.

ASCENT FROM WRYNOSE PASS
1650 feet of ascent : 2¾ miles

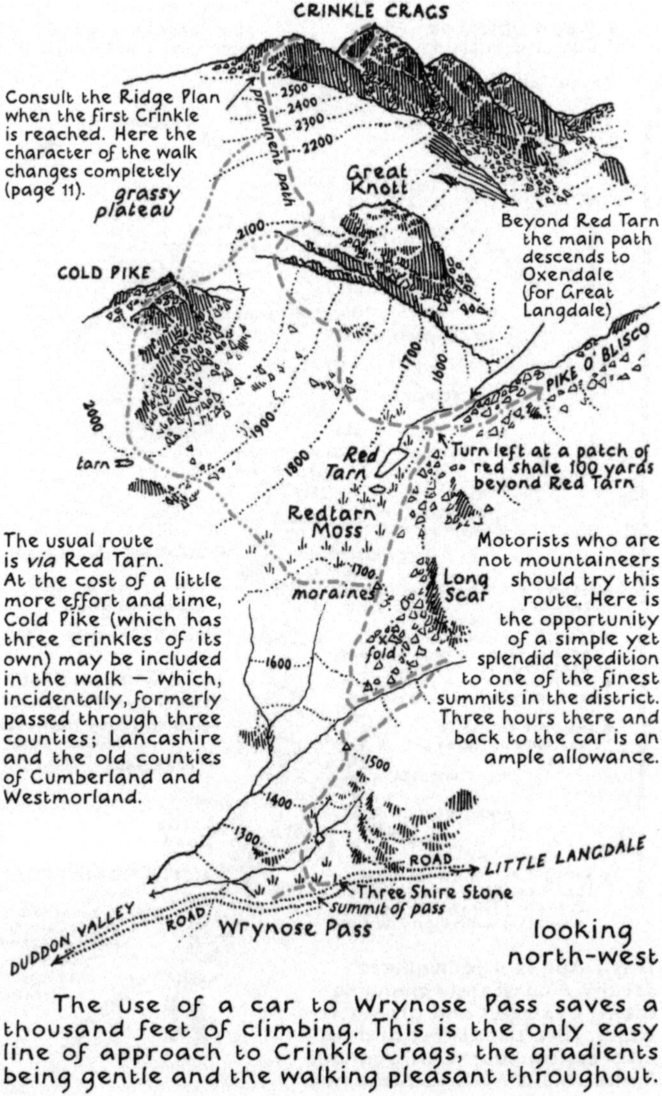
CRINKLE CRAGS
Consult the Ridge Plan when the first Crinkle is reached. Here the character of the walk changes completely (page 11).
prominent path
2500
2400
2300
2200
grassy plateau
Great Knott
Beyond Red Tarn the main path descends to Oxendale (for Great Langdale)
2100
COLD PIKE
PIKE O' BLISCO
1700
1600
2000
1900
1800
tarn
Red Tarn
Turn left at a patch of red shale 100 yards beyond Red Tarn
Redtarn Moss
The usual route is *via* Red Tarn. At the cost of a little more effort and time, Cold Pike (which has three crinkles of its own) may be included in the walk — which, incidentally, formerly passed through three counties; Lancashire and the old counties of Cumberland and Westmorland.
Motorists who are not mountaineers should try this route. Here is the opportunity of a simple yet splendid expedition to one of the finest summits in the district. Three hours there and back to the car is an ample allowance.
1700
moraines
Long Scar
fold
1600
1500
1400
1300
ROAD
LITTLE LANGDALE
Three Shire Stone
summit of pass
DUDDON VALLEY
ROAD
Wrynose Pass
looking north-west

The use of a car to Wrynose Pass saves a thousand feet of climbing. This is the only easy line of approach to Crinkle Crags, the gradients being gentle and the walking pleasant throughout.

RIDGE PLAN

for use when traversing the ridge from SOUTH to NORTH

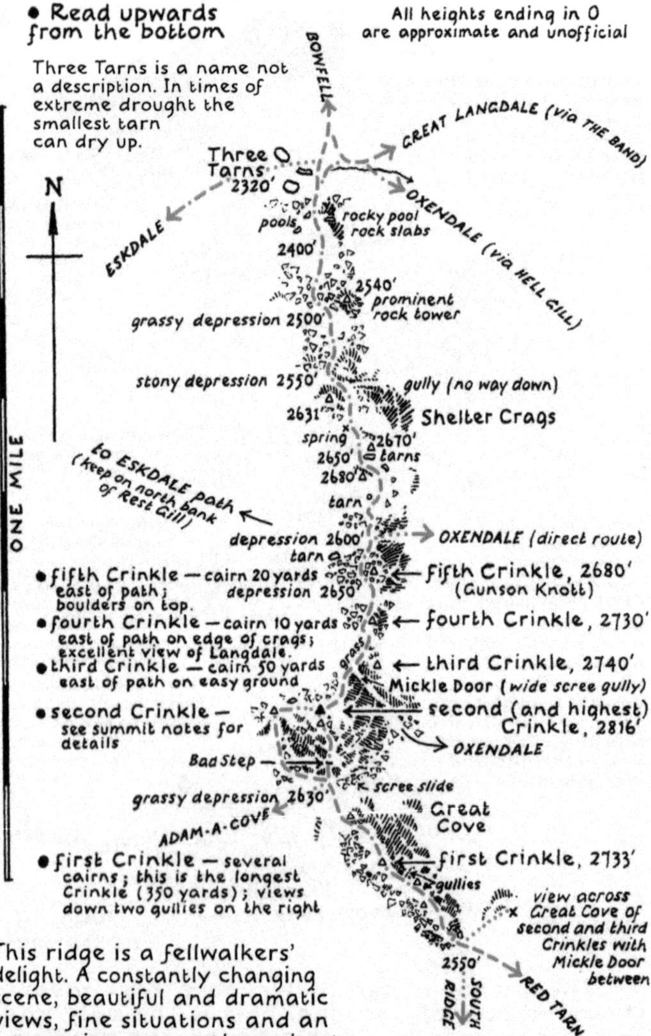
• Read upwards from the bottom
All heights ending in 0 are approximate and unofficial
Three Tarns is a name not a description. In times of extreme drought the smallest tarn can dry up.
BOWFELL
GREAT LANGDALE (via THE BAND)
Three Tarns 2320'
OXENDALE (via HELL GILL)
N
ESKDALE
pools
rocky pool
rock slabs
2400'
2540'
prominent rock tower
grassy depression 2500'
stony depression 2550'
gully (no way down)
2631'
Shelter Crags
spring
2670'
2650'
tarns
2680'
ONE MILE
to ESKDALE path (keep on north bank of Rest Gill)
tarn
depression 2600'
OXENDALE (direct route)
tarn
• fifth Crinkle — cairn 20 yards east of path; boulders on top.
depression 2650'
fifth Crinkle, 2680' (Gunson Knott)
• fourth Crinkle — cairn 10 yards east of path on edge of crags; excellent view of Langdale.
fourth Crinkle, 2730'
grass
• third Crinkle — cairn 50 yards east of path on easy ground
third Crinkle, 2740'
Mickle Door (wide scree gully)
• second Crinkle — see summit notes for details
second (and highest) Crinkle, 2816'
OXENDALE
Bad Step
scree slide
grassy depression 2630'
ADAM-A-COVE
Great Cove
• first Crinkle — several cairns; this is the longest Crinkle (350 yards); views down two gullies on the right
first Crinkle, 2733'
gullies
view across Great Cove of second and third Crinkles with Mickle Door between
2550'
SOUTH RIDGE
RED TARN

This ridge is a fellwalkers' delight. A constantly changing scene, beautiful and dramatic views, fine situations and an interesting course throughout make this a walk to remember.

Looking NORTH along the ridge........

The second (and highest) Crinkle, Mickle Door, and the third Crinkle, seen across Great Cove

The fourth and fifth Crinkles (Shelter Crags and Bowfell behind), seen from the third Crinkle

RIDGE PLAN

for use when traversing the ridge from NORTH to SOUTH

• Read upwards from the bottom

This is, of course, the same plan as that already given for the south to north traverse but reversed for easier reference. Reading upwards, left and right on the plan will agree with left and right as they appear to the walker.

All heights ending in 0 are approximate and unofficial.

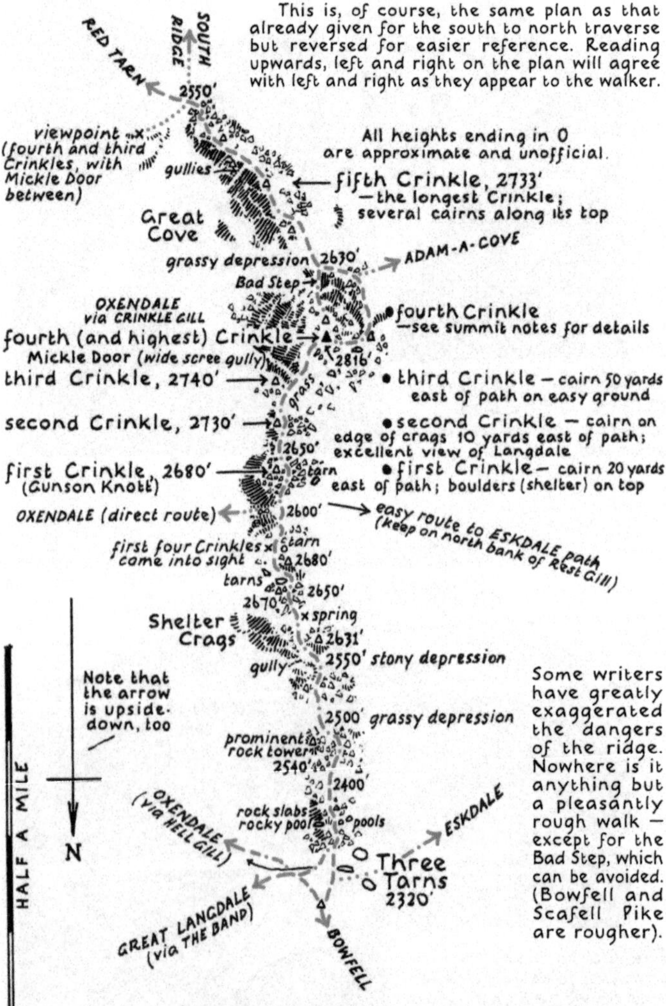
RED TARN
SOUTH RIDGE
2550'
viewpoint x (fourth and third Crinkles, with Mickle Door between)
gullies
fifth Crinkle, 2733' — the longest Crinkle; several cairns along its top
Great Cove
grassy depression 2630'
ADAM-A-COVE
Bad Step
OXENDALE via CRINKLE GILL
• fourth Crinkle — see summit notes for details
fourth (and highest) Crinkle
Mickle Door (wide scree gully)
2816'
third Crinkle, 2740'
grass
• third Crinkle — cairn 50 yards east of path on easy ground
second Crinkle, 2730'
• second Crinkle — cairn on edge of crags 10 yards east of path; excellent view of Langdale
2650'
first Crinkle, 2680' (Gunson Knott)
tarn
• first Crinkle — cairn 20 yards east of path; boulders (shelter) on top
OXENDALE (direct route)
2600'
easy route to ESKDALE path (keep on north bank of Rest Gill)
first four Crinkles x come into sight
tarn
2680'
tarns
2650'
2670'
x spring
Shelter Crags
2631'
gully
2550' stony depression
Note that the arrow is upside-down, too
N
HALF A MILE
2500' grassy depression
prominent rock tower
2540'
2400'
OXENDALE (via HELL GILL)
rock slabs
rocky pool
pools
ESKDALE
Three Tarns 2320'
GREAT LANGDALE (via THE BAND)
BOWFELL

Some writers have greatly exaggerated the dangers of the ridge. Nowhere is it anything but a pleasantly rough walk — except for the Bad Step, which can be avoided. (Bowfell and Scafell Pike are rougher).

Introducing Lakeland's best ridge-mile!

Looking SOUTH along the ridge........

Four Crinkles come suddenly into view from the path as it rounds a corner of Shelter Crags

The fifth Crinkle as seen from the main Crinkle on the descent to the Bad Step

THE SUMMIT

There are five Crinkles (not counting Shelter Crags) and therefore five summits, each with its own summit cairn. The highest is, however, so obviously the highest that the true top of the fell is not in doubt in clear visibility, and this is the Crinkle (the fourth from the north and second from the south) with which these notes are concerned. It is not the stoniest of the five, nor the greatest in girth, but, unlike the others, it extends a considerable distance as a lateral ridge (Long Top) descending westwards, where there is a tarn (unnamed) which has a high claim to being the highest in Lakeland. On the actual summit are two principal cairns separated by 40 yards of easy ground; that to the north, standing on a rock platform, is slightly the more elevated. The eastern face descends in precipices from the easy grass terraces above it; there are crags running down steeply from the south cairn also, but in other directions the top terrain is not difficult although everywhere rough.

1
2
3
4
1
2
4

1 : grassy rake (easy way)
2 : direct route (steep scree)
3 : the Bad Step (*see next page*)
4 : detour to avoid the Bad Step.

The highest Crinkle, from the south

continued

THE SUMMIT

continued

DESCENTS

to GREAT LANGDALE: The orthodox routes are (1) *via* Red Tarn and Brown How, and (2) *via* Three Tarns and the Band, both excellent walks, and in normal circumstances no other ways should be considered. If time is very short, however, or if it is necessary to escape quickly from stormy conditions on the ridge, quick and sheltered routes are provided by (3) the scree gully of Mickle Door or (4) the Gunson Knott gully, which is easier: both are very rough initially but lead to open slopes above Oxendale.

to ESKDALE: Much the easiest way, and much the quickest, is to descend from Adam-a-Cove (no path) keeping *left* of Swinsty Gill where it enters a ravine. Long Top is a temptation to be resisted, for it leads only to trouble,

to COCKLEY BECK BRIDGE: The south ridge is interesting (no path and *not safe in mist*), but tired limbs had better take advantage of the easy way down from Adam-a-Cove, inclining left below Ray Crag into Moasdale

to WRYNOSE PASS: Reverse the route of ascent. Cold Pike may be traversed with little extra cost in energy.

In mist, take good care to keep to the ridge path, which, in many places, is no more than nail scratches on rocks and boulders but is generally simple to follow. Go nowhere unless there is evidence that many others have passed that way before. (The exception to this golden rule is Adam-a-Cove, which is perfectly safe *if it is remembered to keep to the left bank of the stream*).

The Bad Step

Caution is needed on the descent southwards from the summit. A walker crossing the top from the north will naturally gravitate to the south cairn and start his descent here. A steep path goes down rock ledges to a slope of loose scree, which spills over the lip of a chockstone (two, really) bridging and blocking a little gully. Anyone descending at speed here is asking for a nasty fall. The impasse is usually avoided and the gully regained below the chockstone by an awkward descent of the rock wall to the left, which deserves the name 'The Bad Step', for it is 10 feet high and as near vertical as makes no difference. This is the sort of place that everybody would get down in a flash if a £20 note was waiting to be picked up on the scree below, but, without such an inducement, there is much wavering on the brink. Chicken-hearted walkers, muttering something about discretion being the better part of valour, will sneak away and circumvent the difficulty by following the author's footsteps around the left flank of the buttress forming the retaining wall of the gully, where grassy ledges enable the foot of the gully to be reached without trouble; here they may sit and watch, with ill-concealed grins, the discomfiture of other tourists who may come along.

The Bad Step is the most difficult obstacle met on any of the regular walkers' paths in Lakeland.

The Bad Step from below

continued

THE SUMMIT

continued

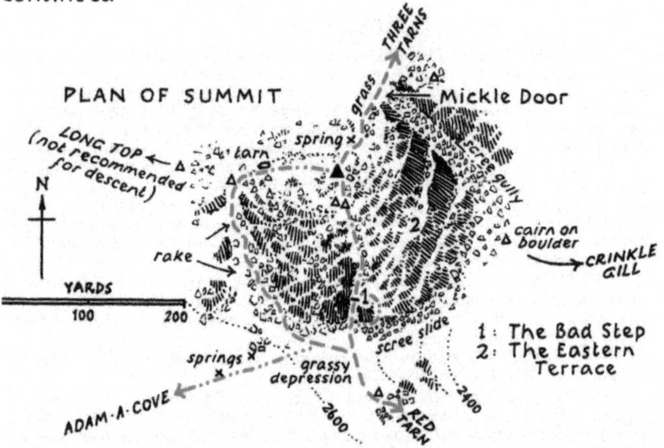
PLAN OF SUMMIT
THREE TARNS
grass
Mickle Door
spring
tarn
LONG TOP (not recommended for descent)
N
scree gully
cairn on boulder
CRINKLE GILL
rake
YARDS
100
200
1
2
scree slide
springs
grassy depression
ADAM-A-COVE
2600
RED TARN
2400
1: The Bad Step
2: The Eastern Terrace

Note that the steep direct descent from the south cairn may be by-passed altogether (it was formerly customary to do so) by proceeding west from the main cairn for 140 yards to another on grass in a slight depression, whence a path leads down a stony rake on the left, skirting completely the rocks of the Crinkle, to join the direct route at its base.

The welcome spring on the summit (usually reliable after recent rain) is remarkable for its proximity to the top cairn (30 yards north-east, in the bend of the path); it is only 20 feet lower than the cairn, and has a very limited gathering ground. Find it by listening for it — it emerges as a tiny waterfall from beneath a boulder. This is not the highest spring in the district but it is the nearest to a high summit.

The Eastern Terrace

A conspicuous grass terrace slants at an angle of 30° across the eastern cliffs of the main Crinkle, rising from the screes of the Mickle Door gully to the direct ridge route just above the Bad Step. It is not seen from the ridge but appears in views of the east face clearly, being the middle of three such terraces and most prominent. It is of little use to walkers, except those who (in defiance of advice already given) are approaching the summit from Crinkle Gill: for them it offers a way of escape from the final screes. The terrace (identified by a little wall at the side of the gully) is wide and without difficulties but is no place for loitering, being subject to bombardments of stones by bloody fools, if any, on the summit above. It is well to remember, too that the terrace is bounded by a precipice At the upper end the terrace becomes more broken near the Bad Step and is not quite easy to locate when approached from this direction.

1
2
3
4
cairn on boulder

1: the Bad Step
2: the Eastern Terrace
3: Mickle Door
4: scree slide

The Eastern Face

RIDGE ROUTES

To BOWFELL, 2960′ : 1½ miles : Generally N, then WNW
Five depressions; final one (Three Tarns) at 2320′: 850 feet of ascent

Positively one of the finest ridgewalks in Lakeland. The rough stony ground makes progress slow, but this walk is, in any case, deserving of a leisurely appreciation; it is much too good to be done in a hurry. Every turn of the fairly distinct track is interesting, and in places even exciting, although no difficulty is met except for an occasional awkward stride on rock. In mist, the walker will probably have to descend to Three Tarns anyway, but should give Bowfell a miss, especially if the route is unfamiliar. For more details, see the ridge plan on *page 11*.

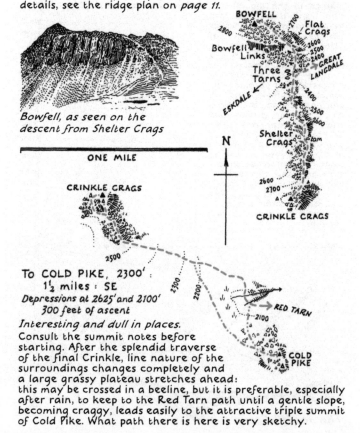

Bowfell, as seen on the descent from Shelter Crags

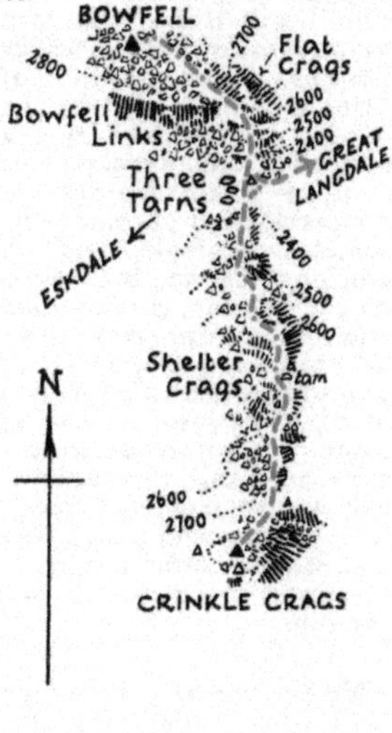

BOWFELL
2700
Flat
Crags
2800
Bowfell
Links
2600
2500
2400
GREAT
LANGDALE
Three
Tarns
ESKDALE
2400
2500
2600
Shelter
Crags
tarn
N
2600
2700
CRINKLE CRAGS

ONE MILE

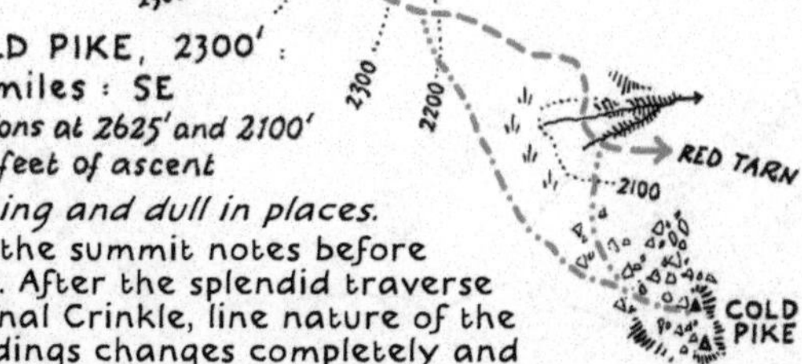

CRINKLE CRAGS
2500
2300
2200
RED TARN
2100
COLD
PIKE

To COLD PIKE, 2300′ : 1½ miles : SE
Depressions at 2625′ and 2100′
300 feet of ascent

Interesting and dull in places.
Consult the summit notes before starting. After the splendid traverse of the final Crinkle, line nature of the surroundings changes completely and a large grassy plateau stretches ahead: this may be crossed in a beeline, but it is preferable, especially after rain, to keep to the Red Tarn path until a gentle slope, becoming craggy, leads easily to the attractive triple summit of Cold Pike. What path there is here is very sketchy.

THE VIEW

The view is not quite as comprehensive as might be expected, the western and north-western fells (with the exception of Eel Crag) being out of sight behind the bulky Scafell group and Bowfell, but is excellent nevertheless. Of special distinction is the supremely beautiful view of the valleys of the Duddon and the Esk winding down to the sea: from no other summit are they so well seen. There is a more dramatic but less attractive picture of Great Langdale, best seen from the edge of the eastern cliffs.

Intruding in the fine array of mountains and lakes and valleys and sea is a comparatively new feature — the towers of the Sellafield nuclear reprocessing plant, neatly framed in the dip of the skyline between Whin Rigg and Illgill Head, the two heights above Wastwater Screes. The summit of Crinkle Crags is ageless, the towers are symbols of one particular age. Here, on this rugged mountain-top, is an everlasting permanence, something simple, and we can understand; but *there*, on the horizon, is something that is temporary, and complicated beyond our comprehension. Those modern structures, out of place in a landscape that is constant and unchanging, will vanish from the scene with the passing years. The mountains, nature's symbols of power and strength, will remain.

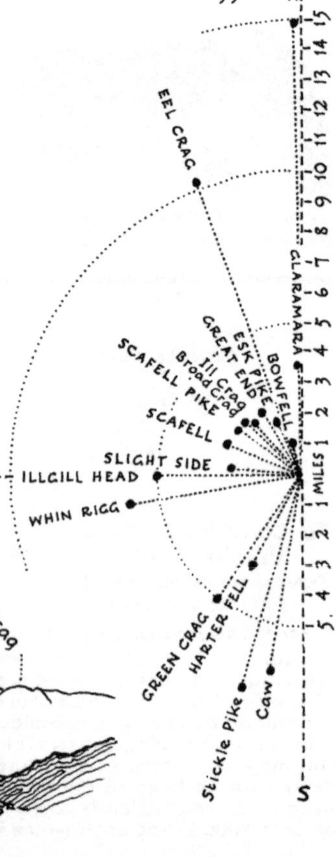
N
ULLOCK PIKE
EEL CRAG
GLARAMARA
BOWFELL
ESK PIKE
GREAT END
Ill Crag
Broad Crag
SCAFELL PIKE
SCAFELL
SLIGHT SIDE
ILLGILL HEAD
WHIN RIGG
W
HARTER FELL
GREEN CRAG
Caw
Stickle Pike
S
MILES
1 2 3 4 5 6 7 8 9 10 11 12 13 14 15
1 2 3 4 5

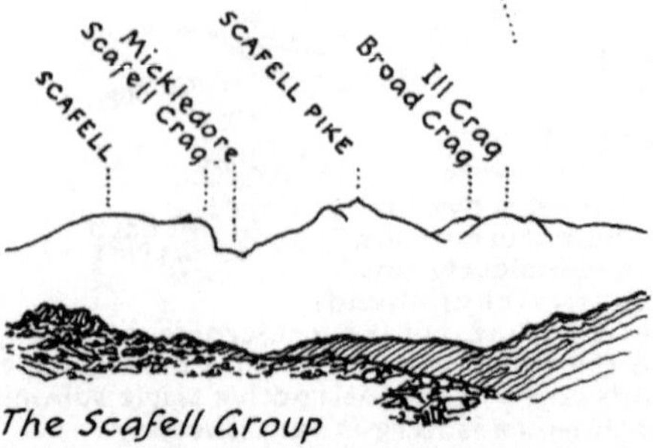
SCAFELL
Mickledore
Scafell Crag
SCAFELL PIKE
Ill Crag
Broad Crag

The Scafell Group

THE VIEW

Principal Fells

Just in case anybody wonders why, in these diagrams of views, certain fells are named in small letters although CAPITALS are the general rule, the reason is that those in small letters are not given separate chapters in this series of books (e.g. Broad Crag, Ill Crag) or are outside its boundaries (e.g. Stickle Pike, Caw). An inconsistency must be admitted, however, before observant and over-critical readers take up their pens: Helvellyn Lower Man (Book One) has been named in all views in capitals although not given a separate chapter; but it did, at least, occupy *much of a page* in the Helvellyn chapter (page 20).

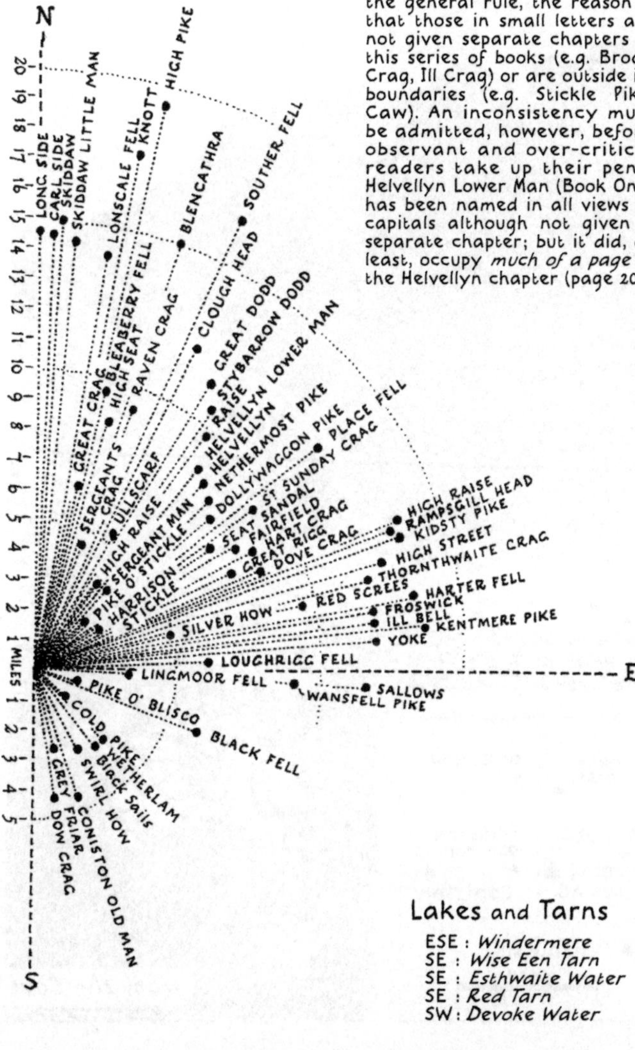
N
E
S
MILES
1
2
3
4
5
6
7
8
9
10
11
12
13
14
15
16
17
18
19
20
LONG SIDE
CARL SIDE
SKIDDAW
SKIDDAW LITTLE MAN
LONSCALE FELL
KNOTT
HIGH PIKE
BLENCATHRA
SOUTHER FELL
CLOUGH HEAD
GREAT DODD
STYBARROW DODD
HELVELLYN LOWER MAN
HELVELLYN
RAISE
BLEABERRY FELL
HIGH SEAT
RAVEN CRAG
GREAT CRAG
SERGEANTS CRAG
ULLSCARF
HIGH RAISE
SERGEANT MAN
PIKE O' STICKLE
HARRISON STICKLE
NETHERMOST PIKE
DOLLYWAGGON PIKE
PLACE FELL
ST SUNDAY CRAG
SEAT SANDAL
FAIRFIELD
HART CRAG
GREAT RIGG
DOVE CRAG
HIGH RAISE
RAMPSGILL HEAD
KIDSTY PIKE
HIGH STREET
THORNTHWAITE CRAG
RED SCREES
HARTER FELL
FROSWICK
ILL BELL
KENTMERE PIKE
YOKE
SILVER HOW
LOUGHRIGG FELL
LINGMOOR FELL
WANSFELL PIKE
SALLOWS
PIKE O' BLISCO
BLACK FELL
COLD PIKE
WETHERLAM
Black Sails
SWIRL HOW
GREY FRIAR
CONISTON OLD MAN
DOW CRAG

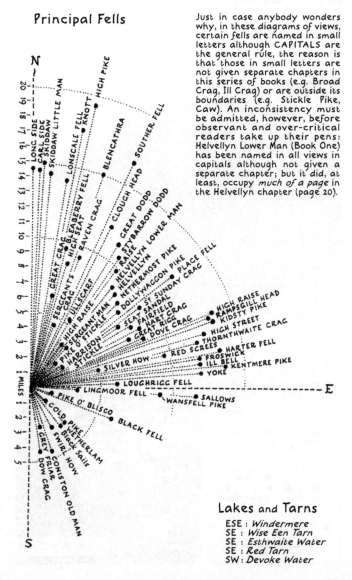

Lakes and Tarns

ESE : *Windermere*
SE : *Wise Een Tarn*
SE : *Esthwaite Water*
SE : *Red Tarn*
SW : *Devoke Water*

Dow Crag

2555'

OS grid ref: SD263978

GREY FRIAR
SWIRL HOW
Troutal
CONISTON OLD MAN
DOW CRAG
Coniston
Seathwaite
MILES
0 1 2 3

from the Cove

NATURAL FEATURES

Second only to Scafell Crag in the magnificence of its rock architecture is the imposing precipice towering above the stony hollow of Goat's Water, a favourite climbing ground hallowed by memories of the earliest and greatest of Lakeland cragsmen and so obviously the supreme natural attraction hereabouts that its name is given to the whole of the fell of which it is a part. Controversy raged at one time on the spelling of the name, DOW or DOE, but the former is now generally accepted.

The fell is extensive, and in marked contrast to the near-vertical eastern face is the smooth and gentle contour of the western slope descending to the little valley of Tarn Beck. The northern flank is easy too, except for a fringe of crag overlooking Seathwaite Tarn. South of the top, on a well defined ridge, are the subsidiary summits of Buck Pike and Brown Pike, and beyond the latter is the lofty pass of Walna Scar, not now a traffic route since the closing of nearby quarries but remaining a most excellent walkers highway.

looking north

1 : *The summit*
2 : *Buck Pike*
3 : *Brown Pike*

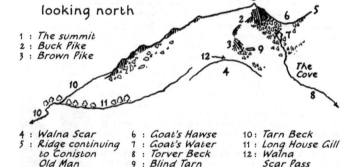
1
2
3
4
5
6
7
8
9
10
10
11
12
The Cove

4 : *Walna Scar*
5 : *Ridge continuing to Coniston Old Man*
6 : *Goat's Hawse*
7 : *Goat's Water*
8 : *Torver Beck*
9 : *Blind Tarn*
10 : *Tarn Beck*
11 : *Long House Gill*
12 : *Walna Scar Pass*

Although really beyond the boundaries of fellwalking country, and therefore outside the area covered by this book, the ridge continuing south-west from the Walna Scar Pass deserves some attention. The 2000' contour occurs twice on Walna Scar itself and then across a wide depression rises the splendid little peak of Caw (1735') followed by a switchback ridge over the miniature Matterhorn of Stickle Pike (1231') and so ultimately, in a wealth of bracken, down to Duddon Bridge at the head of the estuary.

For seven miles this ridge forms the eastern watershed of the Duddon Valley and offers to strong walkers starting from Duddon Bridge a natural high-level approach to Dow Crag. Anyone doing this walk — a day's march in itself — will have fully merited his feeling of achievement when the top rocks are finally reached.

NATURAL FEATURES

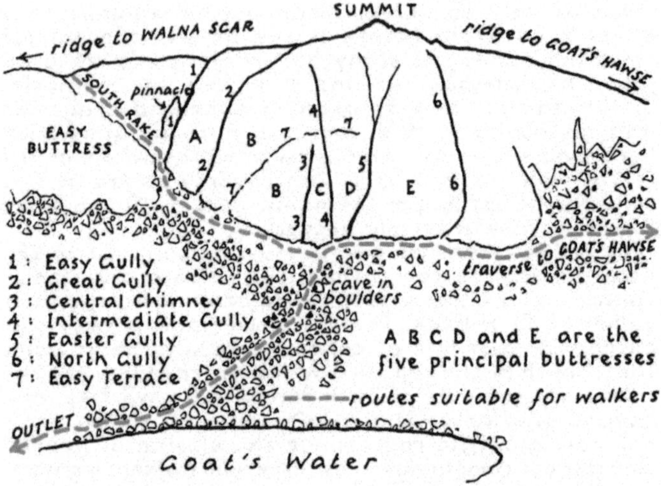
SUMMIT
← ridge to WALNA SCAR
ridge to GOAT'S HAWSE
SOUTH RAKE
pinnacle
EASY BUTTRESS
A B B C D E
1 2 3 4 5 6 7
cave in boulders
traverse to GOAT'S HAWSE
1 : Easy Gully
2 : Great Gully
3 : Central Chimney
4 : Intermediate Gully
5 : Easter Gully
6 : North Gully
7 : Easy Terrace
A B C D and E are the five principal buttresses
routes suitable for walkers
OUTLET
Goat's Water

THE PATTERN OF DOW CRAG
as seen from the slopes of Coniston Old Man

The Crag is the preserve of rock-climbers, but walkers may visit the base of the great cliff by taking the climbers' path from the outlet of Goat's Water. A simple traverse to the right across a scree slope then leads to the ridge just above Goat's Hawse. This route, although involving boulder-hopping, is much more interesting than the usual way to the Hawse on the eastern shore of the tarn.

Easy Buttress, *Easy* Gully and *Easy* Terrace are easy by rock-climbing, not walking, standards. Rock-climbers don't seem to know the meaning of easy. True, most walkers would manage to get up these places if a mad bull was in pursuit, but, if there is no such compelling circumstance, better they should reflect soberly .... and turn away.

There is, however, a coward's way to the top of the crag. From the lowest point of the cliff turn up left past the striking entrance to Great Gully and then more roughly up to the foot of Easy Gully, which is choked with stones. Here, unexpectedly, (it is not seen until reached) a straight ribbon of scree in a shallow gully goes up to the left (at a right-angled tangent to Easy Gully) — this route, although steep and loose, leads directly to the ridge above all difficulties. Climbers often use this as a quick way down, and it is comfortably within the capacity of most walkers. Lacking a name, but deserving one, SOUTH RAKE is suggested.

The entrance to Great Gully

Cove Bridge
carries the Walna Scar 'road' (once a green path, now mainly stones) across Torver Beck

The big cave, Blind Tarn Quarry

A shelter alongside the Walna Scar road, east of the pass,
just big enough for one person or a honeymoon couple

Brown Pike and Blind Tarn from Buck Pike
Brown Pike has a fine cairn. Blind Tarn is one of the few tarns without an outlet — hence its name

Dow Crag 5

MAP

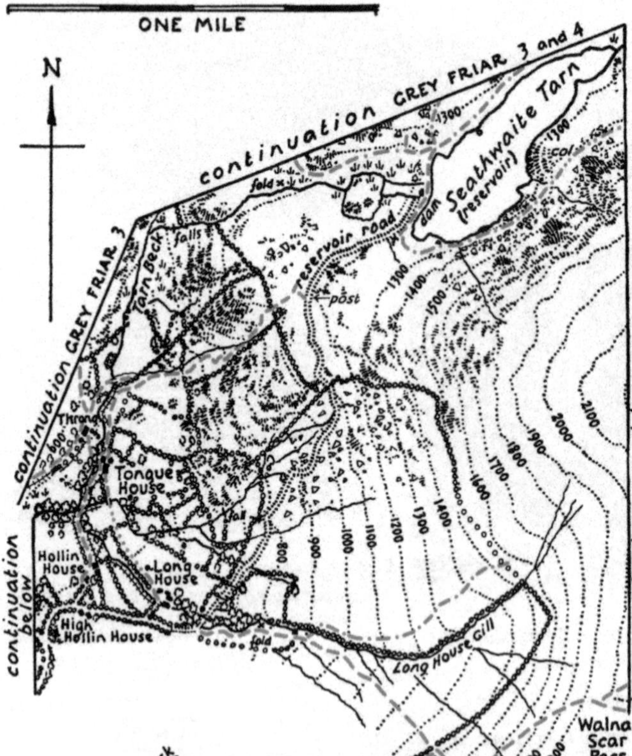
ONE MILE
N
continuation GREY FRIAR 3 and 4
continuation GREY FRIAR 3
continuation on opposite page
continuation below
Seathwaite Tarn
(reservoir)
dam
col
reservoir road
fold
falls
Tarn Beck
post
Throng
Tongue House
Hollin House
Long House
High Hollin House
fall
fold
Long House Gill
Walna Scar Pass
Walna Scar Quarries
(disused)

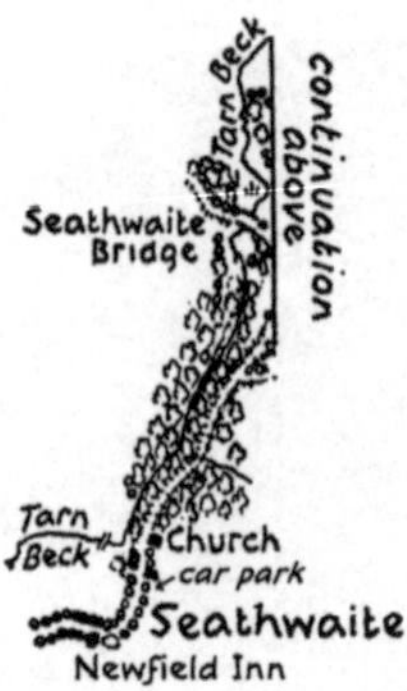
continuation above
Tarn Beck
Seathwaite Bridge
Tarn Beck
Church
car park
Seathwaite
Newfield Inn

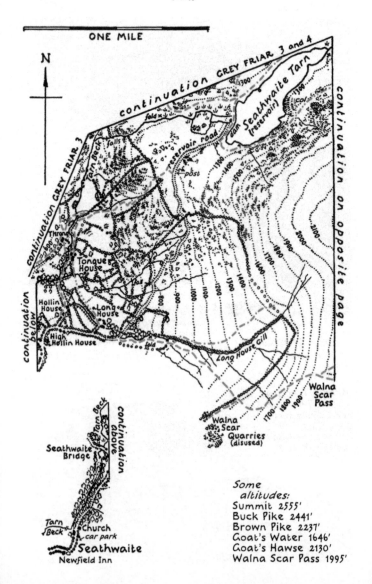

Some altitudes:
Summit 2555'
Buck Pike 2441'
Brown Pike 2237'
Goat's Water 1646'
Goat's Hawse 2130'
Walna Scar Pass 1995'

MAP

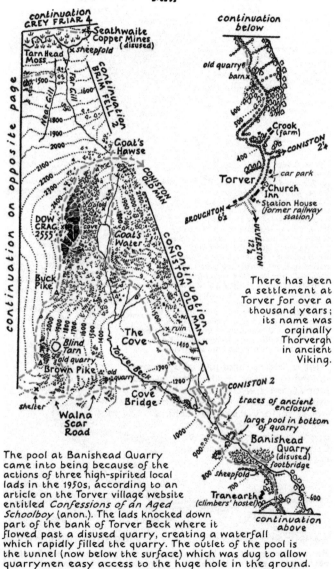

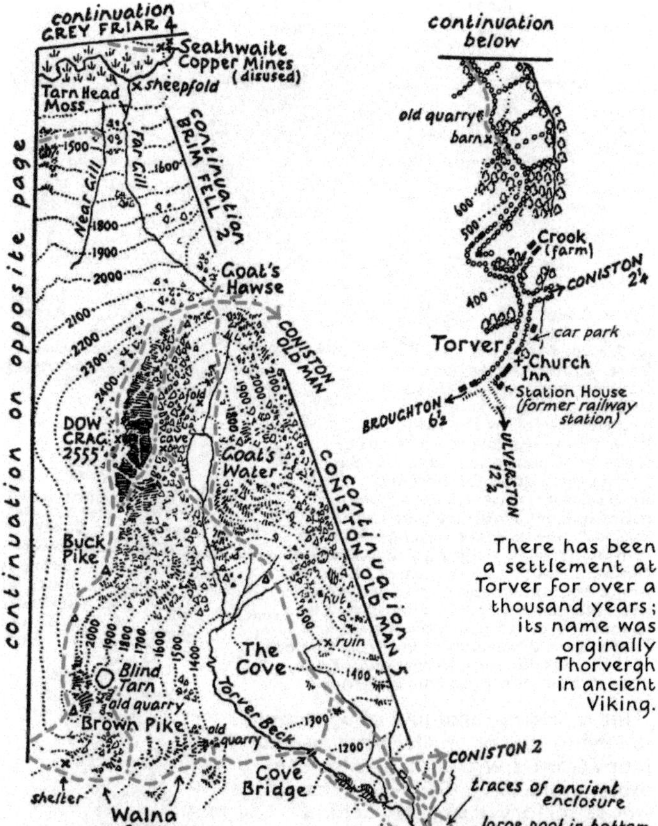
continuation GREY FRIAR 4
Seathwaite Copper Mines (disused)
sheepfold
Tarn Head Moss
continuation BRIM FELL 2
Near Gill
Far Gill
1500
1600
1800
1900
2000
2100
2200
2300
2400
Goat's Hawse
CONISTON OLD MAN
continuation on opposite page
fold
cave
DOW CRAG 2555'
Goat's Water
continuation CONISTON OLD MAN 5
Buck Pike
hut
ruin
The Cove
Blind Tarn
old quarry
Brown Pike
old quarry
Torver Beck
1400
1300
1200
Cove Bridge
CONISTON 2
shelter
Walna Scar Road
traces of ancient enclosure
large pool in bottom of quarry
Banishead Quarry (disused)
footbridge
1000
900
800
700
sheepfold
Tranearth (climbers' hostel)
600
continuation above
continuation below
old quarry
barn
600
500
400
Crook (farm)
CONISTON 2¼
car park
Torver
Church
Inn
Station House (former railway station)
BROUGHTON 6½
ULVERSTON 12½

There has been a settlement at Torver for over a thousand years; its name was orginally Thorvergh in ancient Viking.

The pool at Banishead Quarry came into being because of the actions of three high-spirited local lads in the 1950s, according to an article on the Torver village website entitled *Confessions of an Aged Schoolboy* (anon.). The lads knocked down part of the bank of Torver Beck where it flowed past a disused quarry, creating a waterfall which rapidly filled the quarry. The outlet of the pool is the tunnel (now below the surface) which was dug to allow quarrymen easy access to the huge hole in the ground.

ASCENT FROM TORVER
2250 feet of ascent : 3¾ miles

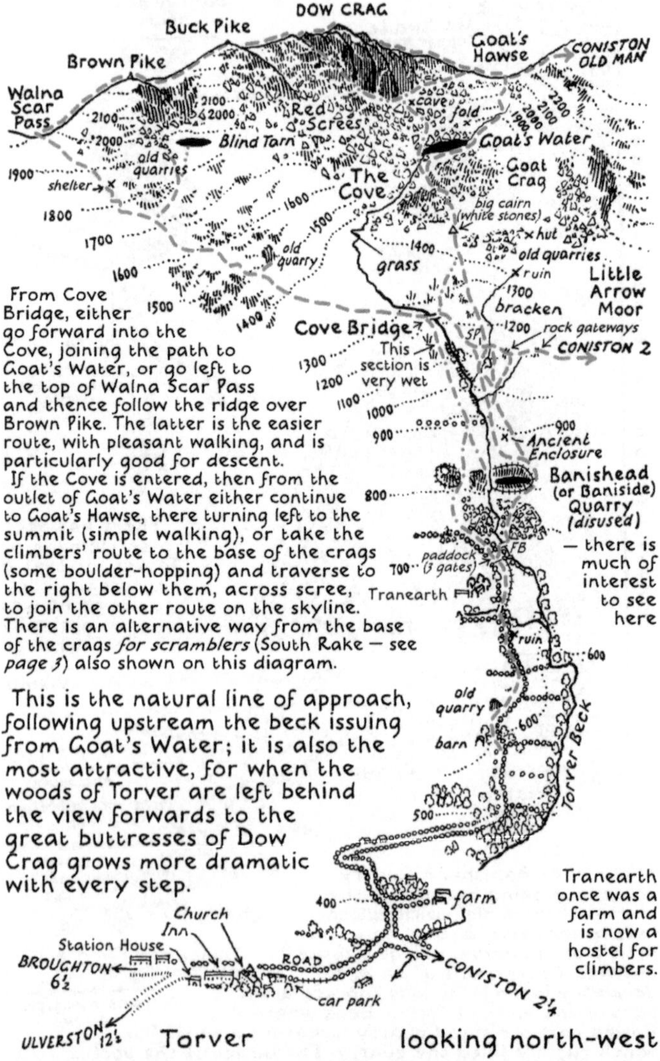
DOW CRAG
Buck Pike
Brown Pike
Walna Scar Pass
Goat's Hawse
CONISTON OLD MAN
2200
2100
2000
1900
1800
1700
1600
1500
1400
1300
1200
1100
1000
900
800
700
600
500
400
cave
fold
Red Screes
Blind Tarn
old quarries
Goat's Water
shelter
The Cove
Goat Crag
big cairn (white stones)
hut
old quarry
grass
old quarries
ruin
Little Arrow Moor
bracken
Cove Bridge
rock gateways
CONISTON 2
SP
This section is very wet
Ancient Enclosure
Banishead (or Baniside) Quarry (disused)
— there is much of interest to see here
FB
paddock (3 gates)
Tranearth
ruin
3
old quarry
barn
Torver Beck
farm
Church Inn
Station House
BROUGHTON 6½
ROAD
CONISTON 2¼
car park
ULVERSTON 12½
Torver
looking north-west

From Cove Bridge, either go forward into the Cove, joining the path to Goat's Water, or go left to the top of Walna Scar Pass and thence follow the ridge over Brown Pike. The latter is the easier route, with pleasant walking, and is particularly good for descent.

If the Cove is entered, then from the outlet of Goat's Water either continue to Goat's Hawse, there turning left to the summit (simple walking), or take the climbers' route to the base of the crags (some boulder-hopping) and traverse to the right below them, across scree, to join the other route on the skyline. There is an alternative way from the base of the crags *for scramblers* (South Rake — see *page 3*) also shown on this diagram.

This is the natural line of approach, following upstream the beck issuing from Goat's Water; it is also the most attractive, for when the woods of Torver are left behind the view forwards to the great buttresses of Dow Crag grows more dramatic with every step.

Tranearth once was a farm and is now a hostel for climbers.

Many walkers will not be familiar with this approach but it has long been popular with rock-climbers — a favourite way to a favourite crag!

ASCENT FROM CONISTON
2350 feet of ascent : 4 miles

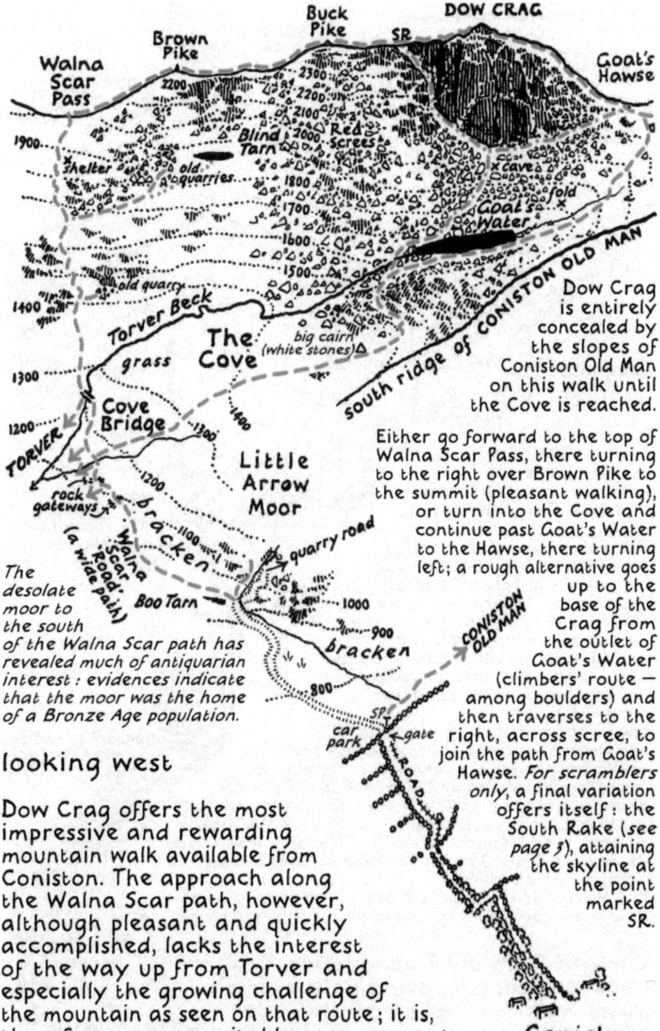
Buck Pike
DOW CRAG
Brown Pike
SR
Walna Scar Pass
Goat's Hawse
2300
2200
2100
2000
1900
Red Screes
Blind Tarn
shelter
old quarries
cave
fold
1800
1700
Goat's Water
1600
1500
CONISTON OLD MAN
old quarry
1400
Torver Beck
The Cove
big cairn (white stones)
grass
south ridge of CONISTON OLD MAN
1300
Cove Bridge
1400
1200
1300
TORVER
Little Arrow Moor
1200
rock gateways
bracken
Walna Scar 'Road' (a wide path)
1100
quarry road
Boo Tarn
1000
900
bracken
CONISTON OLD MAN
800
SP
car park
gate
ROAD
Coniston

The desolate moor to the south of the Walna Scar path has revealed much of antiquarian interest : evidences indicate that the moor was the home of a Bronze Age population.

Dow Crag is entirely concealed by the slopes of Coniston Old Man on this walk until the Cove is reached.

Either go forward to the top of Walna Scar Pass, there turning to the right over Brown Pike to the summit (pleasant walking), or turn into the Cove and continue past Goat's Water to the Hawse, there turning left; a rough alternative goes up to the base of the Crag from the outlet of Goat's Water (climbers' route — among boulders) and then traverses to the right, across scree, to join the path from Goat's Hawse. *For scramblers only*, a final variation offers itself : the South Rake (*see page 3*), attaining the skyline at the point marked SR.

looking west

Dow Crag offers the most impressive and rewarding mountain walk available from Coniston. The approach along the Walna Scar path, however, although pleasant and quickly accomplished, lacks the interest of the way up from Torver and especially the growing challenge of the mountain as seen on that route; it is, therefore, a more suitable arrangement to start the walk from Torver and return direct to Coniston along the Walna Scar path.

ASCENT FROM THE DUDDON VALLEY

2300 feet of ascent : 3¾ miles from Seathwaite

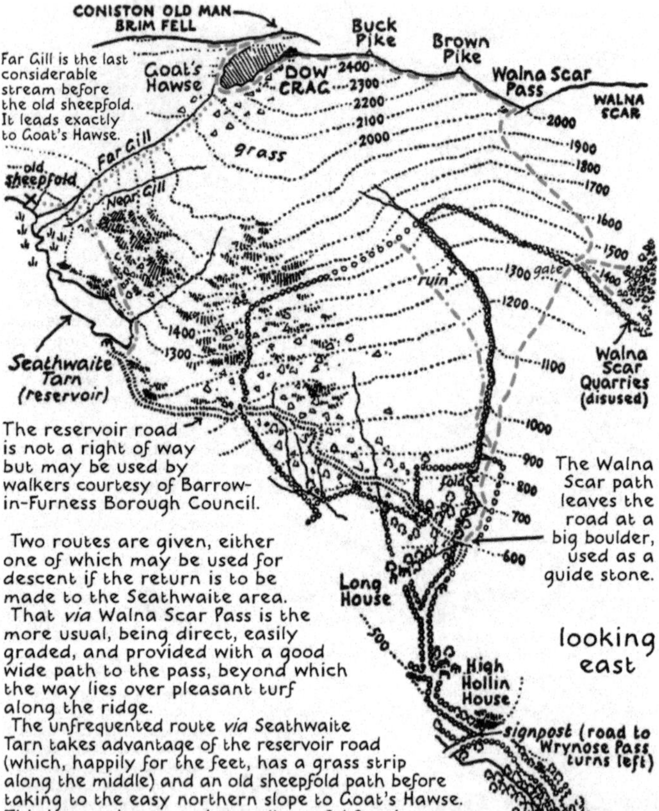
CONISTON OLD MAN
BRIM FELL
Buck Pike
Brown Pike
Walna Scar Pass
WALNA SCAR
Far Gill is the last considerable stream before the old sheepfold. It leads exactly to Goat's Hawse.
Goat's Hawse
DOW CRAG
2400
2300
2200
2100
2000
grass
Far Gill
old sheepfold
Near Gill
2000
1900
1800
1700
1600
1500
1400
1300
gate
ruin
1200
1400
1300
1100
1000
900
800
700
600
500
400
400
Seathwaite Tarn (reservoir)
Walna Scar Quarries (disused)
fold
The Walna Scar path leaves the road at a big boulder, used as a guide stone.
Long House
High Hollin House
looking east
signpost (road to Wrynose Pass turns left)
car park
Church
Tarn Beck
Newfield Inn
Seathwaite

The reservoir road is not a right of way but may be used by walkers courtesy of Barrow-in-Furness Borough Council.

Two routes are given, either one of which may be used for descent if the return is to be made to the Seathwaite area.

That *via* Walna Scar Pass is the more usual, being direct, easily graded, and provided with a good wide path to the pass, beyond which the way lies over pleasant turf along the ridge.

The unfrequented route *via* Seathwaite Tarn takes advantage of the reservoir road (which, happily for the feet, has a grass strip along the middle) and an old sheepfold path before taking to the easy northern slope to Goat's Hawse. This interesting route is equally useful for the ascent of Coniston Old Man — in fact it is the only way to the Old Man from the Duddon Valley that does not involve a considerable descent.

The Walna Scar route is a particularly easy and rapid way down, one of the quickest in the district.

Climbed from the Duddon, Dow Crag is innocuous enough, being only a simple grassy walk. The views from the ridge down the eastern precipice are sensational but give no impression, unfortunately, of the magnificent proportions of the front of the Crag.

THE SUMMIT

Count this amongst the most delectable and exhilarating of Lakeland summits, for the sublime architecture of the great crag directly below is manifest in the topmost rocks also, forming an airy perch on a fang of naked stone elevated high above the tremendous precipice: a scene that cannot fail to exalt the minds of those who have lifted their bodies to it. An easy scramble gives access to the highest point: there is no room for a cairn. For peeps down the vertical rifts of Great Gully and Easy Gully follow a crumbled wall south along the ridge for 200 yards.

DESCENTS: Use the two ridges only: north curving east to Goat's Hawse (fair path) for Coniston Old Man or Seathwaite Tarn, keeping steep ground on the right hand; or south over the summits of Buck Pike and Brown Pike to Walna Scar Pass for Coniston or the Duddon, keeping steep ground on the left hand. Both routes are easy.

The head of Great Gully

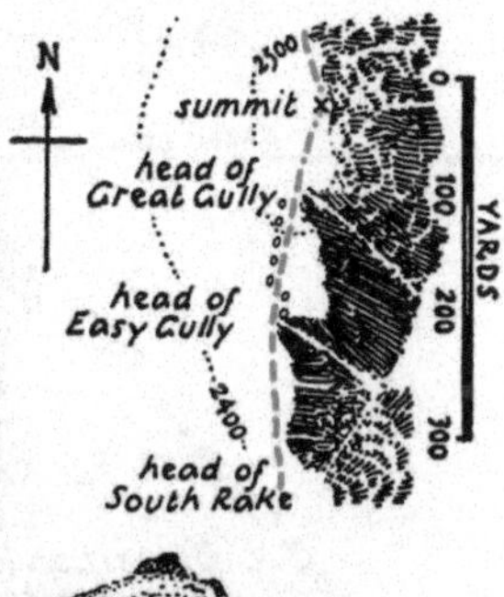
N
2500
summit
head of Great Gully
head of Easy Gully
2400
head of South Rake
0
100
200
300
YARDS

looking down Easy Gully to the pinnacle

SOUTH RAKE

The summit ridge from the top of South Rake

THE VIEW

This is not the best of mountain views, but the outlook over the foothills of the Duddon and Esk is unexcelled, while across the southern horizon is a wide sweep of glittering sea beyond an interesting coastline. The Isle of Man when visible, appears over Devoke Water.

Lakes and Tarns

E : *Goat's Water*
ESE : *Windermere*
E–S : *Coniston Water*
S : *Beacon Tarn*
W : *Devoke Water*

Principal Fells

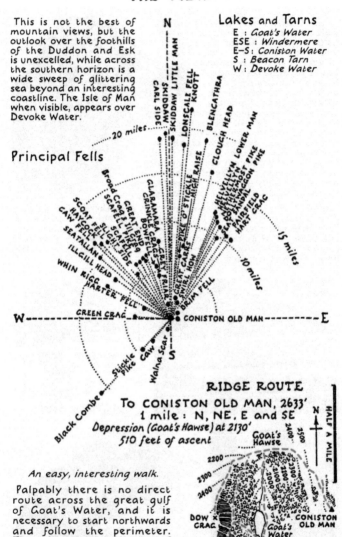

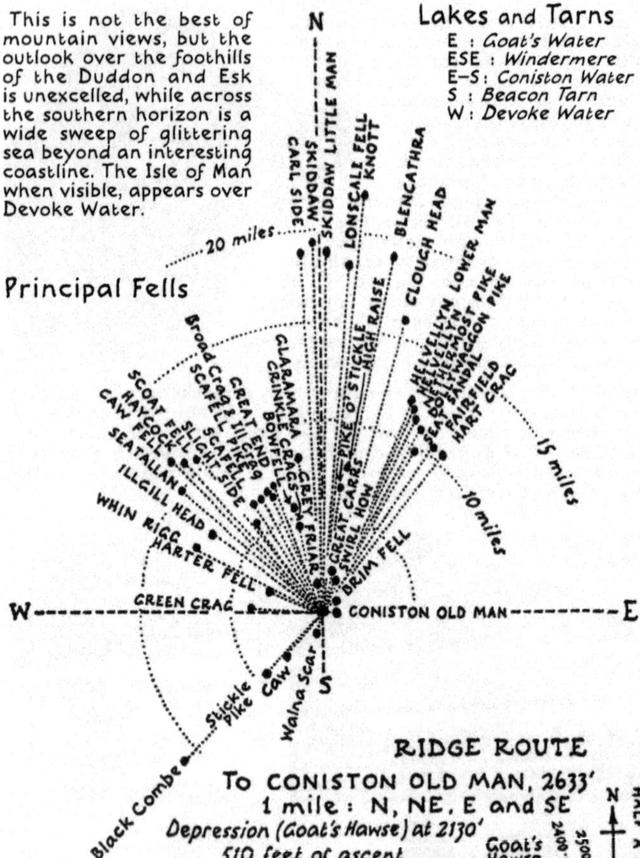
N
S
W
E
20 miles
15 miles
10 miles
SKIDDAW LITTLE MAN
SKIDDAW
CARL SIDE
LONSCALE FELL
KNOTT
BLENCATHRA
CLOUGH HEAD
LOWER MAN
HELVELLYN LOWER MAN
HELVELLYN
NETHERMOST PIKE
CATSTYCAM
DOLLYWAGGON PIKE
SEAT SANDAL
FAIRFIELD
HART CRAG
HIGH RAISE
PIKE O' STICKLE
GREAT CARRS
SWIRL HOW
BRIM FELL
CONISTON OLD MAN
GREY FRIAR
CRINKLE CRAGS
GLARAMARA
BOWFELL
GREAT END
Broad Crag & Ill Crag
SCAFELL PIKE
SCAFELL
SLIGHT SIDE
SCOAT FELL
HAYCOCK
CAW FELL
SEATALLAN
ILLGILL HEAD
WHIN RIGG
HARTER FELL
GREEN CRAG
Caw
Walna Scar
Stickle Pike
Black Combe

RIDGE ROUTE

To CONISTON OLD MAN, 2633'
1 mile : N, NE, E and SE

Depression (Goat's Hawse) at 2130'
510 feet of ascent

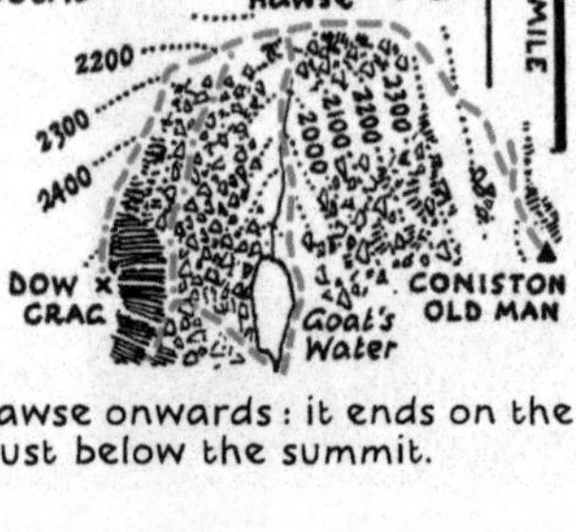
N
HALF A MILE
Goat's Hawse
2200
2300
2400
2500
DOW CRAG
Goat's Water
CONISTON OLD MAN

An easy, interesting walk.

Palpably there is no direct route across the great gulf of Goat's Water, and it is necessary to start northwards and follow the perimeter. There is a good path most of the way, very wide from Goat's Hawse onwards : it ends on the easy upper slope of the Old Man just below the summit.

Dow Crag from Goat's Water

Esk Pike 2903'

OS grid ref: NY237075

from Rest Gill,
Crinkle Crags

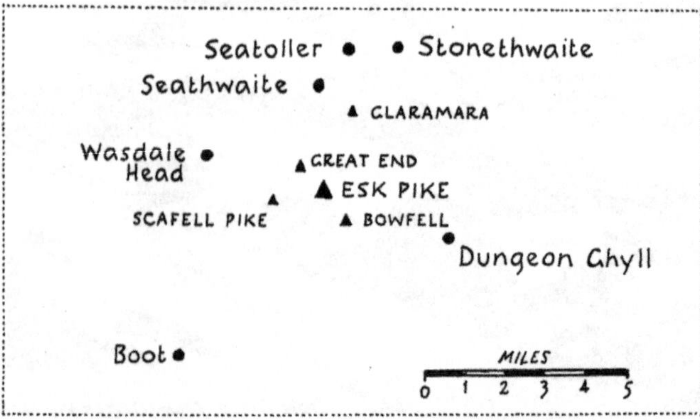
Seatoller
Stonethwaite
Seathwaite
CLARAMARA
Wasdale Head
GREAT END
ESK PIKE
SCAFELL PIKE
BOWFELL
Dungeon Ghyll
Boot
MILES
0 1 2 3 4 5

NATURAL FEATURES

The central height in the semi-circle of fine peaks around the lonely head of upper Eskdale has long been known to walkers as Esk Pike, but was only in the latter half of the twentieth century that its name appeared on Ordnance Survey maps. In the splendid panorama of the Eskdale skyline the fell is the least prominent, not because it competes for attention with popular favourites such as the Scafells and Bowfell and the Crinkles but rather because its top is the furthest removed from the valley and appears dwarfed in relation to the others. Yet this is, in fact, a most attractive summit, deserving of a separate ascent but invariably combined with a greater objective, Bowfell. Did it but stand alone, away from such enticing neighbours, Esk Pike would rank highly among the really worthwhile mountain climbs.

The outstanding feature is a lengthy south ridge, bounded by the River Esk westwards, and to the east by Yeastyrigg Gill and Lingcove Beck: a ridge with many abrupt crags. Northwards a short steep tongue of land goes down into Langstrath, enclosed between Allencrags Gill and Angletarn Gill. Lofty ridges, crossed by the passes of Esk Hause and Ore Gap, connect with Great End and Bowfell.

1 : *The summit*
2 : *Ridge continuing to Great End*
3 : *Ridge continuing to Bowfell*
4 : *Esk Hause*
5 : *Ore Gap*
6 : *Pike de Bield*
7 : *Yeastyrigg Crags*
8 : *Greenhole Crags*
9 : *High Gait Crags*
10 : *Low Gait Crags*
11 : *Long Crag*
12 : *Pianet Knott*

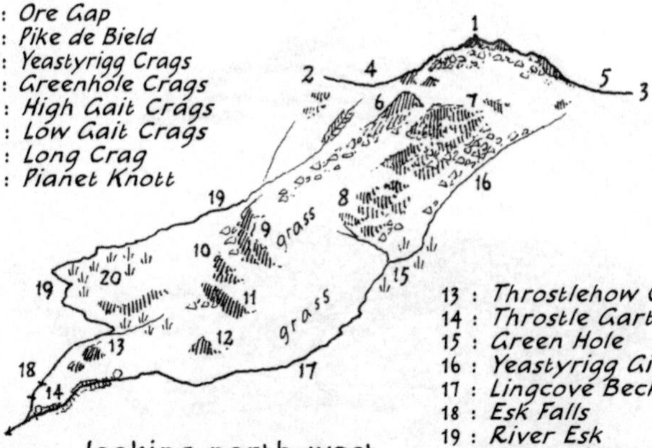
1
2
3
4
5
6
7
8
9
10
11
12
13
14
15
16
17
18
19
19
19
20
grass
grass

looking north-west

13 : *Throstlehow Crag*
14 : *Throstle Garth*
15 : *Green Hole*
16 : *Yeastyrigg Gill*
17 : *Lingcove Beck*
18 : *Esk Falls*
19 : *River Esk*
20 : *Great Moss*

Esk Hause

Sooner or later every fellwalker finds himself for the first time at Esk Hause, the highest, best known and most important of Lakeland foot passes, and he will probably have read, or been told, that this is a place where it is easy to go astray. There should be no danger of this, however, even in bad conditions.

Nevertheless the lie of the land is curious (but not confusing). Esk Hause is a tilted grass plateau, high among the mountains. The unusual thing about it is that *two* passes have their summits on the plateau, two passes carrying entirely different routes; in fact, in general direction they are at right angles. If these routes crossed at the highest point of the plateau there would be a simple 'crossroads', but they do not: one is a hundred feet higher than the other and 300 yards distant.

The name Esk Hause is commonly but incorrectly applied to the lower of the passes, a much-trodden route, but properly belongs to the higher and less-favoured pass. What is almost always referred to as Esk Hause is not Esk Hause at all; the true Esk Hause is rarely so named except by the cartographers. The true Esk Hause (2490') is the head of Eskdale, a shallow depression between Esk Pike and Great End, and is an infrequently used pass between Eskdale and Borrowdale; the general direction is south-west to north-east. The false Esk Hause (2386' with a wall shelter in the form of a cross) is a shallow depression in the high skyline between the true Esk Hause and Allen Crags, and is a much-used pass between Great Langdale and Wasdale, general direction being south-east to north-west.

Esk Pike, from the wall shelter

Esk Hause
path to Scafell Pike

continued

Esk Hause

continued

The likeliest mistake in bad weather is that a walker approaching from Langdale and bound for Wasdale may bear left along the plain path beyond the shelter and so unwittingly be ascending Scafell Pike when he should be going down to Wasdale. (The path to Scafell Pike from the shelter, incidentally, first goes up to the true Esk Hause and there swings away to the right; fortunately there is barely a sketchy path leading down into Eskdale from the Hause, otherwise it might be thought that the valley below is Wasdale — which would be a still worse mistake.) The correct continuation to Wasdale turns distinctly left off the path heading north-east from shelter, as shown on the map. Here is an example of a bifurcation (to Scafell Pike) having become better marked on the ground than the original path (to Wasdale). It is well to remember that the shelter is the *highest* point attained on the Langdale–Wasdale route.

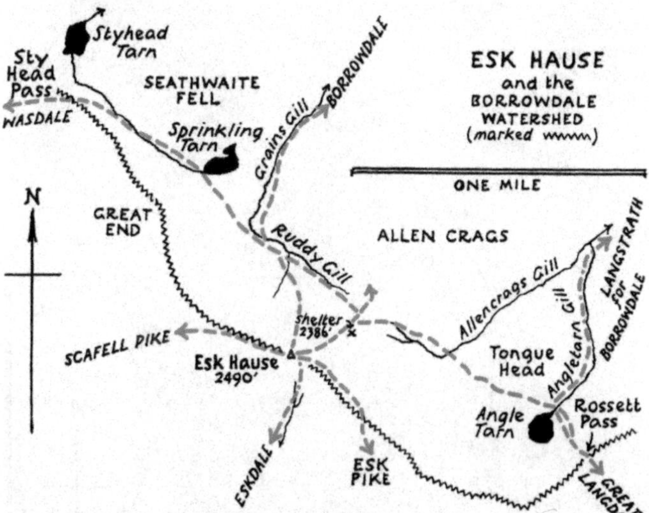
ESK HAUSE
and the
BORROWDALE
WATERSHED
(marked wwww)
ONE MILE
N
Styhead Tarn
Sty Head Pass
WASDALE
SEATHWAITE FELL
Sprinkling Tarn
Grains Gill
BORROWDALE
GREAT END
Ruddy Gill
ALLEN CRAGS
Allencrags Gill
LANGSTRATH for BORROWDALE
shelter 2386'
SCAFELL PIKE
Esk Hause 2490'
Tongue Head
Angletarn Gill
Angle Tarn
Rossett Pass
ESKDALE
ESK PIKE
GREAT LANGDALE

The greater importance of the higher pass as a watershed is well seen from a study of the map. All streams crossed on the Langdale–Wasdale route within the area between Rossett Pass and Sty Head Pass find their way into Borrowdale, although the latter valley is largely screened by Allen Crags. No water from this wide area flows into Langdale or Wasdale, and the lower pass therefore has little geographical significance: it is merely an intrusion in the vast system of the Eskdale–Borrowdale gathering grounds. The one function of the spurious Esk Hause is to deflect the plateau's waters into Borrowdale either by way of Langstrath or Grains Gill.

Esk Pike (centre)
Lining Crag (left)
Allen Crags (right)
from Langstrath

MAP

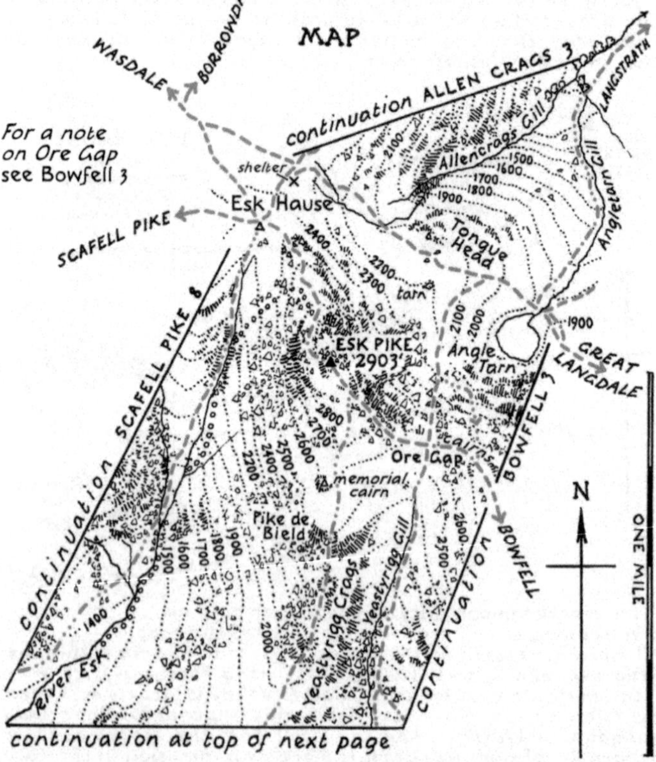
WASDALE
BORROWDALE
continuation ALLEN CRAGS 3
LANGSTRATH
shelter
Esk Hause
SCAFELL PIKE
Allencrags Gill
Tongue Head
Angletarn Gill
tarn
ESK PIKE
2903'
Angle Tarn
GREAT LANGDALE
continuation SCAFELL PIKE 8
BOWFELL 3
cairns
Ore Gap
memorial cairn
BOWFELL
Pike de Bield
Yeastyrigg Crags
Yeastyrigg Gill
River Esk
continuation
N
ONE MILE

For a note on Ore Gap see Bowfell 3

continuation at top of next page

The memorial cairn commemorates Gerry Charnley, a member of South Ribble Orienteering Club who died on Helvellyn in 1982 aged 53. The cairn is on The Charnley Way, a long-distance route devised by friends.

MAP

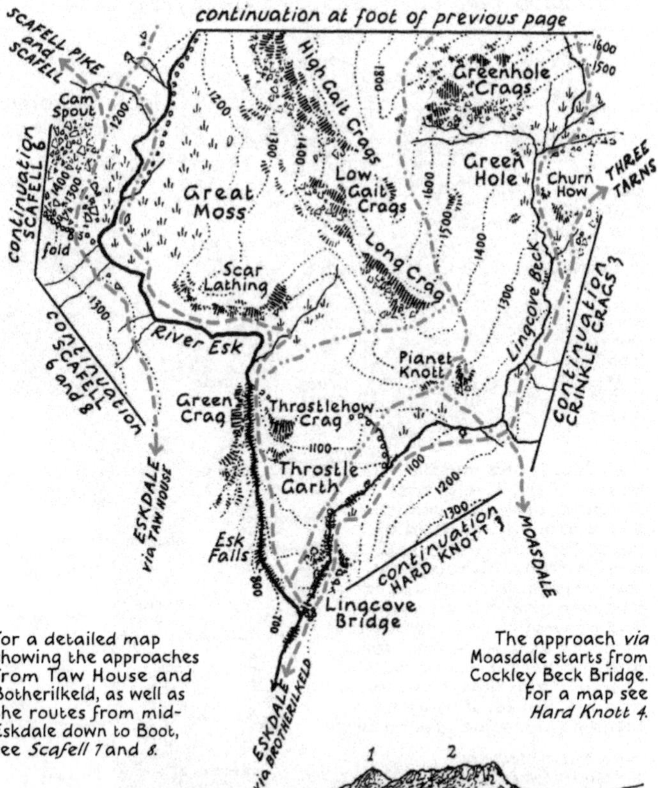
continuation at foot of previous page
SCAFELL PIKE and SCAFELL
Cam Spout
continuation SCAFELL 6
fold
High Gait Crags
Greenhole Crags
Great Moss
Low Gait Crags
Green Hole
Churn How
THREE TARNS
Long Crag
Scar Lathing
River Esk
continuation SCAFELL 6 and 8
Pianet Knott
Lingcove Beck
continuation CRINKLE CRAGS 3
Green Crag
Throstlehow Crag
Throstle Garth
ESKDALE via TAW HOUSE
Esk Falls
continuation HARD KNOTT 3
MOASDALE
Lingcove Bridge
ESKDALE via BROTHERILKELD

For a detailed map showing the approaches from Taw House and Botherilkeld, as well as the routes from mid-Eskdale down to Boot, see *Scafell 7* and *8*.

The approach *via* Moasdale starts from Cockley Beck Bridge. For a map see *Hard Knott 4*.

1
2
3

The approach to the summit along the south ridge (from near Low Gait Crags)

1 : *Pike de Bield*
2 : *Yeastyrigg Crags*
3 : *Greenhole Crags*

ASCENT FROM ESKDALE

2800 feet of ascent : 8½ miles from Boot

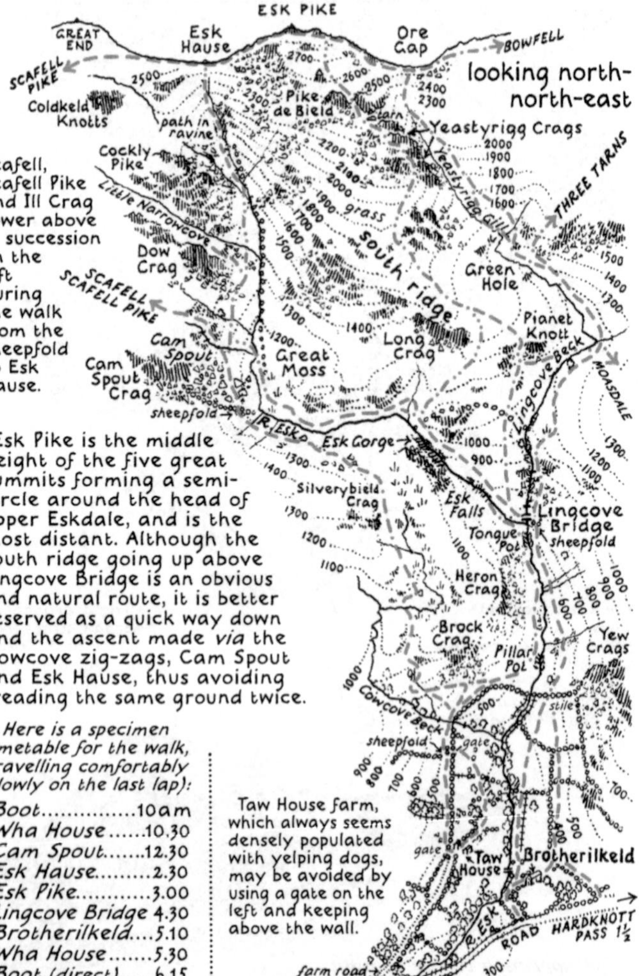
ESK PIKE
GREAT END
Esk Hause
Ore Gap
BOWFELL
SCAFELL PIKE
looking north-north-east
Coldkeld Knotts
path in ravine
Pike de Bield
tarn
Yeastyrigg Crags
Yeastyrigg Gill
Cockly Pike
Little Narrowcove
THREE TARNS
grass
south ridge
Dow Crag
Green Hole
SCAFELL
SCAFELL PIKE
Pianet Knott
Cam Spout
Great Moss
Long Crag
Lingcove Beck
MOASDALE
Cam Spout Crag
sheepfold
R. Esk
Esk Gorge
Silverybield Crag
Esk Falls
Lingcove Bridge
Tongue Pot
sheepfold
Heron Crag
Brock Crag
Pillar Pot
Yew Crags
Cowcove Beck
stile
sheepfold
gate
gate
Taw House
Brotherilkeld
R. Esk
ROAD
HARDKNOTT PASS 1½
farm road
BOOT 1½
Whahouse Bridge
Wha House

Scafell, Scafell Pike and Ill Crag tower above in succession on the left during the walk from the sheepfold to Esk Hause.

Esk Pike is the middle height of the five great summits forming a semi-circle around the head of upper Eskdale, and is the most distant. Although the south ridge going up above Lingcove Bridge is an obvious and natural route, it is better reserved as a quick way down and the ascent made *via* the Cowcove zig-zags, Cam Spout and Esk Hause, thus avoiding treading the same ground twice.

Here is a specimen timetable for the walk, travelling comfortably (slowly on the last lap):

Boot..............10am
Wha House......10.30
Cam Spout.......12.30
Esk Hause.........2.30
Esk Pike...........3.00
Lingcove Bridge 4.30
Brotherilkeld....5.10
Wha House.......5.30
Boot (direct)......6.15
Boot (via the bar of the Woolpack Inn) ?

Taw House farm, which always seems densely populated with yelping dogs, may be avoided by using a gate on the left and keeping above the wall.

This is a walk of exceptional beauty and interest, *but make no mistake — it is a very long one.*

ASCENT FROM WASDALE HEAD

2700 feet of ascent : 4¼ miles

This is also the route of ascent to Bowfell from Wasdale Head – it is reached by going on along the ridge from the top of Esk Pike south-east, crossing the depression of Ore Gap.

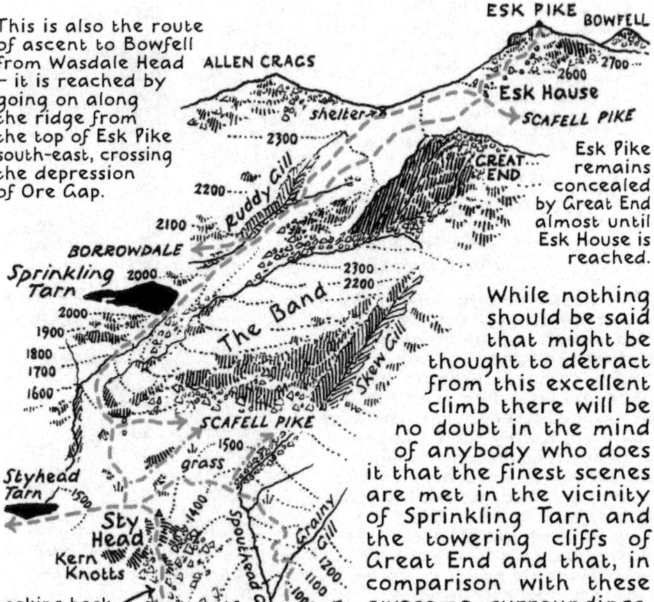
ESK PIKE
BOWFELL
ALLEN CRAGS
2700
2600
Esk Hause
shelter
SCAFELL PIKE
2300
GREAT END
Ruddy Gill
2200
2100
BORROWDALE
Sprinkling Tarn
2000
2300
2200
The Band
2000
1900
1800
1700
1600
Skew Gill
SCAFELL PIKE
1500
grass
Styhead Tarn
1500
Sty Head
1400
Kern Knotts
Spouthead Gill
Grainy Gill
1200
1100
1000
Piers Gill
scree slopes
The fell on the right is LINGMELL
beautiful small pools
900
800
700
600
500
fold
SP
bracken
Lingmell Beck
400
Burnthwaite
INN ½
Wasdale Head

Esk Pike remains concealed by Great End almost until Esk House is reached.

While nothing should be said that might be thought to detract from this excellent climb there will be no doubt in the mind of anybody who does it that the finest scenes are met in the vicinity of Sprinkling Tarn and the towering cliffs of Great End and that, in comparison with these awesome surroundings, the way beyond deteriorates in quality — which is rather a pity, for those climbs are best that grow in interest throughout, the climax coming only as the final steps are taken.

Looking back and upwards to the Napes from this point, the Needle can just be discerned. The prominent rock like a sitting cat on the skyline is the Sphinx. Its other name is Cat Rock.

Towering high into the sky on the left here is GREAT GABLE. The crags are the Napes Ridges.

looking east

Strongly recommended as an alternative to the busy path to Sty Head rising across the screes of Great Gable is the old now-neglected valley track, a route of delightful grassy zig-zags. *(For a description and eulogy of this forgotten path see Great End 1.)*

ASCENT FROM BORROWDALE
2550 feet of ascent : 4¾ miles from Seatoller

BOWFELL
Ore Gap
ESK PIKE
2800
2700
2600
2500
2400
B: Path continues behind Great End to Scafell Pike
GREAT END
Esk Hause
B
A: This path, once just a shortcut, is now the main route to Esk Hause from Ruddy Gill
grass
wall-shelter
2500
Esk Pike now in view
A
2300
C
D
C: South-east Gully
D: Central Gully
2200
2100
ANGLE TARN and GREAT LANGDALE
This is the pass commonly known as Esk Hause
STY HEAD and WASDALE
Ruddy Gill
The fell here (grey rocks) is ALLEN CRAGS

2000
1900
ravine
1800
1700
looking south
1600
1500
1400
old sheepfold
1300
1200
1400
1500
1600
1700
1800
cascades
The fell bounding the valley on the right is SEATHWAITE FELL
Grains Gill
1000
900
800
sheepfold
700
STY HEAD and WASDALE
fine waterfall in wooded ravine is Taylorgill Force
Stockley Bridge
Styhead Gill
600
The fell on the right here is BASE BROWN
River Derwent
500
gate
Sourmilk Gill
long series of cascades
WC
Seathwaite
parking place
SEATOLLER 1¼
There are public toilets at Seathwaite.

The outstanding feature of the walk is the towering precipice of Great End, which is prominent ahead during the ascent of the valley and becomes impressive as it is approached. When seen finally at close quarters across the deep ravine of Ruddy Gill its imposing presence is completely dominant: an awesome picture especially when mist wreathes the top crags. But do not omit, at this point, to look back at the glorious vista of Borrowdale and Derwent Water with Skiddaw beyond. Great Gable is now also in view.

Ruddy Gill (named from its red subsoil) flows in a rocky ravine, so deeply sheltered that meadow and woodland flowers thrive in profusion despite the 2000′ altitude.

The cliff high on the left is Hind Crag

GLARAMARA is the long fell on the left of the valley

If the return is to be made to Borrowdale consider the alternative route of ascent offered by Langstrath (see Bowfell 9), *and reserve Grains Gill for the descent. Done the other way round, Langstrath would seem very long at the end of a hard day. In any case, if time and energy are available, Bowfell should be included in the walk.*

There is space enough only to add that Grains Gill is a delightful way to the tops, and the whole walk is a joy.

ASCENT FROM GREAT LANGDALE

2800 feet of ascent : 4¼ miles (from Dungeon Ghyll Old Hotel)

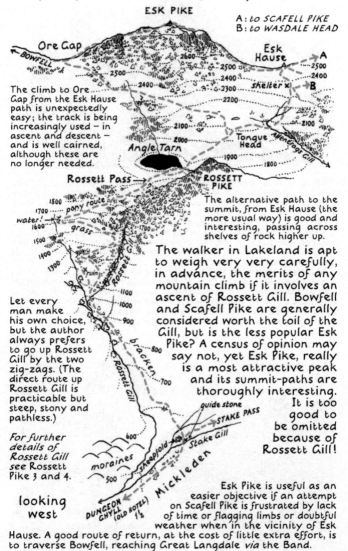

ESK PIKE
A: to SCAFELL PIKE
B: to WASDALE HEAD
Ore Gap
BOWFELL
Esk Hause
A
B
shelter
2600
2500
2400
2300
2200
2100
2000
1900
1800
Tongue Head
Allencrags Gill
Angle Tarn
Rossett Pass
ROSSETT PIKE
pony route
1700
water!
1600
grass
1500
1400
1300
ruin
Rossett Gill
1100
1000
900
800
bracken
700
guide stone
STAKE PASS
Stake Gill
600
moraines
sheepfold
500
Mickleden
DUNGEON GHYLL (OLD HOTEL) 1½
looking west

The climb to Ore Gap from the Esk Hause path is unexpectedly easy; the track is being increasingly used – in ascent and descent – and is well cairned, although these are no longer needed.

The alternative path to the summit, from Esk Hause (the more usual way) is good and interesting, passing across shelves of rock higher up.

The walker in Lakeland is apt to weigh very very carefully, in advance, the merits of any mountain climb if it involves an ascent of Rossett Gill. Bowfell and Scafell Pike are generally considered worth the toil of the Gill, but is the less popular Esk Pike? A census of opinion may say not, yet Esk Pike, really is a most attractive peak and its summit-paths are thoroughly interesting. It is too good to be omitted because of Rossett Gill!

Let every man make his own choice, but the author always prefers to go up Rossett Gill by the two zig-zags. (The direct route up Rossett Gill is practicable but steep, stony and pathless.)

For further details of Rossett Gill see Rossett Pike 3 and 4.

Esk Pike is useful as an easier objective if an attempt on Scafell Pike is frustrated by lack of time or flagging limbs or doubtful weather when in the vicinity of Esk Hause. A good route of return, at the cost of little extra effort, is to traverse Bowfell, reaching Great Langdale *via* the Band.

THE SUMMIT

The summit is characterised by its colourful rocks, which, unlike those of other tops in this area of 'Borrowdale volcanics', are sharp and splintery, in predominantly brown or coppery hues with generous splashes of white and heavily stained with vivid patches of green lichen. These stones are profusely scattered and it is from a debris of flakes and fragments that the highest point, a craggy outcrop, emerges. In the lee of this small crag, which is cut away vertically to the north, there was formerly a summit shelter but it has now fallen into disuse.

There is usually a small cairn clinging to the highest point; there is a modest cairn at the foot of the summit rocks on the south-east side and another on an outcrop to the north-north-east. A quarter of a mile south of the summit is a well-made memorial cairn. The path from Bowfell to Esk Hause once bypassed the summit, but nothing remains of this path except for a few cairns.

The Summit from the top of the north buttress

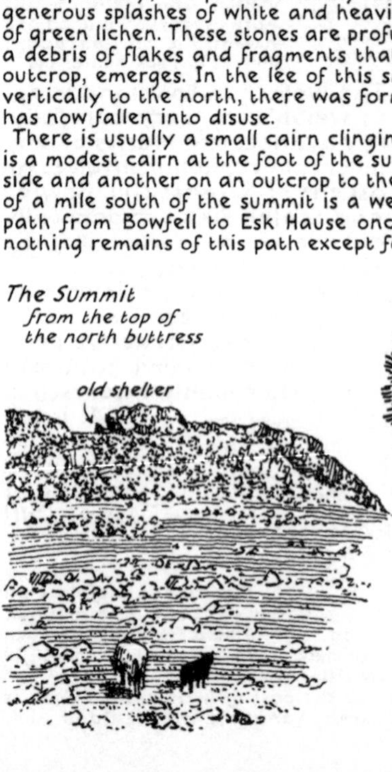
old shelter

PLAN OF SUMMIT
100 YARDS
N
A
old shelter
summit
former bypass
B
2800
C
A : Esk Hause
B : South ridge
C : Ore Gap

RIDGE ROUTES

To BOWFELL, 2960′ : 1 mile
SE, E and SE
Depression (Ore Gap) at 2575′
400 feet of ascent

ESK PIKE
2800
2700
2600
2500
Ore Gap
cairns
Hanging Knotts
2800
2500
2600
2700
BOWFELL

Rough in places but path generally good.

A track skirts the north side of the next prominent outcrop along the top and follows the ridge down to Ore Gap. (Note the red soil here, due to the presence of haematite). From here onwards the walk is straightforward. If the day is clear and time permits, a good alternative from Ore Gap is to bear left and over the top of Hanging Knotts to get views of Angle Tarn and Rossett Pass, which will otherwise not be seen during the walk. There also is a spectacular view of the Great Slab from near the North Buttress; see *Bowfell 12* for details of visiting this location.

To GREAT END, 2984′ :
1¼ miles : N, NNW, W and N
Depression (Esk Hause) at 2490′
525 feet of ascent

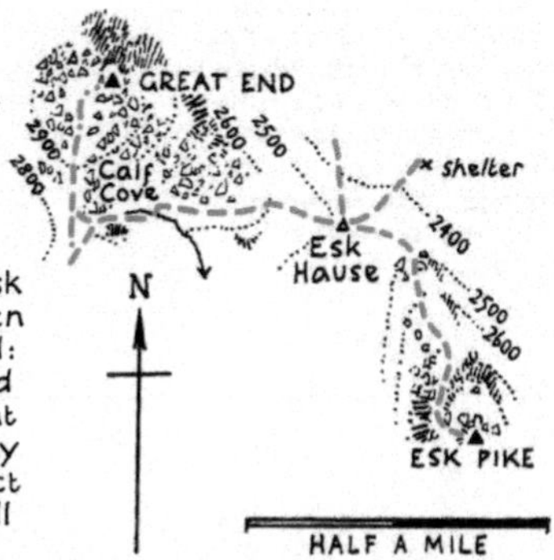
GREAT END
2600
2500
2900
2800
Calf Cove
Esk Hause
N
shelter
2400
2500
2600
ESK PIKE
HALF A MILE

A pleasant high-level walk.

An interesting path goes down to Esk Hause (the *true* Esk Hause) where the well trodden route to Scafell Pike is joined: this may be followed into and out of Calf Cove, when turn right up an easy ridge to the stony top of Great End. A more direct finish, avoiding Calf Cove, will encounter rougher ground.

looking north-west to Great End

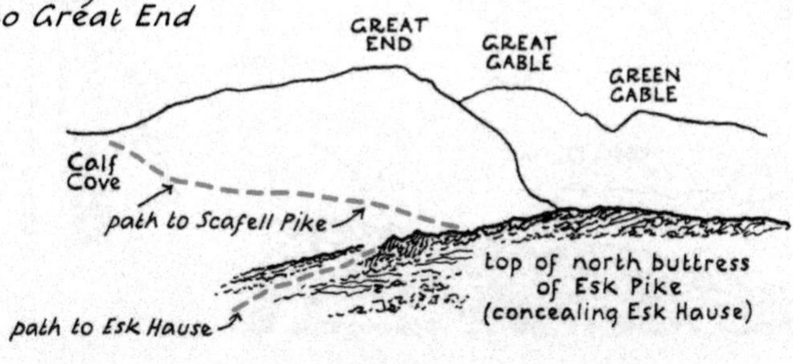
GREAT END
GREAT GABLE
GREEN GABLE
Calf Cove
path to Scafell Pike
top of north buttress of Esk Pike (concealing Esk Hause)
path to Esk Hause

THE VIEW

The excellent view is little inferior to that from the neighbouring Bowfell, and in some respects is even better, notably in the fine sight of the Scafells rising out of the depths of upper Eskdale, while the scene northwards is enhanced by the inclusion of Derwent Water, which is not seen from the loftier Bowfell. Southwards the Duddon estuary makes a pleasing picture over the slender peak of Stickle Pike.

There is an interesting viewpoint 60 yards north of the summit and above a craggy buttress, where upper Langstrath is well displayed beyond and below Tongue Head, the shelf carrying the path between Rossett Pass and Esk Hause, which can also be seen fully. Two other buttresses to the left are easily visited: the further one has a view of Sprinkling Tarn.

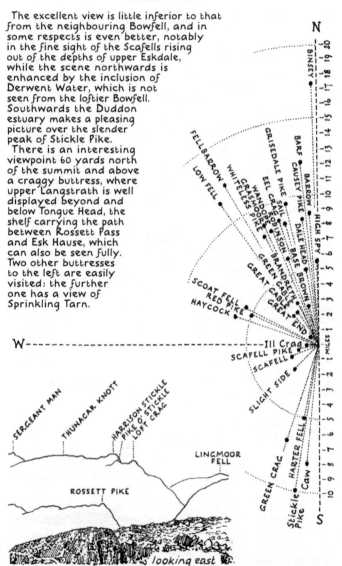

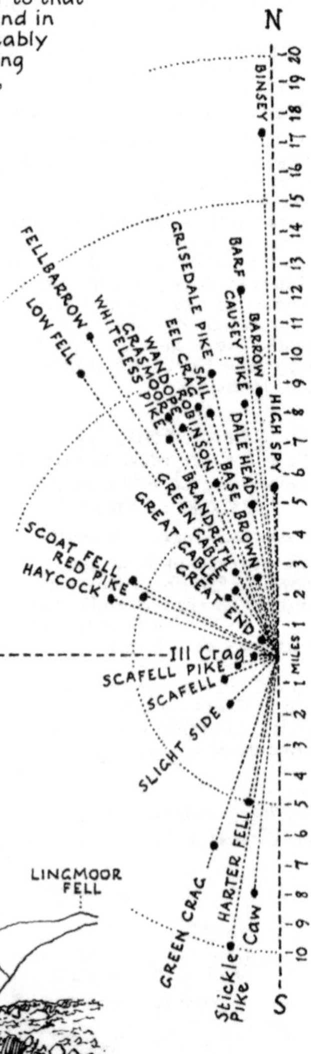
N
W
S
MILES
BINSEY
FELLBARROW
LOW FELL
WHITELESS PIKE
GRASMOOR
WANDOPE
EEL CRAG
GRISEDALE PIKE
SAIL
ROBINSON
BARF
CAUSEY PIKE
BARROW
HIGH SPY
DALE HEAD
BASE BROWN
BRANDRETH
GREEN GABLE
GREAT GABLE
GREAT END
SCOAT FELL
RED PIKE
HAYCOCK
Ill Crag
SCAFELL PIKE
SCAFELL
SLIGHT SIDE
GREEN CRAG
HARTER FELL
Caw
Stickle Pike

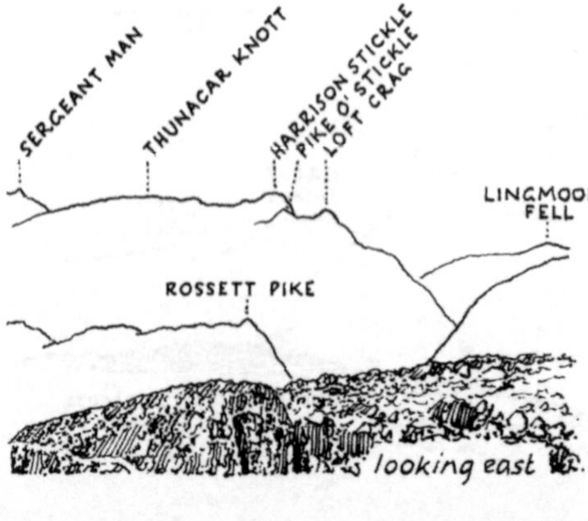
SERGEANT MAN
THUNACAR KNOTT
HARRISON STICKLE
PIKE O' STICKLE
LOFT CRAG
LINGMOOR FELL
ROSSETT PIKE
looking east

THE VIEW

Principal Fells

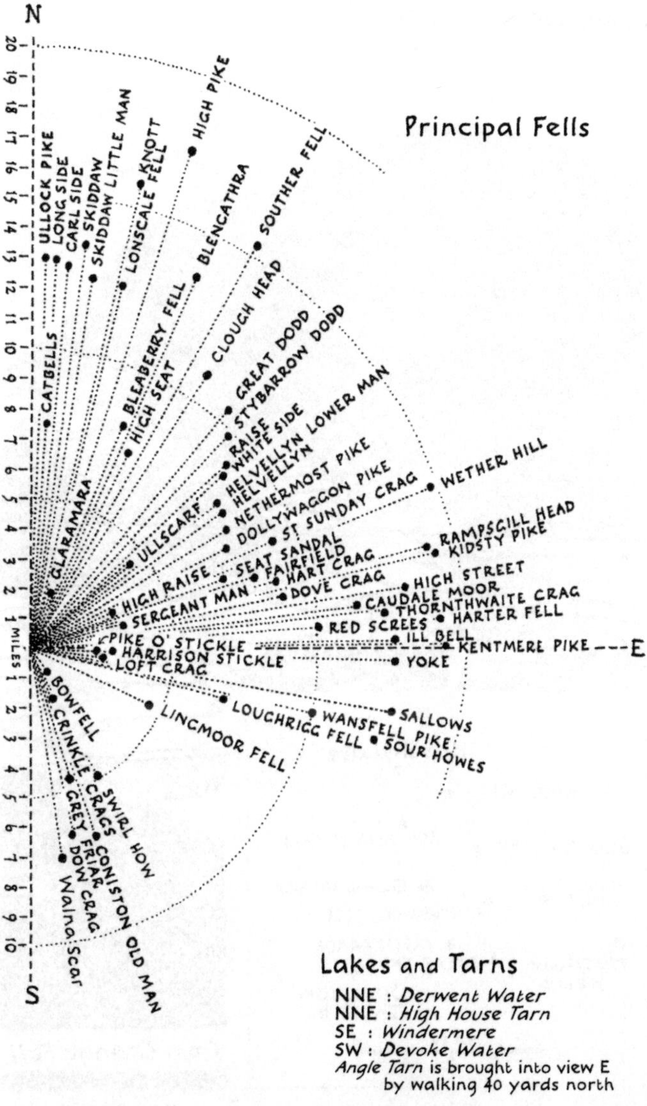
N
S
E
MILES
20
19
18
17
16
15
14
13
12
11
10
9
8
7
6
5
4
3
2
1
1
2
3
4
5
6
7
8
9
10
ULLOCK PIKE
LONG SIDE
CARL SIDE
SKIDDAW
SKIDDAW LITTLE MAN
KNOTT
LONSCALE FELL
HIGH PIKE
BLENCATHRA
SOUTHER FELL
CLOUGH HEAD
GREAT DODD
STYBARROW DODD
CATBELLS
BLEABERRY FELL
HIGH SEAT
RAISE
WHITE SIDE
HELVELLYN LOWER MAN
HELVELLYN
NETHERMOST PIKE
DOLLYWAGGON PIKE
ST SUNDAY CRAG
WETHER HILL
CLARAMARA
ULLSCARF
HIGH RAISE
SERGEANT MAN
SEAT SANDAL
FAIRFIELD
HART CRAG
DOVE CRAG
RAMPSGILL HEAD
KIDSTY PIKE
HIGH STREET
CAUDALE MOOR
THORNTHWAITE CRAG
HARTER FELL
RED SCREES
ILL BELL
KENTMERE PIKE
PIKE O' STICKLE
HARRISON STICKLE
LOFT CRAG
YOKE
BOWFELL
CRINKLE CRAGS
LINGMOOR FELL
LOUGHRIGG FELL
WANSFELL PIKE
SALLOWS
SOUR HOWES
SWIRL HOW
GREY FRIAR
DOW CRAG
CONISTON OLD MAN
Walna Scar

Lakes and Tarns

NNE : *Derwent Water*
NNE : *High House Tarn*
SE : *Windermere*
SW : *Devoke Water*
Angle Tarn is brought into view E
by walking 40 yards north

Glaramara

2569'

OS grid ref: NY247106

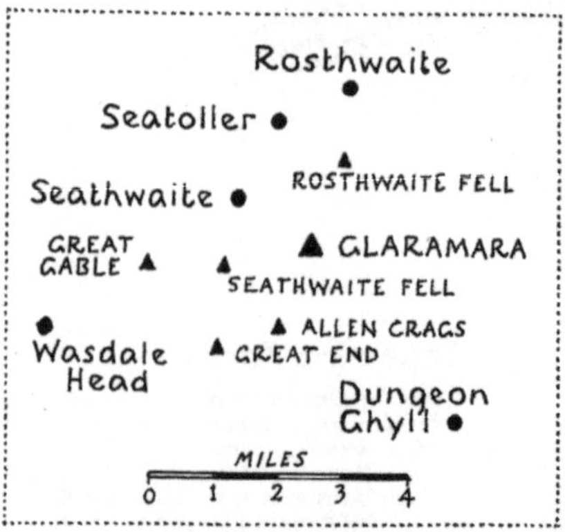

Rosthwaite
Seatoller
ROSTHWAITE FELL
Seathwaite
GREAT GABLE
GLARAMARA
SEATHWAITE FELL
ALLEN CRAGS
Wasdale Head
GREAT END
Dungeon Ghyll
MILES
0 1 2 3 4

from Grange Fell

NATURAL FEATURES

Prominent in the mid-Borrowdale scene is the bulky fell of Glaramara, which, with an ally in Rosthwaite Fell, seems, on the approach from the north, to throw a great barrier across the valley; although in fact the level strath turns away to the right to persist as far as Seathwaite, two miles further, while a shorter branch goes left to Stonethwaite. Seen from the north the most notable feature is a gigantic hollow scooped out of the craggy mountain wall — this is Combe Gill, a splendid example of a hanging valley caused by glacial erosion and containing in its recesses the biggest cave of natural origin in the district. Considering the short distance from the road, the charmingly wooded climb to its portals, and the impressive surround of crags, the Gill is surprisingly little visited.

Combe Gill apart, Glaramara exhibits sterile slopes of scree and rock on both east and west sides, where deep valleys, Langstrath and Grains Gill, effectively sever it from other high ground, but southwards a broad grass ridge continues with many undulations but with little general change in altitude over Allen Crags to join, at Esk Hause, a high link with the Scafell mass, of which, geographically, Glaramara and Rosthwaite Fell form the northern extremity.

The ancient and beautiful name really applies only to the grey turret of rock at the summit but happily has been commonly adopted for the fell as a whole, and it is pleasing to record that no attempt has been made to rob it of this heritage of the past, as in the case of Blencathra.

Much of Lakeland's appeal derives from the very lovely names of its mountains and valleys and lakes and rivers, which fit the scenery so well. These names were given by the earliest settlers, rough men, invaders and robbers: they were here long before Wordsworth — but they, too, surely had poetry in their hearts?

Combe Head and Raven Crag

MAP

There is a National Trust car park at Seatoller; between Seathwaite Bridge and Seathwaite there is ample verge parking. There are public toilets at Seatoller and Seathwaite.

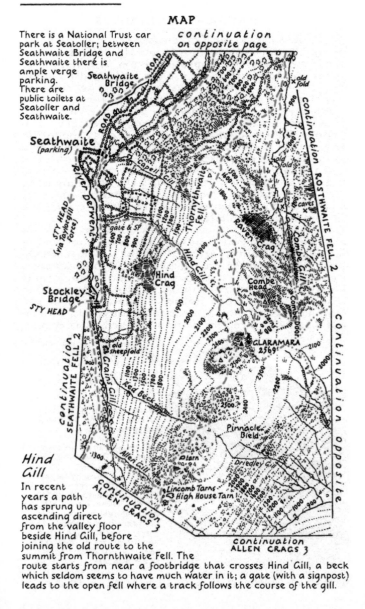

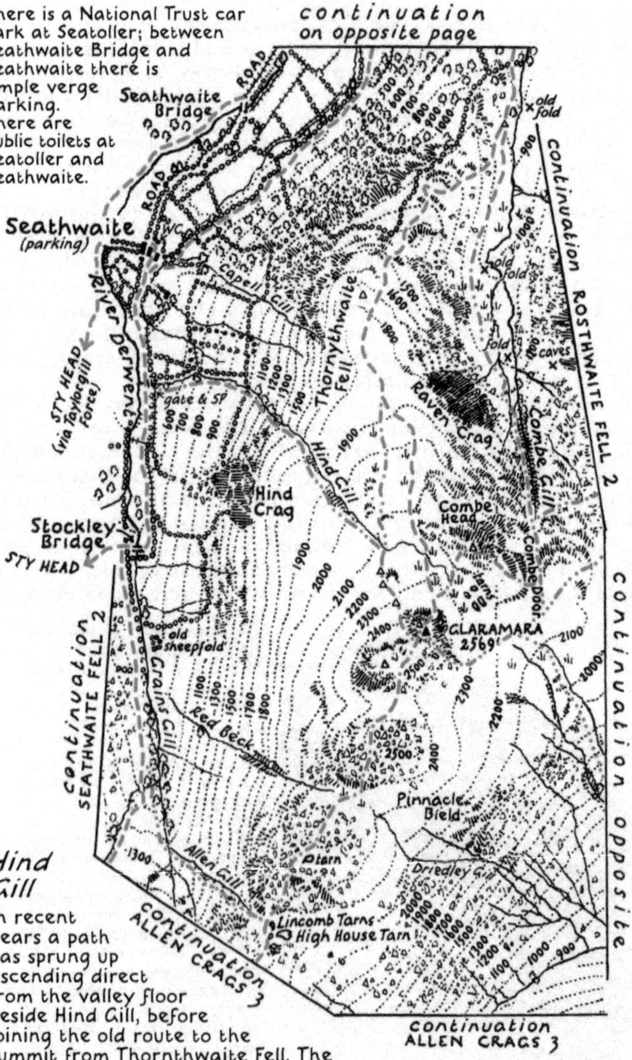
continuation on opposite page
ROAD
Seathwaite Bridge
Seathwaite (parking)
WC
River Derwent
STY HEAD (via Taylorgill Force)
Stockley Bridge
STY HEAD
Capell Gill
Thornythwaite Fell
gate & SP
Hind Gill
Hind Crag
Raven Crag
Combe Gill
Combe Head
Combe Door
old fold
fold
caves
continuation ROSTHWAITE FELL 2
GLARAMARA 2569
old sheepfold
Grains Gill
Red Beck
2500
Pinnacle Bield
continuation SEATHWAITE FELL 2
Allen Gill
tarn
Lincomb Tarns
High House Tarn
Driedley Gill
continuation ALLEN CRAGS 3
continuation opposite
continuation ALLEN CRAGS 3

Hind Gill

In recent years a path has sprung up ascending direct from the valley floor beside Hind Gill, before joining the old route to the summit from Thornthwaite Fell. The route starts from near a footbridge that crosses Hind Gill, a beck which seldom seems to have much water in it; a gate (with a signpost) leads to the open fell where a track follows the course of the gill.

MAP

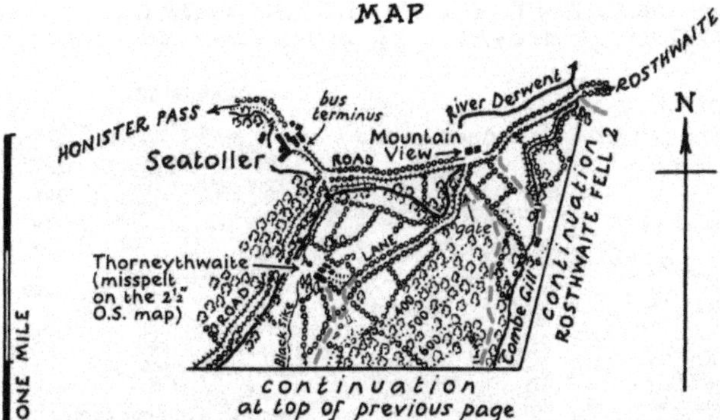
HONISTER PASS
bus terminus
River Derwent
ROSTHWAITE
N
Seatoller
ROAD
Mountain View
gate
LANE
Thorneythwaite (misspelt on the 2½" O.S. map)
ROAD
Black Sike
400
500
600
Combe Gill
continuation ROSTHWAITE FELL 2
continuation at top of previous page
ONE MILE

A new generation seems to have sprung up that knows not the pleasant path from Mountain View to Seathwaite, at first along the lane almost to Thorneythwaite and then on through the fields; indeed it is unusual nowadays to see anyone using it, even though the hard road to Seathwaite yearly becomes busier and busier with pedestrian and motor traffic and, in the season, is a trial to walk upon. The field path is an excellent start to a day's walk on the hills; returning, when one no longer has strength left even to climb stiles and ambition has narrowed to the sole objective of reaching the bus terminus before collapse is complete, the road will be rather the easier.

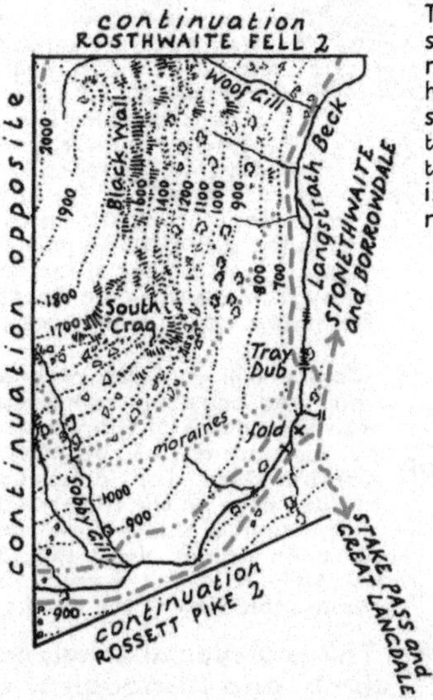
continuation ROSTHWAITE FELL 2
Woof Gill
Langstrath Beck
STONETHWAITE and BORROWDALE
continuation opposite
Black Wall
2000
1900
1600
1400
1200
1100
1000
900
800
700
1800
1700
South Crag
Tray Dub
fold
moraines
Sobby Gill
1000
900
STAKE PASS and GREAT LANGDALE
continuation ROSSETT PIKE 2

Tray Dub

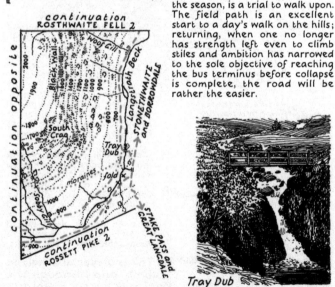

Tray Dub is one of the more distinctive watercourses in Lakeland, where Langstrath Beck flows through a narrow rocky gorge. Just a mile downstream is its twin, Blackmoss Pot.

ASCENT FROM BORROWDALE

2300 feet of ascent : 3¾ miles (from Rosthwaite)

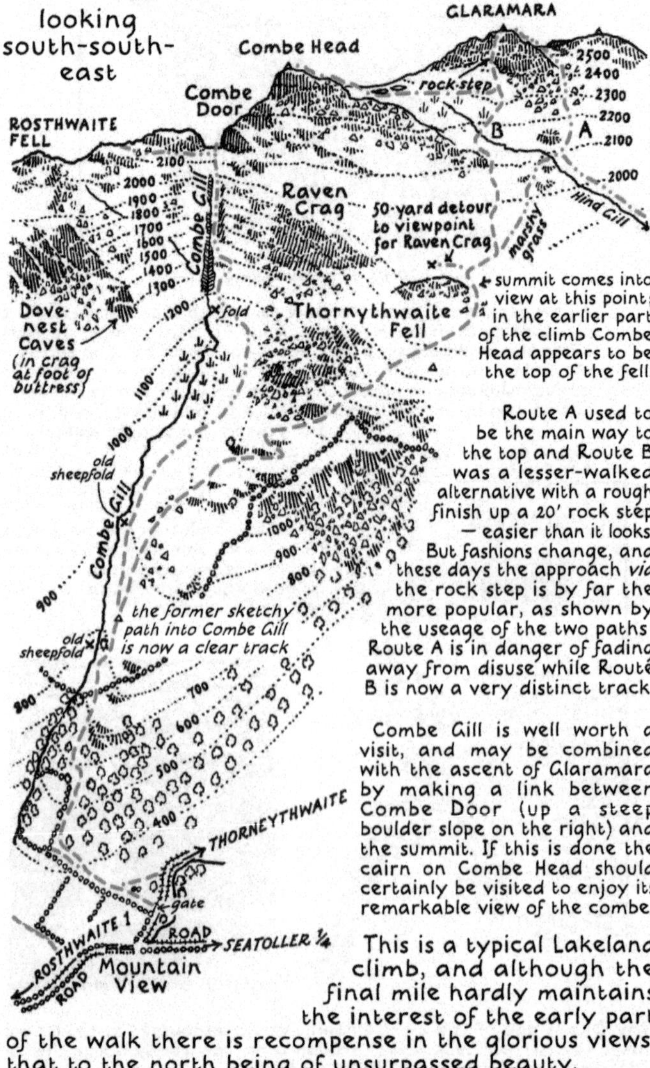
looking south-south-east
GLARAMARA
Combe Head
Combe Door
ROSTHWAITE FELL
rock step
2500
2400
2300
2200
2100
2000
B
A
Hind Gill
2100
2000
1900
1800
1700
1600
1500
1400
1300
1200
1100
1000
900
800
700
600
500
400
Combe Gill
Raven Crag
50-yard detour to viewpoint for Raven Crag
marshy grass
← summit comes into view at this point; in the earlier part of the climb Combe Head appears to be the top of the fell.
Dove nest Caves (in crag at foot of buttress)
fold
Thornythwaite Fell
old sheepfold
the former sketchy path into Combe Gill is now a clear track
THORNEYTHWAITE
gate
ROAD
SEATOLLER ¼
ROSTHWAITE 1
ROAD
Mountain View

Route A used to be the main way to the top and Route B was a lesser-walked alternative with a rough finish up a 20′ rock step — easier than it looks. But fashions change, and these days the approach *via* the rock step is by far the more popular, as shown by the useage of the two paths: Route A is in danger of fading away from disuse while Route B is now a very distinct track.

Combe Gill is well worth a visit, and may be combined with the ascent of Glaramara by making a link between Combe Door (up a steep boulder slope on the right) and the summit. If this is done the cairn on Combe Head should certainly be visited to enjoy its remarkable view of the combe.

This is a typical Lakeland climb, and although the final mile hardly maintains the interest of the early part of the walk there is recompense in the glorious views, that to the north being of unsurpassed beauty.

ASCENT FROM LANGSTRATH

2300 feet of ascent : 4½ miles (from Stonethwaite)

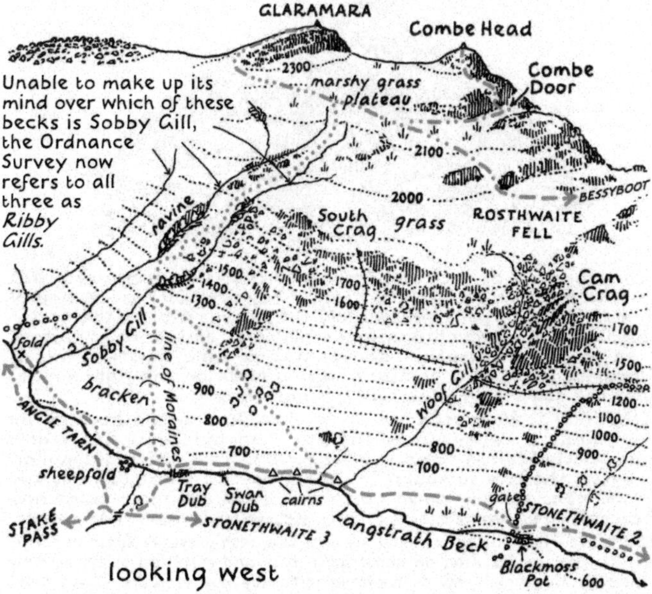
GLARAMARA
Combe Head
Combe Door
2300
marshy grass plateau
Unable to make up its mind over which of these becks is Sobby Gill, the Ordnance Survey now refers to all three as *Ribby Gills.*
2100
2000
BESSYBOOT
ravine
South Crag
grass
ROSTHWAITE FELL
Cam Crag
1500
1400
1300
1700
1600
1700
1500
Sobby Gill
line of Moraines
fold
bracken
900
800
700
Woof Gill
1200
1100
1000
900
800
700
ANGLE TARN
sheepfold
Tray Dub
Swan Dub
cairns
gate
STONETHWAITE 2
STAKE PASS
STONETHWAITE 3
Langstrath Beck
Blackmoss Pot
600

looking west

Sobby Gill marks the first real break in the long escarpment above Langstrath and the climbing here, pathless on grass, is straightforward, simple and trouble-free: in fact the only easy route on this flank. (Woof Gill looks inviting, but is all stones.)

This route is submitted without recommendation that it should be tried: it lacks interest above Tray Dub and does not favourably compare with the usual approach over Thornythwaite Fell. One purpose it serves, and serves well, is to introduce Langstrath but otherwise the climb from the valley floor is dull, although the route will satisfy purists who like to traverse their mountains.

1 : *Bowfell*
2 : *Esk Pike*
3 : *Rossett Pike*
4 : *Tongue Head*
5 : *Allen Crags*
6 : *Angletarn Gill*
7 : *Allencrags Gill*
8 : *Langstrath Beck*
9 : *Ore Gap*

1
2
9
3
4
5
6
7
6
7
8

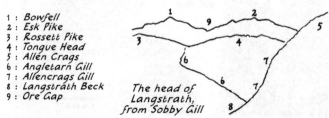

The head of Langstrath, from Sobby Gill

THE SUMMIT

Twin summits of rock rise from a surrounding ocean of grass, each within its own circle of crags. They are much alike, and of similar elevation, but indisputably the finer is that to the north-east, the top of which is a rocky platform with a cairn (bigger than in the illustration above) and a wind shelter: this is Glaramara proper, a pleasant halting-place on the right sort of day. The other summit, strictly, is nameless.

DESCENTS: All descents must lead to Borrowdale because all the flanking valleys flow thereto. The old route (A) starts indistinctly (cairn) down a little ravine from the slight hollow between the two summits. The more popular route (B), initially rough, goes sharply down north-east from the main cairn and breaches the escarpment at a 20' rock-step, which is easier than it looks.

(Ladies wearing skirts, in mixed parties, can best preserve their decorum at this point by insisting on going down first and rejecting offers of male assistance. Conversely, when *ascending* here, they must send the men up first.)

Route B crosses much marshy ground, aided by stepping stones provided by various public benefactors, and joins Route A 150 yards short of the cairn on Thornythwaite Fell. Combe Gill is too rough and bumpy to give a good way down, and takes an hour longer.

In mist, neither route will be easy to follow, but it is most important that, one or the other should be adhered to closely.

the 20' rock-step

PLAN OF SUMMIT

A : **BORROWDALE** *(old route)*

B : **BORROWDALE** *(popular route)*

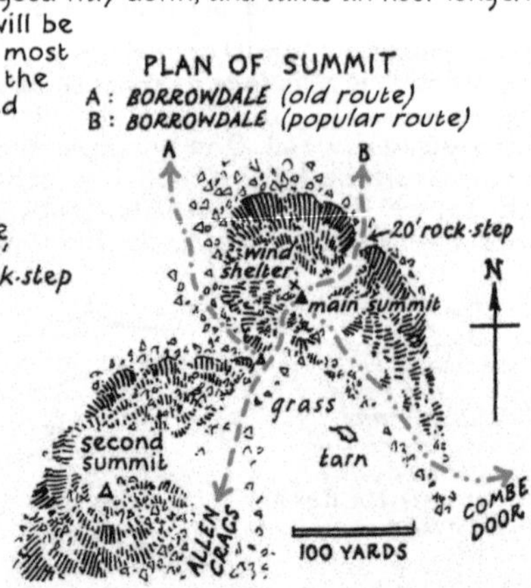
A
B
20' rock-step
wind shelter
main summit
N
grass
second summit
tarn
ALLEN CRAGS
100 YARDS
COMBE DOOR

RIDGE ROUTES

To ALLEN CRAGS, 2572′: 1¾ miles : generally SSW
Five depressions: 500 feet of ascent

A delightful walk along a fascinating path.

The time when this ridge-walk was a rough and disagreeable scramble is long past: the well-cairned and continuous path, skilfully planned so that easy passages are linked together, makes this a simple walk throughout. Time formerly spent in hunting for the route can now be employed in admiring the excellent views. The track, with many twists and undulations, is fairly distinct (more so, for instance, than route A) and can be followed in any weather. Look out for a perfect mountain tarn in a rocky setting; this is easily missed.

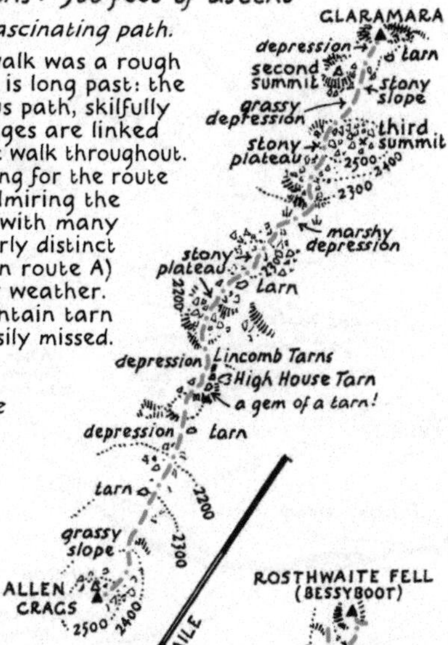
GLARAMARA
depression
tarn
second summit
stony slope
grassy depression
third summit
stony plateau
2500
2400
2300
marshy depression
stony plateau
2200
tarn
depression
Lincomb Tarns
High House Tarn
a gem of a tarn!
depression
tarn
tarn
2200
grassy slope
2300
ALLEN CRAGS
2500
2400
ONE MILE

Which comes first, the line of cairns or the path? Usually, as here, the cairns, the path materialising gradually as walkers aim from one to the next. Paths often become, in due course, so distinct that the cairns lose their function except in deep snow.

To ROSTHWAITE FELL (BESSYBOOT), 1807′: 1¾ miles ESE, then NE and N
200 feet of ascent

Not as good as it looks on the map.

Confusing, marshy, pathless terrain makes this a disappointing walk. (Wanted: a line of cairns!) If the idea is to find an alternative way down to Borrowdale, it should be discarded. The easiest way lies on the Langstrath side. In clear weather a number of prominent outcrops may visited to add interest. See *Rosthwaite Fell 5* for more details about these. *Definitely not a walk to attempt in mist.*

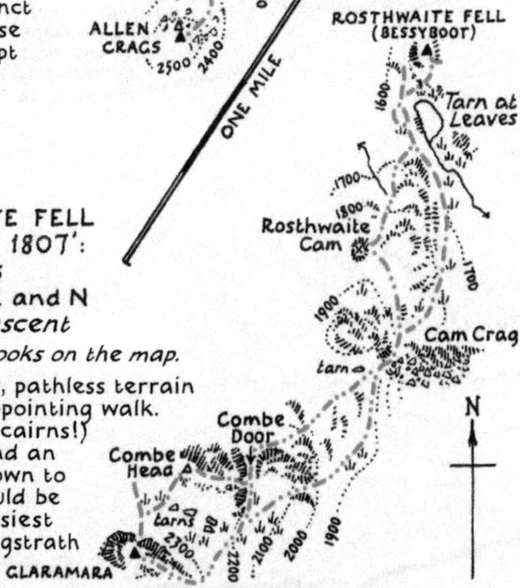
ROSTHWAITE FELL (BESSYBOOT)
1600
Tarn at Leaves
1700
1800
Rosthwaite Cam
1700
1900
Cam Crag
tarn
Combe Door
Combe Head
tarns
2400
2300
2200
2100
2000
1900
GLARAMARA
N

THE VIEW

(with distances in miles)

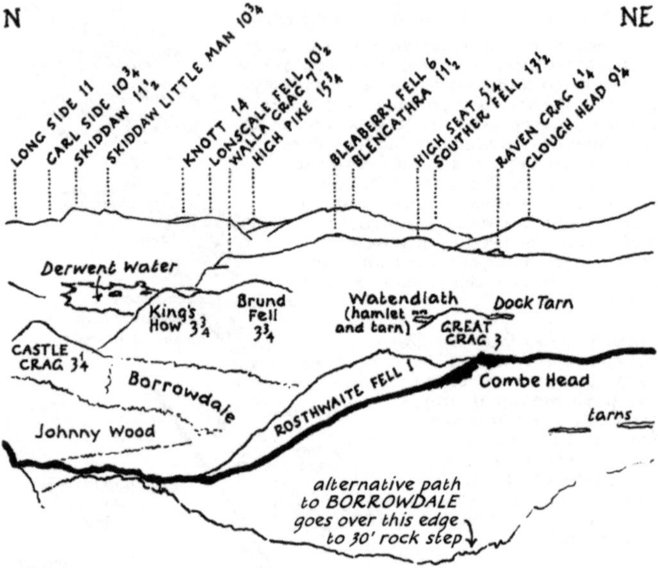
N
NE
LONG SIDE 11
CARL SIDE 10¾
SKIDDAW 11½
SKIDDAW LITTLE MAN 10¾
KNOTT 14
LONSCALE FELL 10½
WALLA CRAG 7
HIGH PIKE 15¾
BLEABERRY FELL 6
BLENCATHRA 11½
HIGH SEAT 5¼
SOUTHER FELL 13½
RAVEN CRAG 6¼
CLOUGH HEAD 9¾
Derwent Water
King's How 3¾
Brund Fell 3¾
Watendlath (hamlet and tarn)
Dock Tarn
GREAT CRAG 3
CASTLE CRAG 3¼
Borrowdale
ROSTHWAITE FELL 1
Combe Head
tarns
Johnny Wood
alternative path to BORROWDALE goes over this edge to 30' rock step

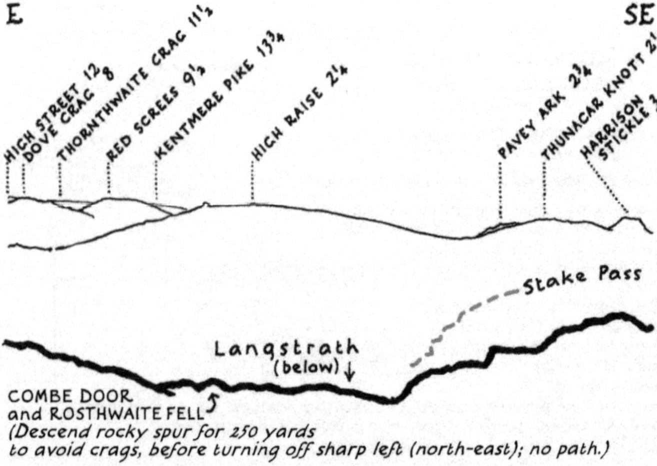
E
SE
HIGH STREET 12
DOVE CRAG 8
THORNTHWAITE CRAG 11½
RED SCREES 9½
KENTMERE PIKE 13¾
HIGH RAISE 2¼
PAVEY ARK 2¾
THUNACAR KNOTT 2½
HARRISON STICKLE 3
Stake Pass
Langstrath (below)
COMBE DOOR and ROSTHWAITE FELL
(Descend rocky spur for 250 yards to avoid crags, before turning off sharp left (north-east); no path.)

THE VIEW

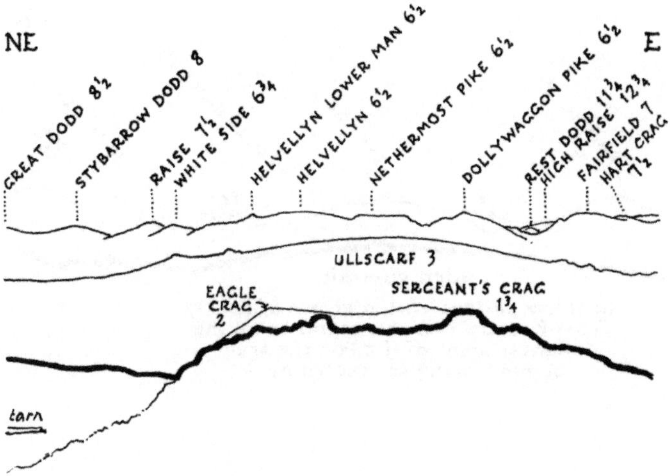
NE
E
GREAT DODD 8½
STYBARROW DODD 8
RAISE 7½
WHITE SIDE 6¾
HELVELLYN LOWER MAN 6½
HELVELLYN 6½
NETHERMOST PIKE 6½
DOLLYWAGGON PIKE 6½
REST DODD 11¾
HIGH RAISE 12¾
FAIRFIELD 7
HART CRAG 7½
ULLSCARF 3
EAGLE CRAG 2
SERGEANT'S CRAG 1¾
tarn

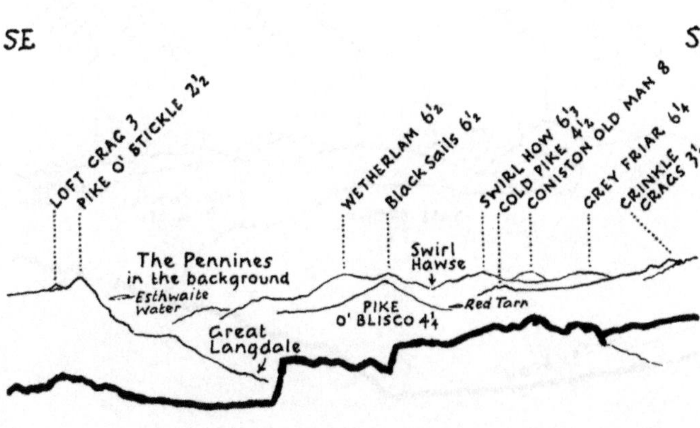
SE
S
LOFT CRAG 3
PIKE O' STICKLE 2½
WETHERLAM 6½
Black Sails 6½
SWIRL HOW 6½
COLD PIKE 4½
CONISTON OLD MAN 8
GREY FRIAR 6¼
CRINKLE CRAGS 3½
The Pennines in the background
Esthwaite Water
Swirl Hawse
Red Tarn
PIKE O' BLISCO 4¼
Great Langdale

The thick black line marks the visible boundaries of the fell from the main cairn

THE VIEW

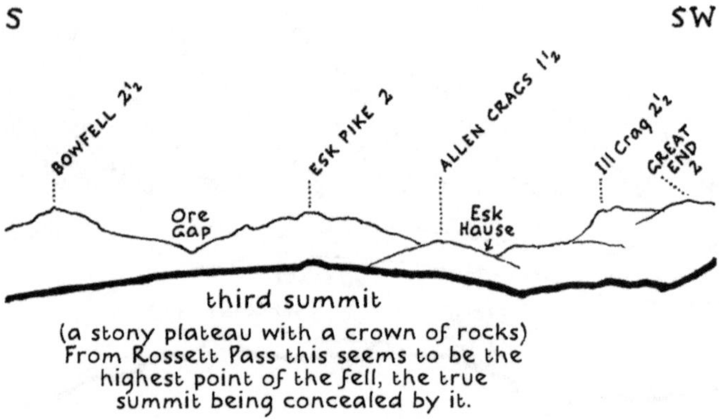
S
SW
BOWFELL 2½
ESK PIKE 2
ALLEN CRAGS 1½
Ill Crag 2½
GREAT END 2
Ore Gap
Esk Hause
third summit
(a stony plateau with a crown of rocks)
From Rossett Pass this seems to be the highest point of the fell, the true summit being concealed by it.

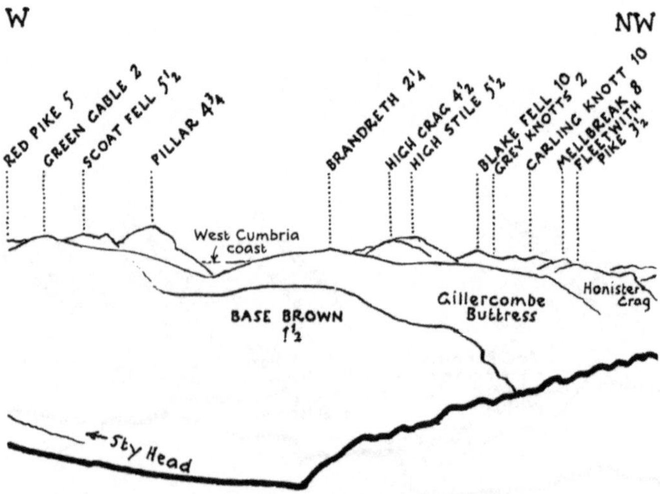
W
NW
RED PIKE 5
GREEN GABLE 2
SCOAT FELL 5½
PILLAR 4¾
BRANDRETH 2¼
HIGH CRAG 4½
HIGH STILE 5½
BLAKE FELL 10
GREY KNOTTS 2
CARLING KNOTT 10
MELLBREAK 8
FLEETWITH PIKE 3½
West Cumbria coast
Gillercombe Buttress
Honister Crag
BASE BROWN 1½
Sty Head

THE VIEW

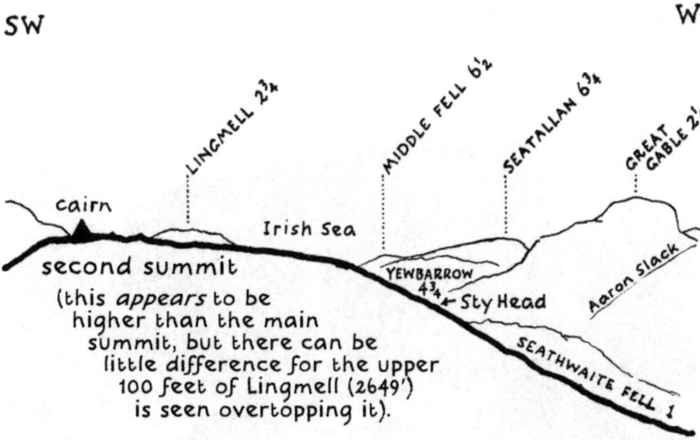
SW
W
LINGMELL 2¾
MIDDLE FELL 6½
SEATALLAN 6¾
GREAT GABLE 2¼
cairn
Irish Sea
second summit
(this *appears* to be higher than the main summit, but there can be little difference for the upper 100 feet of Lingmell (2649') is seen overtopping it).
YEWBARROW 4¾
Sty Head
Aaron Slack
SEATHWAITE FELL 1

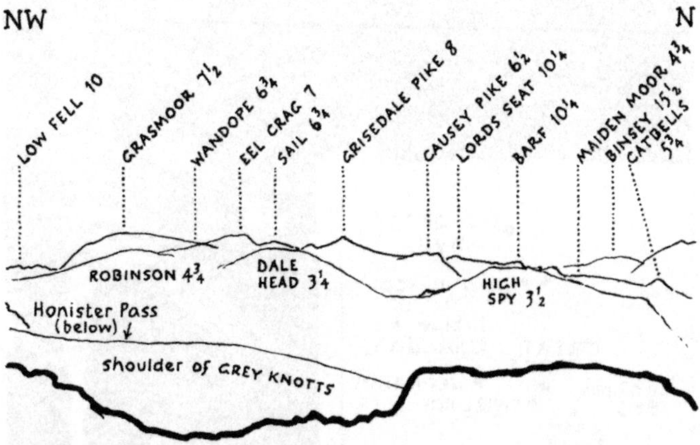
NW
N
LOW FELL 10
GRASMOOR 7½
WANDOPE 6¾
EEL CRAG 7
SAIL 6¾
GRISEDALE PIKE 8
CAUSEY PIKE 6½
LORDS SEAT 10¼
BARF 10¼
MAIDEN MOOR 4¾
BINSEY 15½
CATBELLS 5¾
ROBINSON 4¾
DALE HEAD 3¼
HIGH SPY 3½
Honister Pass (below)
shoulder of GREY KNOTTS

Glaramara's unique situation, in the heart of the district yet isolated by deep valleys, is emphasised by the splendid view. Overtopped by many fells but overshadowed by none, the summit provides a spacious and interesting panorama. But the best scene of all is that of the curve of Borrowdale with Derwent Water and Skiddaw beyond: a superb picture.

Great Carrs

2575'

OS grid ref: NY270009

Dungeon Ghyll
PIKE O' BLISCO
Little Langdale
GREAT CARRS
Cockley Beck
WETHERLAM
SWIRL HOW
GREY FRIAR
CONISTON OLD MAN
Coniston
MILES
0 1 2 3 4

from Greenburn Beck

NATURAL FEATURES

Curved like a scythe, the shapely ridge springing from the fields of Little Langdale to the crest of Rough Crags and climbing gradually thence along the grassy rim of Wet Side Edge to a lofty altitude between deep valleys, has little to arouse interest until the mild excitement of a bouldery stairway skirting the edge of crags promises better things ahead. The airy summit of Great Carrs follows at once, a splendid perch on the edge of the profound abyss of Greenburn. A short distance beyond, the ridge terminates in the peak of Swirl How.

Hell Gill Pike

Apart from its eastern precipice Great Carrs has few features out of the ordinary and the western slopes going down to the valley of the Duddon are generally dull; on this flank the cliffs of Hell Gill Pike, below the subsidiary summit of Little Carrs, are more worthy of note.

The ridge, which bounds Wrynose Pass on the south, separates the waters of the Brathay from those of Greenburn, but they mingle finally in Little Langdale Tarn. Westwards, Hell Gill, in a steep ravine, is the most prominent of the early feeders of the Duddon.

1 : *The summit*
2 : *Swirl How*
3 : *Little Carrs*
4 : *Hell Gill Pike*
5 : *Wet Side Edge*
6 : *Rough Crags*
7 : *Greenburn Res.r (disused)*
8 : *Greenburn Beck*
9 : *Little Langdale Tarn*
10 : *River Brathay*
11 : *River Duddon*
12 : *Wrynose Pass*

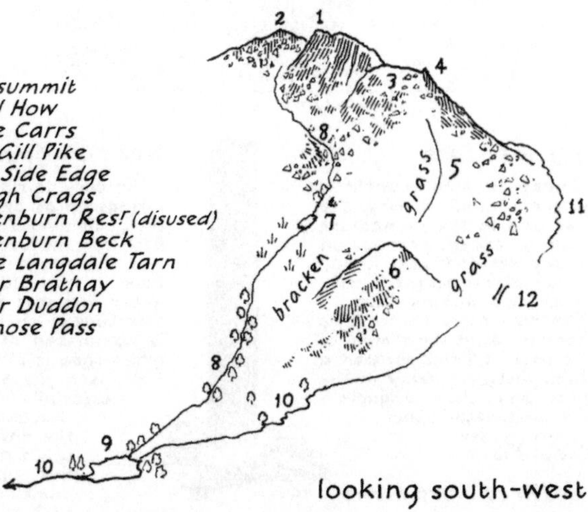
2
1
3
4
8
grass
5
11
7
6
bracken
grass
12
8
10
9
10

looking south-west

MAP

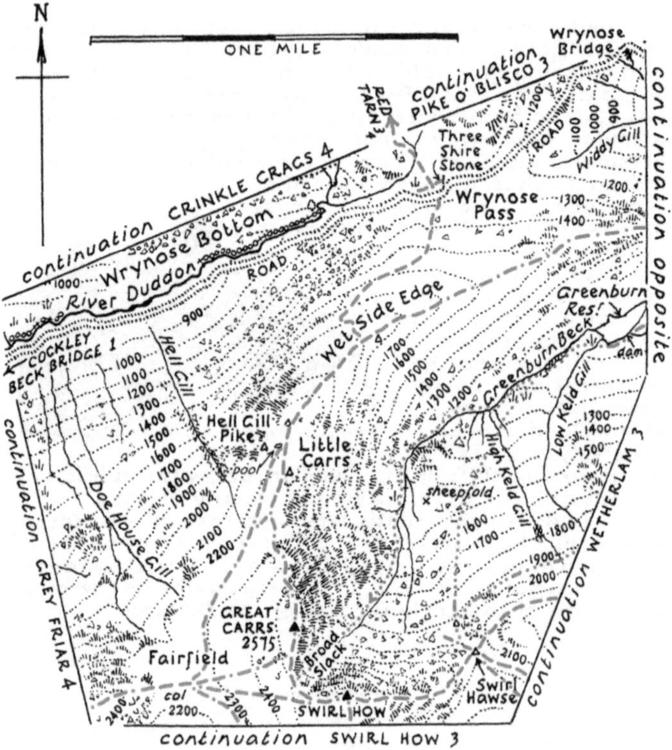
N
ONE MILE
Wrynose Bridge
continuation PIKE O' BLISCO 3
RED TARN 4
continuation CRINKLE CRAGS 4
Three Shire Stone
ROAD
Widdy Gill
Wrynose Pass
Wrynose Bottom
River Duddon
ROAD
Wet Side Edge
Greenburn Res!
Greenburn Beck
dam
COCKLEY BECK BRIDGE 1
Hell Gill
Hell Gill Pike
pool
Little Carrs
Low Keld Gill
High Keld Gill
sheepfold
Doe House Gill
continuation GREY FRIAR 4
GREAT CARRS 2575
Broad Slack
Fairfield
col
SWIRL HOW
Swirl Hawse
continuation WETHERLAM 3
continuation opposite
continuation SWIRL HOW 3

Wrynose Pass

There is ample parking at the summit of Wrynose Pass and in the immediate vicinity, except perhaps on holiday weekends when it may be advisable to get there early to secure a parking place.

The distinctive Three Shire Stone is not at the summit of the pass, it being located a short distance away in the direction of Little Langdale. For some detail about its history, see *Pike o' Bisco 3*.

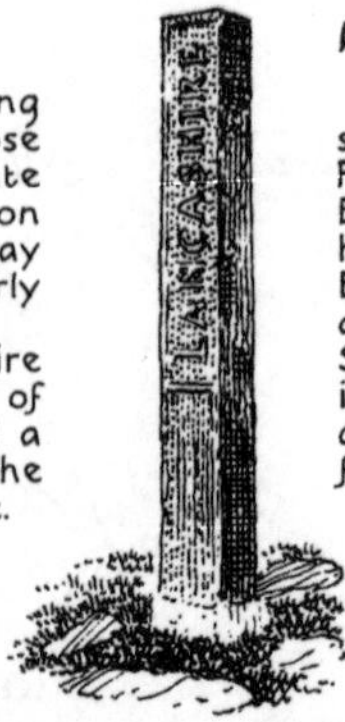
LANCASHIRE

Three Shire Stone

Wet Side Edge

The curving ridge which springs up at beyond Fell Foot, dividing Greenburn Beck from the River Brathay has the name Wet Side Edge in its middle stages above Wrynose Pass; Wet Side Edge is mis-named: it is comprised of springy grass that is *dry*, and, in fact, is a joy to tread, especially in descent.

Rough Crags, at the eastern end of the ridge, *does* live up to its name however.

MAP

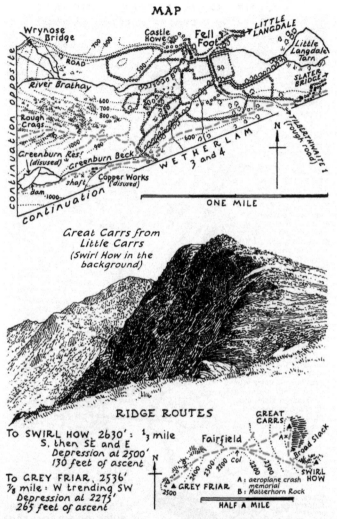

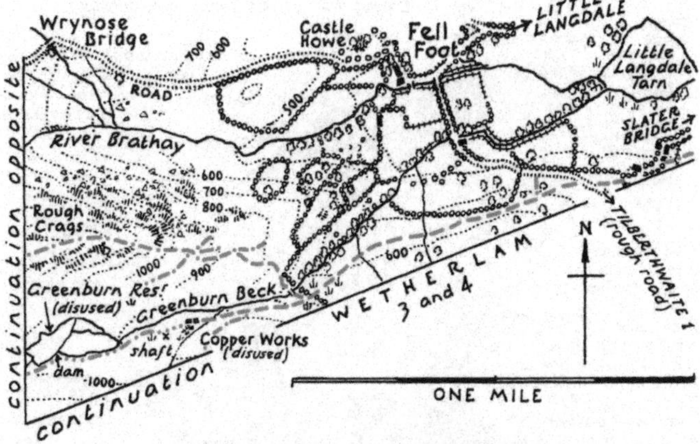
Wrynose Bridge
ROAD
River Brathay
Rough Crags
Greenburn Resr (disused)
Greenburn Beck
Copper Works (disused)
shaft
dam
1000
900
800
700
600
500
Castle Howe
Fell Foot
LITTLE LANGDALE
Little Langdale Tarn
SLATER BRIDGE
TILBERTHWAITE 1 (rough road)
WETHERLAM 3 and 4
N
ONE MILE
continuation opposite
continuation

Great Carrs from Little Carrs
(Swirl How in the background)

RIDGE ROUTES

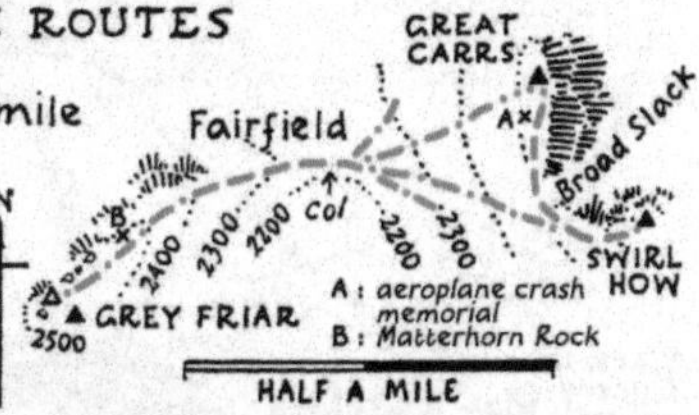
GREAT CARRS
Fairfield
Broad Slack
A
B
col
2500
2400
2300
2200
2200
2300
GREY FRIAR
SWIRL HOW
N
A : aeroplane crash memorial
B : Matterhorn Rock
HALF A MILE

To SWIRL HOW, 2630′ : 1/3 mile
S, then SE and E
Depression at 2500′
130 feet of ascent

To GREY FRIAR, 2536′
7/8 mile : W trending SW
Depression at 2275′
265 feet of ascent

Both easy walks, but Grey Friar is not a place to visit *in mist*. At the start of both routes, take the opportunity to visit the memorial to the airmen killed in crash on the summit plateau in the Second World War; it is a moving experience. Three hundred yards before the summit of Grey Friar look out for the Matterhorn Rock which, from a certain angle, resembles the alpine giant as seen from Zermatt.

ASCENT FROM LITTLE LANGDALE

2350 feet of ascent : 4 miles (from the village)

A short detour to Hell Gill Pike is recommended. The nearby pool is charming.

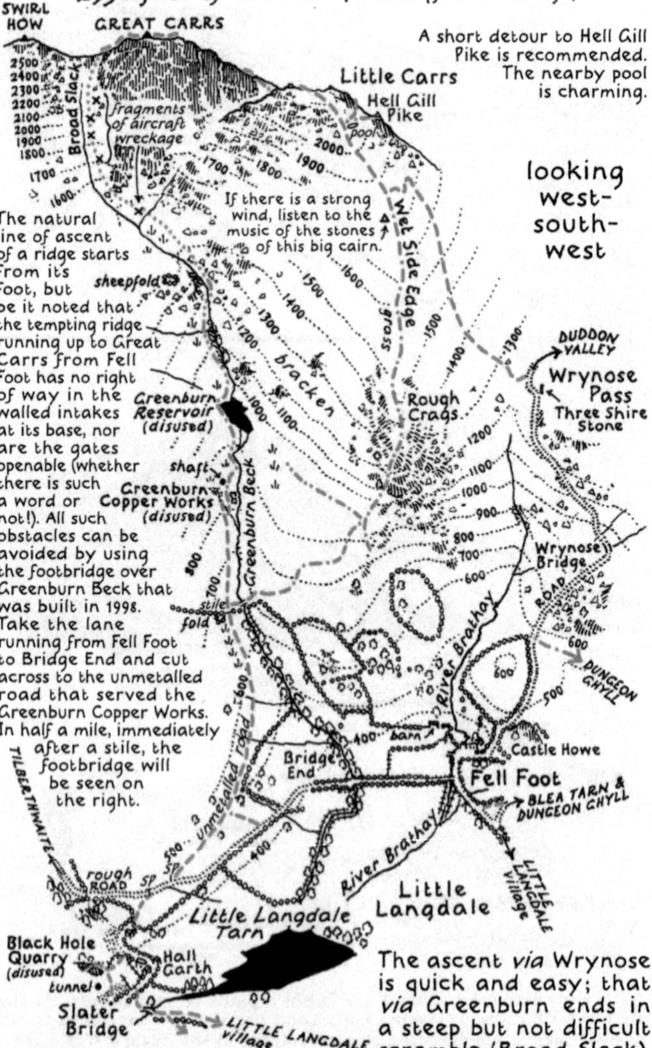
SWIRL HOW
GREAT CARRS
Broad Slack
2500
2400
2300
2200
2100
2000
1900
1800
1700
1600
fragments of aircraft wreckage
Little Carrs
Hell Gill Pike
pool
2000
1900
1800
1700
If there is a strong wind, listen to the music of the stones of this big cairn.
Wet Side Edge
grass
1600
1500
1400
1300
1200
1100
1000
bracken
sheepfold
Greenburn Reservoir (disused)
shaft
Greenburn Copper Works (disused)
Greenburn Beck
Rough Crags
1500
1400
1300
1200
1100
1000
900
800
700
600
DUDDON VALLEY
Wrynose Pass
Three Shire Stone
Wrynose Bridge
ROAD
600
DUNGEON GHYLL
500
600
River Brathay
800
700
stile
fold
600
unmetalled road
400
barn
Bridge End
Castle Howe
Fell Foot
BLEA TARN & DUNGEON GHYLL
River Brathay
LITTLE LANGDALE village
TILBERTHWAITE
500
SP
rough ROAD
SP
400
Little Langdale
Little Langdale Tarn
Black Hole Quarry (disused)
Hall Garth
tunnel
Slater Bridge
LITTLE LANGDALE village

looking west-south-west

The natural line of ascent of a ridge starts from its foot, but be it noted that the tempting ridge running up to Great Carrs from Fell Foot has no right of way in the walled intakes at its base, nor are the gates openable (whether there is such a word or not!). All such obstacles can be avoided by using the footbridge over Greenburn Beck that was built in 1998. Take the lane running from Fell Foot to Bridge End and cut across to the unmetalled road that served the Greenburn Copper Works. In half a mile, immediately after a stile, the footbridge will be seen on the right.

The ascent *via* Wrynose is quick and easy; that *via* Greenburn ends in a steep but not difficult scramble (Broad Slack).

The best way up is *via* Wet Side Edge, a lovely approach. There is no public path direct from Fell Foot.

THE SUMMIT

1 : slope of Swirl How
2 : Coniston Old Man
3 : Brim Fell
4 : Dow Crag
south summit

The easily graded upper western slope of Great Carrs breaks very abruptly into a long eastern precipice, the highest point of the fell therefore being on the rim, and here, on a small outcrop, is the cairn, airily perched in a splendid position high above the great hollow formed by the deep-set Greenburn valley in its circle of peaks. A short tour along the ridge, which is grassy on either side of the cairn, reveals striking gullies failing very steeply in the direction of Greenburn Reservoir.

An unnatural and unwelcome adornment to the top is provided by some wreckage of a Second World War aeroplane, 150 yards south of the cairn. The Royal Canadian Air Force Halifax bomber, travelling from west to east, failed to clear the ridge by a few feet only; at the place of impact the undercarriage was ripped off (and still lies there, built into a memorial cairn for the eight airman who lost their lives on 22nd October, 1944). The remainder of the wreckage was later pushed over the edge to crash far down the precipice. Some of this was taken to the Ruskin Museum in Coniston in 1997.

DESCENTS: Go along the declining ridge, over Little Carrs, to Wet Side Edge, where turn left for Wrynose Pass, or continue along the ridge for the footbridge over Greenburn Beck – an easy descent, safe *in mist*.

The summit ridge, looking north

THE VIEW

looking north-west

1
2
3
4
5
6
7
8
9

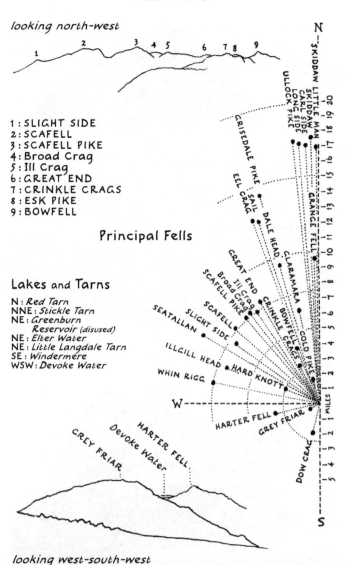

1 : SLIGHT SIDE
2 : SCAFELL
3 : SCAFELL PIKE
4 : Broad Crag
5 : Ill Crag
6 : GREAT END
7 : CRINKLE CRAGS
8 : ESK PIKE
9 : BOWFELL

Principal Fells

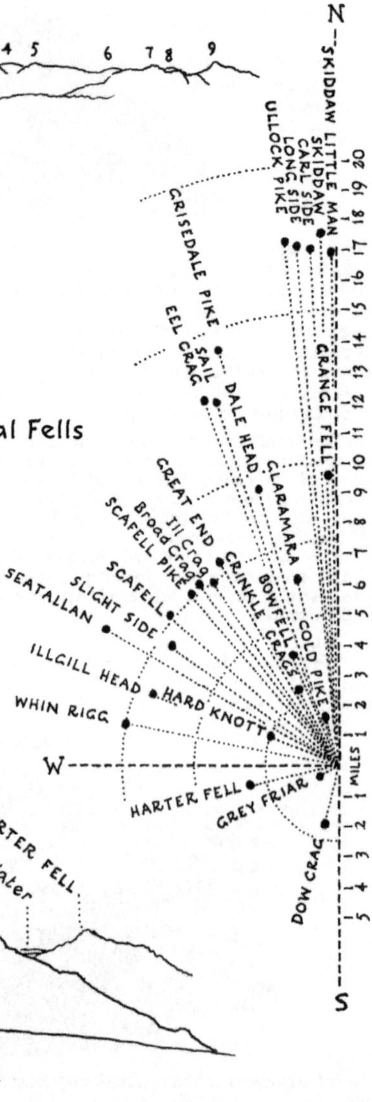
N
SKIDDAW LITTLE MAN
SKIDDAW
CARL SIDE
LONG SIDE
ULLOCK PIKE
GRISEDALE PIKE
EEL CRAG
SAIL
GRANGE FELL
DALE HEAD
GLARAMARA
GREAT END
Ill Crag
Broad Crag
SCAFELL PIKE
CRINKLE CRAGS
BOWFELL
SCAFELL
SLIGHT SIDE
SEATALLAN
COLD PIKE
ILLGILL HEAD
HARD KNOTT
WHIN RIGG
W
HARTER FELL
GREY FRIAR
DOW CRAG
MILES
S

Lakes and Tarns

N : *Red Tarn*
NNE : *Stickle Tarn*
NE : *Greenburn Reservoir (disused)*
NE : *Elter Water*
NE : *Little Langdale Tarn*
SE : *Windermere*
WSW : *Devoke Water*

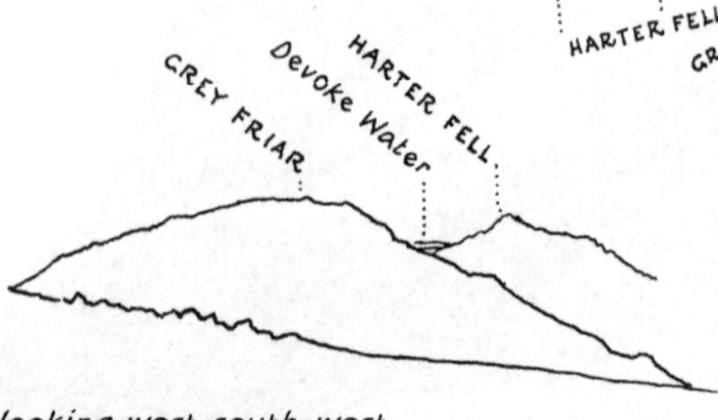
HARTER FELL
Devoke Water
GREY FRIAR

looking west-south-west

THE VIEW

This is an excellent view, well worth the easy walk up from Wrynose Pass, although to some extent unbalanced by the impending mass of Swirl How, which conceals the pleasant Coniston countryside (this defect being quickly remedied by going on to Swirl How itself). The prospect across to the Scafell and Bowfell groups is magnificent. Greenburn is especially well displayed, directly below, but appears as a drab and unattractive hollow until its beck curves to join the Brathay in the brighter pastures of Little Langdale.

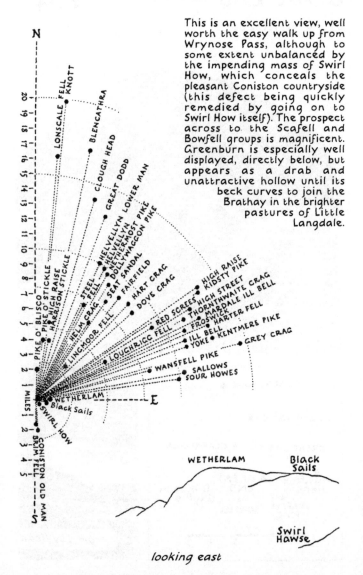

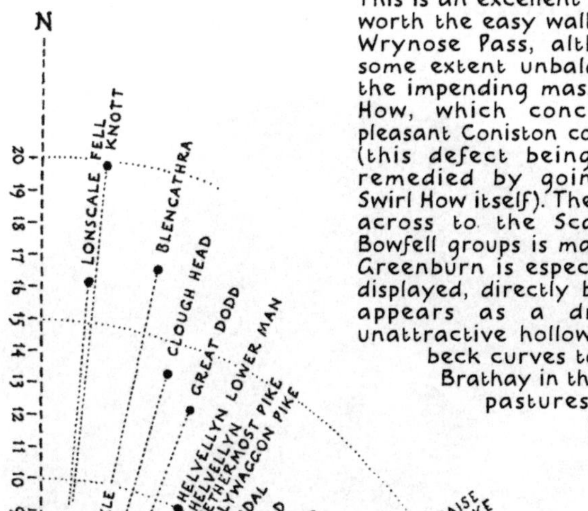
N
E
S
MILES
1
2
3
4
5
6
7
8
9
10
11
12
13
14
15
16
17
18
19
20
LONSCALE FELL
KNOTT
BLENCATHRA
CLOUGH HEAD
GREAT DODD
LOWER MAN
HELVELLYN
NETHERMOST PIKE
DOLLYWAGGON PIKE
SEAT SANDAL
FAIRFIELD
HART CRAG
DOVE CRAG
STEEL FELL
HELM CRAG
LINGMOOR FELL
LOUGHRIGG FELL
RED SCREES
HIGH RAISE
KIDSTY PIKE
HIGH STREET
THORNTHWAITE CRAG
MARDALE ILL BELL
FROSWICK
HARTER FELL
ILL BELL
KENTMERE PIKE
YOKE
GREY CRAG
WANSFELL PIKE
SALLOWS
SOUR HOWES
WETHERLAM
Black Sails
SWIRL HOW
CONISTON OLD MAN
BRIM FELL
PIKE O' BLISCO
PIKE O' STICKLE
HIGH RAISE
HARRISON STICKLE

WETHERLAM
Black Sails
Swirl Hawse

looking east

Great End

2984'

OS grid ref: NY227084

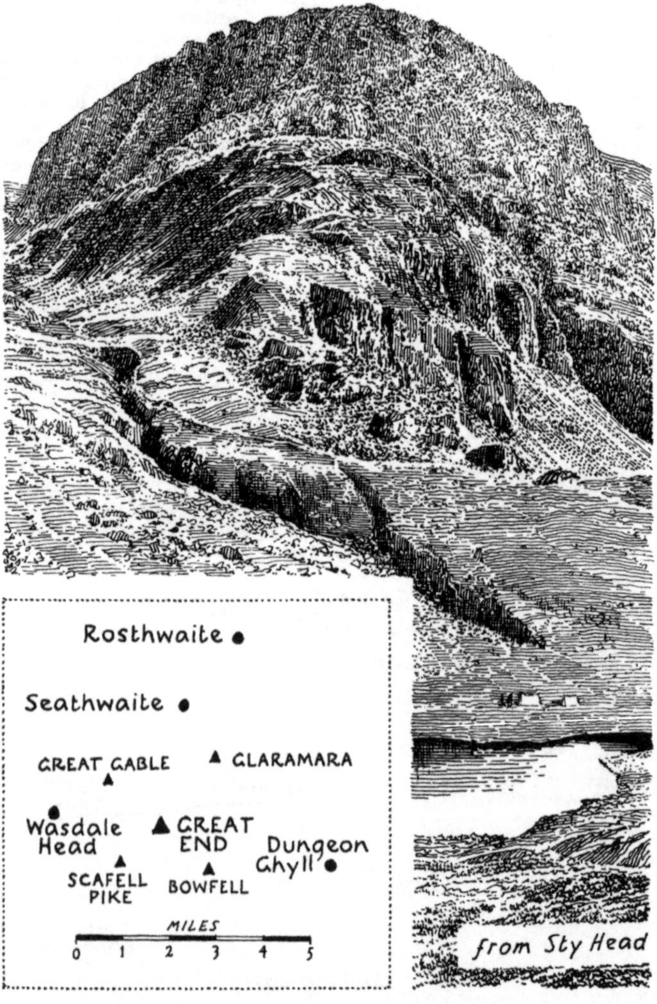
Rosthwaite
Seathwaite
GREAT GABLE
GLARAMARA
Wasdale Head
GREAT END
Dungeon Ghyll
SCAFELL PIKE
BOWFELL
MILES
0 1 2 3 4 5

from Sty Head

NATURAL FEATURES

Nobody who is familiar with the topography of the Scafell area will have any doubts why Great End was so named: there could not have been a more descriptive choice for the tremendous northern buttress of the mass. Great it is, and the end of the highest plateau in the country.

Without losing much altitude, the lofty spine of Scafell Pike extends north-eastwards a mile to the domed summit of Great End, which, when approached in this direction, has little to show other than a bouldery waste, a stony wilderness. But the vast northern fall of the mountain is one of the finest scenes in the district, awe-inspiring in its massive strength and all the more imposing for being eternally in shadow. The summit breaks immediately in a long cliff seamed by dark gullies, below which a broad shelf holds Sprinkling Tarn and continues as Seathwaite Fell, but a shoulder (the Band) also fiercely scarped and severed from the main fell by the deep ravine of Skew Gill, runs down to Sty Head.

When mist wreathes the summit and clings like smoke in the gullies, when ravens soar above the lonely crags, when snow lies deep and curtains of ice bejewel the gaunt cliffs, then Great End is indeed an impressive sight. Sunshine never mellows this grim scene but only adds harshness.

Central Gully
Cust's Gully
South-east Gully
Long Pike
The Band
Skew Gill
footpath
←ESK HAUSE
STY HEAD→
stream from Sprinkling Tarn (usually regarded as the source of the Derwent)
Styhead Tarn

This is the true Lakeland of the fell walker, the sort of terrain that calls people back time after time, the sort of memory that haunts their long winter exile.

It is not the pretty places — the flowery lanes of Grasmere or Derwentwater's wooded bays — that keep walkers restless in their beds; it is the magnificent ones.

Places like Great End .....

Key to drawing opposite

Borrowdale
from the top of
Central Gully

MAP

Sprinkling Tarn is a most attractive sheet of water with an indented rocky shore, its scenic quality enhanced by the massive cliffs of Great End nearby and soaring above. The tarn is a delightful place, well provided with heathery couches amongst grey boulders on the water's edge.

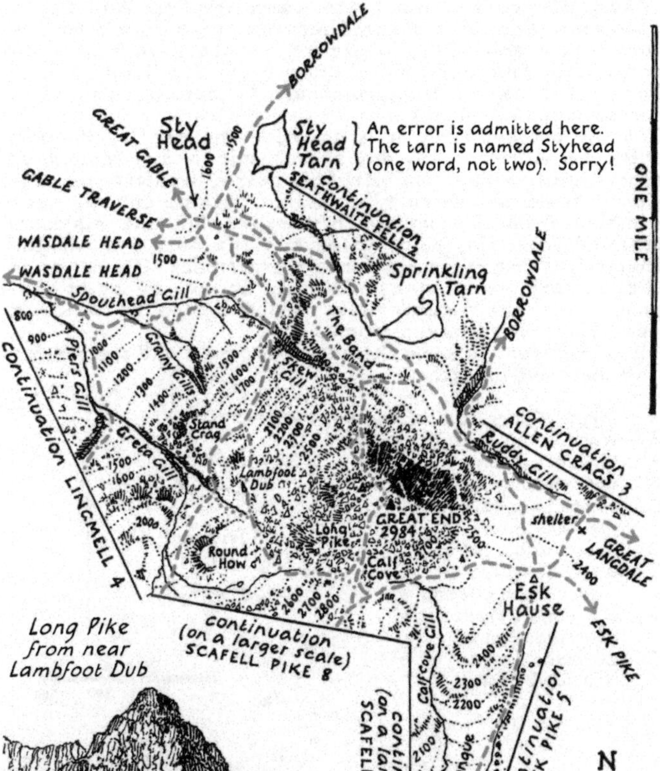
BORROWDALE
Sty Head
Sty Head Tarn
An error is admitted here. The tarn is named Styhead (one word, not two). Sorry!
GREAT GABLE
GABLE TRAVERSE
WASDALE HEAD
WASDALE HEAD
continuation SEATHWAITE FELL 2
Sprinkling Tarn
ONE MILE
Spouthead Gill
The Band
BORROWDALE
Piers Gill
Grainy Gills
Skew Gill
Stand Crag
continuation LINGMELL 4
Greta Gill
Lambfoot Dub
continuation ALLEN CRAGS 3
Ruddy Gill
GREAT END 2984
shelter
Long Pike
Round How
Calf Cove
GREAT LANGDALE
Esk Hause
continuation (on a larger scale) SCAFELL PIKE 8
ESK PIKE
Calfcove Gill
Tongue
continuation (on a larger scale) SCAFELL PIKE 8
continuation ESK PIKE 5
N
River Esk
ESKDALE

Long Pike from near Lambfoot Dub

Sty Head

Once upon a time Sty Head was a simple pass between Wasdale and Borrowdale, providing also a link with Great Langdale: the two routes served the dalesmen sufficiently and no others were needed in the vicinity to carry them about their business.

Then, 150 years or more ago, came the first walkers, in occasional twos and threes, hesitant to venture into this wild place; and later, in greater numbers, with growing confidence and much more, often — for Sty Head became known as a convenient springboard for excursions into the surrounding mountains.

At the present time, it is doubtful whether Sty Head is without a visitor on any day of any year; and on most days scores, and, in high summer, hundreds of walkers pass this way — some, as the early dalesmen, seeking only an easy crossing from one valley to another, but the majority starting from this point to ascend the hills and win for themselves one more memorable experience. The needs of these happy wanderers could only be met by additional paths, and their boots have brought into existence a network of well trodden tracks.

It is important to know these various tracks and the purpose and objective of each.

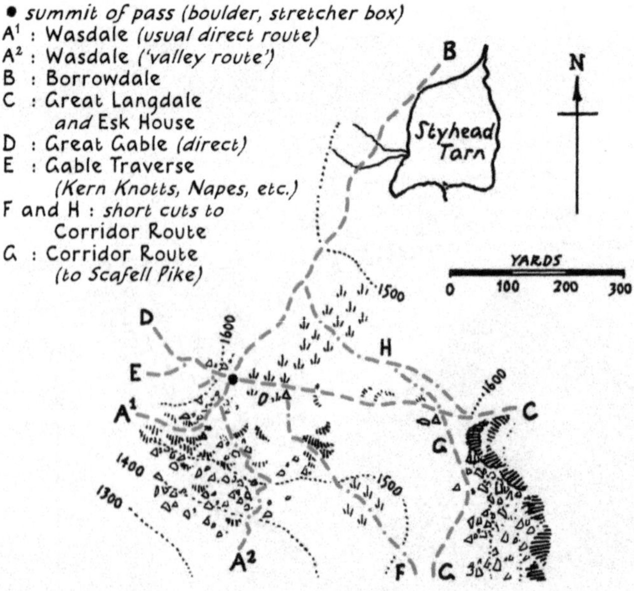

• summit of pass (boulder, stretcher box)
A1 : Wasdale (usual direct route)
A2 : Wasdale ('valley route')
B : Borrowdale
C : Great Langdale and Esk House
D : Great Gable (direct)
E : Gable Traverse (Kern Knotts, Napes, etc.)
F and H : short cuts to Corridor Route
G : Corridor Route (to Scafell Pike)
Styhead Tarn
N
YARDS
0 100 200 300
1500
1600
1400
1300
B
C
D
E
F
G
H
A1
A2

ASCENT FROM STY HEAD

1450 feet of ascent : 1 mile

(from Wasdale Head : 2800 ft : 3¼ miles
from Seathwaite : 2650 ft : 3¼ miles)

A : Cust's Gully
B : branch gully
GREAT END
A
B
2800
2700
2600
2500
2400
2300
2100
2000
1900
1800
1700
1600
1500
1600
1500
head of Skew Gill (here only a shallow trough)
bouldery gully
ESK HAUSE
path follows grassy ridge on right of gully for a short section of the climb
The Band (not to be confused with Bowfell's better-known Band)
Skew Gill
Sprinkling Tarn
grass
boulder
SCAFELL PIKE
Sty Head
note stretcher (just in case it is needed later in the day!)
Styhead Tarn
BORROWDALE
looking south-south-east

The Band is straightforward walking, but the final rugged dome beyond the head of Skew Gill is mountaineering. Cust's Gully and its branch may be inspected from below by a detour (and later from the top) but the recommended route goes up a narrow scree-filled cleft away to the right around an intervening buttress, or follow a sketchy path to the right. Above, a steep slope leads past the upper exit of the branch gully, and then, 50 yards higher and in the midst of boulders (care needed in placing your feet), a short traverse left crosses the head of Cust's Gully and reaches the welcome grass of the summit.

The simplest way onto the ridge of the Band is to first use the Esk Hause path (which continues beyond Sprinkling Tarn) and leave it for a grassy slope on the right at the point where the path crosses the stream. A thin path soon appears.

The alternative route shown is, at first, pathless on grass. Aim for a prominent gully that is littered with boulders but stay on the edge on the right and follow a sketchy track to the top of the gully, joining the usual route at the head of Skew Gill. The striking views of Sprinkling Tarn make this a route worth considering.

Subject to the qualification that the last section is a very rough climb, this is an excellent ascent, giving a satisfying sense of achievement. Both routes shown are within the capacity of energetic walkers; experienced scramblers may vary it by ascending Skew Gill (instead of the Band) and by finishing up the branch gully, both of which entail some handling of easy rocks. *Avoid this way up in mist.*

The Valley Route
(Wasdale Head to Sty Head)

'Stee' (or 'Sty') means 'ladder' and the old original zig-zag path here described may well be the stee that gave the Pass its name.

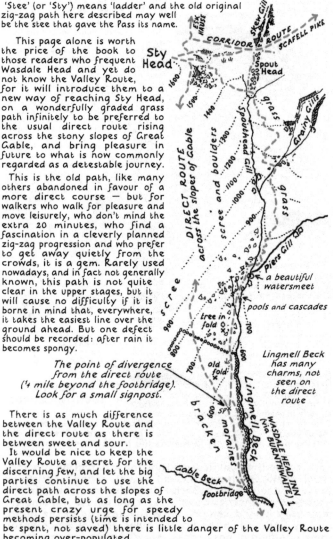

This page alone is worth the price of the book to those readers who frequent Wasdale Head and yet do not know the Valley Route, for it will introduce them to a new way of reaching Sty Head, on a wonderfully graded grass path infinitely to be preferred to the usual direct route rising across the stony slopes of Great Gable, and bring pleasure in future to what is now commonly regarded as a detestable journey.

This is the old path, like many others abandoned in favour of a more direct course — but for walkers who walk for pleasure and move leisurely, who don't mind the extra 20 minutes, who find a fascination in a cleverly planned zig-zag progression and who prefer to get away quietly from the crowds, it is a gem. Rarely used nowadays, and in fact not generally known, this path is not quite clear in the upper stages, but it will cause no difficulty if it is borne in mind that, everywhere, it takes the easiest line over the ground ahead. But one defect should be recorded: after rain it becomes spongy.

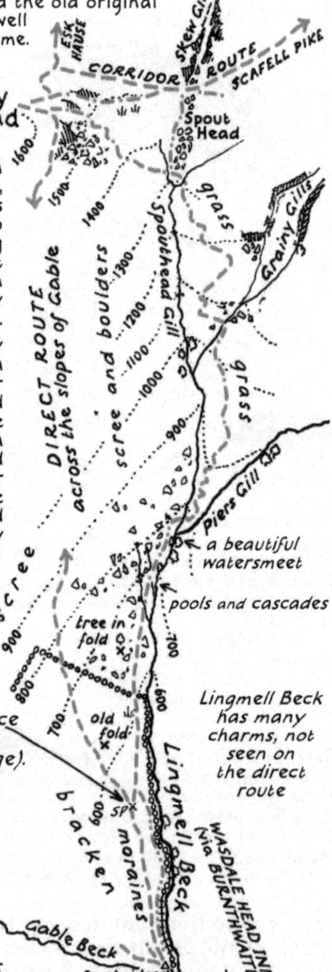
ESK HAUSE
Skew Gill
CORRIDOR ROUTE
SCAFELL PIKE
Sty Head
Spout Head
1600
1500
1400
1300
1200
1100
1000
900
800
700
600
grass
Grainy Gills
Spouthead Gill
DIRECT ROUTE across the slopes of Gable
scree and boulders
scree
Piers Gill
a beautiful watersmeet
pools and cascades
tree in fold
old fold
Lingmell Beck has many charms, not seen on the direct route
The point of divergence from the direct route (¼ mile beyond the footbridge). Look for a small signpost.
SP
bracken
moraines
Lingmell Beck
WASDALE HEAD INN (via BURNTHWAITE) 1
Gable Beck
footbridge

There is as much difference between the Valley Route and the direct route as there is between sweet and sour.

It would be nice to keep the Valley Route a secret for the discerning few, and let the big parties continue to use the direct path across the slopes of Great Gable, but as long as the present crazy urge for speedy methods persists (time is intended to be spent, not saved) there is little danger of the Valley Route becoming over-populated.

ASCENT FROM WASDALE HEAD

2750 feet of ascent : 4 miles

The path to Lambfoot Dub (a beautiful little tarn) has an indistinct start and is actually easier to follow in descent. Beyond the tarn the route passes through a cluster of large boulders. The *col* on the ridge reached by this route is, of course, the one above Calf Cove on the Esk Hause to Scafell Pike path. The final part of the climb to the *col* is steep and stony in places.

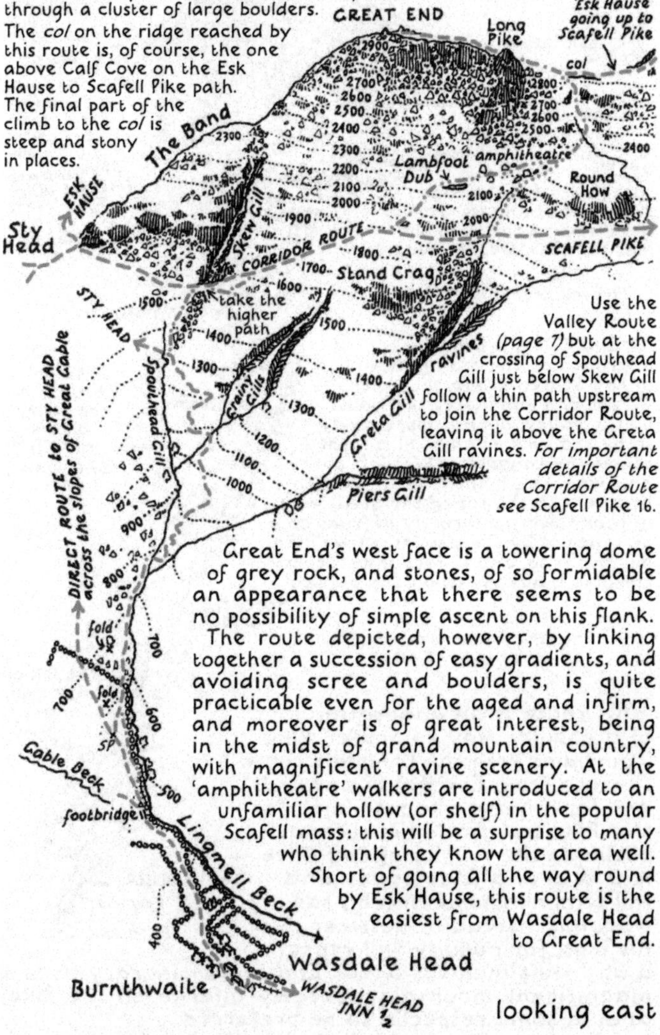
GREAT END
Long Pike
path from Esk Hause going up to Scafell Pike
col
The Band
ESK HAUSE
Sty Head
Lambfoot Dub
amphitheatre
Round How
Skew Gill
CORRIDOR ROUTE
SCAFELL PIKE
Stand Crag
take the higher path
STY HEAD
Spouthead Gill
Grainy Gills
ravines
Greta Gill
Piers Gill
DIRECT ROUTE to STY HEAD across the slopes of Great Gable
fold
Gable Beck
footbridge
Lingmell Beck
Wasdale Head
Burnthwaite
WASDALE HEAD INN ½
2900
2800
2700
2600
2500
2400
2300
2200
2100
2000
1900
1800
1700
1600
1500
1400
1300
1200
1100
1000
900
800
700
600
500
400

Use the Valley Route (page 7) but at the crossing of Spouthead Gill just below Skew Gill follow a thin path upstream to join the Corridor Route, leaving it above the Greta Gill ravines. *For important details of the Corridor Route* see Scafell Pike 16.

Great End's west face is a towering dome of grey rock, and stones, of so formidable an appearance that there seems to be no possibility of simple ascent on this flank. The route depicted, however, by linking together a succession of easy gradients, and avoiding scree and boulders, is quite practicable even for the aged and infirm, and moreover is of great interest, being in the midst of grand mountain country, with magnificent ravine scenery. At the 'amphitheatre' walkers are introduced to an unfamiliar hollow (or shelf) in the popular Scafell mass: this will be a surprise to many who think they know the area well. Short of going all the way round by Esk Hause, this route is the easiest from Wasdale Head to Great End.

looking east

ASCENT FROM BORROWDALE

2650 feet of ascent : 5 miles from Seatoller

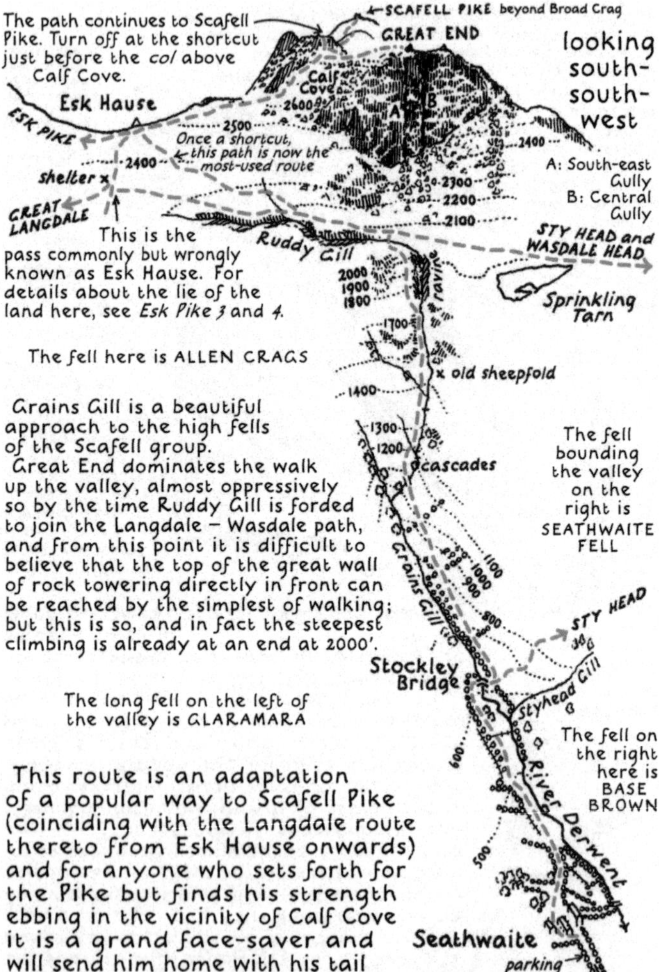

SCAFELL PIKE beyond Broad Crag
The path continues to Scafell Pike. Turn off at the shortcut just before the *col* above Calf Cove.
GREAT END
looking south-south-west
Calf Cove
2600
Esk Hause
ESK PIKE
2500
Once a shortcut, this path is now the most-used route
2400
A
B
A: South-east Gully
B: Central Gully
shelter
2400
2300
2200
2100
GREAT LANGDALE
This is the pass commonly but wrongly known as Esk Hause. For details about the lie of the land here, see *Esk Pike 3* and *4*.
Ruddy Gill
STY HEAD and WASDALE HEAD
ravine
2000
1900
1800
Sprinkling Tarn
1700
The fell here is ALLEN CRAGS
old sheepfold
1400
1300
1200
cascades
The fell bounding the valley on the right is SEATHWAITE FELL
Grains Gill
1100
1000
900
800
STY HEAD
Stockley Bridge
Styhead Gill
The long fell on the left of the valley is GLARAMARA
The fell on the right here is BASE BROWN
600
River Derwent
500
Seathwaite
parking
SEATOLLER 1¼

Grains Gill is a beautiful approach to the high fells of the Scafell group.
Great End dominates the walk up the valley, almost oppressively so by the time Ruddy Gill is forded to join the Langdale – Wasdale path, and from this point it is difficult to believe that the top of the great wall of rock towering directly in front can be reached by the simplest of walking; but this is so, and in fact the steepest climbing is already at an end at 2000'.

This route is an adaptation of a popular way to Scafell Pike (coinciding with the Langdale route thereto from Esk Hause onwards) and for anyone who sets forth for the Pike but finds his strength ebbing in the vicinity of Calf Cove it is a grand face-saver and will send him home with his tail wagging instead of between his legs, for nobody will regret a day that includes Great End in its itinerary: it is a magnificent mountain, scarcely inferior to the Pike, and, in some respects, to be preferred.

ASCENT FROM GREAT LANGDALE

2900 feet of ascent : 5 miles (from Dungeon Ghyll Old Hotel)

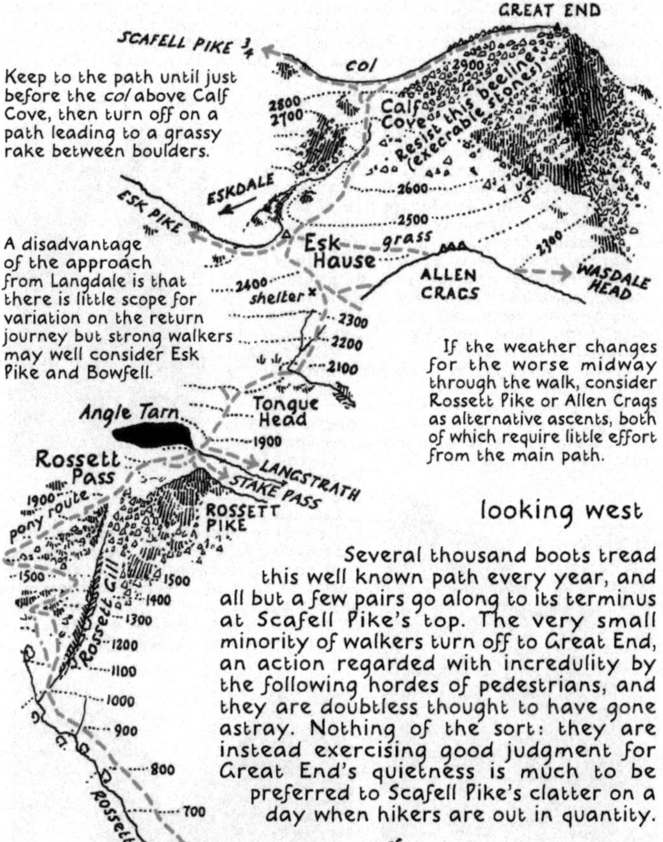

GREAT END
SCAFELL PIKE 3/4
col
2900
Resist this beeline (execrable stones)
2800
2700
Calf Cove
ESKDALE
ESK PIKE
2600
2500
Esk Hause
grass
2300
WASDALE HEAD
ALLEN CRAGS
2400
shelter
2300
2200
2100
Tongue Head
Angle Tarn
1900
Rossett Pass
LANGSTRATH
STAKE PASS
1900
pony route
ROSSETT PIKE
1500
1500
Rossett Gill
1400
1300
1200
1100
1000
900
800
700
Rossett Gill
guide stone
STAKE PASS
Stake Gill
sheepfold
moraines
Mickleden
DUNGEON GHYLL (OLD HOTEL) 1½

Keep to the path until just before the *col* above Calf Cove, then turn off on a path leading to a grassy rake between boulders.

A disadvantage of the approach from Langdale is that there is little scope for variation on the return journey but strong walkers may well consider Esk Pike and Bowfell.

If the weather changes for the worse midway through the walk, consider Rossett Pike or Allen Crags as alternative ascents, both of which require little effort from the main path.

looking west

Several thousand boots tread this well known path every year, and all but a few pairs go along to its terminus at Scafell Pike's top. The very small minority of walkers turn off to Great End, an action regarded with incredulity by the following hordes of pedestrians, and they are doubtless thought to have gone astray. Nothing of the sort: they are instead exercising good judgment for Great End's quietness is much to be preferred to Scafell Pike's clatter on a day when hikers are out in quantity.

For further details of Rossett Gill see Rossett Pike 3 *and* 4.

Although this is not the finest approach to Great End it is an excellent walk nevertheless; but it should be undertaken out of season if the idea is to get away from others of the species and commune with nature.

Cust's Gully

Sooner or later, every Lakeland walker hears mention of Cust's Gully, but written references to it are confined to rock-climbing literature, which dismiss the place as of little consequence although grudgingly conceding that there is one small and insignificant pitch.

Looking up from the path near Sprinkling Tarn, Cust's Gully is situated high to the western end of the Great End cliffs, a clue to its position being given by the long conspicuous tongue of light-coloured stones debouching from it. On this approach the gully is concealed until its foot is reached, when it is revealed suddenly and impressively as a straight rising channel of scree between vertical walls that wedge a great boulder high above the bed of the gully and thereby provide a sure means of identification. There is no mistaking Cust's Gully.

the pitch

Progress up the stony bed of the gully is easy but very rough for 50 yards to the pitch, where a chockstone blocks the way. Sloping shelves of rock, one on each side, lead up beyond the obstruction, that on the left requiring an awkward final movement, that on the right steepening for a few critical feet. The walls of the gully are here quite vertical, and directly above is poised the wedged boulder.

This pitch is the one difficulty: above there is nothing but simple scrambling to the top of the gully. The pitch may therefore be visited from either exit and the splendid rock-scenes certainly justify an inspection.

from below

The author after twice timorously attempting to climb the pitch with no real hope of succeeding, retired from Cust's Gully with a jeering conscience and went home to write, in capital letters, on page 11 of his Great End chapter:

NO WAY FOR WALKERS

from above

Note that the wedged boulder itself supports a number of smaller stones which can only be at *temporary* rest. Heaven help anybody in Cust's Gully when they fall off. It won't be the author, anyway: *he's not going again.*

The branch gully

On the direct climb from the path below, Cust's Gully slants away to the left, but an ill-defined branch gully continues the line of ascent, its course after 20 yards being interrupted by a chockstone pitch, mossy and of formidable appearance. This can be avoided, but not easily and only by handling rocks, over broken ground (steep) immediately to the right; beyond is scree to the open fellside.

The branch gully cannot be described as a walkers route, either.

The pitch, branch gully

The pedestrian route

Frustrated and humbled by defeats in Cust's and the branch gully, the dispirited pedestrian, his ego in shreds, can still find a way to the top of the fell without losing more than 100 feet in height, by sneaking round the toe of the buttress to the right (west) of both gullies and ascending the first obvious breach in the crags, a short scree-filled ravine, which will be found easy after what has just been endured and which gives access to a steep, simple slope above, where an incipient track will be found; alternatively, further to the right is a thin path. Halfway up the slope the top exit of the branch gully is passed and higher a fringe of boulders is reached; by stumbling upwards over these wretched stones for 50 further yards and then traversing left the open top of Cust's Gully will be skirted and the grassy summit of the fell reached, with sighs of relief, immediately beyond.

main cairn
north-west cairn
Central Gully
Cust's Gully
pedestrian route
A
B
C
D
scree
SKEW GILL
THE BAND
SPRINKLING TARN

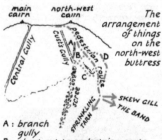

The arrangement of things on the north-west buttress

A : *branch gully*
B : *short cut to pedestrian route*
C : *link with pedestrian route*
D : *alternative to pedestrian route*

Skew Gill

Skew Gill is a tremendous gash in the Wasdale side of Great End with proportions little inferior to those of Piers Gill. The floor of the ravine is littered with stones of all shapes and sizes which can be negotiated by agile walkers, but in the upper reaches the bed of the gill is composed of naked rock at an easy angle, calling for care; the final climb out, round a corner, is rather steeper. The sides of the ravine are loose; it is important to keep throughout in the company of the stream. In good conditions this may be regarded as a way for experienced scramblers. The author managed to ascend the gill (on the end of the publisher's rope) so there seems to be no good reason why everybody shouldn't, but his sufferings were such that he can NOT recommend it as a route for decent walkers.

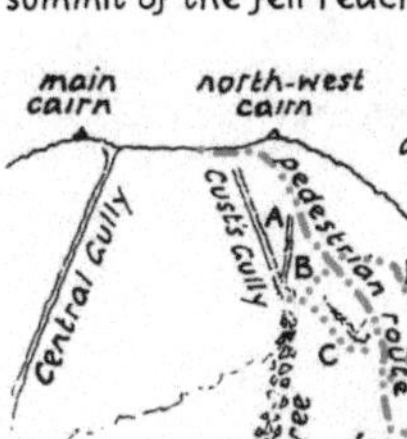

in Skew Gill

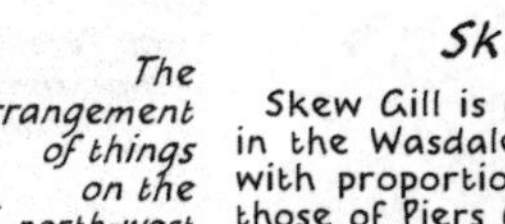

the lower entrance, Skew Gill

THE SUMMIT

There are two insignificant cairns, linked by a grassy saddle of slightly lower, altitude. The main cairn (trigonometrical station) is that to the south-east, although the difference in elevation between the two can be a matter of inches only. There is little interest on the actual top of the fell but it would be almost a sin to go away without searching for the various upper exits of the gullies. Only the gaping main exit of Central Gully is likely to be noticed on a walk across the summit; the others have to be hunted and each in turn provides an excitement with its startling downward plunge and fine rock scenery.

north-west cairn
GREAT GABLE

The cliff is broken into small crags with areas of vegetation. Except at the rim, the angle of the slope is, in general, not excessive. This explains the wide extent of the cliff on the plan. Thus, although the two main gullies have a vertical height of 600 feet, it is that distance also horizontally between top and bottom — an average of 45°.

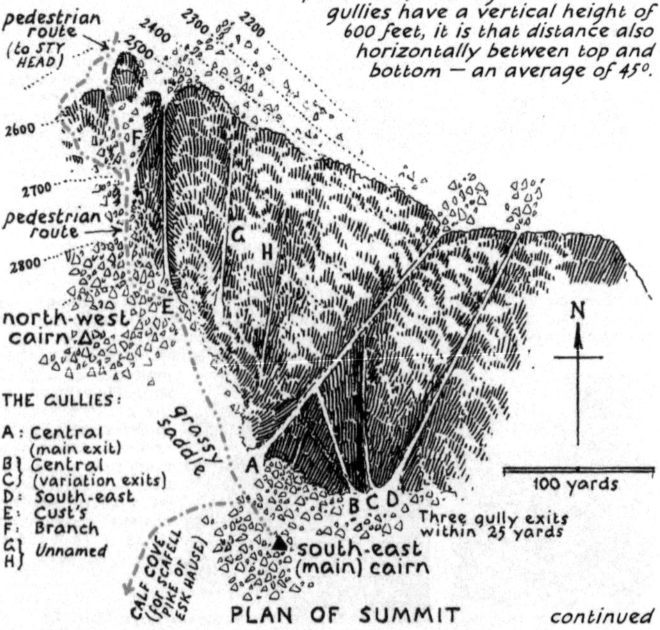

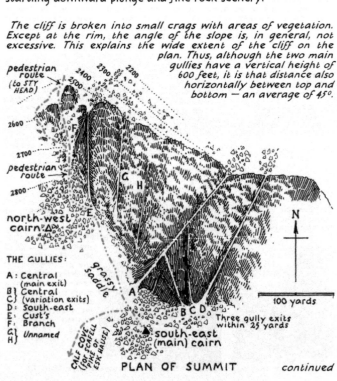

pedestrian route (to STY HEAD)
2400
2300
2200
2500
2600
F
2700
pedestrian route
G
H
2800
E
north-west cairn
N
THE GULLIES:
A: Central (main exit)
B} Central
C} (variation exits)
D: South-east
E: Cust's
F: Branch
G} Unnamed
H}
grassy saddle
A
100 yards
B C D
Three gully exits within 25 yards
south-east (main) cairn
CALF COVE (for SCAFELL PIKE or ESK HAUSE)

PLAN OF SUMMIT

continued

THE SUMMIT

continued

DESCENTS: There is only one simple way off Great End, and that is to proceed south-south-west, keeping to a grass strip between acres of stones, to the Calf Cove depression, where the path from Scafell Pike may be followed to Esk Hause for whatever destination is required. Although this way is roundabout and long, it is possible to work up a spanking pace on the easy gradient to Esk Hause.

The way down *via* Lambfoot Dub and the Corridor Route is easy underfoot after an initially steep descent from the depression.

The pedestrian route below the north-west cairn is not quite easy to determine from above, the stony ground is very rough, and progress is painfully slow. This route goes down parallel to and 30 yards west of Cust's Gully.

In mist, do be careful and sensible. Go round by Calf Cove to Esk Hause. The inviting openings in the edge of the cliff are all traps and will quickly lead to serious trouble. The pedestrian route is out of the question unless its location is already well known and its course has been followed recently.

RIDGE ROUTES

To ESK PIKE, 2903':

$1\frac{1}{4}$ miles: S, E, ESE and S

Depression (Esk Hause) at 2490'

425 feet of ascent

A pleasant high-level walk.

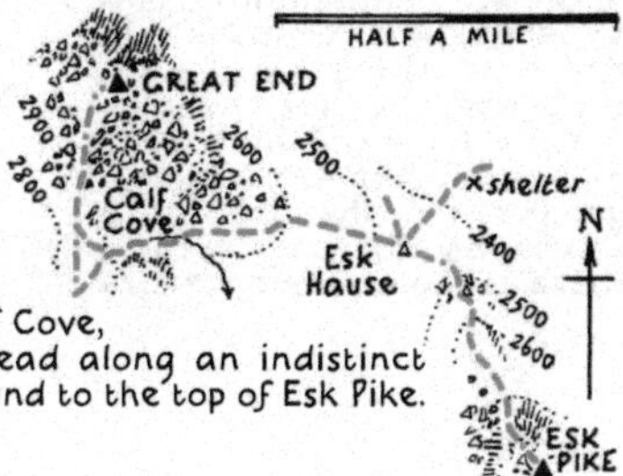
HALF A MILE
GREAT END
2900
2800
2600
2500
Calf Cove
shelter
Esk Hause
N
2400
2500
2600
ESK PIKE

Don't try a beeline (acres of boulders). Join the path from Scafell Pike to Esk Hause at Calf Cove, and at the Hause continue ahead along an indistinct track ascending interesting ground to the top of Esk Pike.

To SCAFELL PIKE, 3210':

$1\frac{1}{3}$ miles: S, then SW

Three depressions (Calf Cove col, 2830', Ill Crag col, 2900', Broad Crag col, 2900')

600 feet of ascent

Easy at first, beoming very rough.

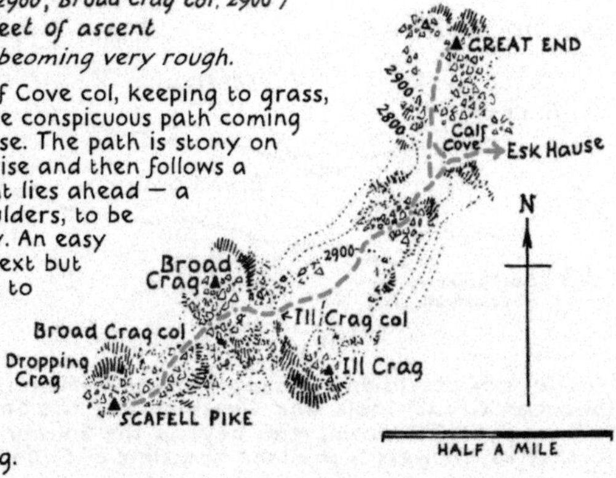
GREAT END
2900
2800
Calf Cove
Esk Hause
N
2900
Broad Crag
Ill Crag col
Broad Crag col
Dropping Crag
Ill Crag
SCAFELL PIKE
HALF A MILE

Go down to Calf Cove col, keeping to grass, and there join the conspicuous path coming up from Esk Hause. The path is stony on the first abrupt rise and then follows a foretaste of what lies ahead — a pavement of boulders, to be trodden carefully. An easy plateau comes next but after a descent to Ill Crag *col*, conditions underfoot deteriorate, the traverse of Broad Crag being very trying.

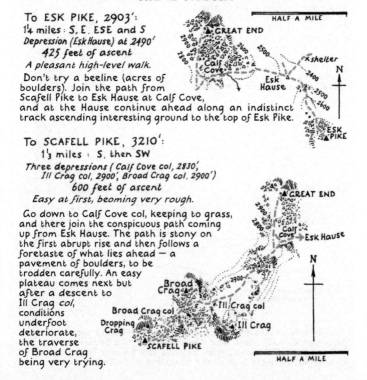

THE VIEW

While the multitudes are milling around the top of nearby Scafell Pike, trying to find elbow room to manipulate their field glasses and telescopes, the cairn on Great End often remains lonely and here one may enjoy, uninterrupted, a view scarcely less extensive or interesting and certainly not less beautiful than that from the Pike. In one direction, to the north, the view is near perfection: this scene of Borrowdale and Derwent Water, backed by Skiddaw, is best surveyed from the crest of the cliff and is among the fairest of Lakeland pictures. The only intrusion on the wide landscape is the nuclear reprocessing and decommissioning site at Sellafield, a reminder that, down on the plains, men's thoughts are not, as they are up here, of mountains and peace and the bountiful goodness of the Creator of this lovely district. Here, not there, is the supreme artistry.

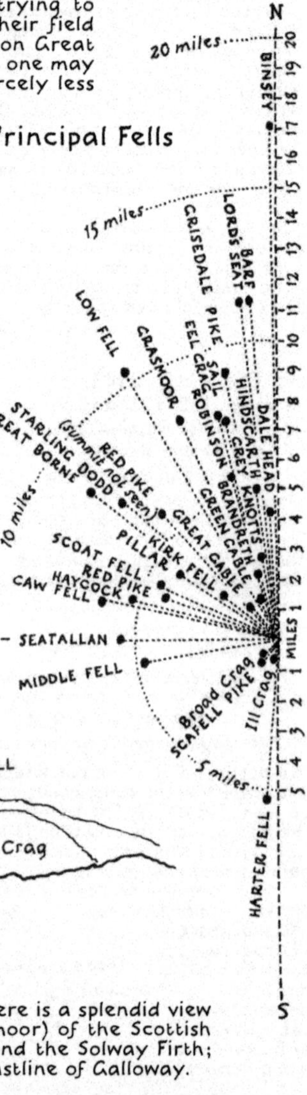

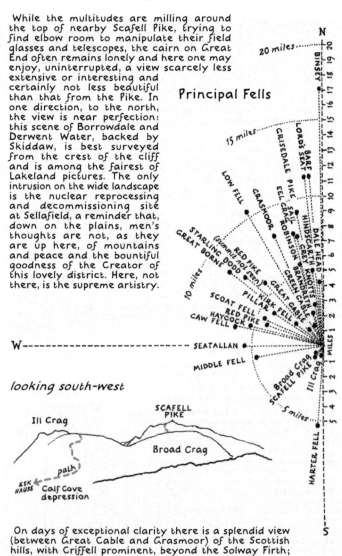

Principal Fells
N
W
S
20 miles
15 miles
10 miles
5 miles
MILES
BINSEY
LORD'S SEAT
BARF
GRISEDALE PIKE
LOW FELL
GRASMOOR
EEL CRAG
SAIL
HINDSCARTH
DALE HEAD
ROBINSON
GREY KNOTTS
BRANDRETH
GREEN GABLE
GREAT GABLE
KIRK FELL
RED PIKE (summit not seen)
STARLING DODD
GREAT BORNE
PILLAR
SCOAT FELL
RED PIKE
HAYCOCK
CAW FELL
SEATALLAN
MIDDLE FELL
Broad Crag
SCAFELL PIKE
Ill Crag
HARTER FELL

looking south-west

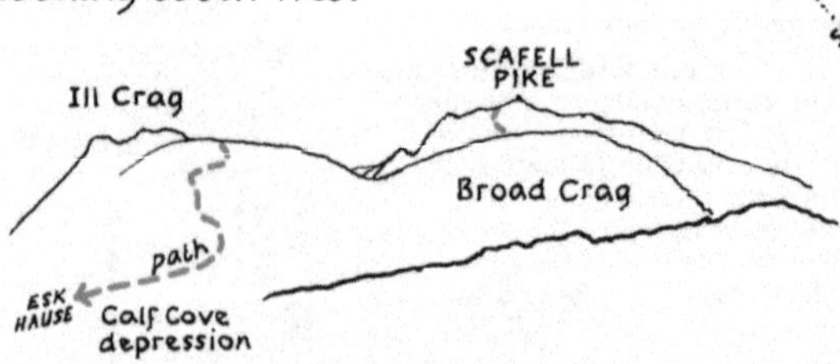

SCAFELL PIKE
Ill Crag
Broad Crag
path
ESK HAUSE
Calf Cove depression

On days of exceptional clarity there is a splendid view (between Great Gable and Grasmoor) of the Scottish hills, with Criffell prominent, beyond the Solway Firth; further to the west is the long coastline of Galloway.

THE VIEW

Lakes and Tarns

NNE : *Derwent Water*
NE: *High House Tarn*
SE : *Windermere*

Watendlath hamlet is in view NE, but it needs keen eyes to see the tarn.

From the north-west cairn, *Styhead Tarn* is well seen NNW. This, and *Sprinkling Tarn*, N, are in view at several points along the cliff.

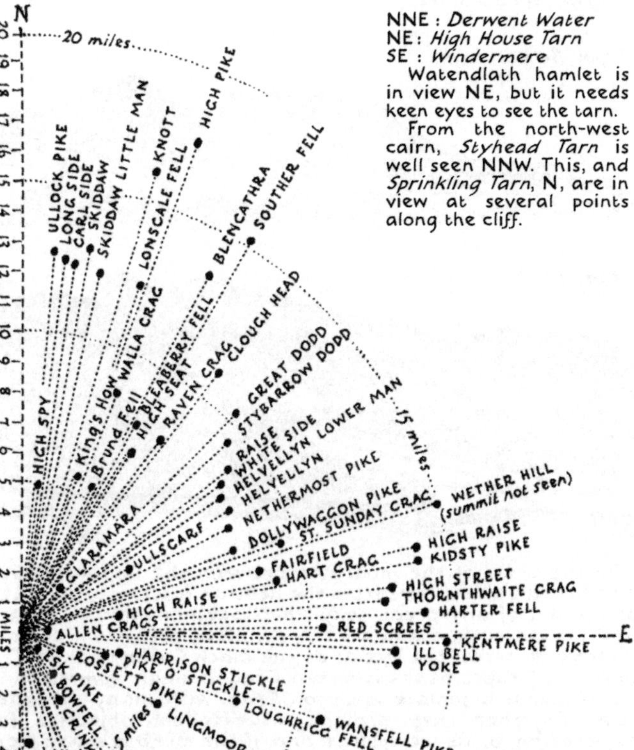
N
S
E
20 miles
15 miles
10 miles
5 miles
MILES
20 19 18 17 16 15 14 13 12 11 10 9 8 7 6 5 4 3 2 1
1 2 3 4 5 6 7 8 9 10
HIGH PIKE
SOUTHER FELL
BLENCATHRA
KNOTT
LONSCALE FELL
SKIDDAW LITTLE MAN
SKIDDAW
CARL SIDE
LONG SIDE
ULLOCK PIKE
CLOUGH HEAD
GREAT DODD
STYBARROW DODD
BLEABERRY FELL
HIGH SEAT
RAVEN CRAG
WALLA CRAG
King's How
Brund Fell
HIGH SPY
RAISE SIDE
WHITE SIDE
HELVELLYN LOWER MAN
HELVELLYN
NETHERMOST PIKE
DOLLYWAGGON PIKE
ST. SUNDAY CRAG
WETHER HILL
(summit not seen)
HIGH RAISE
KIDSTY PIKE
CLARAMARA
ULLSCARF
FAIRFIELD
HART CRAG
HIGH STREET
THORNTHWAITE CRAG
HARTER FELL
HIGH RAISE
ALLEN CRAGS
RED SCREES
KENTMERE PIKE
ILL BELL
YOKE
HARRISON STICKLE
PIKE O' STICKLE
ROSSETT PIKE
LOUGHRIGG FELL
WANSFELL PIKE
LINGMOOR FELL
ESK PIKE
BOWFELL
CRINKLE CRAGS
WETHERLAM
Black Sails
SWIRL HOW
GREY FRIAR
DOW CRAG
CONISTON OLD MAN
HARDKNOTT
Walna Scar
Caw

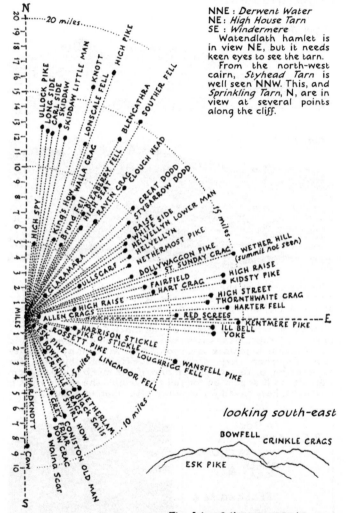

looking south-east

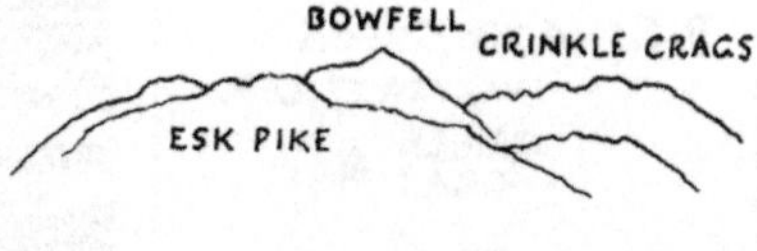
BOWFELL
CRINKLE CRAGS
ESK PIKE

The Isle of Man cannot be seen without looking at Sellafield, the one being directly above the other.

Green Crag 1602′

OS grid ref: SD200983

from Birker Fell

from Boot

On the crest of the moorland between the Duddon Valley and Eskdale there rises from the heather a series of serrated peaks, not of any great height but together forming a dark and jagged outline against the sky that, seen from certain directions, arrest the eye as do the Black Coolin of Skye. The highest of these peaks is Green Crag, a single summit, and its principal associate is Crook Crag, with many separate tops. Together they provide an excellent objective for exploration, or as viewpoints, and, if the climb is made from Eskdale, as it should be for full enjoyment, the whole walk is a delight, best saved for a sunny afternoon in August.

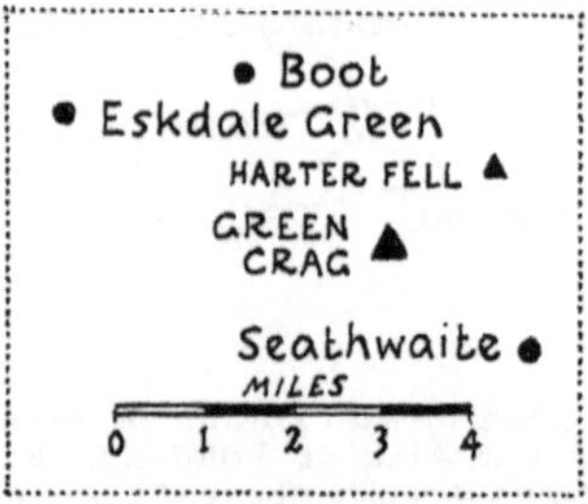

Boot
Eskdale Green
HARTER FELL
GREEN CRAG
Seathwaite
MILES
0
1
2
3
4

on the approach from Eskdale

MAP

The path beside the rocky summits of Crook Crag is relatively recent. It is somewhat easier to follow from south to north, *i.e.* in descent from the summit of Green Crag.

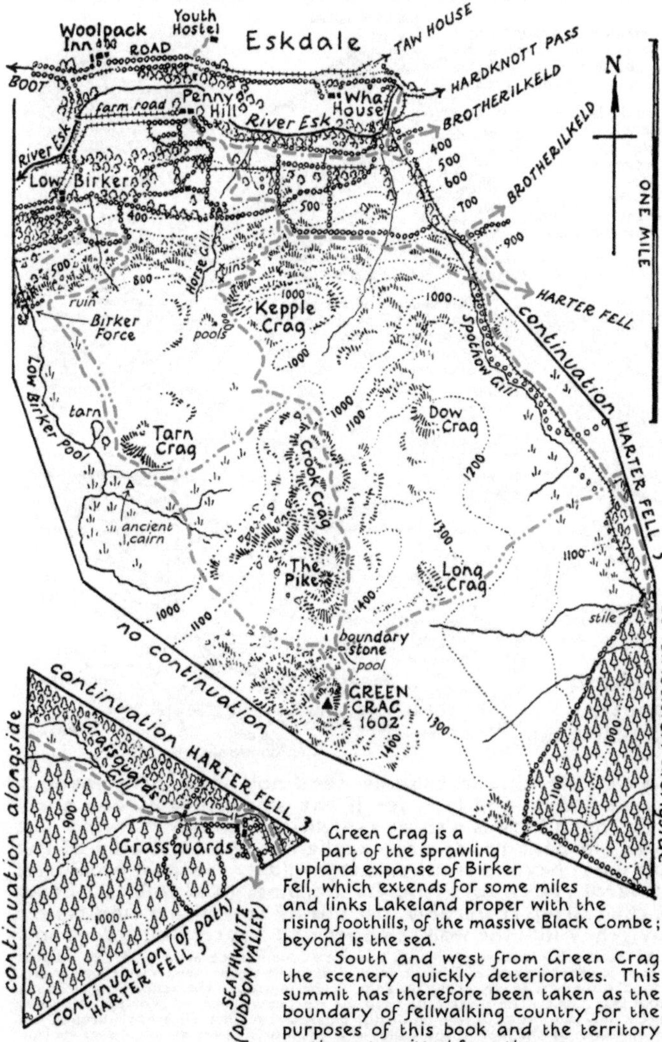
Youth Hostel
Woolpack Inn
ROAD
Eskdale
TAW HOUSE
BOOT
HARDKNOTT PASS
BROTHERILKELD
Penny Hill
Wha House
farm road
River Esk
River Esk
BROTHERILKELD
BROTHERILKELD
N
Low Birker
400
500
600
700
900
ONE MILE
Horse Gill
ruins
800
ruin
Birker Force
pools
1000
Kepple Crag
HARTER FELL
continuation
Spothow Gill
Low Birker Pool
tarn
Tarn Crag
Crook Crag
Dow Crag
1100
1200
continuation HARTER FELL 3
ancient cairn
1300
The Pike
Long Crag
1400
stile
no continuation
boundary stone
pool
GREEN CRAG 1602'
continuation HARTER FELL 3
continuation alongside
continuation alongside
Grassguards Gill
Grassguards
continuation (of path) HARTER FELL 5
SEATHWAITE (DUDDON VALLEY)

Green Crag is a part of the sprawling upland expanse of Birker Fell, which extends for some miles and links Lakeland proper with the rising foothills, of the massive Black Combe; beyond is the sea.

South and west from Green Crag the scenery quickly deteriorates. This summit has therefore been taken as the boundary of fellwalking country for the purposes of this book and the territory south-west omitted from the map.

ASCENT FROM ESKDALE

1450 feet of ascent : 2½ miles from the Woolpack Inn

The rocky top can be gained from the rear or, better still, *via* a grassy rake (boulders easily sidestepped) that leads conveniently to the summit.

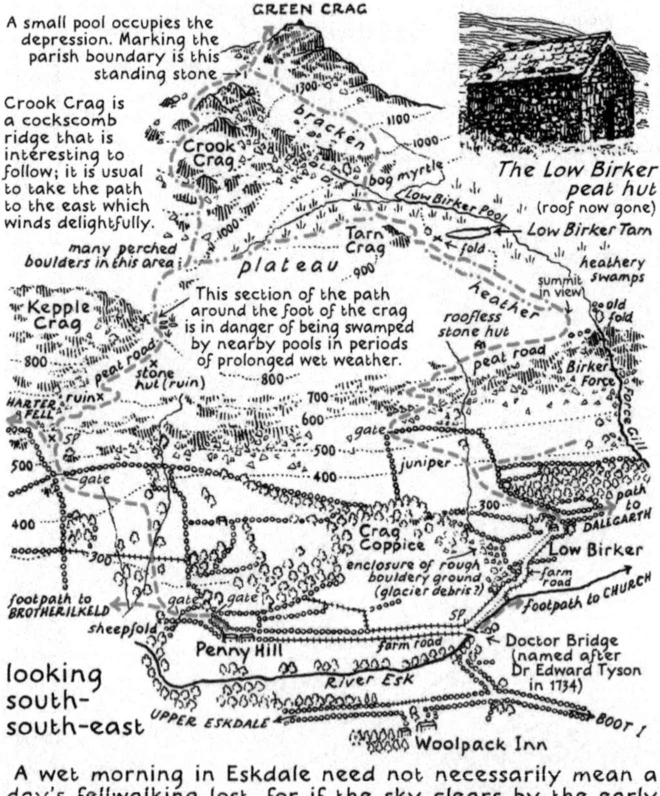
GREEN CRAG
A small pool occupies the depression. Marking the parish boundary is this standing stone
Crook Crag is a cockscomb ridge that is interesting to follow; it is usual to take the path to the east which winds delightfully.
The Low Birker peat hut (roof now gone)
1300
1100
1000
bracken
Crook Crag
bog myrtle
Low Birker Pool
Low Birker Tarn
fold
1000
Tarn Crag
many perched boulders in this area
plateau
900
heathery swamps
summit in view
heather
old fold
Kepple Crag
This section of the path around the foot of the crag is in danger of being swamped by nearby pools in periods of prolonged wet weather.
roofless stone hut
peat road
800
peat road
stone hut (ruin)
800
Birker Force
ruin
700
HARTER FELL
600
Force Gill
SP
gate
500
juniper
500
gate
400
300
path to DALEGARTH
400
Crag Coppice
Low Birker
300
enclosure of rough bouldery ground (glacier debris?)
farm road
footpath to BROTHERILKELD
gate
gate
footpath to CHURCH
SP
sheepfold
farm road
Doctor Bridge (named after Dr Edward Tyson in 1734)
Penny Hill
looking south-south-east
River Esk
UPPER ESKDALE
BOOT
Woolpack Inn

A wet morning in Eskdale need not necessarily mean a day's fellwalking lost, for if the sky clears by the early afternoon here is a short expedition well worth trying. The two old peat roads are excellent ways to the lip of the plateau; beyond is a heathery wilderness from which rise several rocky tors, the furthermost (and loftiest) being Green Crag. Preferably, ascend by Low Birker and return by Penny Hill: the walk is easier and less confusing done so.

An interesting feature of this walk is the acquaintance made with the old peat roads so characteristic of Eskdale. From most of the valley farms a wide, well graded 'road' (usually a grassy path) zig-zags up the fellside to the peaty heights above, and there ends; the stone huts used for storing a supply of peat are still to be seen, now in ruins or decay, on or just below the skyline. Time has marched fast in Eskdale: at the foot of the valley was the world's first atomic power station, now the site of a nuclear reprocessing plant, and peat is out of fashion. Alas!

OTHER ASCENTS

FROM THE DUDDON VALLEY

Reach Grassguards by one of the four routes mentioned on *Harter Fell 5*, continuing onwards by the Eskdale path until the end of the plantation on the right. There, turn south-west, finding then following a sketchy path up a grassy, often wet, and very easy slope.

FROM THE BIRKER FELL ROAD

An obvious starting point is the top of the unenclosed road between Ulpha and Eskdale Green, whence simple and straightforward walking leads to the summit. There are two routes that avoid swamps: *to the south* keep to the heights over Rough Crag, Great Worm Crag and White How; *to the north*, the way lies over Little Crag, Great Crag (*via* a steep grassy rake at its southern end) and Broad Crag.

THE SUMMIT

A ring of crags gives the appearance of impregnability to the summit, but an easy scramble from either way up reveals the highest point, a fine place of vantage, as a small grassy sward, with a cairn occupying the place of honour. A second cairn, east of the summit, marks the easier way down.

THE VIEW

DESCENTS *in mist*: Get down, with care, to the grassy depression between Green Crag and Crook Crag (a small pool marks the lowest point) and walk east on a sketchy path, down a gentle gradient to join the path connecting the Duddon Valley (right) and Eskdale (left).

The view is better than will generally be expected, and in some respects even surpasses that from Harter Fell, the high Mosedale Fells being seen to advantage over the wide depression of Burnmoor Tarn, while the Scafell–Bowfell groups lose nothing in majesty at this greater distance. Seawards there is a fine prospect interrupted only by the bulky Black Combe.

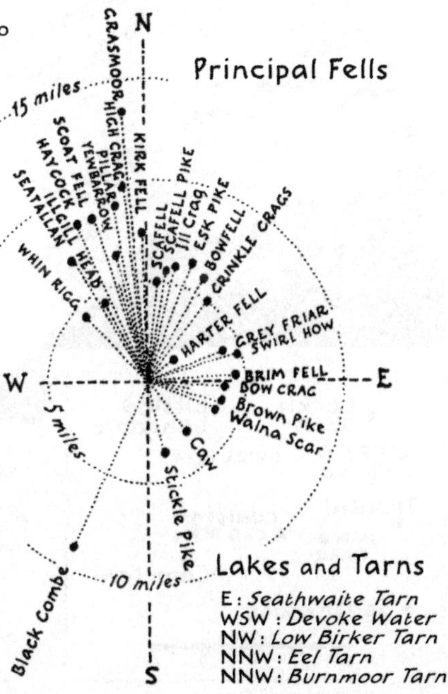
N
Principal Fells
15 miles
GRASMOOR
HIGH CRAG
KIRK FELL
PILLAR
YEWBARROW
SCOAT FELL
HAYCOCK
ILLGILL
SEATALLAN
HEAD
WHIN RIGG
SCAFELL PIKE
SCAFELL
Ill Crag
ESK PIKE
BOWFELL
CRINKLE CRAGS
HARTER FELL
GREY FRIAR
SWIRL HOW
BRIM FELL
DOW CRAG
Brown Pike
Walna Scar
W
E
5 miles
Caw
Stickle Pike
10 miles
Black Combe
S
Lakes and Tarns
E: Seathwaite Tarn
WSW: Devoke Water
NW: Low Birker Tarn
NNW: Eel Tarn
NNW: Burnmoor Tarn

Grey Friar 2536'

OS grid ref: NY260004

Cockley Beck
Little Langdale
GREY FRIAR
SWIRL HOW
Troutal
CONISTON OLD MAN
DOW CRAG
Coniston
Seathwaite
MILES
0 1 2 3 4

from Hell Gill Pike

NATURAL FEATURES

Grey Friar, like Dow Crag, stands aloof from the main spine of the Coniston Fells, but, unlike Dow Crag, has no great single natural feature to attract attention and is consequently the least-frequented of the group. Yet it is a fine mountain of considerable bulk, and forms the eastern wall of the Duddon Valley for several miles, rising high above the foothill series of knobbly tors and hanging crags that so greatly contribute to the unique beauty of that valley. In topographical fact, Grey Friar belongs exclusively to the Duddon, to which all its waters drain, and not to Coniston. Great Blake Rigg and Little Blake Rigg are extensive rock faces in the neighbourhood of Seathwaite Tarn, and there are others, but generally the higher reaches are grassy and the summit assumes the shape of a rounded dome, which is of no particular interest except as a viewpoint, the scene westwards to the Scafells being magnificent.

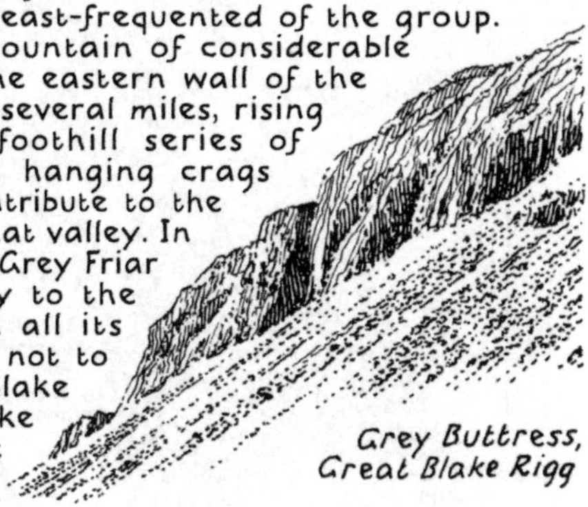

Grey Buttress, Great Blake Rigg

1 : *The summit*
2 : *Wet Side Edge*
3 : *Great Blake Rigg*
4 : *Little Blake Rigg*
5 : *Troutal Tongue*
6 : *High Tongue*
7 : *Hollin House Tongue*
8 : *Hinning House Plantation (Hardknott Forest)*
9 : *Seathwaite Tarn*
10 : *Tarn Beck*
11 : *The valley of Tarn Beck*
12 : *Cockley Beck*
13 : *River Duddon*
14 : *Wallowbarrow Gorge*

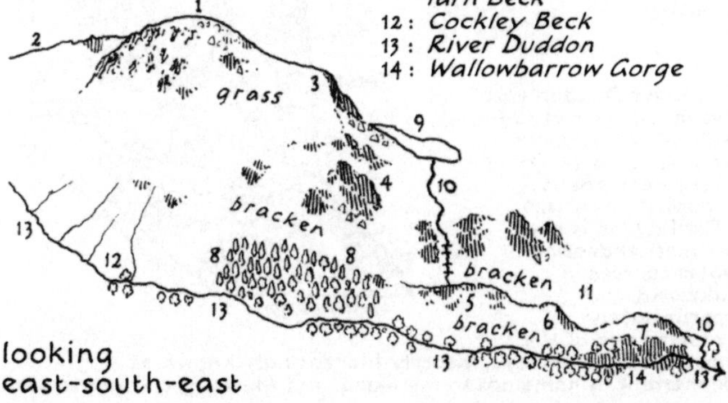
1
2
3
grass
9
4
10
bracken
13
8
8
12
bracken
11
5
13
bracken
6
7
10
13
14
13

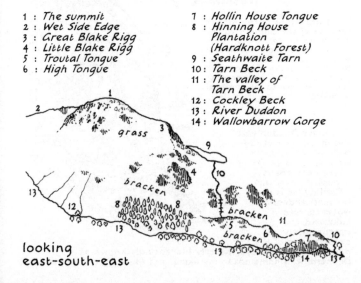

looking east-south-east

Grey Friar 3

MAP

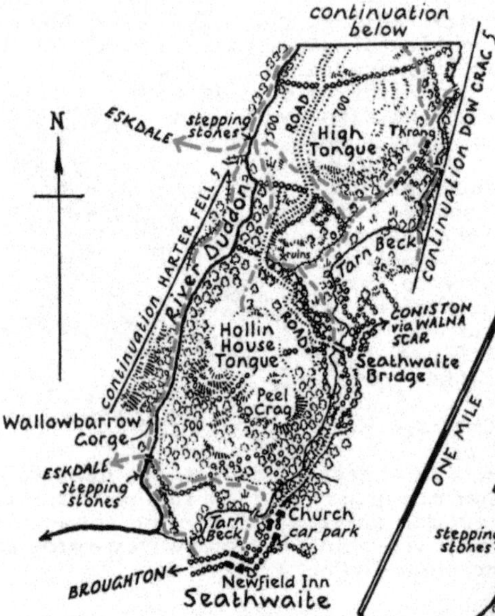

continuation below
N
ESKDALE
stepping stones
ROAD
500
700
High Tongue
T'krang
continuation DOW CRAG 5
continuation HARTER FELL 5
River Duddon
ruins
Tarn Beck
Hollin House Tongue
CONISTON via WALNA SCAR
Seathwaite Bridge
Peel Crag
Wallowbarrow Gorge
ESKDALE
stepping stones
Tarn Beck
Church
car park
BROUGHTON
Newfield Inn
Seathwaite
ONE MILE

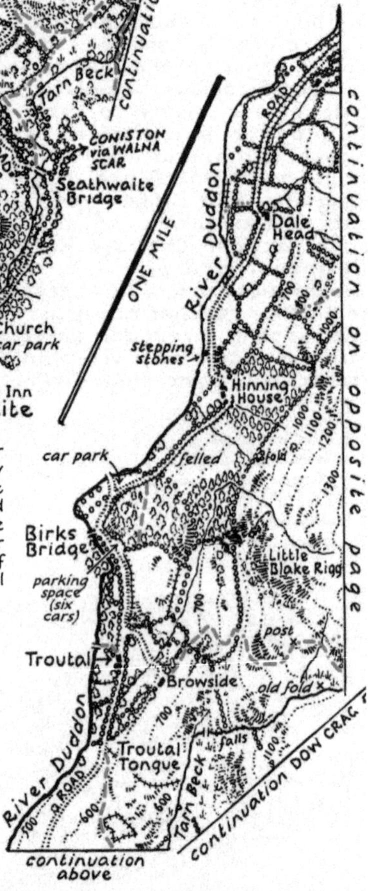

ROAD
continuation on opposite page
River Duddon
Dale Head
stepping stones
Hinning House
car park
felled
fold
Birks Bridge
parking space (six cars)
Little Blake Rigg
post
Troutal
Browside
old fold
River Duddon
Troutal Tongue
falls
Tarn Beck
continuation DOW CRAG
continuation above

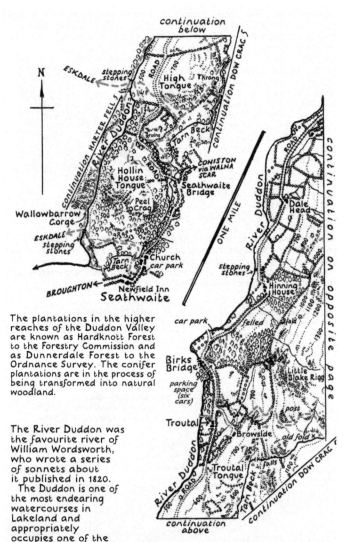

The plantations in the higher reaches of the Duddon Valley are known as Hardknott Forest to the Forestry Commission and as Dunnerdale Forest to the Ordnance Survey. The conifer plantations are in the process of being transformed into natural woodland.

The River Duddon was the favourite river of William Wordsworth, who wrote a series of sonnets about it published in 1820.

The Duddon is one of the most endearing watercourses in Lakeland and appropriately occupies one of the most beautiful valleys, latterly increasingly known as Dunnerdale, a name not to my liking, and which I prefer not to use.

MAP

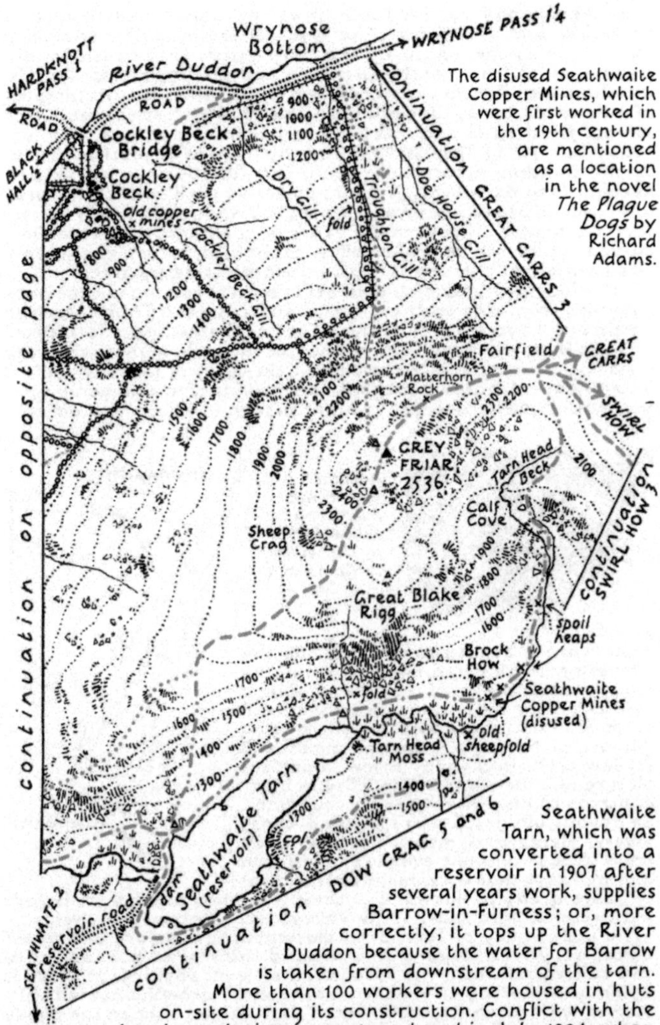

Wrynose Bottom
WRYNOSE PASS 1¼
HARDKNOTT PASS 1
River Duddon
ROAD
ROAD
BLACK HALL ½
Cockley Beck Bridge
Cockley Beck
old copper mines
Cockley Beck Gill
Dry Gill
fold
Troughton Gill
Doe House Gill
continuation GREAT CARRS 3
Fairfield
GREAT CARRS
Matterhorn Rock
SWIRL HOW
GREY FRIAR 2536
Tarn Head Beck
Calf Cove
Sheep Crag
continuation SWIRL HOW 3
Great Blake Rigg
spoil heaps
Brock How
Seathwaite Copper Mines (disused)
fold
Old sheepfold
Tarn Head Moss
Seathwaite Tarn (reservoir)
col
dam
reservoir road
SEATHWAITE 2
continuation DOW CRAG 5 and 6
continuation on opposite page

The disused Seathwaite Copper Mines, which were first worked in the 19th century, are mentioned as a location in the novel *The Plague Dogs* by Richard Adams.

Seathwaite Tarn, which was converted into a reservoir in 1907 after several years work, supplies Barrow-in-Furness; or, more correctly, it tops up the River Duddon because the water for Barrow is taken from downstream of the tarn. More than 100 workers were housed in huts on-site during its construction. Conflict with the local population came to a head in July 1904, when the Newfield Hotel at Seathwaite was besieged by a mob of workers after the landlord refused to serve them. Three workers were shot, one of whom died a day later. An inquest recorded a verdict of justifiable homicide in the case.

The Valley of Tarn Beck

The geography of the Duddon Valley above Seathwaite is confusing, and calls for a close study of the map. The tributary Tarn Beck is the cause of the perplexity: this considerable stream issues from Seathwaite Tarn and at first heads directly for the River Duddon in accordance with the natural instinct of all water to go downhill by the shortest route and has almost finished the journey when it runs up against the low rocky barrier of Troutal Tongue, which turns it south, parallel to the Duddon. A continuation of the Tongue then persists in keeping Tarn Beck away from its objective until gentler pastures are reached below Seathwaite, where the waters are finally united. Tarn Beck, after thousands of years of constant frustration, has carved out its own beautiful valley, so that for two miles the dale has twin parallel troughs running closely side by side.

Confusion is worse confounded because the road along the valley switches from one to the other, unobtrusively. Thus the river bordering the road north of the village of Seathwaite is Tarn Beck, not the Duddon as is commonly supposed, while higher, after the road has crossed again to the Duddon, the valley of Tarn Beck widens into a neat cultivated strath with a small farming community, but the main river hereabouts remains hidden in its wooded gorge.

Ancient footbridge over Long House Gill in the valley of Tarn Beck

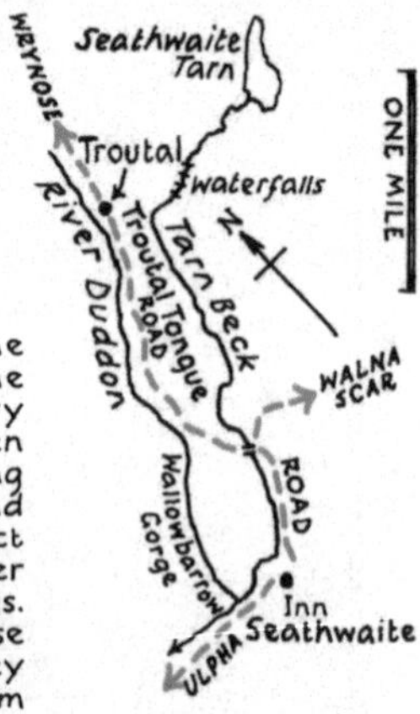
WRYNOSE
Seathwaite Tarn
ONE MILE
Troutal
waterfalls
N
River Duddon
Troutal Tongue
ROAD
Tarn Beck
WALNA SCAR
ROAD
Wallowbarrow Gorge
Inn
Seathwaite
ULPHA

Man rarely beautifies nature, but the exception most certainly occurs in the cultivated valleys of Lakeland. Every walker on the hills must often have been stopped in his tracks by some entrancing glimpse of beautiful green pastures and stately trees in a valley below, a perfect picture of charm and tranquillity in utter contrast to his own rugged surroundings. So delightfully fresh and sparkling, those lovely, fields and meadows, that they seem to be in sunshine even in rain; so trim and well kept that they might be the lawns of some great parkland. But they were not always so. Before man settled here these same valleys were dreary marshes.

The little valley of Tarn Beck illustrates the 'before and after' effect very well. Beyond and around the walled boundaries of the cultivated area — a patchwork of level pastures — there is at once a morass of bracken and coarse growth littered with stones, with much standing water that cannot escape the choke of vegetation. Once all the dale was like this. So was Borrowdale, and Langdale, and other valleys that today enchant the eye. Hard work and long perseverance have brought fertility from sterility. Rough hands have won a very rare beauty from the wilderness.... Man here has improved on nature.

ASCENT FROM THE DUDDON VALLEY

2200 feet of ascent : 4 miles from Seathwaite
(2000 feet : 2¼ miles from Troutal)

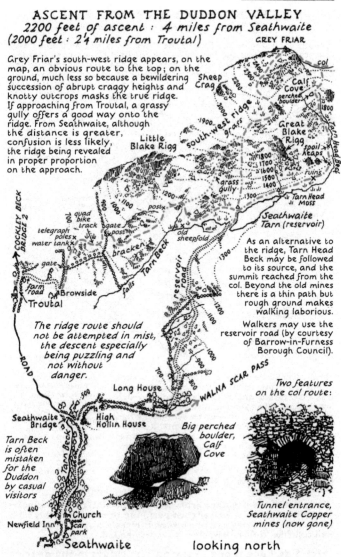

Grey Friar's south-west ridge appears, on the map, an obvious route to the top; on the ground, much less so because a bewildering succession of abrupt craggy heights and knotty outcrops masks the true ridge. If approaching from Troutal, a grassy gully offers a good way onto the ridge. From Seathwaite, although the distance is greater, confusion is less likely, the ridge being revealed in proper proportion on the approach.

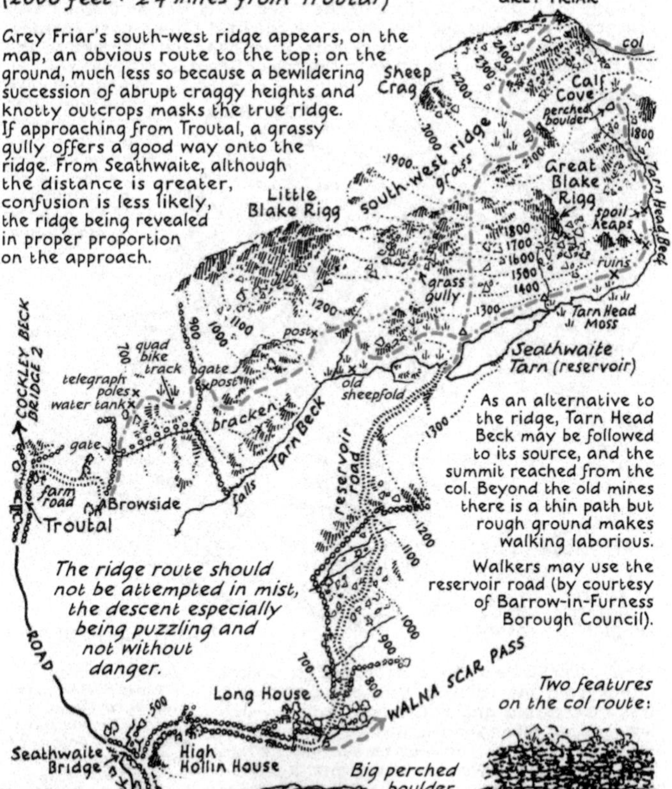
GREY FRIAR
col
Sheep Crag
Calf Cove
perched boulder
2400
2300
2200
2100
2000
1900
1800
south-west ridge
grass
Great Blake Rigg
Little Blake Rigg
spoil heaps
Tarn Head Beck
1700
1600
1500
1400
1300
ruins
grass gully
Tarn Head Moss
1200
1100
1000
900
post
Seathwaite Tarn (reservoir)
COCKLEY BECK BRIDGE 2
700
quad bike track
gate
post
telegraph poles
water tank
old sheepfold
bracken
Tarn Beck
gate
farm road
Browside
Troutal
falls
reservoir road
800
ROAD
WALNA SCAR PASS
Long House
500
Seathwaite Bridge
High Hollin House
Tarn Beck
400
Church
Newfield Inn
car park
Seathwaite
looking north

As an alternative to the ridge, Tarn Head Beck may be followed to its source, and the summit reached from the col. Beyond the old mines there is a thin path but rough ground makes walking laborious.

Walkers may use the reservoir road (by courtesy of Barrow-in-Furness Borough Council).

The ridge route should not be attempted in mist, the descent especially being puzzling and not without danger.

Tarn Beck is often mistaken for the Duddon by casual visitors

Two features on the col route:

Big perched boulder, Calf Cove

Tunnel entrance, Seathwaite Copper mines (now gone)

Grey Friar is fully in view from the road outside the inn and is easily accessed *via* the road to Seathwaite Tarn.

ASCENT FROM WRYNOSE PASS
1350 feet of ascent : 2¼ miles

Turn off the ridge at the foot of the steep stony rise on Great Carrs and traverse across the fellside to the Fairfield col, an easy passage, or, even easier, take the grassy path from near Hell Gill Pike to the col. It is not necessary to go up to the top of Great Carrs. Fairfield, well named, is a wide gently-contoured grassy expanse, and a favourite sheep-walk, sloping to a shallow col between Grey Friar and the main ridge.

SWIRL HOW
GREAT CARRS
GREY FRIAR
Matterhorn Rock
col
Fairfield
2300
2200
Hell Gill Pike
2100
2000
1900
1800
Little Carrs
pool
Greenburn Valley
sheepfold
gate
Cockley Beck
Wet Side Edge
1700
1600
1500
1400
1300
1200
1100
1000
900
800
Hell Gill
Troughton Gill
FELL FOOT
bield
bields
River Duddon
Wrynose Bottom
Wrynose Pass
ROAD
LITTLE LANGDALE
Three Shire Stone

looking south

The alternative route depicted (a direct climb from the road in Wrynose Bottom) is less interesting and rather spoiled by much wet ground alongside the wall (which, usefully, points straight to the unseen summit). When the wall turns away to the right, keep on ahead, first up a grassy rake between crags and then selecting a route between the several outcrops below the top.

There is ample parking at Wrynose Pass. For details about the Three Shire Stone see *Pike o' Blisco 3*.

Travellers along Wrynose Bottom may have their curiosity aroused by the short stone, walls, only a few yards in length, built at intervals at right angles to the road and not far distant from it. These walls are BIELDS, shelters for sheep from strong winds and drifting snow.

Once the ridge is gained from the Pass (a matter of 15 minutes simple climbing on a well pitched path) the remainder of this walk, with views improving the whole way, is merely a stroll. A detour to Hell Gill Pike, a fine viewpoint, is recommended.

Wet Side Edge is one of the easiest ridges in the district, and, in spite of its name, quite dry underfoot. *In mist*, keep to the ridge and be content with Great Carrs instead.

THE SUMMIT

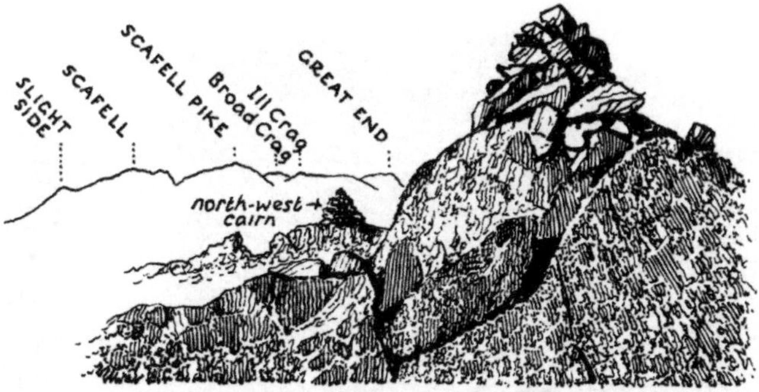
SLIGHT SIDE
SCAFELL
SCAFELL PIKE
Broad Crag
Ill Crag
GREAT END
north-west cairn

On the usual approach to the summit, from the Fairfield *col*, a long level promenade of excellent turf precedes a stonier area where two rock outcrops 40 yards apart, each bearing a cairn, are slightly elevated above the plateau: the one to the south-east is the true summit, having an advantage of a few feet in altitude, but the one north-west (which may be reached by a simple 20' rock-climb, if so desired) commands the better view. There are other outcrops (without cairns) in the summit area.

DESCENTS: In clear weather there should be no difficulty in getting down by any of the routes given for ascent. The start of the path along the south-west ridge is marked by a cairn.

In mist it is advisable to go down first to the Fairfield *col*, whatever the ultimate aim, and take bearings there. The track to the *col* is reasonably distinct, but a few more cairns would be useful here: if in doubt, incline slightly right rather than left where the descent from the summit-plateau commences.

RIDGE ROUTES

To SWIRL HOW, 2630': 1 mile: NE, then E and ESE
Depression (Fairfield col) at 2275'
355 feet of ascent

To GREAT CARRS, 2575'
⅞ mile: NE, then E
Depression (Fairfield col) at 2275'
300 feet of ascent

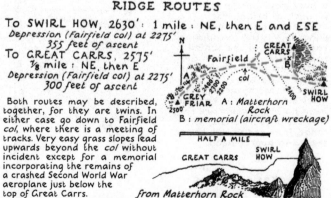

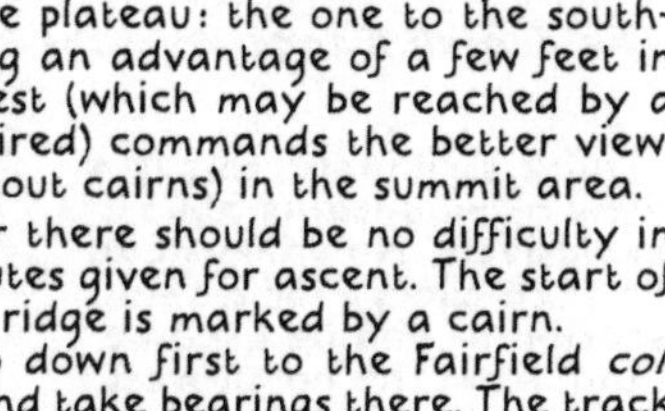
N
GREAT CARRS
Fairfield
B
A
col
2400
2300
2200
2400
SWIRL HOW
GREY FRIAR
2500
A: Matterhorn Rock
B: memorial (aircraft wreckage)
HALF A MILE

Both routes may be described together, for they are twins. In either case go down to Fairfield *col*, where there is a meeting of tracks. Very easy grass slopes lead upwards beyond the *col* without incident except for a memorial incorporating the remains of a crashed Second World War aeroplane just below the top of Great Carrs.

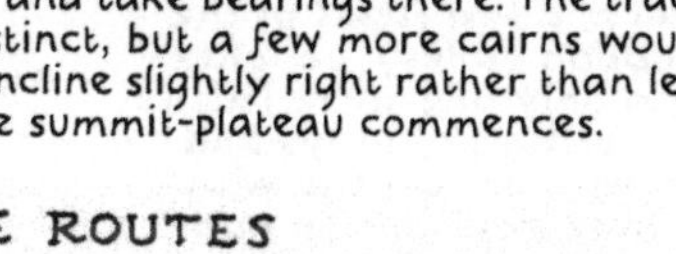
SWIRL HOW
GREAT CARRS
from Matterhorn Rock

THE VIEW

The Scafell Range, from the north-west cairn

Quite strikingly, this is a view of mountains almost exclusively. No valleys can be seen except for a small section of middle Eskdale (and, from the north-west cairn, a few fields in the Duddon Valley), no lakes and only one tarn. This is a picture of greys and browns, not greens, with a wide seascape to add a touch of brightness.

Outstanding in the panorama is the splendid eastern wall of the Scafell range, best viewed from the north-west cairn. Nothing is lost of the majesty of this rugged mass by being five miles distant; on the contrary, from no other point are the correct proportions of the range, from end to end, better seen and appreciated.

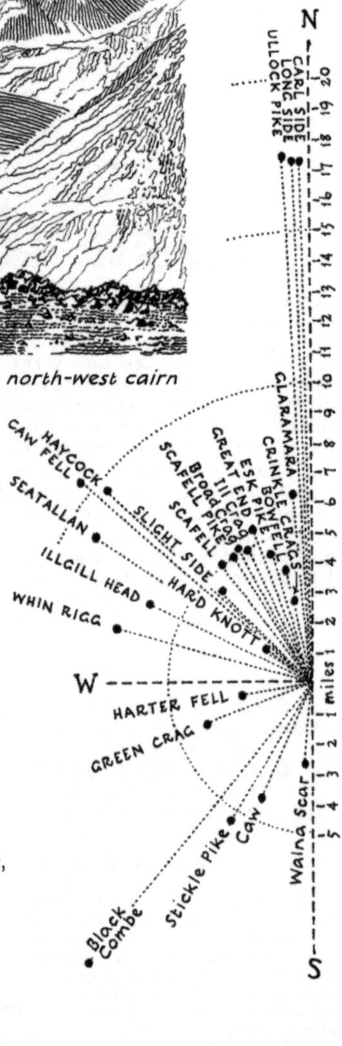
N
CARL SIDE
LONG SIDE
ULLOCK PIKE
GLARAMARA
CRINKLE CRAGS
BOWFELL
ESK PIKE
GREAT END
Ill Crag
Broad Crag
SCAFELL PIKE
SCAFELL
SLIGHT SIDE
HAYCOCK
CAW FELL
SEATALLAN
ILLGILL HEAD
HARD KNOTT
WHIN RIGG
W
HARTER FELL
GREEN CRAG
miles
Walna Scar
Caw
Stickle Pike
Black Combe
S

Lakes and Tarns

WSW : *Devoke Water*

THE VIEW

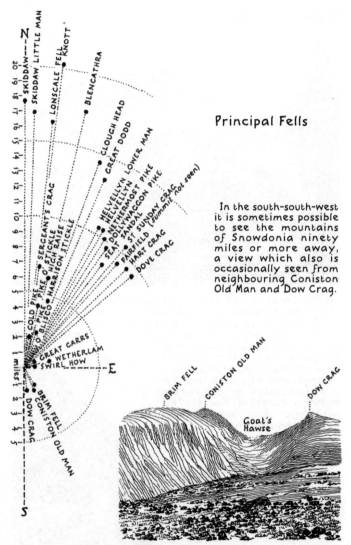

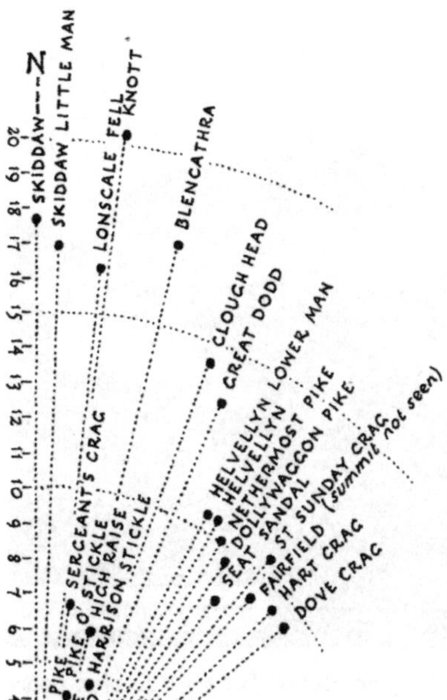
N
S
E
miles
SKIDDAW
SKIDDAW LITTLE MAN
KNOTT
LONSCALE FELL
BLENCATHRA
CLOUGH HEAD
GREAT DODD
LOWER MAN
HELVELLYN
NETHERMOST PIKE
DOLLYWAGGON PIKE
ST SUNDAY CRAG (summit not seen)
SEAT SANDAL
FAIRFIELD
HART CRAG
DOVE CRAG
SERGEANT'S CRAG
PIKE O' STICKLE
HIGH RAISE
HARRISON STICKLE
COLD PIKE
PIKE O' BLISCO
GREAT CARRS
WETHERLAM
SWIRL HOW
BRIM FELL
CONISTON OLD MAN
DOW CRAG

Principal Fells

In the south-south-west it is sometimes possible to see the mountains of Snowdonia ninety miles or more away, a view which also is occasionally seen from neighbouring Coniston Old Man and Dow Crag.

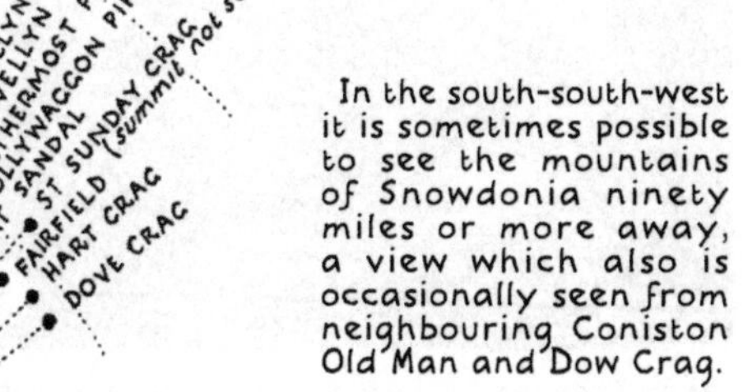
BRIM FELL
CONISTON OLD MAN
DOW CRAG
Goat's Hawse

The Coniston Fells, from the south-east cairn

Hard Knott 1803'

OS grid ref: NY232024

From Whahouse Bridge

Hard Knott is well known for three features: the pass of the same name, a Roman camp, and the view of the Scafells from its summit. The fell itself is not especially remarkable, and is best described as a wedge of high ground dividing Eskdale and Moasdale, the latter running down into the Duddon Valley.

Geographically, Hard Knott is a continuation of the north-eastern ridge of Harter Fell, with the pass occupying a depression thereon.

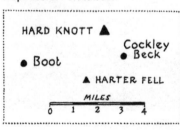

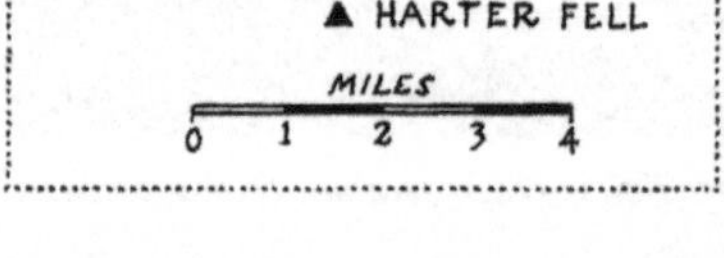
HARD KNOTT
Cockley Beck
Boot
HARTER FELL
MILES
0 1 2 3 4

Hardknott Pass

The Roman Fort

On the south-western slope of Hard Knott the rocky cliffs of Border End fall steeply to an inclined grassy shelf, which extends for half a mile and then breaks abruptly in a line of crags overlooking the Esk. This shelf, a splendid place of vantage commanding a view of the valley from the hills down to the sea, was selected by the Romans towards the end of the first century A.D. as a site for the establishment of a garrison to reinforce their military occupation of the district. Here they built a fort, MEDIOBOGDVM, which today is more usually, and certainly more easily, referred to as HARDKNOTT CASTLE. The main structure and outbuildings have survived the passing years sufficiently to provide a valuable source of information and study for the expert and an object of considerable interest for the layman. In 1959 the walls of the fort were rebuilt by the Ministry of Works, a slate course indicating the original wall below and the restored portion above. There is divided opinion as to whether this physical reconstruction is desirable: would not the mouldering ruins, left to their natural decay, have had a greater appeal to the imagination?

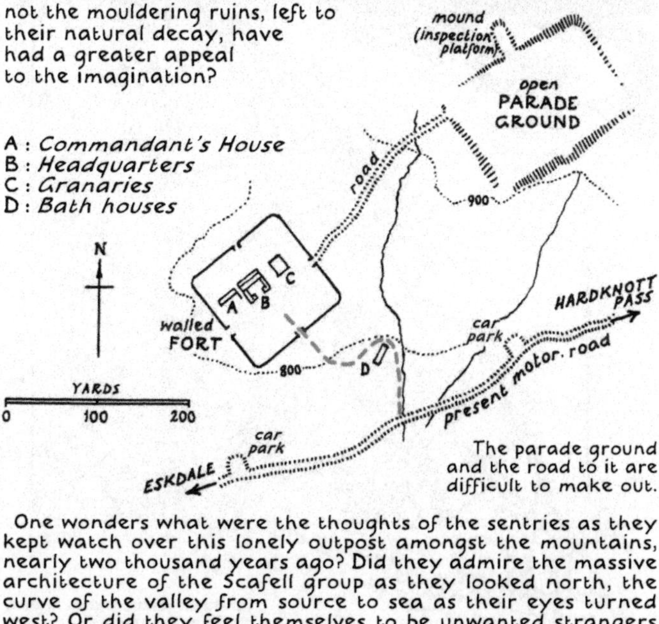
mound
(inspection platform)
open
PARADE
GROUND
A : Commandant's House
B : Headquarters
C : Granaries
D : Bath houses
N
road
900
walled
FORT
A
B
C
D
800
YARDS
0
100
200
HARDKNOTT PASS
car park
present motor road
car park
ESKDALE

The parade ground and the road to it are difficult to make out.

One wonders what were the thoughts of the sentries as they kept watch over this lonely outpost amongst the mountains, nearly two thousand years ago? Did they admire the massive architecture of the Scafell group as they looked north, the curve of the valley from source to sea as their eyes turned west? Or did they feel themselves to be unwanted strangers in a harsh and hostile land? Did their hearts ache for the sunshine of their native country, for their families, for their homes?

Many plaques giving information about the site for visitors have been provided at the fort.

Hard Knott 3

MAP

Walkers bound for Eskdale who start their day in the Ambleside area should make a note of Moasdale; it offers nearly as quick a way to Lingcove Bridge as from Brotherilkeld (although admittedly nowhere near as beautiful), but means the crossing of Hardknott Pass by car, twice, is not necessary. Moasdale, of course, means dreary valley, and it lives up to its name. Gradients are easy, however.

Lingcove Bridge

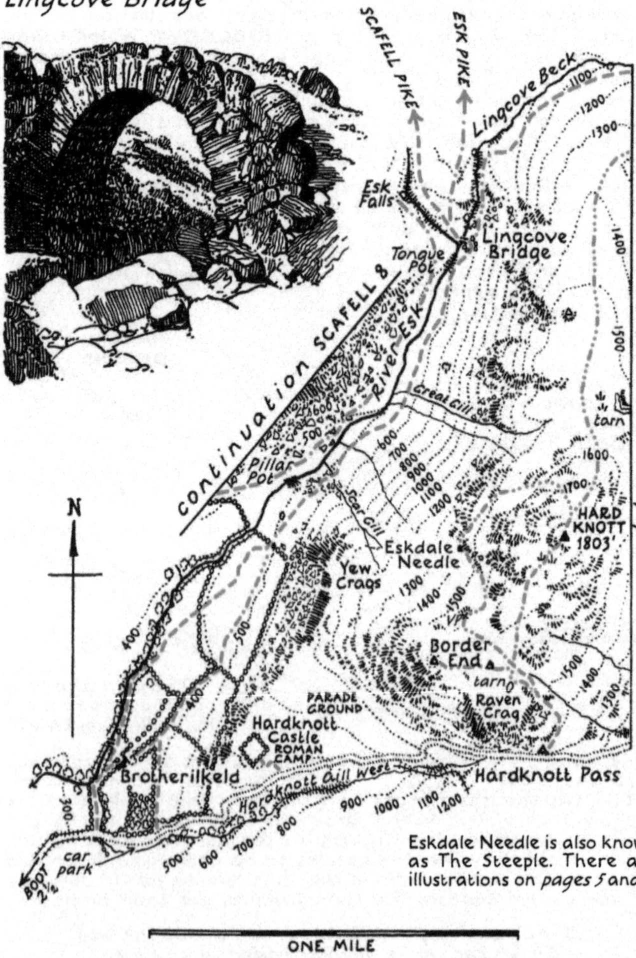

SCAFELL PIKE
ESK PIKE
Lingcove Beck
1100
1200
1300
1400
1500
1600
1700
continuation opposite
Esk Falls
Lingcove Bridge
Tongue Pot
continuation SCAFELL 8
River Esk
Great Gill
tarn
600
700
800
900
1000
Pillar Pot
Scar Gill
HARD KNOTT 1803'
N
Eskdale Needle
Yew Crags
VP
Border End
tarn
Raven Crag
400
500
PARADE GROUND
Hardknott Castle
ROMAN CAMP
Brotherilkeld
Hardknott Gill West
Hardknott Pass
300
car park
BOOT 2½
ONE MILE

Eskdale Needle is also known as The Steeple. There are illustrations on *pages 5* and *6*.

MAP

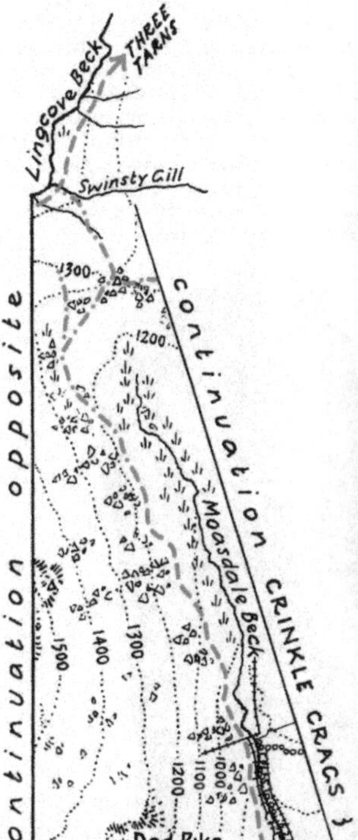
Lingcove Beck
THREE TARNS
Swinsty Gill
continuation opposite
continuation
CRINKLE CRAGS
Moasdale Beck
1300
1200
1500
1400
1100
1000
900
800
700
Dod Pike
River Duddon
WRYNOSE PASS
Cockley Beck Bridge
ROAD
BLACK HALL
DUDDON VALLEY

Lingcove Beck

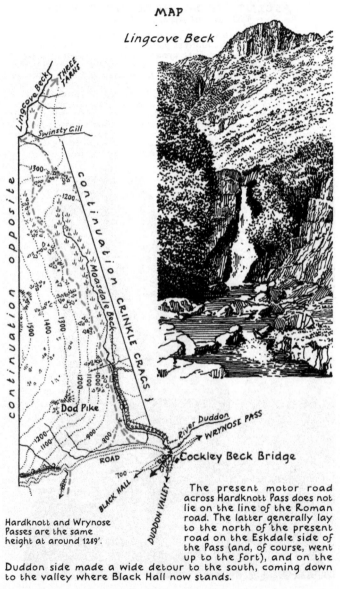

Hardknott and Wrynose Passes are the same height at around 1289′.

The present motor road across Hardknott Pass does not lie on the line of the Roman road. The latter generally lay to the north of the present road on the Eskdale side of the Pass (and, of course, went up to the fort), and on the Duddon side made a wide detour to the south, coming down to the valley where Black Hall now stands.

ASCENT FROM HARDKNOTT PASS
550 feet of ascent : ¾ mile

This short climb hardly calls for a diagram. Leave the road at the pile of stones on the highest point of the Pass — not from the rocky defile to the west, where crags bar the way. From the cairn a grass track slants up to the right, then left to a run of scree, above which a shallow grassy valley is reached amongst outcrops. A path goes right to the summit along an indefinite ridge, but this misses three of the fell's finest features: a delectable tarn to the north of Raven Crag; Border End, with its glorious prospect of Eskdale; and Eskdale Needle, which can be 'threaded' on its shorter side. Paths visit all these places (see map on *page 3*): it is suggested the Needle is visited in *ascent* because it is easier to locate that way, and the tarn in *descent* because its alluring shoreline is not an easy place to leave on a fine day.

Eskdale Needle also known as *The Steeple* (about 50' high on its longest side facing the valley). This is the view from the north.

THE SUMMIT

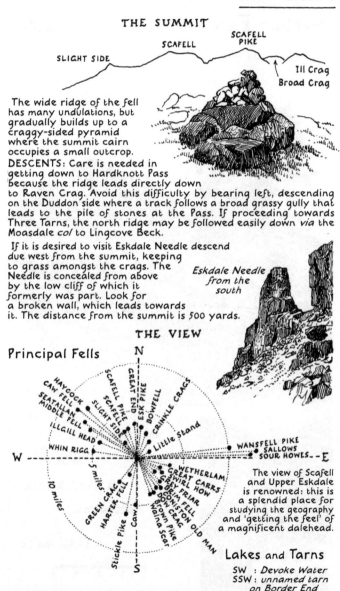

SLIGHT SIDE
SCAFELL
SCAFELL PIKE
Ill Crag
Broad Crag

The wide ridge of the fell has many undulations, but gradually builds up to a craggy-sided pyramid where the summit cairn occupies a small outcrop.

DESCENTS: Care is needed in getting down to Hardknott Pass because the ridge leads directly down to Raven Crag. Avoid this difficulty by bearing left, descending on the Duddon side where a track follows a broad grassy gully that leads to the pile of stones at the Pass. If proceeding towards Three Tarns, the north ridge may be followed easily down *via* the Moasdale *col* to Lingcove Beck.

If it is desired to visit Eskdale Needle descend due west from the summit, keeping to grass amongst the crags. The Needle is concealed from above by the low cliff of which it formerly was part. Look for a broken wall, which leads towards it. The distance from the summit is 500 yards.

Eskdale Needle from the south

THE VIEW

Principal Fells

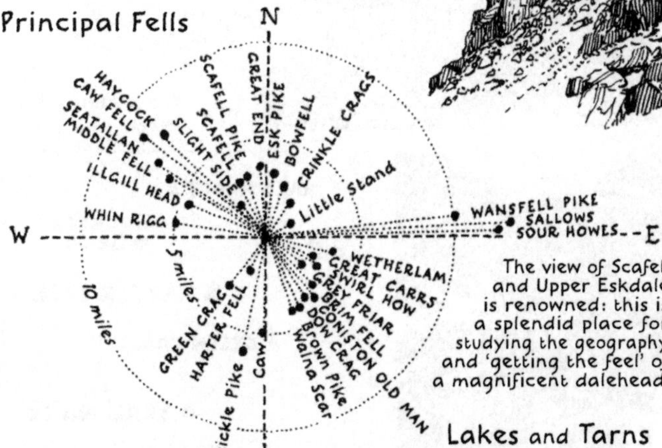
N
E
S
W
HAYCOCK
CAW FELL
SEATALLAN
MIDDLE FELL
ILLGILL HEAD
WHIN RIGG
SLIGHT SIDE
SCAFELL
SCAFELL PIKE
GREAT END
ESK PIKE
BOWFELL
CRINKLE CRAGS
Little Stand
WANSFELL PIKE
SALLOWS
SOUR HOWES
WETHERLAM
GREAT CARRS
SWIRL HOW
GREY FRIAR
BRIM FELL
CONISTON OLD MAN
DOW CRAG
Brown Pike
Walna Scar
Caw
Stickle Pike
HARTER FELL
GREEN CRAG
5 miles
10 miles

The view of Scafell and Upper Eskdale is renowned: this is a splendid place for studying the geography and 'getting the feel' of a magnificent dalehead.

Lakes and Tarns

SW : *Devoke Water*
SSW : *unnamed tarn on Border End*

Harter Fell

2140'

OS grid ref: SD219997

from Penny Hill

Birks Bridge

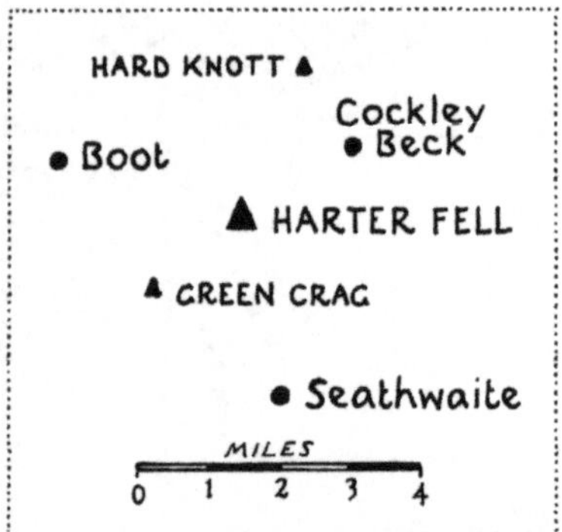

HARD KNOTT
Cockley Beck
Boot
HARTER FELL
GREEN CRAG
Seathwaite
MILES
0 1 2 3 4

NATURAL FEATURES

Not many fells can be described as *beautiful*, but the word fits Harter Fell, especially so when viewed from Eskdale. The lower slopes on this flank climb steeply from the tree-lined curves of the River Esk in a luxurious covering of bracken, higher is a wide belt of heather, and finally spring grey turrets and ramparts of rock to a neat and shapely pyramid.

The Duddon slopes, once extensively planted, have largely been cleared to the east and north-east of the summit. Only south-west do deciduous trees and evergreens still make a colourful picture.

Harter Fell from the Walna Scar path

The fell is not only good to look at, but good to climb, interest being well sustained throughout and reaching a climax in the last few feet, an upthrust of naked rock where the walker must turn cragsman if he is to enjoy the magnificent panorama from the uttermost point.

Harter Fell rises between the mid-valleys of the Esk and the Duddon, not at the head, and is therefore not the source of either river although it feeds both.

The head of Eskdale, from the summit of Harter Fell

Harter Fell 3

MAP

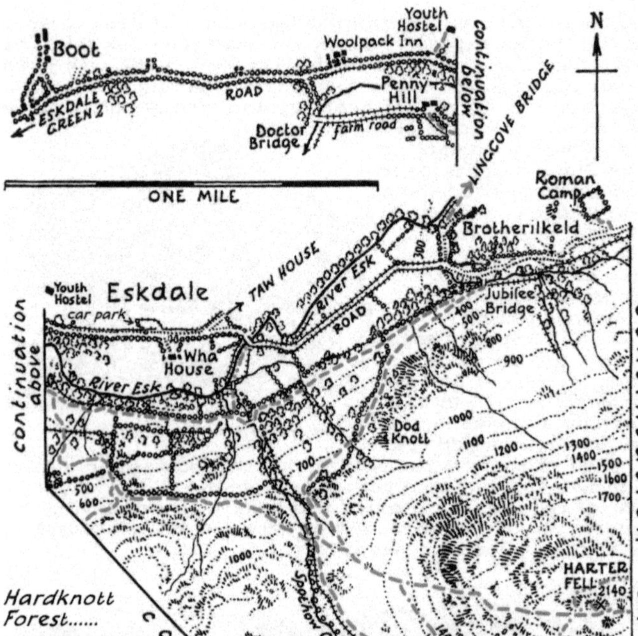

Youth Hostel
Boot
Woolpack Inn
ROAD
ESKDALE GREEN 2
Penny Hill
Doctor Bridge
farm road
continuation below
LINGCOVE BRIDGE
N
ONE MILE
Roman Camp
Brotherilkeld
TAW HOUSE
River Esk
Youth Hostel
Eskdale
car park
ROAD
Jubilee Bridge
Wha House
River Esk
continuation above
Dod Knott
HARTER FELL 2140
Spothow Gill
Dow Crag
Kepple Crag
stile
Grassguards Gill
continuation GREEN CRAG 2
continuation on opposite page

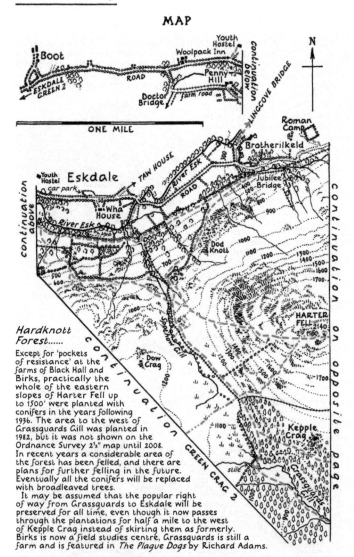

Hardknott Forest......

Except for 'pockets of resistance' at the farms of Black Hall and Birks, practically the whole of the eastern slopes of Harter Fell up to 1500' were planted with conifers in the years following 1936. The area to the west of Grassguards Gill was planted in 1982, but it was not shown on the Ordnance Survey 2½" map until 2008. In recent years a considerable area of the forest has been felled, and there are plans for further felling in the future. Eventually all the conifers will be replaced with broadleaved trees.

It may be assumed that the popular right of way from Grassguards to Eskdale will be preserved for all time, even though it now passes through the plantations for half a mile to the west of Kepple Crag instead of skirting them as formerly. Birks is now a field studies centre, Grassguards is still a farm and is featured in *The Plague Dogs* by Richard Adams.

The other Harter Fell

...is situated in the Far Eastern Fells, between the valleys of Mardale, Kentmere and Longsleddale. Its altitude is 2552'.

MAP

Of the two sets of steppings stones shown below, the one near Hinning House is more difficult to cross and the one near Dale Head requires an awkward crossing of a subsidiary beck and climbing over two stiles.

Cockley Beck Bridge
WRYNOSE PASS
Hardknott Pass
HARD KNOTT ROAD 3 & 4
continuation
ROAD
Hardknott Gill West
Hardknott Gill East
Black Hall
River Duddon
ROAD
gate
gate
felled area
felled area
felled area
felled area
felled area
stepping stones
Dale Head
stiles
Castle How
Skelly Crags
stile
stile
Demming Crag
Castlehow Beck
The Duddon Valley
stepping stones
Hinning House (outdoor education centre)
Crook Crags
car park
stiles
stiles
Buck Crag
stile and gate
Maiden Castle
Birks Bridge
Birks
forest road
Troutal
Long Crag
felled
ROAD
THRANG
Grassguards
continuation on opposite page
continuation HARTER FELL 5

TAKE CARE
DO NOT START
FIRE

and so waste the effort spent in drawing all the little trees on this map. The Forestry Commission, too, will be annoyed.

The illustration and note, right, were made in 1958 at a time when much of the map on this page was covered with trees.

MAP

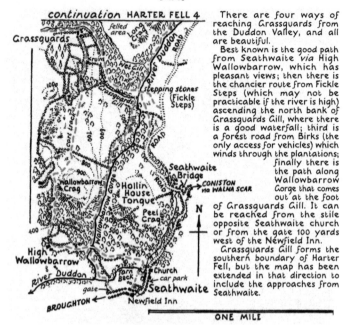

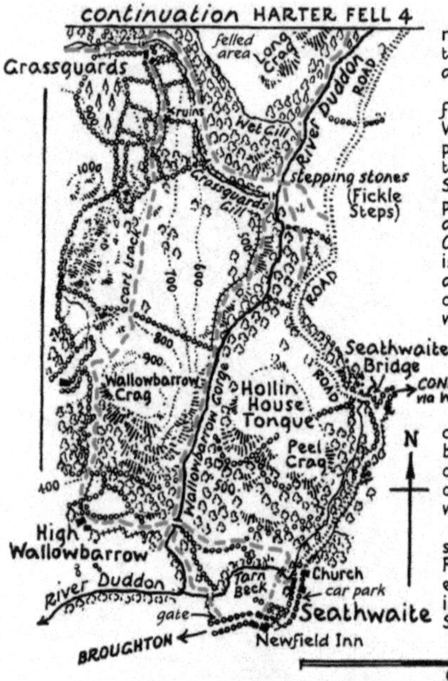
continuation HARTER FELL 4
Grassguards
felled area
Long Crag
River Duddon
ROAD
ruins
Wet Gill
1000
Grassguards Gill
stepping stones
(Fickle Steps)
cart track
700
600
500
ROAD
800
900
Seathwaite Bridge
CONISTON via WALNA SCAR
Wallowbarrow Crag
Hollin House Tongue
Wallowbarrow Gorge
Peel Crag
N
400
500
High Wallowbarrow
River Duddon
Tarn Beck
Church
car park
gate
Seathwaite
BROUGHTON
Newfield Inn
ONE MILE

There are four ways of reaching Grassguards from the Duddon Valley, and all are beautiful.

Best known is the good path from Seathwaite *via* High Wallowbarrow, which has pleasant views; then there is the chancier route from Fickle Steps (which may not be practicable if the river is high) ascending the north bank of Grassguards Gill, where there is a good waterfall; third is a forest road from Birks (the only access for vehicles) which winds through the plantations; finally there is the path along Wallowbarrow Gorge that comes out at the foot of Grassguards Gill. It can be reached from the stile opposite Seathwaite church or from the gate 100 yards west of the Newfield Inn.

Grassguards Gill forms the southern boundary of Harter Fell, but the map has been extended in that direction to include the approaches from Seathwaite.

ASCENT FROM THE DUDDON VALLEY

For a long time free and open access to the fellside from the Duddon has been restricted because of the plantations, but there are two established routes to the summit and one new one which has come into being because of felling between Black Hall and Birks.

FROM FICKLE STEPS – *via Grassguards: 1700 feet of ascent : 2¼ miles*
FROM SEATHWAITE – *via Grassguards: 1800 feet of ascent : 3 miles*

This is the time-honoured route to Eskdale. At the end of the plantation follow the good path up to the right to avoid the considerable descent and ascent involved in joining the route from Eskdale.

FROM BIRKS BRIDGE – *via Maiden Castle : 1650 feet of ascent : 1½ miles*

The route to Birks for vehicles now starts at the car park, and the former drive to Birks from Birks Bridge has become a footpath. Above Birks the path is signposted; it is initially wet through some bushes, followed by a short stony section on the rise to the prominent crag of Maiden Castle. Beyond is an easy grassy slope to the summit.

FROM BIRKS BRIDGE – *via Castlehow Beck : 1700 feet of ascent : 3½ miles*

A roundabout route that joins the ridge from Hardknott Pass; a clear path has sprung up through the felled plantations, most probably from walkers descending from Harter Fell. In fact, this route is excellent in descent and, combined with the shorter direct route described above, makes a good round trip of the fell from the Duddon side.

ASCENT FROM ESKDALE

2000 feet of ascent : 3½ miles from Boot

A longer variation is to continue along the Duddon bridleway until the edge of the plantation is reached and turn left up a grassy path beside the fence. It is not to be preferred to the route shown, however.

At about 1250' the path to the left can be missed. If that happens continue to the wall and ascend from there.

The beautiful Doctor Bridge is Grade II listed. It was so named in 1734 when it was widened to allow local surgeon Dr Edward Tyson to cross in his pony and trap.

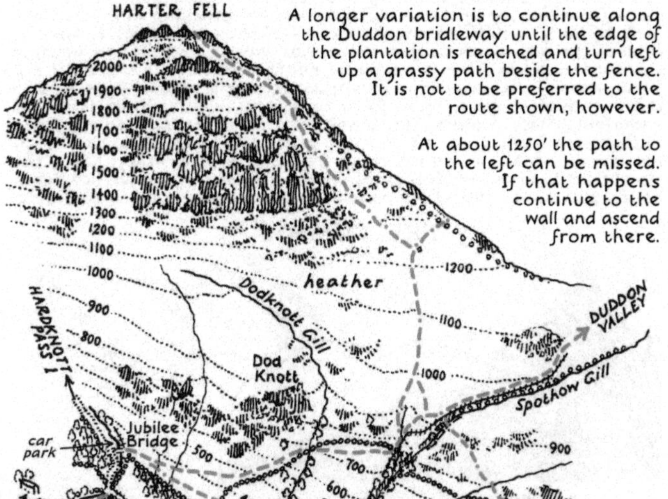
HARTER FELL
2000
1900
1800
1700
1600
1500
1400
1300
1200
1100
1000
900
800
heather
Dodknott Gill
Dod Knott
HARDKNOTT PASS
1200
1100
1000
DUDDON VALLEY
Spothow Gill
900
Jubilee Bridge
car park
500
700
600
400
ROAD
Brotherilkeld
TAW HOUSE
Eskdale
Wha House
GREEN CRAG
gate
SP (Harter Fell)
500
400
Penny Hill (farm)
farm road
LOW BIRKER
River Esk
car park
Youth Hostel
ROAD
Doctor Bridge
Woolpack Inn
BOOT ¾

looking east-south-east

On the approach *via* Penny Hill, doubts may arise in the little tangle of rough country in the vicinity of Spothow Gill, above the walls of the enclosures, where footsteps will tend to gravitate in error to the path going across to the Duddon Valley. It is better to use the path from Jubilee Bridge.

There is not a more charming ascent than this, which is a delight from start to finish. Harter Fell's grand rocky pyramid gives an air of real mountaineering to the climb, the views of Eskdale are glorious and the immediate surroundings richly colourful.

ASCENT FROM HARDKNOTT PASS
900 feet of ascent : 1½ miles

Little can be said in favour of the obvious route along the swampy ridge from the top of Hardknott Pass, which is lacking in interest for most of its length. However, the clarity of the path, which is distinct most of the way, suggests this is a popular way up, undoubtedly because the ascent starts from a height of nearly 1300′. Leave the road 200 yards west of the pass (signposted); go right at a second signpost and then through a gate. From here to a stile over a fence it is wet underfoot unless in a drought, conditions that persist beyond the fence until a prominent gully is crossed. A grass path ascends to the left of the summit crags, joining the route from the Duddon Valley. Resist the temptation to follow any tracks that make a beeline for the terrace shown on the plan at the foot of the page – the lie of the land is too confusing.

THE SUMMIT

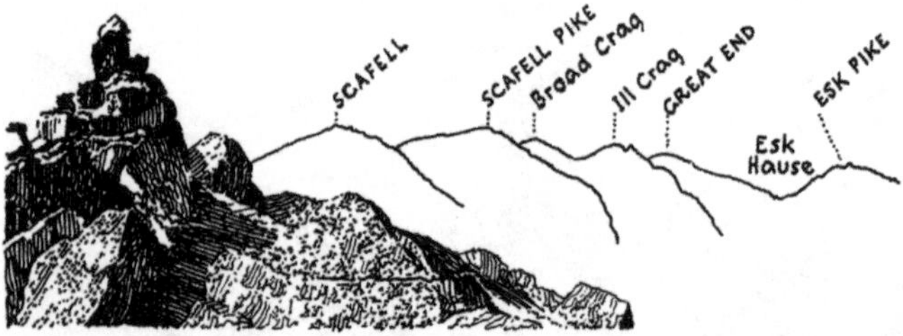
SCAFELL
SCAFELL PIKE
Broad Crag
Ill Crag
GREAT END
ESK PIKE
Esk Hause

An Ordnance Survey triangulation column gives an air of authenticity to the craggy rise it occupies, but this is clearly not the highest point. Near at hand, east, is a steep-sided outcrop extending several feet nearer to heaven, and beyond that is another, similar but of lower elevation. The middle one of these three rocky tors is therefore the true summit, although it carries no decorations; at first glance it looks unassailable but an investigation on its east side discloses there a breach: the crest may then be reached by simple climbing. The third turret also offers, on its south edge, an easy access to its top.

The true summit from the 'official'

All told, this is a grand and entertaining summit, a place one is loth to leave.

DESCENTS: Crags are continuous along the north edge of the fell and scattered elsewhere, so that the path going down to Eskdale, which is distinct enough to be found and followed in mist, should be adhered to closely. For the Duddon Valley it is best to use the path to Birks.

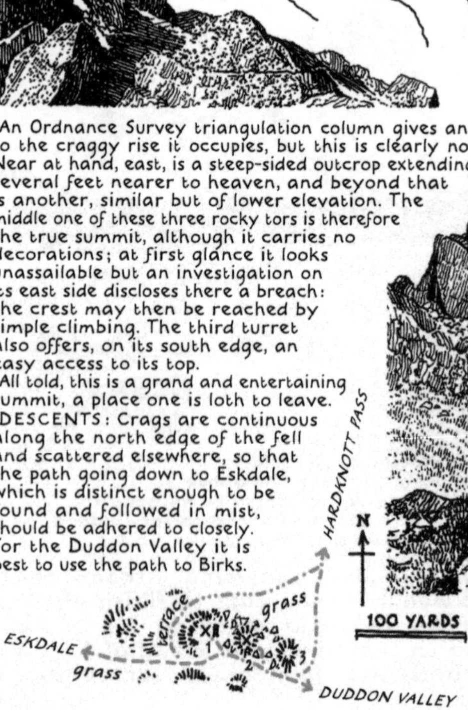
HARDKNOTT PASS
N
100 YARDS
grass
terrace
ESKDALE
grass
1
2
3
DUDDON VALLEY

1: *'official' summit*
2: *true summit*
3: *third outcrop*

THE VIEW

Having exercised himself by scrambling up and down the three summits, the visitor can settle himself on the sharp arête of the highest and enjoy a most excellent view. The Scafell group and Upper Eskdale dominate the scene, appearing not quite in such detail as when surveyed from Hard Knott but in better balance — added distance often adds quality to a picture. Over Wrynose Pass there is an array of faraway fells in the Kirkstone area, which will not surprise walkers familiar with that district, where Harter Fell often pops into the views therefrom. Near at hand, east, the Coniston fells bulk largely but unattractively. Lower Eskdale and the Duddon Valley lead the eye to golden sands and glittering sea.

Principal Fells

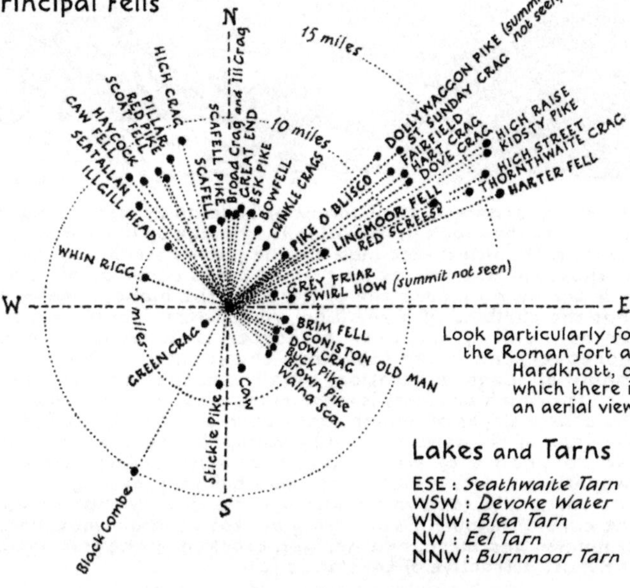
N
E
S
W
15 miles
10 miles
5 miles
Broad Crag and Ill Crag
HIGH CRAG
PILLAR
RED PIKE
SCOAT FELL
HAYCOCK
CAW FELL
SEATALLAN
ILLGILL HEAD
SCAFELL
SCAFELL PIKE
GREAT END
ESK PIKE
BOWFELL
CRINKLE CRAGS
DOLLYWAGGON PIKE (summit not seen)
ST. SUNDAY CRAG
FAIRFIELD
HART CRAG
DOVE CRAG
HIGH RAISE
KIDSTY PIKE
HIGH STREET
THORNTHWAITE CRAG
HARTER FELL
PIKE O' BLISCO
LINGMOOR FELL
RED SCREES
WHIN RIGG
GREY FRIAR
SWIRL HOW (summit not seen)
BRIM FELL
CONISTON OLD MAN
DOW CRAG
Buck Pike
Brown Pike
Walna Scar
CAW
Stickle Pike
GREEN CRAG
Black Combe

Look particularly for the Roman fort at Hardknott, of which there is an aerial view.

Lakes and Tarns

ESE : *Seathwaite Tarn*
WSW : *Devoke Water*
WNW: *Blea Tarn*
NW : *Eel Tarn*
NNW: *Burnmoor Tarn*

RIDGE ROUTES

To HARD KNOTT, 1803' : 2½ miles : NE then N by E
Depression (Hardknott Pass) at 1265' : 700' of ascent

This is an easy walk although wet in places; there is a fairly clear path most of the way. Consult the summit plan on the facing page to reach the ridge to Hardknott Pass, from whence the route onwards has been described as a separate ascent (see *Hard Knott 5* and map on *Hard Knott 2*).

To GREEN CRAG, 1602' : 1¾ miles : SW
Depression at 1150' : 600' of ascent

There is no defined ridge seawards, the route from Harter Fell to Green Crag being on the flanks of both fells. Take the Eskdale path and turn left shortly to descend a grassy path to the side of a plantation. At the bridleway continue up the facing grassy slope. See *page 3* and *Green Crag 2*.

Holme Fell 1040'

OS grid ref: NY315007

from Tunnel Quarry Low Fell

It is a characteristic of many of Lakeland's lesser heights that what they lack in elevation they make up in ruggedness. Slopes a thousand feet high can be just as steep and rough as those three times as long, while crags occur at all levels and are by no means the preserve of the highest peaks, so that the climbing of a small hill, what there is of it, can call for as much effort, over a shorter time, as a big one; moreover, the lower tops have the further defence of a tangle of tough vegetation, usually heather and bracken, through which progress is a far more laborious task than on the grassy slopes of higher zones. Such a one is Holme Fell, at the head of Yewdale, isolated by valleys but very much under the dominance of Wetherlam. A craggy southern front, a switchback ridge, a cluster of small but very beautiful tree-girt tarns (old reservoirs), and a great quarry that reveals the core of colourful slate lying beneath the glorious jungle of juniper and birch, heather and bracken, make this one of the most attractive of Lakeland's fells.

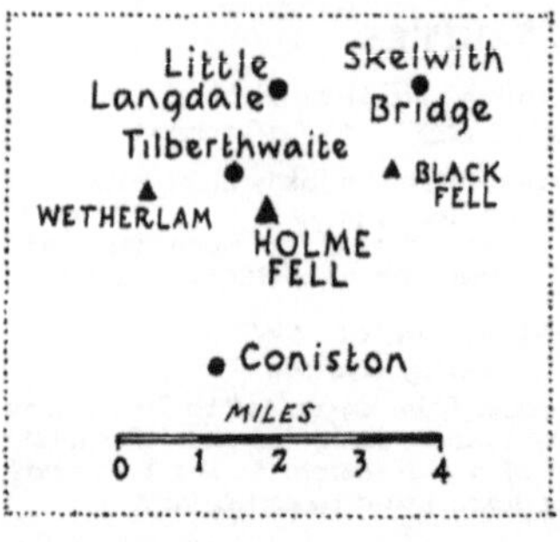
Little Langdale
Skelwith Bridge
Tilberthwaite
BLACK FELL
WETHERLAM
HOLME FELL
Coniston
MILES
0 1 2 3 4

the big cairn on Ivy Crag
(there are uncairned outcrops nearby at a slightly higher elevation)

MAP

The car park south-west of Hodge Close is accessible *via* the single-track road from Shepherd's Bridge, and is a popular spot for artists and photographers. The road from Oxen Fell ends at High Oxen Fell farm – a rough track continues to Hodge Close.

A : High Tilberthwaite
B : Low Tilberthwaite
C : Holme Ground Cottages
D : Holme Ground
E : Shepherd's Bridge
F : High Yewdale
G : Yew Tree Farm
H : Yew Tree Tarn
I : Low Oxen Fell
J : High Oxen Fell
K : Quarry pool

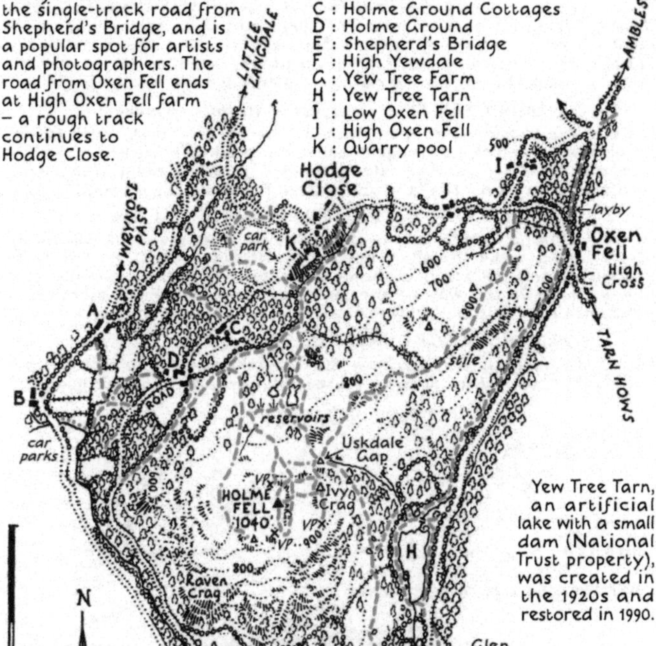
LITTLE LANGDALE
AMBLESIDE
Hodge Close
WRYNOSE PASS
car park
Oxen Fell
layby
High Cross
TARN HOWS
ROAD
stile
reservoirs
car parks
Uskdale Gap
HOLME FELL 1040'
Ivy Crag
VP
Raven Crag
N
ONE MILE
Glen Mary Bridge
car park
Yewdale
TARN HOWS
CONISTON 1½
500
600
700
800
900

Yew Tree Tarn, an artificial lake with a small dam (National Trust property), was created in the 1920s and restored in 1990.

from the north ridge (Ivy Crag on the left)

ASCENTS

FROM YEW TREE FARM – *850 feet of ascent : 1 mile*

The ascent from pretty Yew Tree Farm is popular, with the benefit of a National Trust car park nearby. The climb is in three sections: a rising, wooded path to the col of Uskdale Gap; left up to the subsidiary of Ivy Crag; then a choice of paths across a heathery valley to the summit ridge, of which the one on the right up a pleasant edge is to be preferred.

FROM OXEN FELL – *800 feet of ascent : 1¾ miles*

There is limited parking on the A593 at the start of this route, which follows the little-known north-east ridge of Holme Fell to Uskdale Gap where the Yew Tree Farm route is joined. The ridge is an up-and-down delight, with a good path all the way from the lane above Oxen Fell, accessed through a gate.

FROM HODGE CLOSE – *650 feet of ascent : 1 mile*

Plentiful parking nearby makes this a popular starting point, but many people fail to make the short pre-ascent detour to visit the two huge quarries nearby, which is a shame because they are spectacular *(see facing page)*. On the way up the larger of the two former reservoirs is worth visiting – this is a perfect picnic spot on a sunny day.

FROM HOLME GROUND – *550 feet of ascent : ⅔ mile*

This is the shortest way up from the Tilberthwaite side of the fell but lacking the charm of the previous route (and the drama of the big quarries).

THE SUMMIT

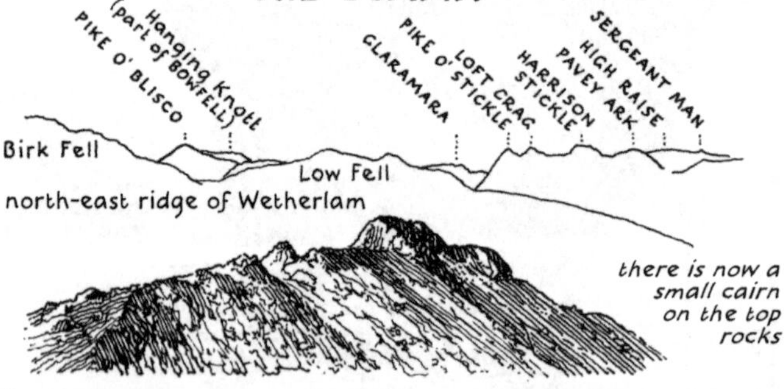
PIKE O' BLISCO
Hanging Knott (part of BOWFELL)
CLARAMARA
PIKE O' STICKLE
LOFT CRAG
HARRISON STICKLE
PAVEY ARK
HIGH RAISE
SERGEANT MAN
Birk Fell
Low Fell
north-east ridge of Wetherlam
there is now a small cairn on the top rocks

The highest point is a platform of naked rock, set at the top of slabs, in the middle of a summit ridge with a near-continuous escarpment on the east side. There is one breach in this broken cliff, from where a path in a rocky groove descends to a heathery plateau that sits between the main ridge and a parallel ridge 200 yards to the east. At the northern end of this ridge is the subsidiary summit of Ivy Crag; at the southern end is a rocky outcrop from which Coniston Water is well seen.

DESCENTS: Uskdale Gap is the key to the descents to Oxen Fell on the north-east ridge and Yew Tree Farm; the two reservoirs also may be reached from here.

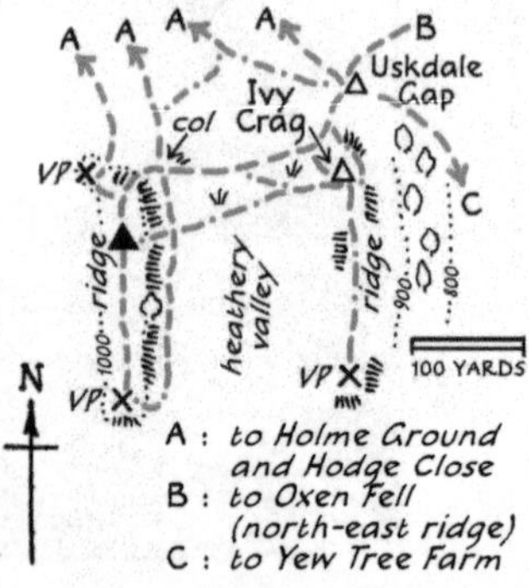
A
A
A
A
B
Uskdale Gap
Ivy Crag
col
VP
VP
VP
C
ridge
heathery valley
ridge
1000
900
800
100 YARDS
N
A : to Holme Ground and Hodge Close
B : to Oxen Fell (north-east ridge)
C : to Yew Tree Farm

THE VIEW

Outstanding in a moderate view is the striking full length of Coniston Water; this is the best place for viewing the lake.

Principal Fells

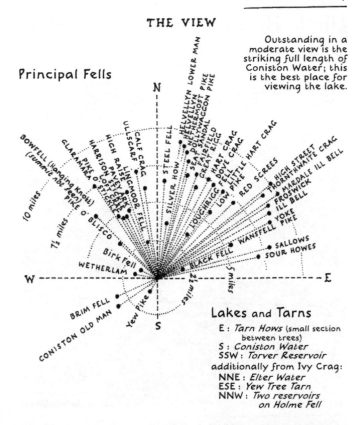

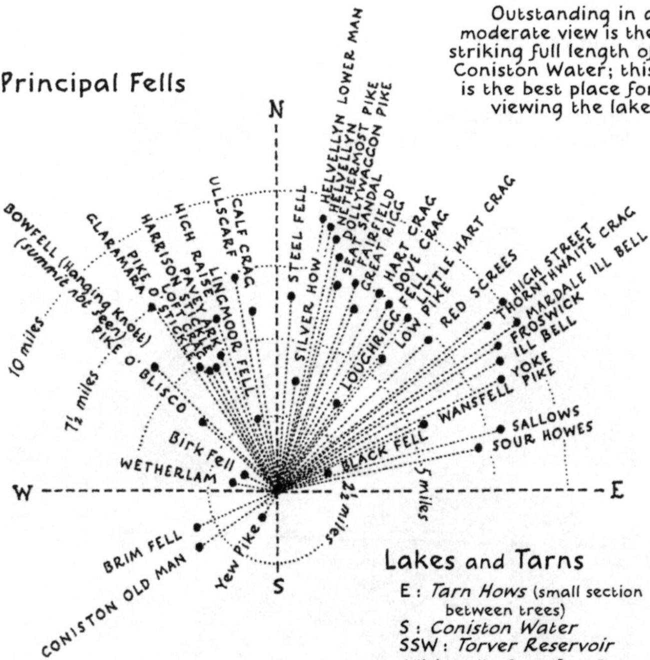
N
S
E
W
HELVELLYN LOWER MAN
HELVELLYN
NETHERMOST PIKE
DOLLYWAGGON PIKE
SEAT SANDAL
FAIRFIELD
GREAT RIGG
HART CRAG
DOVE CRAG
HART CRAG
LITTLE HART CRAG
RED SCREES
HIGH STREET
THORNTHWAITE CRAG
MARDALE ILL BELL
FROSWICK
ILL BELL
YOKE
PIKE
LOW PIKE
LOUGHRIGG FELL
WANSFELL
SALLOWS
SOUR HOWES
BLACK FELL
STEEL FELL
SILVER HOW
CALF CRAG
ULLSCARF
LINGMOOR FELL
HIGH RAISE
SERGEANT MAN
PAVEY ARK
HARRISON STICKLE
LOFT CRAG
PIKE O'STICKLE
GLARAMARA
BOWFELL (Hanging Knott)
(summit not seen)
PIKE O' BLISCO
Birk Fell
WETHERLAM
BRIM FELL
CONISTON OLD MAN
Yew Pike
10 miles
7½ miles
5 miles
2½ miles

Lakes and Tarns

E : *Tarn Hows* (small section between trees)
S : *Coniston Water*
SSW : *Torver Reservoir*

additionally from Ivy Crag:

NNE : *Elter Water*
ESE : *Yew Tree Tarn*
NNW : *Two reservoirs on Holme Fell*

The Hodge Close quarries were worked from the 19th century until the 1960s. The travelling crane and mineral railway have gone, but there is still an emerald lake, and the two tremendous holes are extremely impressive and they can be visited by walkers. The disused northern quarry may be entered by a steep path at the northern end and its stony floor crossed to the arch connecting with the second quarry and the green lake; occasionally the floor below this arch can flood. Much of the quarry waste has been colonised by birches.

The arch

When the quarry was working, water from the two reservoirs to the south of the quarry was used to operate the funicular railway, which raised slate from the quarry floors to ground level.

Illgill Head

1983'

OS grid ref: NY169049

often referred to as Wastwater Screes

from Green How

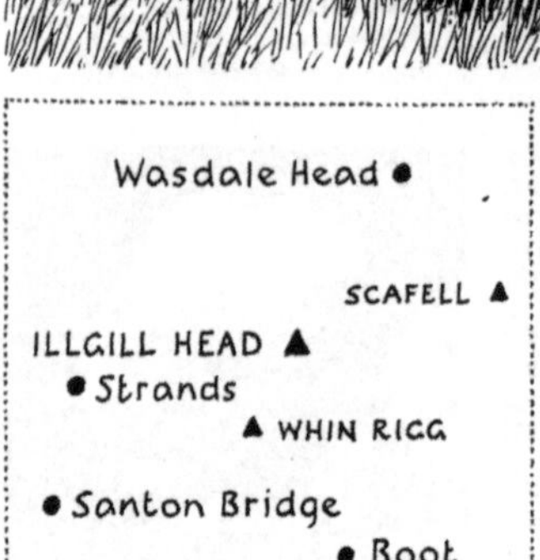
Wasdale Head
SCAFELL
ILLGILL HEAD
Strands
WHIN RIGG
Santon Bridge
Boot
MILES
0 1 2 3 4

from Miterdale

NATURAL FEATURES

Illgill Head is known to most visitors to Lakeland as Wastwater Screes, although this latter title is strictly appropriate only to the stone-strewn flank that falls so spectacularly into the depths of Wast Water. Much of this north-western slope, however, is bracken-covered and grassy, the screes descending only from the actual summit and its southerly continuation to Whin Rigg. It is here that the fellside from top to bottom, down even to the floor of the lake 250' below the surface, is piled deep with stones lying at their maximum angle of rest, 35°–40°, through a vertical height of almost 2000'. The top of the fell is a smooth sheepwalk; these many acres of loose and shifting debris must therefore have resulted from the disintegration of crags that, ages ago, rimmed the top of the fell: some rocks remain still in a state of dangerous decay. The screes, when seen in the light of an evening sun, make a picture of remarkable colour and brilliance: a scene unique in this country.
The opposite flank, descending to Burnmoor and the shy little valley of Miterdale in patches of heather and bracken, has, in contrast, nothing of interest to show.

Wastwater Screes

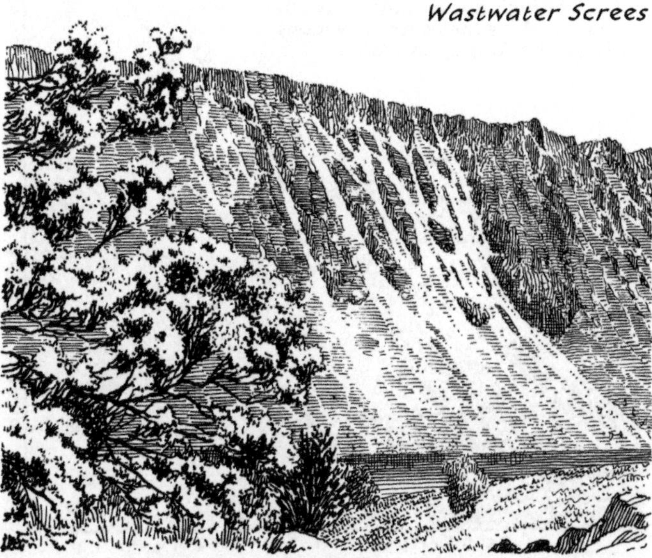

Illgill Head 3

MAP

The Lakeside Path

From Wasdale Head Hall the lakeside path starts innocuously as a broad avenue in the bracken, and although it soon climbs a little and narrows to a track the way continues quite easy, even when the first screes are reached and for a mile beyond, during which section the path returns almost to the lakeside, crossing successive bands of stony debris which cause no trouble. Then just as the walker who has been forewarned of the difficulties of the route is beginning to wonder what all the fuss is about, and with the end almost in sight, there comes a vicious quarter-mile compared with which the top of Scafell Pike is like a bowling green — here the screes take the form of big awkward boulders, loosely piled at a steep angle and avoidable only by a swim in the lake; it has been impossible to tread out a path here despite a brave effort by somebody to cairn a route. This section is really trying and progress is slow, laborious and just a little dangerous unless the feet are placed carefully; ladies wearing stiletto heels will be gravely inconvenienced and indeed many a gentle pedestrian must have suffered nightmares in this dreadful place and looked with hopelessness and envy at people striding along the smooth road on the opposite shore. The boulders end abruptly at a little copse of trees, and here, in between giving thanks for deliverance, the tremendous cliffs and gullies high above may be studied in comfort. A distinct path now leads easily to the foot of the lake.

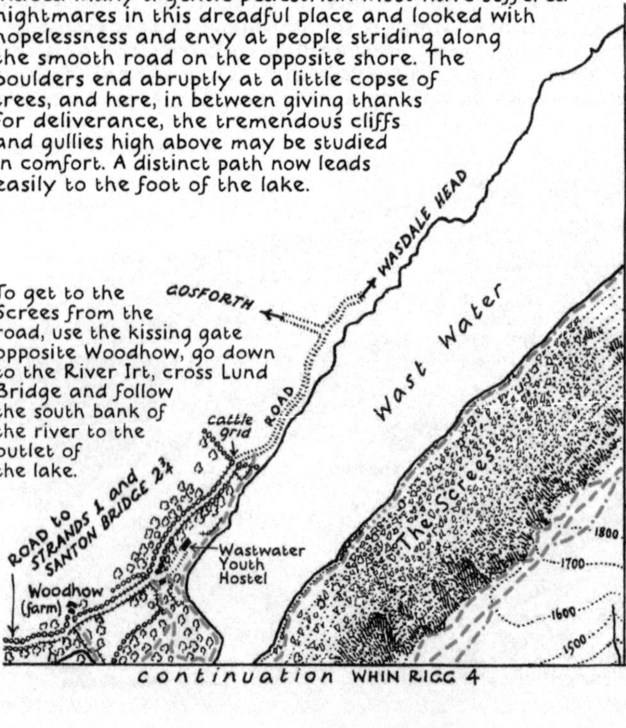

To get to the Screes from the road, use the kissing gate opposite Woodhow, go down to the River Irt, cross Lund Bridge and follow the south bank of the river to the outlet of the lake.
WASDALE HEAD
GOSFORTH
Wast Water
ROAD
cattle grid
ROAD to STRANDS 1 and SANTON BRIDGE 2¾
Wastwater Youth Hostel
Woodhow (farm)
The Screes
1800
1700
1600
1500
continuation on opposite page
continuation WHIN RIGG 4

MAP

In the map below five cairns are shown on the Old Corpse Road immediately to the north of the pass – in reality there are probably six times that number, one of the highest concentrations in Lakeland. The reason for this proliferation is unclear: perhaps it is to mark the route in deep snow. Another mystery is why are there so many paths from the main track up the steep and grassy eastern flank of the fell.

The steepness of the fellside is maintained to the bottom of the lake, 258' below the surface, and Lakeland's deepest (58' below sea level).

The ruined buildings to the south-east of Wasdale Head Hall were once peat huts.

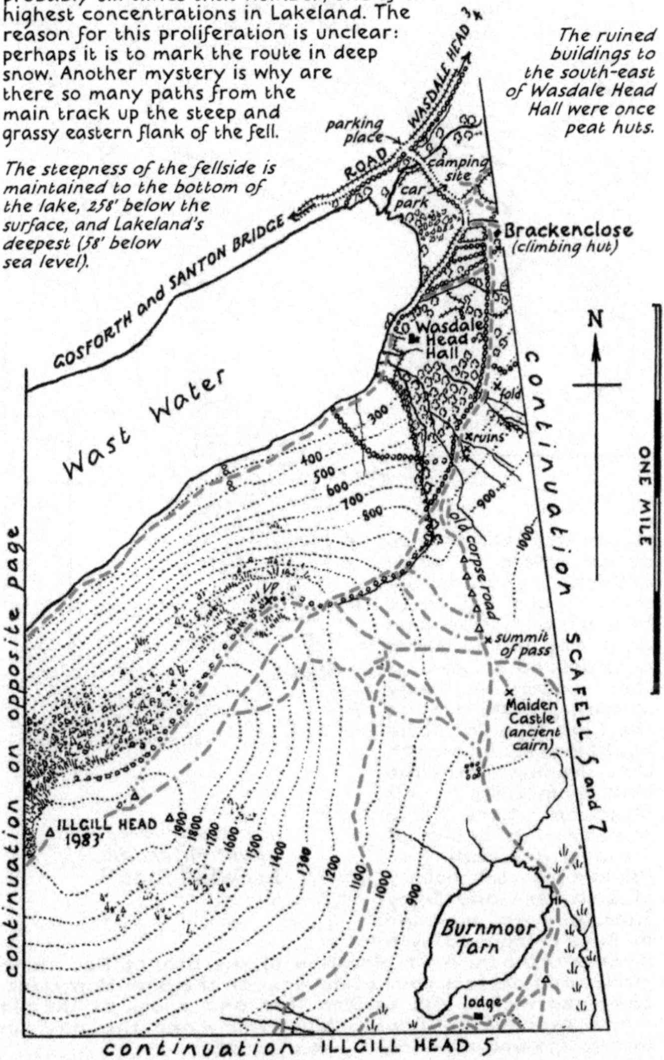
WASDALE HEAD 3
ROAD
parking place
camping site
car park
GOSFORTH and SANTON BRIDGE
Brackenclose
(climbing hut)
Wasdale Head Hall
fold
ruins
Wast Water
300
400
500
600
700
800
900
1000
old corpse road
VP
summit of pass
Maiden Castle
(ancient cairn)
ILLGILL HEAD
1983'
1900
1800
1700
1600
1500
1400
1300
1200
1100
1000
900
Burnmoor Tarn
lodge
N
ONE MILE
continuation
SCAFELL 5 and 7
continuation on opposite page
continuation ILLGILL HEAD 5

MAP

continuation ILLGILL HEAD 4

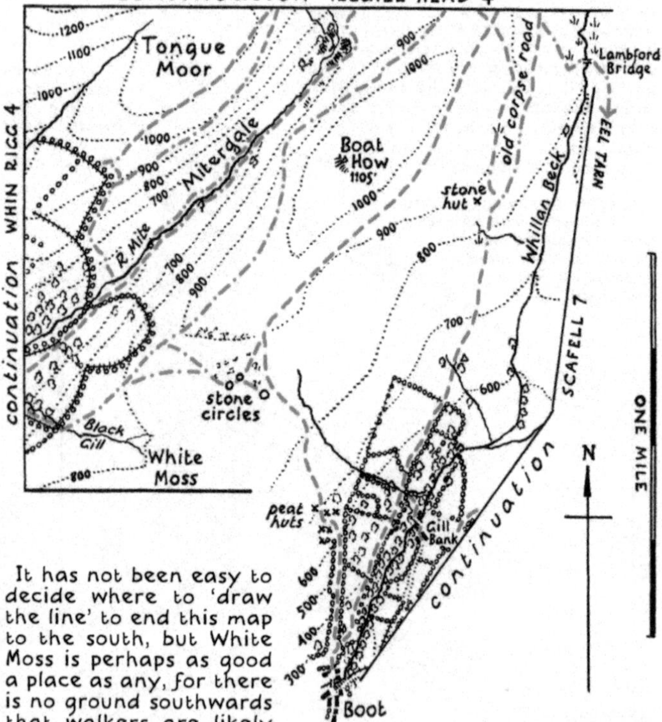
continuation WHIN RIGG 4
1200
1100
1000
Tongue Moor
1000
900
800
700
Mitergale
R. Mite
700
800
900
900
1000
Boat How
1105'
1000
900
800
old corpse road
stone hut
Lambford Bridge
EEL TARN
Whillan Beck
SCAFELL 7
700
600
stone circles
Black Gill
White Moss
800
peat huts
Gill Bank
600
500
400
300
Boot
continuation
N
ONE MILE

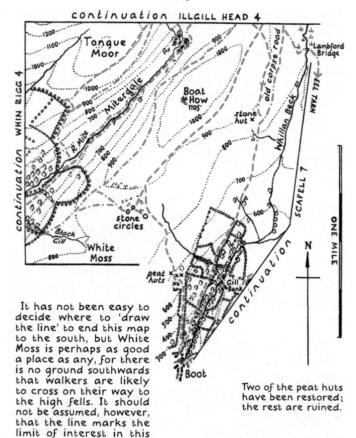

It has not been easy to decide where to 'draw the line' to end this map to the south, but White Moss is perhaps as good a place as any, for there is no ground southwards that walkers are likely to cross on their way to the high fells. It should not be assumed, however, that the line marks the limit of interest in this direction, there being a charming group of foothills descending to Eskdale from the vicinity of Blea Tarn and Siney Tarn. If a wet morning at Boot is followed by a clear afternoon, an exploration of the Bronze Age stone circles and ancient cairns and walls on the Boat How ridge, combined with a visit to Blea Tarn and a look at the old mines overtopping Boot village, will make the day an interesting and memorable one after all.

Two of the peat huts have been restored; the rest are ruined.

for some notes about Miterdale see Whin Rigg 3

ASCENT FROM WASDALE HEAD

1750 feet of ascent : 4 miles (from Wasdale Head Inn)

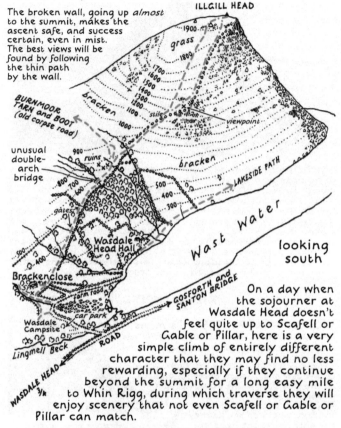

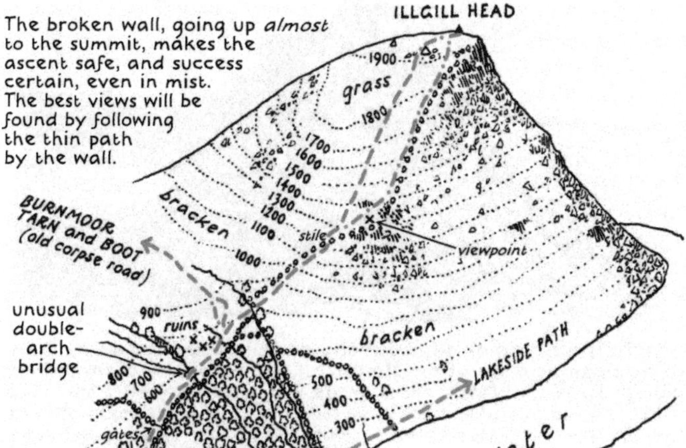
The broken wall, going up *almost* to the summit, makes the ascent safe, and success certain, even in mist. The best views will be found by following the thin path by the wall.
ILLGILL HEAD
1900
grass
1800
1700
1600
1500
1400
1300
1200
1100
1000
900
800
700
600
500
400
300
bracken
stile
viewpoint
BURNMOOR TARN and BOOT (old corpse road)
unusual double-arch bridge
ruins
gates
LAKESIDE PATH
Wast Water
looking south
Wasdale Head Hall
Brackenclose
farm road
car park
Wasdale Campsite
Lingmell Beck
ROAD
GOSFORTH and SANTON BRIDGE
WASDALE HEAD 3/4

On a day when the sojourner at Wasdale Head doesn't feel quite up to Scafell or Gable or Pillar, here is a very simple climb of entirely different character that they may find no less rewarding, especially if they continue beyond the summit for a long easy mile to Whin Rigg, during which traverse they will enjoy scenery that not even Scafell or Gable or Pillar can match.

ASCENTS FROM ESKDALE

from Boot via *old corpse road : 2000 feet of ascent : 4 miles*

The climb may be made with equal facility from Boot by using the old corpse road to and beyond Burnmoor Tarn until an old walled enclosure is passed on the left. Beyond it there are a number of short cuts to the broken wall, as shown on the map on *page 4*.

from Eskdale Green via *Whin Rigg : 2100 feet of ascent : 5 miles*

From Eskdale, a more rewarding plan is to climb Whin Rigg first, then go on to Illgill Head and return *via* the broken wall and Burnmoor Tarn: a splendid round. See *Whin Rigg 6* and *8*.

THE SUMMIT

There is nothing at all about the actual summit to give a hint of its dramatic situation almost on the lip of the tremendous plunge to Wast Water. All is grass — dry springy turf that, on a hot day, cries aloud for a siesta; but heavy sleepers should not so position themselves that they can slide down the gradual decline to the rim of the cliffs, 35 yards from the cairn. This remarkable point of vantage, high above the lake, should be visited nevertheless: if it is omitted the whole ascent becomes purposeless. There is a second cairn in a rash of stones nearer to Wasdale Head: this is slightly higher than what is generally regarded as the true summit.

RIDGE ROUTE

TO WHIN RIGG, 1755′ : 1⅓ miles : SW

Depression at 1550′ : 240 feet of ascent

A magnificent walk.

There is a faint path in the short grass of the summit. It soon becomes clearer on the long slope to the depression and continues all the way to Whin Rigg with a choice of routes. In three places on the journey the path skirts the head of big gullies down which are thrilling views; otherwise its course along the grassy ridge is uneventful. But scenery of a very high order may be obtained throughout by following a track, a little sketchy in places, that skirts the escarpment closely. Indicated on the diagram are two viewpoints, both at the edge of vertical crags and needing caution in high winds.

ILLGILL HEAD
1900
N
HALF A MILE
1800
1700
grass
1600
two viewpoints
limestone sinks: a series of small potholes, not more than a few feet deep, in an unexpected vein of limestone.
tarns
heads of gullies
head of Great Gully
WHIN RIGG
1600
For better identification of the two viewpoints, see Whin Rigg 8.

THE VIEW

This summit is the only really satisfactory viewpoint for Wasdale Head — a finely proportioned scene, with gaunt mountains soaring up suddenly from the level strath of this grandest of all daleheads. (It is better seen from the north cairn.) Scafell is disappointing: a vast and featureless mass, showing its dullest side. Visitors will, *of course*, walk across to the rim of the escarpment for the view down the screes into Wast Water far below; an impressive scene indeed.

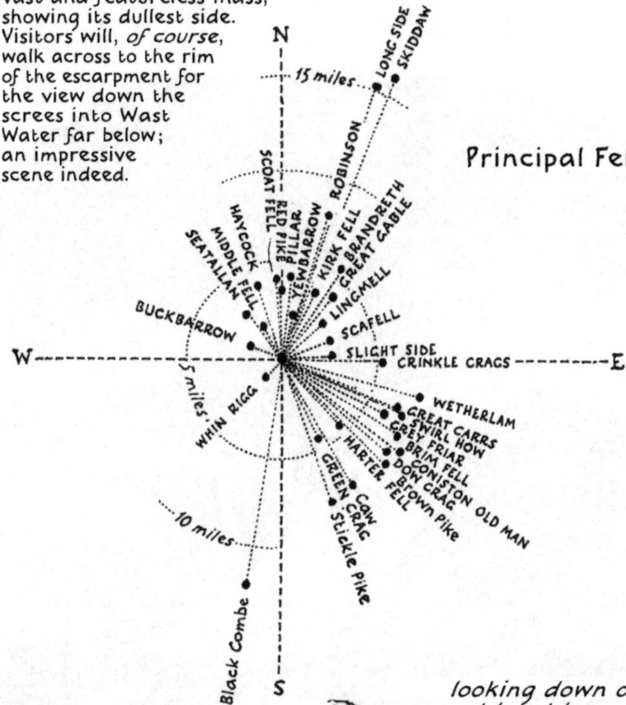

N
15 miles
LONG SIDE
SKIDDAW
ROBINSON
SCOAT FELL
RED PIKE
PILLAR
YEWBARROW
KIRK FELL
BRANDRETH
GREAT GABLE
HAYCOCK
MIDDLE FELL
SEATALLAN
LINGMELL
BUCKBARROW
SCAFELL
SLIGHT SIDE
W
E
CRINKLE CRAGS
5 miles
WHIN RIGG
WETHERLAM
GREAT CARRS
SWIRL HOW
GREY FRIAR
BRIM FELL
CONISTON OLD MAN
DOW CRAG
Brown Pike
HARTER FELL
GREEN CRAG
CAW
Stickle Pike
10 miles
Black Combe
S

Principal Fells

Lakes and Tarns

The summit cairn is not the best place for viewing lakes and tarns, the only sheets of water clearly seen (apart from the sea) being those in the depression south-west below Whin Rigg, and an easterly perambulation of the top will be necessary if it is desired to view the Eskdale tarns. But the *piece de resistance* is Wast Water, which comes amazingly into the picture after a walk of only 35 yards west.

looking down on Wast Water from the summit

Lingmell 2649′

OS grid ref: NY209081

Seathwaite
GREAT GABLE
Wasdale Head
LINGMELL
SCAFELL PIKE
SCAFELL
MILES
0 1 2 3

from the Corridor route, Great End

NATURAL FEATURES

Following the general pattern of the fells, Lingmell has a smooth outline to the south and west but exhibits crags and steep rough slopes to the north and east. The distinction is very marked, the ground falling away precipitously from the gentle western rise to the watershed as though severed by a great knife and laying naked a decaying confusion of crags and arêtes, screes and boulders. On this flank is the huge cleft of Piers Gill, a natural chute for the stones that pour down the thousand-foot declivity, and the finest ravine in the district. Eastwards, a high saddle connects the fell with Scafell Pike, but on other sides steep slopes descend abruptly from the wide top. Lingmell Beck and Lingmell Gill are its streams, both flowing into Wast Water in wide channels and boulder-choked courses, testimony to the fury of the storms and cloudbursts that have riven the fellsides in past years; there is, indeed, a vast area of denudation (Lingmell Scars) on the slope overlooking Brown Tongue, and the devastated lakeside fields below Brackenclose add their witness to the power of the floods that have carried the debris down to the valley.

1 : *The summit*
2 : *Lingmell Col*
3 : *Ridge continuing to Scafell Pike*
4 : *Lingmell Scars*
5 : *Brown Tongue*
6 : *Hollow Stones*
7 : *Wasdale Head*
8 : *Lingmell Beck*
9 : *Lingmell Gill*
10 : *Wast Water*

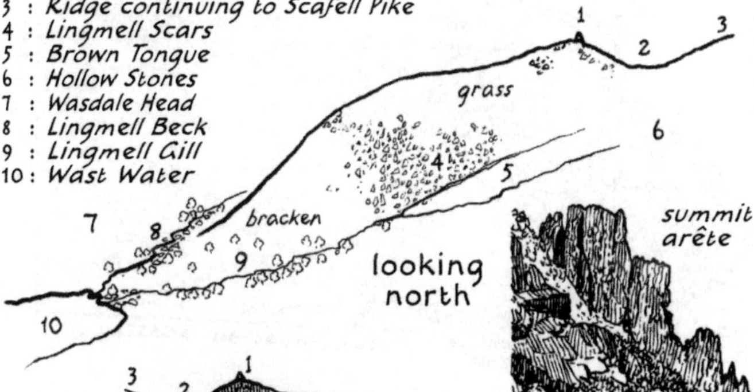

1
2
3
grass
6
4
5
bracken
7
8
9
looking north
10
summit arête

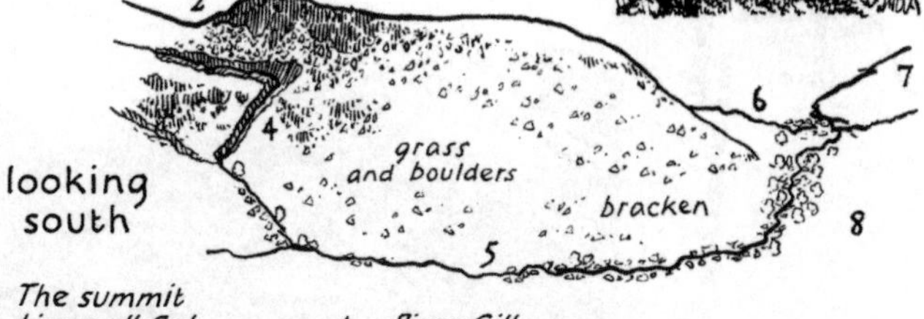

3
2
1
4
grass and boulders
6
7
looking south
bracken
8
5

1 : *The summit*
2 : *Lingmell Col*
3 : *Ridge continuing to Scafell Pike*
4 : *Piers Gill*
5 : *Lingmell Beck*
6 : *Lingmell Gill*
7 : *Wast Water*
8 : *Wasdale Head*

Lingmell 3

MAP

The hamlet of Wasdale Head is traditionally regarded as possessing the highest mountain, the deepest lake, the smallest church and the greatest liar in England, these being Scafell Pike, Wast Water, St. Olaf's Church, and Will Ritson, a former landlord of the Wasdale Head Inn. The inn was originally called the Huntsman's Inn, and later the Wastwater Hotel.

Ritson (1808-1890) paradoxically claimed that he was the greatest liar in England. The World's Biggest Liar competition is held annually in his memory.

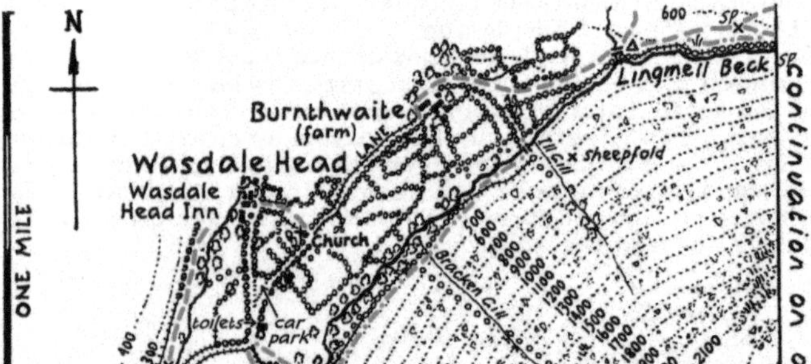

N
ONE MILE
Burnthwaite
(farm)
LANE
Wasdale Head
Wasdale
Head Inn
Church
toilets
car
park
gates
fold
Lingmell Beck
sheepfold
Bracken Gill
Mosedale Beck
GOSFORTH and SANTON BRIDGE ROAD
Wasdale
Campsite
car
park
stile
gate
Lingmell
Scars
Brown Tongue
old
fold
Lingmell Gill
Wast
Water
Brackenclose
(climbing hut)
Wasdale
Head
Hall
(farm)
ESKDALE
via BURNMOOR TARN
continuation on opposite page
continuation SCAFELL 5

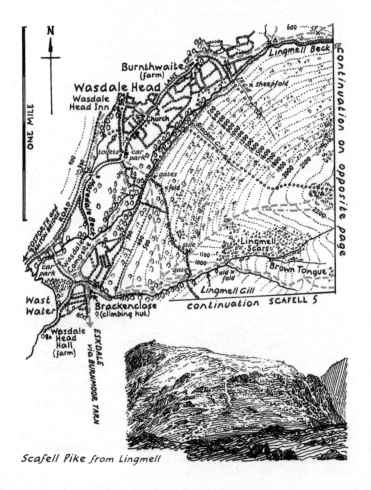

Scafell Pike from Lingmell

MAP

Wasdale Head is the starting point for the ascent of Scafell Pike as part of the Three Peaks Challenge; this is a 24-hour vehicle-supported walk of the highest peaks of Scotland (Ben Nevis), England (Scafell Pike) and Wales (Snowdon).

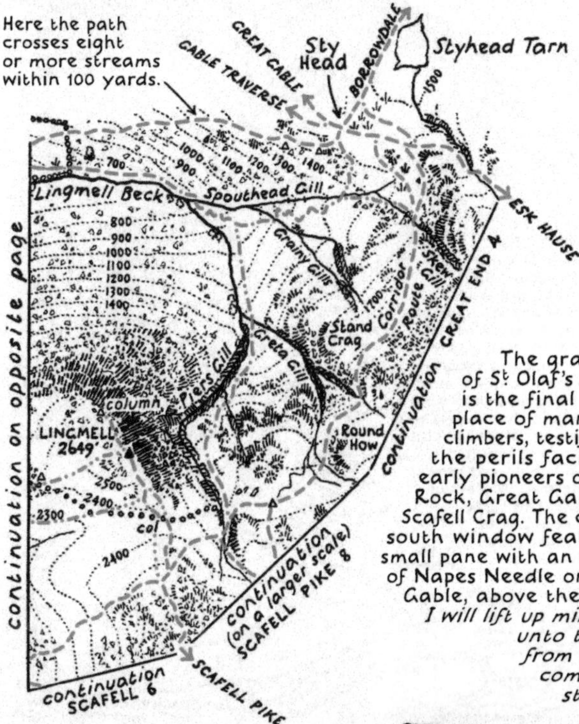
Here the path crosses eight or more streams within 100 yards.
GREAT GABLE
GABLE TRAVERSE
Sty Head
BORROWDALE
Styhead Tarn
1500
700
1000
900
1100
1200
1300
1400
Lingmell Beck
Spouthead Gill
ESK HAUSE
800
900
1000
1100
1200
1300
1400
Grainy Gills
Skew Gill
Corridor Route
1700
GREAT END 4
continuation
Stand Crag
Greta Gill
Piers Gill
column
LINGMELL 2649'
Round How
continuation
2500
2400
2300
col
2400
continuation (on a larger scale) SCAFELL PIKE 8
continuation on opposite page
continuation SCAFELL 6
SCAFELL PIKE

The graveyard of St. Olaf's Church is the final resting place of many rock climbers, testifying to the perils facing the early pioneers on Pillar Rock, Great Gable and Scafell Crag. The church's south window features a small pane with an etching of Napes Needle on Great Gable, above the words: *I will lift up mine eyes unto the hills from whence cometh my strength.*

Mickledore and Scafell Crag from Lingmell

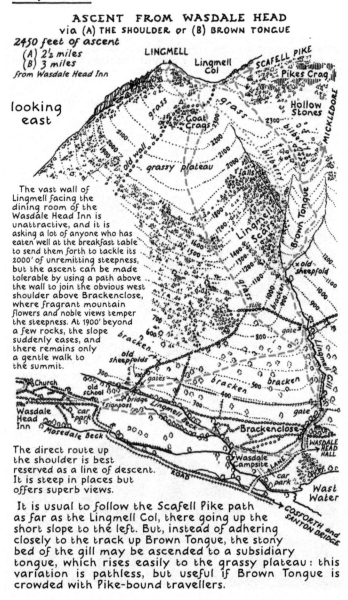

ASCENT FROM WASDALE HEAD
via (A) THE SHOULDER or (B) BROWN TONGUE

2450 feet of ascent
(A) 2½ miles
(B) 3 miles
from Wasdale Head Inn

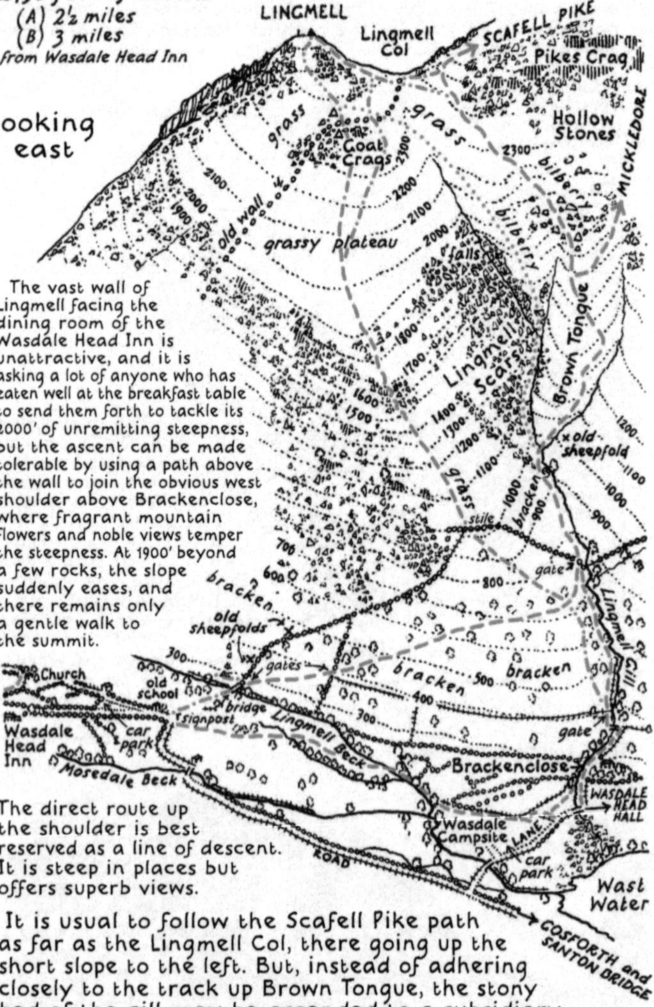
looking east
LINGMELL
Lingmell Col
SCAFELL PIKE
Pikes Crag
Hollow Stones
MICKLEDORE
grass
Goat Crags
old wall
grassy plateau
bilberry
falls
Lingmell Scars
Brown Tongue
old sheepfold
stile
bracken
gate
Lingmell Gill
old sheepfolds
gates
Church
old school
bridge
signpost
Lingmell Beck
car park
Wasdale Head Inn
Mosedale Beck
Brackenclose
WASDALE HEAD HALL
Wasdale Campsite
LANE
ROAD
car park
Wast Water
GOSFORTH and SANTON BRIDGE
2300
2200
2100
2000
1900
1800
1700
1600
1500
1400
1300
1200
1100
1000
900
800
700
600
500
400
300

The vast wall of Lingmell facing the dining room of the Wasdale Head Inn is unattractive, and it is asking a lot of anyone who has eaten well at the breakfast table to send them forth to tackle its 2000′ of unremitting steepness, but the ascent can be made tolerable by using a path above the wall to join the obvious west shoulder above Brackenclose, where fragrant mountain flowers and noble views temper the steepness. At 1900′ beyond a few rocks, the slope suddenly eases, and there remains only a gentle walk to the summit.

The direct route up the shoulder is best reserved as a line of descent. It is steep in places but offers superb views.

It is usual to follow the Scafell Pike path as far as the Lingmell Col, there going up the short slope to the left. But, instead of adhering closely to the track up Brown Tongue, the stony bed of the gill may be ascended to a subsidiary tongue, which rises easily to the grassy plateau: this variation is pathless, but useful if Brown Tongue is crowded with Pike-bound travellers.

ASCENT FROM WASDALE HEAD
via PIERS GILL
2450 feet of ascent : 3½ miles (from Wasdale Head Inn)

From the *col* the top of Lingmell is easily reached by a grass slope behind the edge of the crags.

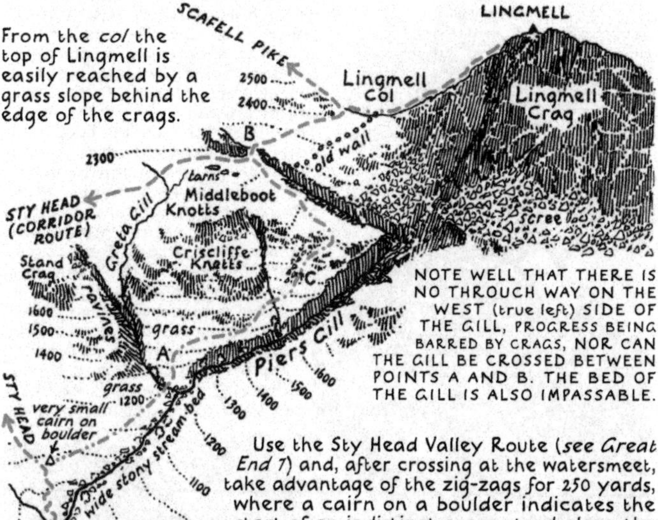
LINGMELL
SCAFELL PIKE
Lingmell Col
Lingmell Crag
2500
2400
2300
B
old wall
tarns
Middleboot Knotts
STY HEAD (CORRIDOR ROUTE)
Greta Gill
Criscliffe Knotts
scree
Stand Crag
C
ravines
1600
1500
1400
grass
A
Piers Gill
1600
1500
1400
1300
1200
grass
1200
STY HEAD
very small cairn on boulder
wide stony stream bed
1100
1000
a beautiful watersmeet
pools and cascades
900
800
800
700
STY HEAD (direct route)
600
SP
500
Lingmell Beck
looking south
bracken
moraines
SP
FB
Burnthwaite
500
Wasdale Head
WASDALE HEAD INN ½

NOTE WELL THAT THERE IS NO THROUGH WAY ON THE WEST (true left) SIDE OF THE GILL, PROGRESS BEING BARRED BY CRAGS, NOR CAN THE GILL BE CROSSED BETWEEN POINTS A AND B. THE BED OF THE GILL IS ALSO IMPASSABLE.

Use the Sty Head Valley Route (*see Great End 7*) and, after crossing at the watersmeet, take advantage of the zig-zags for 250 yards, where a cairn on a boulder indicates the start of an indistinct grassy trod along the east bank. A little doubt is likely to arise at point C, where a steepish wall of broken crag needs to be negotiated, but there is easy scrambling only and no real difficulty in finding a way up. The edge of the great ravine may be, and should be, visited at opportune places for the striking views into its depths — *but extreme care is necessary, as the sheer walls are badly eroded and dangerously loose.*

The 'very small cairn' on a boulder at the top of the zig-zags is sometimes just a stone!

The north face of Lingmell and the great ravine of Piers Gill make as wild a scene as will be found anywhere, and the walk here described is impressive. But the way is virtually pathless alongside the gill, and unreliably cairned; clear weather is advisable for ascent and essential for descent by this route.

THE SUMMIT

Summit cairns are welcome sights, but they are seldom objects of beauty or admiration. Here, however, on the highest point of Lingmell, was one of singular elegance, a graceful ten-foot spire that quite put to shame the squat and inartistic edifice crowning the neighbouring very superior Scafell Pike. The cairn illustrated has been replaced by one much broader, but just as well built, while 250 yards to the north-west is a column looking much like the one illustrated. Both cairns are poised on the brink of a great precipice.

The summit area is stony, but not too stony to hamper progress unduly, and a short exploration along the top of the cliff northwards earns a reward of magnificent views.

DESCENTS:

TO WASDALE HEAD: The shoulder route is a quick and easy way down, with excellent views right left and centre, and much better than the longer alternative *via* Lingmell Col and the Brown Tongue path. *In mist* the latter is to be preferred, as the shoulder at first is too broad to give direction naturally and the path is too sketchy to be a reliable guide.

TO BORROWDALE: The only way is to join the Corridor Route just beyond Lingmell Col.

RIDGE ROUTE

To SCAFELL PIKE, 3210′:
⅞ mile : SSE
Depression (Lingmell Col) at 2370′
850 feet of ascent

A tedious half-hour.

With steep ground on the left hand descend the grass slope following a path to Lingmell Col, where cross the broken wall and join the cairned path coming up from Brown Tongue; this is distinct over stones and boulders to the summit.

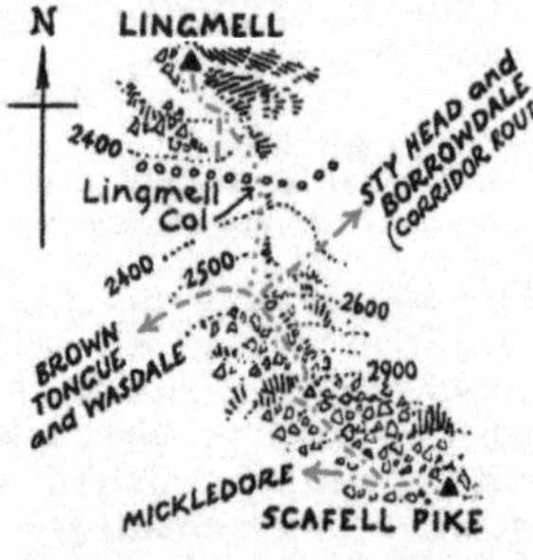
HALF A MILE
N
LINGMELL
2400
Lingmell Col
STY HEAD and BORROWDALE (CORRIDOR ROUTE)
2400
2500
2600
BROWN TONGUE and WASDALE
2900
MICKLEDORE
SCAFELL PIKE

THE VIEW

Scafell Pike dominates the scene, but from this side is the dullest of mountains; Scafell is better, but the grouping of the western fells around Mosedale is best of all. The views of Borrowdale and down Wast Water to the coastal plain and the sea are also good.

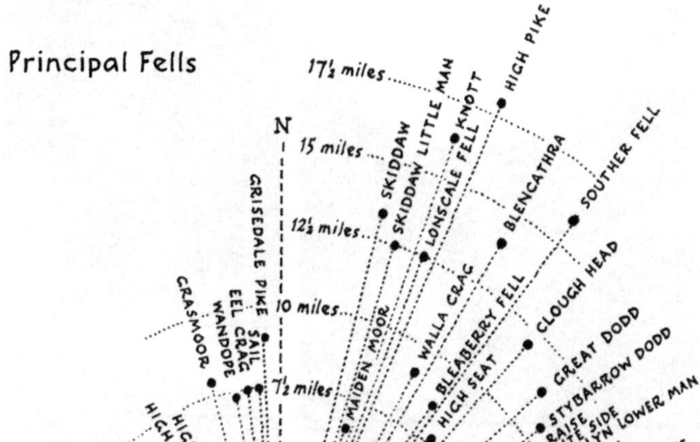
Principal Fells
N
S
W
E
17½ miles
15 miles
12½ miles
10 miles
7½ miles
5 miles
2½ miles
HIGH PIKE
KNOTT
SKIDDAW LITTLE MAN
SKIDDAW
LONSCALE FELL
BLENCATHRA
SOUTHER FELL
CLOUGH HEAD
GREAT DODD
STYBARROW DODD
RAISE
WHITE SIDE
HELVELLYN LOWER MAN
HELVELLYN
NETHERMOST PIKE
DOLLYWAGGON PIKE
WALLA CRAG
BLEABERRY FELL
HIGH SEAT
MAIDEN MOOR
BASE BROWN
GLARAMARA
GREAT GABLE
GREAT END
Broad Crag
SCAFELL PIKE
SCAFELL
GRISEDALE PIKE
SAIL
EEL CRAG
WANDOPE
GRASMOOR
HIGH CRAG
HIGH STILE
PILLAR
KIRK FELL
SCOAT FELL
RED PIKE
HAYCOCK
CAW FELL
YEWBARROW
SEATALLAN
MIDDLE FELL
ILLGILL HEAD

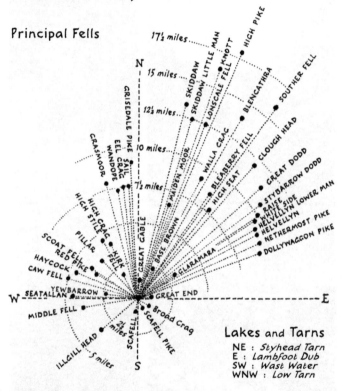

Lakes and Tarns

NE : *Styhead Tarn*
E : *Lambfoot Dub*
SW : *Wast Water*
WNW : *Low Tarn*

Two features of the view deserve special mention. The first is the surprising aspect of Great Gable across the deep gulf of Lingmell Beck (seen more fully from the summit ridge north of the main cairn), the eye being deceived into seeing its half-mile of height as quite perpendicular: a remarkable picture. The other is the astonishing downward view into the stony depths of Piers Gill, a thousand-foot drop which again is not nearly so vertical as it appears at first sight to the startled beholder.

Piers Gill

above
the upper section (looking down from the Corridor Route)

right
the lower section (looking up)

top right
pinnacles and spires in the gill

Great Gable from Lingmell

Lingmoor Fell 1539′

OS grid ref: NY303046

from Elter Water

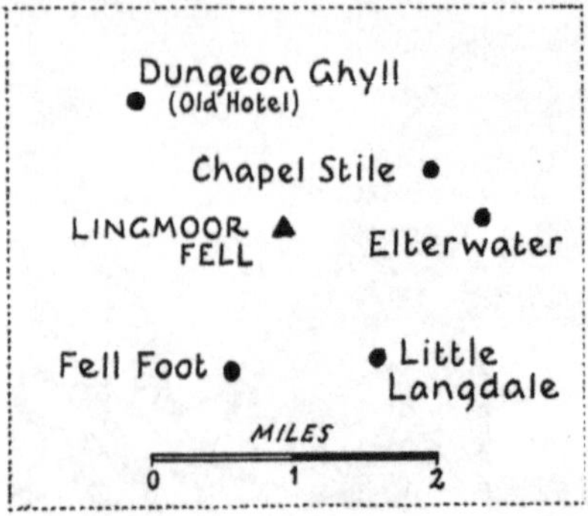
Dungeon Ghyll
(Old Hotel)
Chapel Stile
LINGMOOR FELL
Elterwater
Fell Foot
Little Langdale
MILES
0
1
2

Oak Howe Needle

NATURAL FEATURES

A crescent-shaped ridge of high ground rises to the west from Elterwater's pleasant pastures, climbs to a well defined summit, a fine vantage point, and then curves northwards as it descends to valley-level near Dungeon Ghyll. Within the crescent lies Great Langdale, the longer outside curve sloping down into Little Langdale and the Blea Tarn depression. The mass is Lingmoor Fell, so named because of the extensive zone of heather clothing the northern flanks below the summit. The fell has contributed generously to the prosperity of the surrounding valleys, for not only has it nurtured the sheep but it has also been quarried extensively for many generations, yielding a very beautiful and durable green stone. Bracken and heather, some ragged patches of juniper and well timbered estate woods, many crags and a delectable little tarn, all combine to make this fell a colourful addition to the varied attractions of the Langdale area.

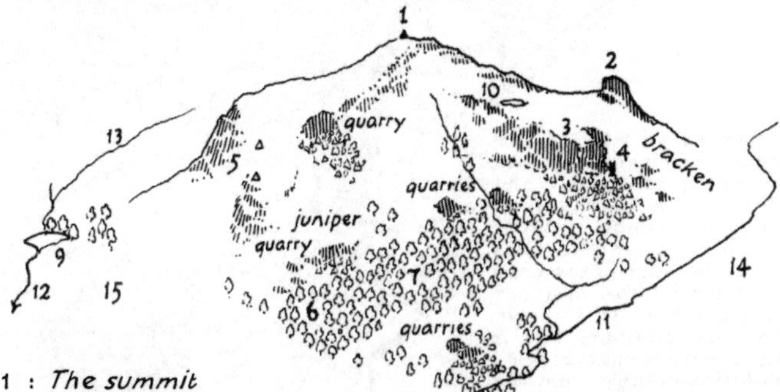
1
2
10
quarry
13
3
4
bracken
5
quarries
juniper
quarry
9
7
14
12
15
6
11
quarries
8

looking west

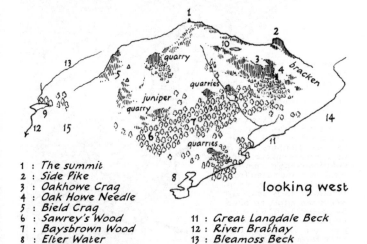

1 : *The summit*
2 : *Side Pike*
3 : *Oakhowe Crag*
4 : *Oak Howe Needle*
5 : *Bield Crag*
6 : *Sawrey's Wood*
7 : *Baysbrown Wood*
8 : *Elter Water*
9 : *Little Langdale Tarn*
10 : *Lingmoor Tarn*
11 : *Great Langdale Beck*
12 : *River Brathay*
13 : *Bleamoss Beck*
14 : *Great Langdale*
15 : *Little Langdale*

Side Pike

The rocky Side Pike (NY293054) is one of the most impressive of Lakeland's subsidiary summits, and at 1188' is not an insignificant height. More visitors to its summit than not would agree this is one of the finest viewpoints of the head of Great Langdale.

Lingmoor Fell 3

MAP

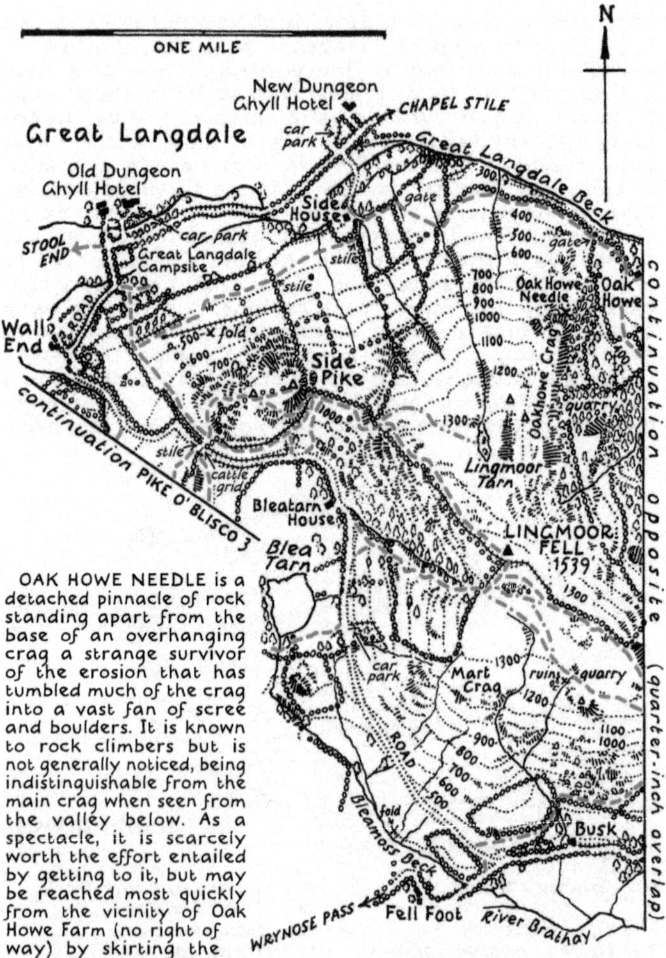

ONE MILE
N
New Dungeon Ghyll Hotel
CHAPEL STILE
Great Langdale
car park
Great Langdale Beck
Old Dungeon Ghyll Hotel
Side House
gate
STOOL END
car park
Great Langdale Campsite
stile
stile
Oak Howe Needle
Oak Howe
ROAD
Wall End
fold
Side Pike
Oakhowe Crag
quarry
continuation PIKE O' BLISCO 3
stile
cattle grid
Lingmoor Tarn
Bleatarn House
LINGMOOR FELL 1539'
Blea Tarn
car park
Mart Crag
ruin
quarry
ROAD
Bleamoss Beck
fold
Busk
WRYNOSE PASS
Fell Foot
River Brathay
continuation opposite (quarter-inch overlap)

OAK HOWE NEEDLE is a detached pinnacle of rock standing apart from the base of an overhanging crag a strange survivor of the erosion that has tumbled much of the crag into a vast fan of scree and boulders. It is known to rock climbers but is not generally noticed, being indistinguishable from the main crag when seen from the valley below. As a spectacle, it is scarcely worth the effort entailed by getting to it, but may be reached most quickly from the vicinity of Oak Howe Farm (no right of way) by skirting the scree slope on its west side. Locating the Needle from the top of Lingmoor Fell is a dangerous and difficult proceeding, for it cannot be seen from the heathery slope above the crag, which breaks away suddenly in a vertical cliff: the safest course is to descend the east bank of the beck issuing from Lingmoor Tarn until a big area of juniper is seen on the right, whence by walking eastwards above it, a small bracken col is reached — and there, directly in front and quite close, is Oak Howe Needle.

MAP

Great Langdale is probably the most frequented valley in the district, with a heavy inflow of visitors summer and winter alike, most of them bound for Dungeon Ghyll. In former years the whole of the traffic, both on foot and a wheel, was confined to the one road in the valley, on the north side, while the south side, along the base of Lingmoor Fell, seldom saw a soul. In 1960 the author commented on this and said how much pleasanter it would be if there were public rights of way linking Baysbrown, Oak Howe, Side House and Wall End. Today there is a public bridleway from Baysbrown to Oak Howe, a public footpath from Oak Howe to Side House, and a permitted footpath from Side House to within a quarter of a mile of Wall End.

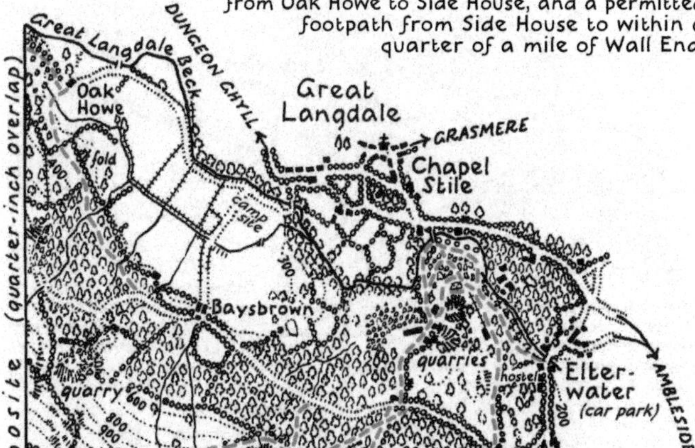
continuation opposite (quarter-inch overlap)
Great Langdale Beck
DUNGEON GHYLL
Oak Howe
fold
camp site
Great Langdale
GRASMERE
Chapel Stile
Baysbrown
quarries
hostel
Elter-water
(car park)
AMBLESIDE 4
CONISTON 4¾
quarry
quarry
quarry
Bield Crag
Bield
Dale End
Little Langdale
Three Shires Inn
COLWITH 1
Little Langdale Tarn
Slater Bridge
R. Brathay
200
300
400
500
600
700
800
900
1000
1100
1200

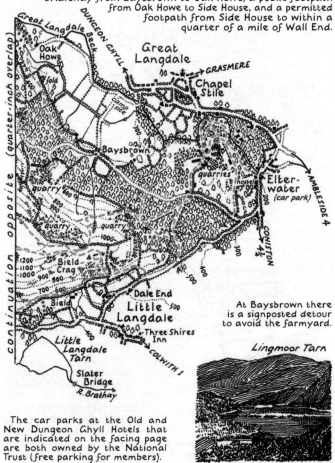

At Baysbrown there is a signposted detour to avoid the farmyard.

Lingmoor Tarn

The car parks at the Old and New Dungeon Ghyll Hotels that are indicated on the facing page are both owned by the National Trust (free parking for members).

ASCENT FROM DUNGEON GHYLL

1250 feet of ascent : 2 miles

(Add 250 feet and ½ mile if Side Pike is included)

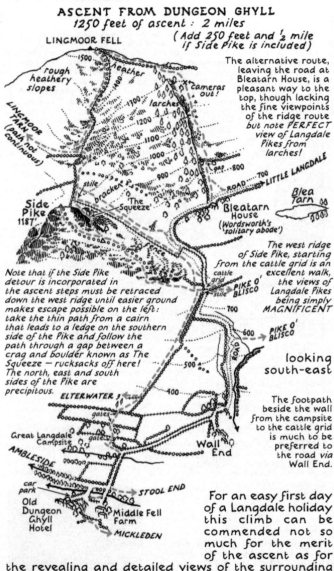

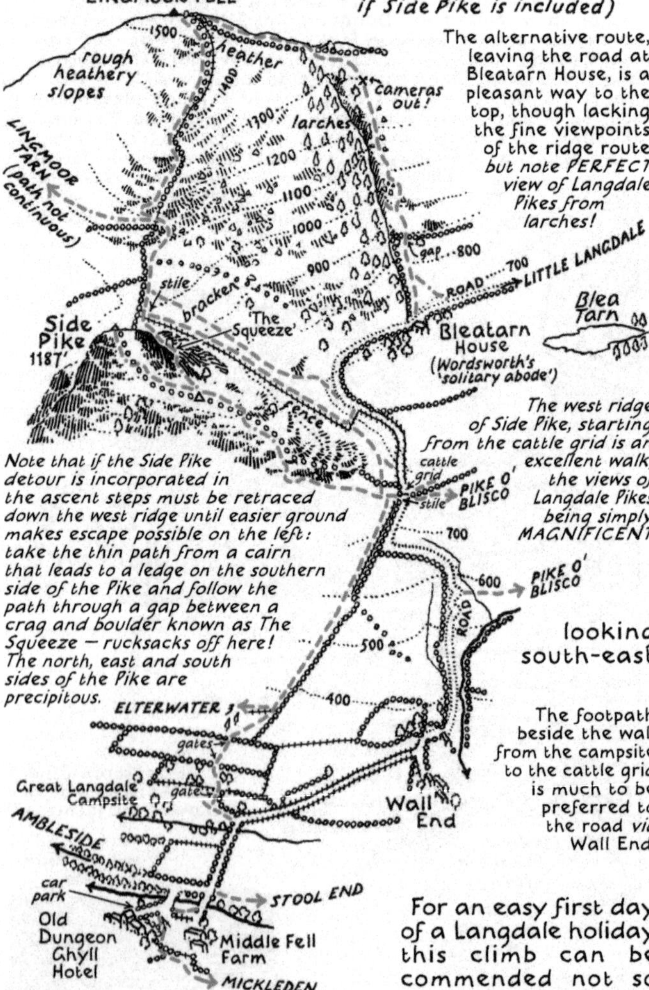
LINGMOOR FELL
1500
1400
1300
1200
1100
1000
900
800
700
600
500
400
rough heathery slopes
heather
cameras out!
larches
LINGMOOR TARN (path not continuous)
gap
stile
bracken
'The Squeeze'
Side Pike 1187'
fence
ROAD → LITTLE LANGDALE
Blea Tarn
Bleatarn House
(Wordsworth's 'solitary abode')
cattle grid
stile
PIKE O' BLISCO
ROAD
looking south-east
ELTERWATER 3
gates
gate
Great Langdale Campsite
AMBLESIDE
car park
Old Dungeon Ghyll Hotel
STOOL END
Middle Fell Farm
MICKLEDEN
Wall End

The alternative route, leaving the road at Bleatarn House, is a pleasant way to the top, though lacking the fine viewpoints of the ridge route *but note PERFECT view of Langdale Pikes from larches!*

The west ridge of Side Pike, starting from the cattle grid is an excellent walk, the views of Langdale Pikes being simply MAGNIFICENT

Note that if the Side Pike detour is incorporated in the ascent steps must be retraced down the west ridge until easier ground makes escape possible on the left: take the thin path from a cairn that leads to a ledge on the southern side of the Pike and follow the path through a gap between a crag and boulder known as The Squeeze — rucksacks off here! The north, east and south sides of the Pike are precipitous.

The footpath beside the wall from the campsite to the cattle grid is much to be preferred to the road *via* Wall End.

For an easy first day of a Langdale holiday this climb can be commended not so much for the merit of the ascent as for the revealing and detailed views of the surrounding giants — worthy objectives for later days of the holiday.

'The Squeeze'
x

Side Pike
from the ridge running up to Lingmoor Fell

Side Pike is accessible to the walker by its west ridge only, and there is no other safe way off. When descending from the cairn do not be tempted by a track going, down eastwards: this ends suddenly above a vertical drop, with easy ground tantalisingly close, but out of reach. On the drawing above, this dangerous trap is seen directly below the X. The route of the path that utilises a ledge on the southern face and the location of The Squeeze is indicated above; this is the only chink in Side Pike's rocky armour on this side.

Langdale Pikes
from Side Pike

1 : *Pike o' Stickle*
2 : *Loft Crag*
3 : *Thorn Crag*
4 : *Harrison Stickle*
5 : *Pavey Ark*

1
2
3
4
5

ASCENTS FROM ELTERWATER AND CHAPEL STILE

1350 feet of ascent : 2½ miles

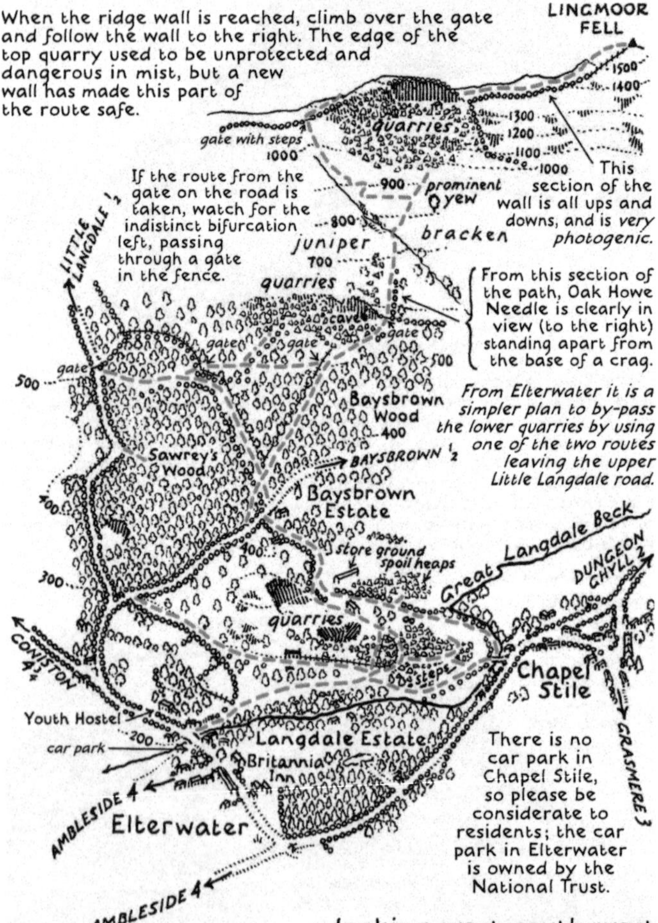
LINGMOOR FELL
1500
1400
1300
1200
1100
1000
quarries
gate with steps
1000
900
prominent yew
800
bracken
juniper
700
quarries
cave
gate
gate
gate
500
gate
500
LITTLE LANGDALE ½
Baysbrown Wood
400
Sawrey's Wood
BAYSBROWN ½
Baysbrown Estate
400
400
store ground
spoil heaps
300
Great Langdale Beck
DUNGEON GHYLL 2
quarries
CONISTON 4¼
steps
Chapel Stile
Youth Hostel
200
car park
Langdale Estate
Britannia Inn
GRASMERE 3
AMBLESIDE 4
Elterwater
AMBLESIDE 4

When the ridge wall is reached, climb over the gate and follow the wall to the right. The edge of the top quarry used to be unprotected and dangerous in mist, but a new wall has made this part of the route safe.

If the route from the gate on the road is taken, watch for the indistinct bifurcation left, passing through a gate in the fence.

This section of the wall is all ups and downs, and is *very photogenic.*

From this section of the path, Oak Howe Needle is clearly in view (to the right) standing apart from the base of a crag.

From Elterwater it is a simpler plan to by-pass the lower quarries by using one of the two routes leaving the upper Little Langdale road.

There is no car park in Chapel Stile, so please be considerate to residents; the car park in Elterwater is owned by the National Trust.

looking west-south-west

The lower quarries are a labyrinth of paths and cart tracks, confusing on a first visit. The extensive spoil heaps are not pretty, the many trees being an ineffective screen; nevertheless, this is an interesting and attractive approach to the ridge.

ASCENT FROM LITTLE LANGDALE

1100 feet of ascent : 1½ miles (from Dale End)

The quarry track may be followed (easy walking) to its terminus at some ruins, disused workings, whence the same direction may be continued along a shallow trough to join the Bleatarn House route at a wall or the track may be left when it turns towards the ridge wall beyond the big cairn above Bield Crag, and the ridge then followed to the top. Watch for the junction or it will be missed.

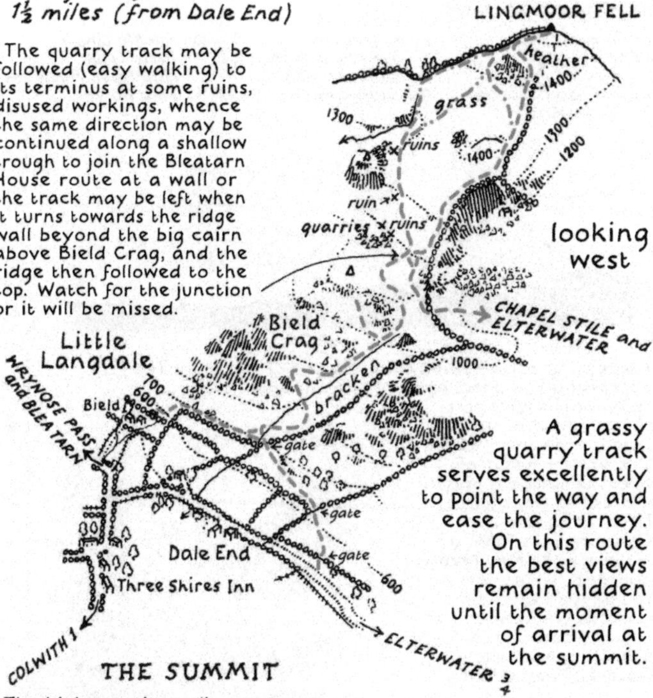
LINGMOOR FELL
heather
1400
grass
1300
ruins
1400
1300
1200
ruin
quarries
ruins
looking west
CHAPEL STILE and ELTERWATER
Bield Crag
Little Langdale
WRYNOSE PASS and BLEA TARN
700
600
Bield
bracken
1000
gate
gate
gate
Dale End
Three Shires Inn
600
COLWITH 1
ELTERWATER 3/4

A grassy quarry track serves excellently to point the way and ease the journey. On this route the best views remain hidden until the moment of arrival at the summit.

THE SUMMIT

The highest point, adjacent to an angle in the summit wall, is a stony mound superimposed on a dome dark with heather (Brown How), and owns a large cairn. 150 yards east, along the line of a fence, are the remains of a second cairn, a good viewpoint.

DESCENTS: Routes of ascent may be reversed, with the old wall as guide initially. *In mist*, when descending the south-east ridge, care should be taken near the quarry; a new wall makes this section much safer than before.

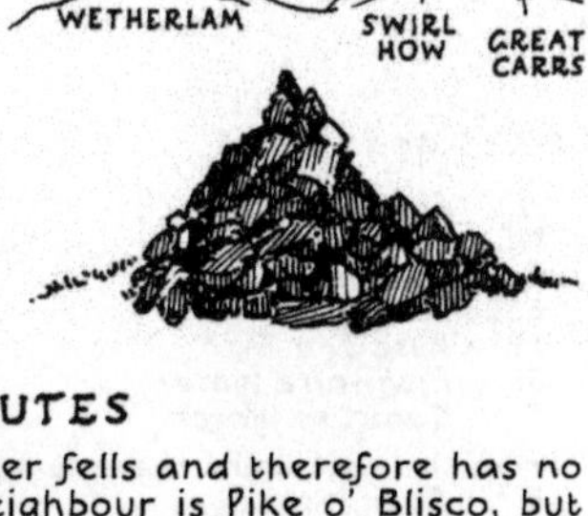
The Coniston Fells
WETHERLAM
SWIRL HOW
GREAT CARRS

RIDGE ROUTES

Lingmoor Fell is isolated from other fells and therefore has no connecting ridges. Its nearest neighbour is Pike o' Blisco, but the considerable descent to the Bleatarn road makes a climb therefrom virtually a complete ascent.

THE VIEW

looking north-west

1 : *Pike o' Stickle*	6 : *High Raise*	10: *Stickle Ghyll*
2 : *Loft Crag*	7 : *Sergeant Man*	11 : *Tarn Crag*
3 : *Thorn Crag*	8 : *Gimmer Crag*	12: *Middlefell Buttress*
4 : *Harrison Stickle*	9 : *Dungeon Ghyll*	13 : *Pike Howe*
5 : *Pavey Ark*		

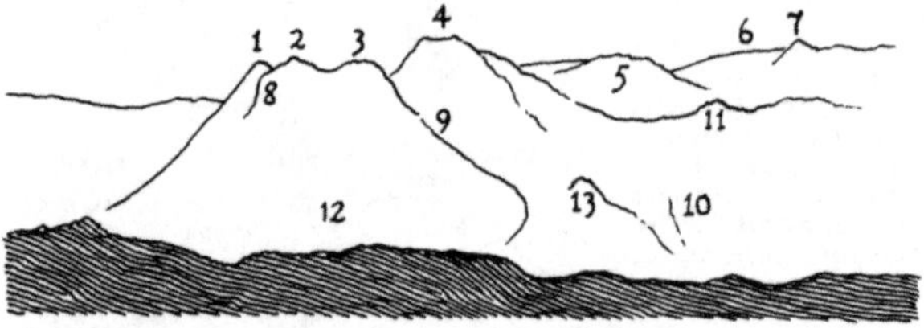
1
2
3
4
5
6
7
8
9
10
11
12
13

There is no better place than the top of Lingmoor Fell for appraising the geography of the Langdale district. From this viewpoint the surround of rugged heights towering above the valley head of Great Langdale is most impressive, while across Little Langdale the Coniston fells form a massive wall. In marked contrast is the low countryside extending towards Windermere, richly wooded and sparkling with the waters of many lakes.

Principal Fells

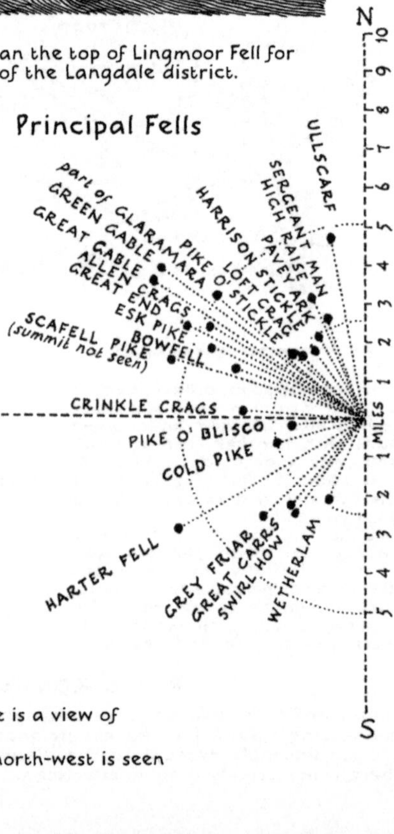
N
ULLSCARF
SERGEANT MAN
HIGH RAISE
PAVEY ARK
HARRISON STICKLE
LOFT CRAG
PIKE O' STICKLE
part of GLARAMARA
GREEN GABLE
GREAT GABLE
ALLEN CRAGS
GREAT END
ESK PIKE
BOWFELL
SCAFELL PIKE
(summit not seen)
W
CRINKLE CRAGS
PIKE O' BLISCO
COLD PIKE
HARTER FELL
GREY FRIAR
GREAT CARRS
SWIRL HOW
WETHERLAM
MILES
10 9 8 7 6 5 4 3 2 1
1 2 3 4 5
S

Lakes and Tarns

N : *Lingmoor Tarn*
NE : *Lang How Tarn*
E : *Loughrigg Tarn*
ESE: *Windermere*
SE : *Wise Een Tarn*
SE : *Esthwaite Water*
S : *Coniston Water*

From the east cairn there is a view of
E : *Elter Water*

From the wall 250 yards north-west is seen
W : *Blea Tarn*

THE VIEW

Bowfell

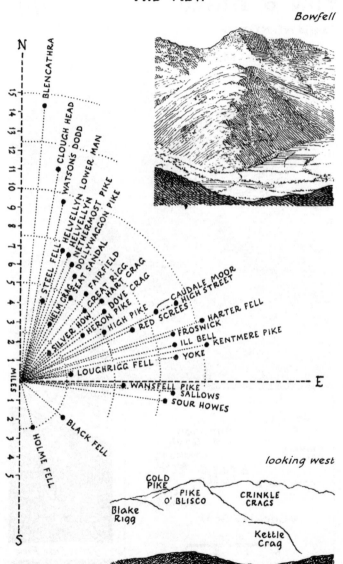

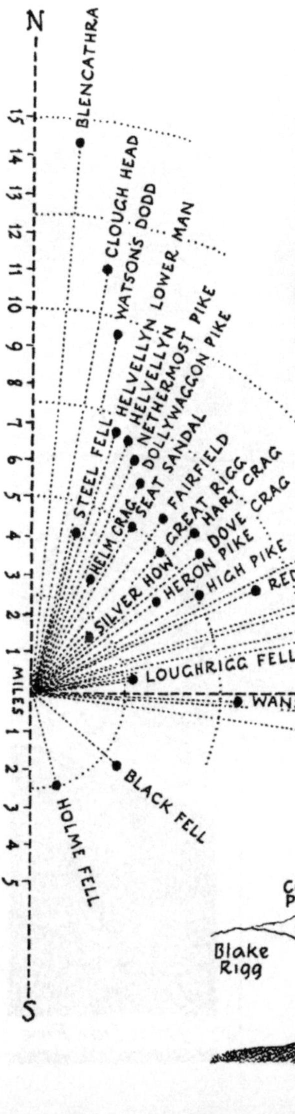
N
S
E
MILES
15
14
13
12
11
10
9
8
7
6
5
4
3
2
1
1
2
3
4
5
BLENCATHRA
CLOUGH HEAD
WATSON'S DODD
HELVELLYN LOWER MAN
HELVELLYN
NETHERMOST PIKE
DOLLYWAGGON PIKE
STEEL FELL
SEAT SANDAL
FAIRFIELD
HELM CRAG
GREAT RIGG
HART CRAG
DOVE CRAG
SILVER HOW
HERON PIKE
HIGH PIKE
RED SCREES
CAUDALE MOOR
HIGH STREET
HARTER FELL
FROSWICK
ILL BELL
KENTMERE PIKE
YOKE
LOUGHRIGG FELL
WANSFELL PIKE
SALLOWS
SOUR HOWES
BLACK FELL
HOLME FELL

looking west

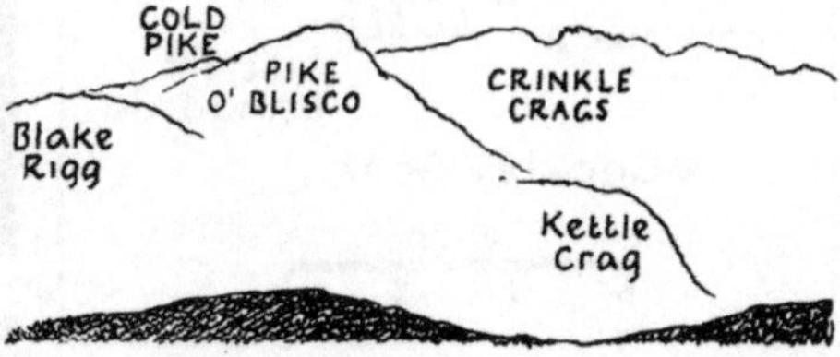
COLD PIKE
PIKE O' BLISCO
CRINKLE CRAGS
Blake Rigg
Kettle Crag

Pike o' Blisco 2313'

OS grid ref: NY271042

Sunday name: Pike OF Blisco

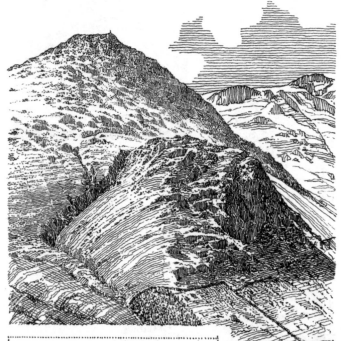

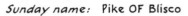

BOWFELL
Dungeon Ghyll
CRINKLE CRAGS
LINGMOOR FELL
PIKE O' BLISCO
COLD PIKE
Little Langdale
Cockley Beck
MILES
0
1
2
3

from Side Pike

NATURAL FEATURES

A mountain has added merit if its highest point can be seen from the valley below, instead of being hidden beyond receding upper slopes as is often the case, for then the objective is clear to the climber, there is no deception about height or steepness, and the full stature from base to summit can readily be comprehended. Such a mountain is Pike o' Blisco, with a well constructed cairn plainly in view from the floor of Great Langdale and perched high above the steep and rugged flank that forms a massive south wall to the side valley of Oxendale. This peak has great character, for shapeliness and a sturdy strength combine well in its appearance, and that splendid cairn etched against the sky is at once an invitation and a challenge — while the man has no blood in his veins who does not respond eagerly to its fine-sounding swashbuckling name, savouring so much of buccaneers and the Spanish Main. There are higher summits all around, some of far greater altitude; but height alone counts for nothing, and Pike o' Blisco would hold its own in any company.

Easy routes to the top can be worked out between the crags, which are in abundance. Kettle Crag above Wall End, and Blake Rigg towering over Blea Tarn, are notable. Except for minor runnels near the top of Wrynose Pass, all streams from the fell join ultimately in the River Brathay.

1 : *The summit*
2 : *Black Wars*
3 : *Kettle Crag*
4 : *Blake Rigg*
5 : *Long Crag*
6 : *Little Horse Crag*
7 : *Great Horse Crag*
8 : *Hollin Crag*
9 : *Castle Howe*
10 : *Black Crag*
11 : *Widdy Gill*
12 : *Wrynose Beck*
13 : *River Brathay*
14 : *Blea Tarn*
15 : *Redacre Gill*
16 : *Oxendale Beck*
17 : *Wrynose Pass*

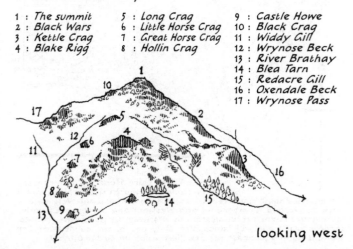

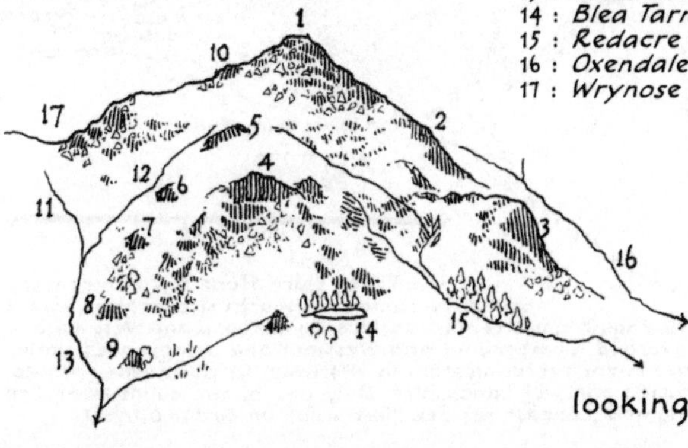
1
2
3
4
5
6
7
8
9
10
11
12
13
14
15
16
17

looking west

Pike o' Blisco 3

MAP

Stool End is a traditional Lakeland farm with shire horses and chickens in the yard. It is the starting point of popular routes to Bowfell and Crinkle Crags as well as Pike o' Blisco.

Old Dungeon Ghyll Hotel
car park
AMBLESIDE
Great Langdale Beck
farm road
Great Langdale Campsite
Stool End
BOWFELL
400
500
ELTERWATER 3
Wall End
footbridge
800
700
fold
Oxendale Beck
Redacre Gill
600
ROAD
500
600
700
800
900
1000
1100
1200
1300
1400
1500
Kettle Crag
1000
1100
1200
1300
Brown Howe
Browney Gill
PIKE O' BLISCO 2313'
1600
Black Wars
tarn
1500
1600
2100
2000
1900
1800
1700
Red Tarn
Black Crag
Long Scar
fold
Long Crag
fold
Blake Rigg
1600
Little Horse Crag
Great Horse Crag
Hollin Crag
1800
1700
1600
1500
1400
1300
1200
1100
1000
Wrynose Bridge
ROAD
Widdy Gill
Three Shire Stone
ROAD
Wrynose Pass
continuation CRINKLE CRAGS 4
continuation opposite
continuation COLD PIKE 2
N
DUDDON VALLEY
ONE MILE

The Three Shire Stone is a 19th century boundary stone that marks the location where the historic English counties of Lancashire, Cumberland and Westmorland once converged. Cumberland and Westmorland disappeared under local government reorganisation in 1974 when Cumbria was created, incorporating parts of Lancashire. Only one of the counties on the stone is named (Lancashire). See illustration on *Great Carrs 3*.

Blea Tarn's once well wooded western shore is now denuded of many of its trees, although a fringe has been left by the water's edge (including the pines that have graced many a thousand photographs).

Once rhododendrons were rampant in this area, but now most of them have been cut down, leaving only the stumps. Larches and spruces are more recent additions to the scene.

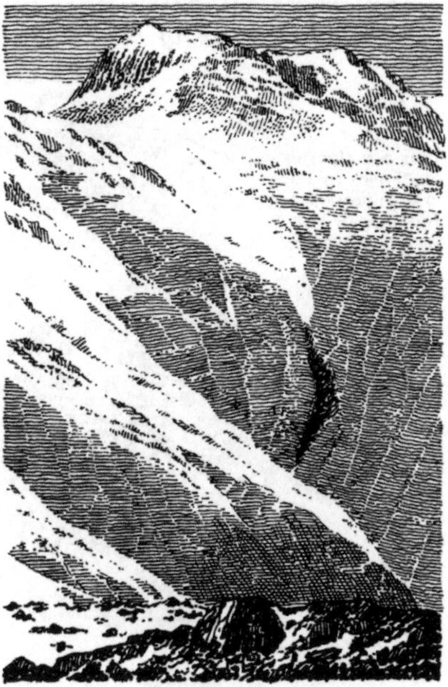

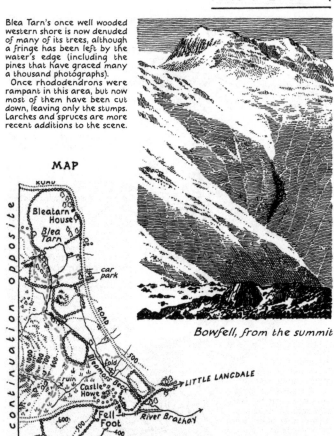

Bowfell, from the summit

MAP

ROAD
Bleatarn House
Blea Tarn
car park
ROAD
500
fold
Bleamoss Beck
LITTLE LANGDALE
ruin
Castle Howe
Fell Foot
River Brathay
1000
800
700
600
600
500
400
continuation opposite

Fell Foot was once an inn, provided for the benefit of people crossing the passes of Wrynose and Hardknott. In 1958 it was acquired by the National Trust. Behind the house is a Viking 'thing mount' or 'ting mound' where open air meetings took place more than a thousand years ago.

Kettle Crag

ASCENT FROM DUNGEON GHYLL (via WALL END)
2100 feet of ascent : 2¼ miles

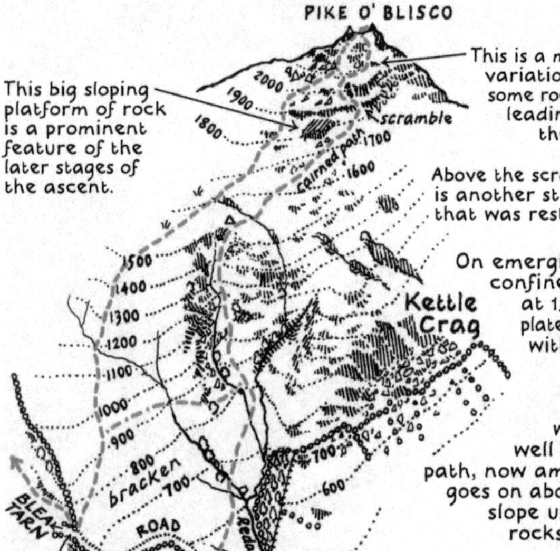
PIKE O' BLISCO
2000
1900
1800
scramble
1700
cairned path
1600
1500
1400
1300
1200
1100
1000
900
800
bracken
700
Kettle Crag
700
600
BLEA TARN
ROAD
cattle grid
Redacre Gill
500
600
500
400
Wall End
ROAD
STOOL END
MICKLEDEN
Great Langdale Campsite
AMBLESIDE
car park
Old Dungeon Ghyll Hotel

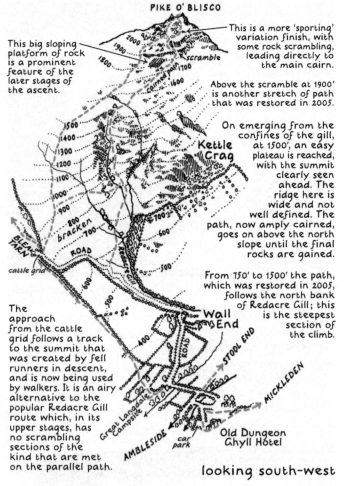

This big sloping platform of rock is a prominent feature of the later stages of the ascent.

This is a more 'sporting' variation finish, with some rock scrambling, leading directly to the main cairn.

Above the scramble at 1900' is another stretch of path that was restored in 2005.

On emerging from the confines of the gill, at 1500', an easy plateau is reached, with the summit clearly seen ahead. The ridge here is wide and not well defined. The path, now amply cairned, goes on above the north slope until the final rocks are gained.

From 750' to 1500' the path, which was restored in 2005, follows the north bank of Redacre Gill; this is the steepest section of the climb.

The approach from the cattle grid follows a track to the summit that was created by fell runners in descent, and is now being used by walkers. It is an airy alternative to the popular Redacre Gill route which, in its upper stages, has no scrambling sections of the kind that are met on the parallel path.

looking south-west

This is a good natural route, much easier than is suggested by the formidable appearance of the objective. The well used path by the gill is generally excellent underfoot. The variation from the cattle grid is an interesting and quiet alternative.

ASCENT FROM DUNGEON GHYLL (via STOOL END)
2100 feet of ascent : 2½ miles

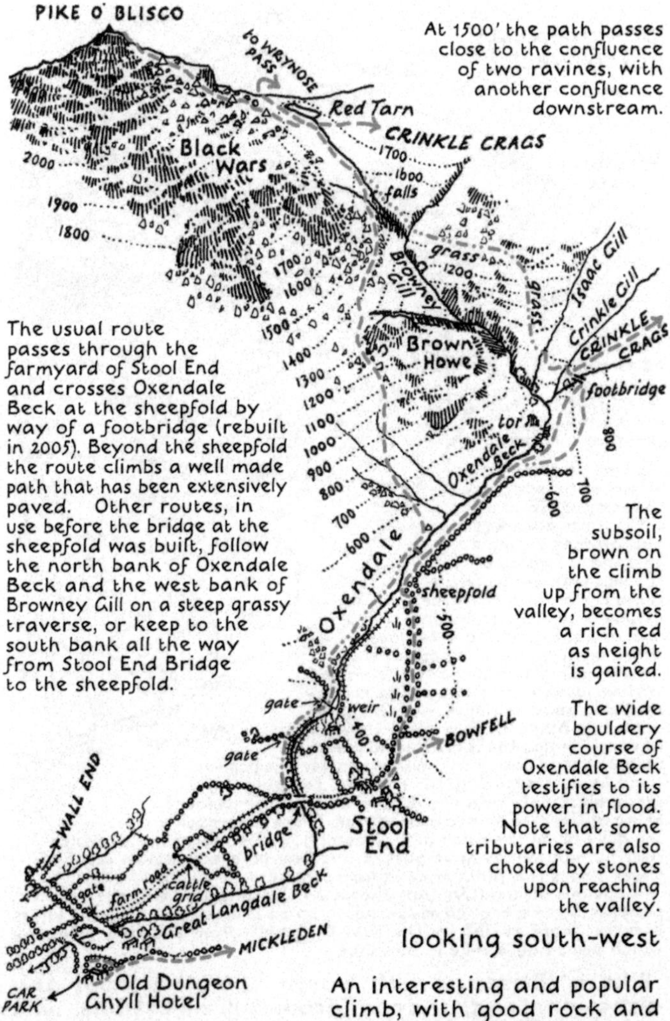
PIKE O' BLISCO
to WRYNOSE PASS
Red Tarn
CRINKLE CRAGS
Black Wars
2000
1900
1800
1700
1600
falls
grass
1200
Browney Gill
grass
Isaac Gill
Crinkle Gill
Brown Howe
CRINKLE CRAGS
footbridge
800
tor
Oxendale Beck
1700
1600
1500
1400
1300
1200
1100
1000
900
800
700
600
700
600
Oxendale
sheepfold
500
gate
weir
400
gate
BOWFELL
WALL END
Stool End
bridge
farm road
cattle grid
gate
Great Langdale Beck
MICKLEDEN
Old Dungeon Ghyll Hotel
CAR PARK

At 1500' the path passes close to the confluence of two ravines, with another confluence downstream.

The usual route passes through the farmyard of Stool End and crosses Oxendale Beck at the sheepfold by way of a footbridge (rebuilt in 2005). Beyond the sheepfold the route climbs a well made path that has been extensively paved. Other routes, in use before the bridge at the sheepfold was built, follow the north bank of Oxendale Beck and the west bank of Browney Gill on a steep grassy traverse, or keep to the south bank all the way from Stool End Bridge to the sheepfold.

The subsoil, brown on the climb up from the valley, becomes a rich red as height is gained.

The wide bouldery course of Oxendale Beck testifies to its power in flood. Note that some tributaries are also choked by stones upon reaching the valley.

looking south-west

An interesting and popular climb, with good rock and ravine scenery. The section between Oxendale Beck and Brown Howe, which was once bumpy and rough, is now well maintained.

ASCENT FROM LITTLE LANGDALE

1800 feet of ascent : 2½ miles from Fell Foot

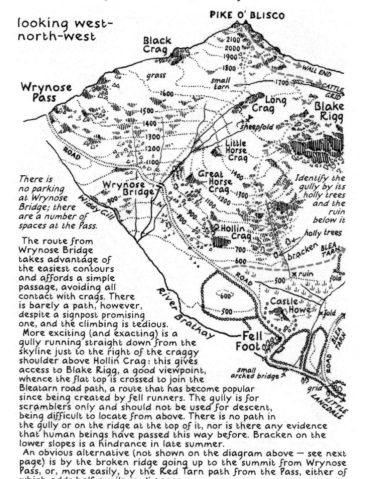

looking west-north-west

PIKE O' BLISCO
Black Crag
Wrynose Pass
grass
small tarn
WALL END
CATTLE GRID
Long Crag
Blake Rigg
sheepfold
Little Horse Crag
Great Horse Crag
Hollin Crag
ROAD
Wrynose Bridge
Widdy Gill
holly trees
bracken
BLEA TARN
ruin
fold
Castle Howe
River Brathay
Fell Foot
small arched bridge
BLEA TARN ROAD
grid
LITTLE LANGDALE
2100
2000
1900
1800
1700
1600
1500
1400
1300
1200
1100
1000
900
800
700
600
500

There is no parking at Wrynose Bridge; there are a number of spaces at the Pass.

Identify the gully by its holly trees and the ruin below it

The route from Wrynose Bridge takes advantage of the easiest contours and affords a simple passage, avoiding all contact with crags. There is barely a path, however, despite a signpost promising one, and the climbing is tedious.

More exciting (and exacting) is a gully running straight down from the skyline just to the right of the craggy shoulder above Hollin Crag: this gives access to Blake Rigg, a good viewpoint, whence the flat top is crossed to join the Bleatarn road path, a route that has become popular since being created by fell runners. The gully is for scramblers only and should not be used for descent, being difficult to locate from above. There is no path in the gully or on the ridge at the top of it, nor is there any evidence that human beings have passed this way before. Bracken on the lower slopes is a hindrance in late summer.

An obvious alternative (not shown on the diagram above — see next page) is by the broken ridge going up to the summit from Wrynose Pass, or, more easily, by the Red Tarn path from the Pass, either of which adds half a mile in distance.

Pike o' Blisco is well worth climbing from any direction, and, indeed, from all directions. The approach from Little Langdale by the usual way leaving Wrynose Bridge, however, is rather dull in comparison with those from Great Langdale.

ASCENT FROM WRYNOSE PASS
1100 feet of ascent : 1¼ miles

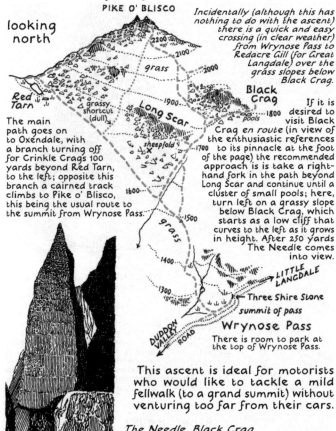

PIKE O' BLISCO
looking north
2200
2100
2000
grass
Red Tarn
grassy shortcut (dull)
Black Crag
1900
Long Scar
1800
pools
sheepfold
1700
1600
1500
grass
1400
1300
LITTLE LANGDALE
Three Shire Stone
summit of pass
Wrynose Pass
DUDDON VALLEY
ROAD

Incidentally (although this has nothing to do with the ascent) there is a quick and easy crossing (in clear weather) from Wrynose Pass to Redacre Gill (for Great Langdale) over the grass slopes below Black Crag.

The main path goes on to Oxendale, with a branch turning off for Crinkle Crags 100 yards beyond Red Tarn, to the left; opposite this branch a cairned track climbs to Pike o' Blisco, this being the usual route to the summit from Wrynose Pass.

If it is desired to visit Black Crag *en route* (in view of the enthusiastic references to its pinnacle at the foot of the page) the recommended approach is is take a right-hand fork in the path beyond Long Scar and continue until a cluster of small pools; here, turn left on a grassy slope below Black Crag, which starts as a low cliff that curves to the left as it grows in height. After 250 yards The Needle comes into view.

There is room to park at the top of Wrynose Pass.

This ascent is ideal for motorists who would like to tackle a mild fellwalk (to a grand summit) without venturing too far from their cars.

The Needle, Black Crag

This smooth and slender pinnacle, detached from the face of Black Crag, is precariously balanced on a massive plinth of rock, 12ft. high, the total height to the tip being 35ft. Well off the beaten track (although only a long half-mile from Wrynose Pass) it may have escaped the notice of cragsmen, there being no evidence of ascent on the pinnacle or in the rock-climbing literature at present available for the area. It seems (to a novice who hasn't tried) that the tip may be gained by 'bridging' the gap with the main crag. He will be a good man who can stand erect on the point of the needle.

The author feels rather proud of this 'discovery' and hopes people will not write to claim (i) a knowledge of the pinnacle (since they were children), (ii) that they have climbed it (blindfolded), and (iii) stood for hours on its point (on their heads).

THE SUMMIT

see "Some Personal Notes in conclusion"

This is a beautiful 'top' and a colourful one, with pinky-grey rocks outcropping everywhere from dark heather and green mosses. The main cairn is a shapely edifice (although not as shapely as in the illustration), which is gloriously situated on a platform of naked rock at the north-western terminus of a summit ridge 100 yards long. At the south-east extremity is another cairn, less imposing; this too crowns a craggy pyramid.

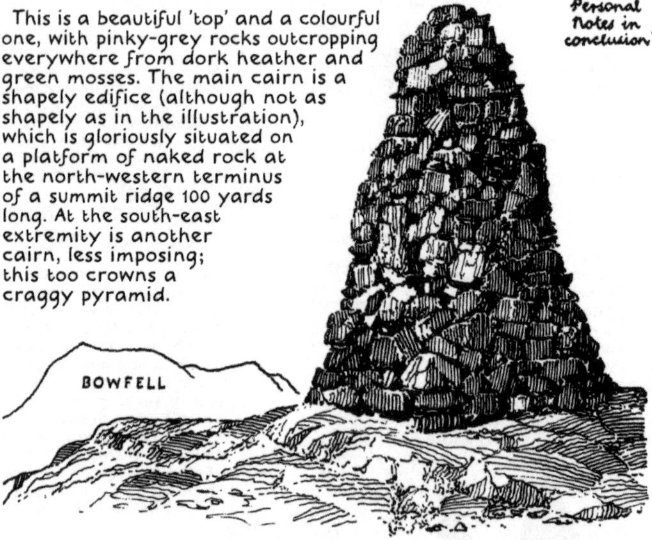
BOWFELL

PLAN OF SUMMIT

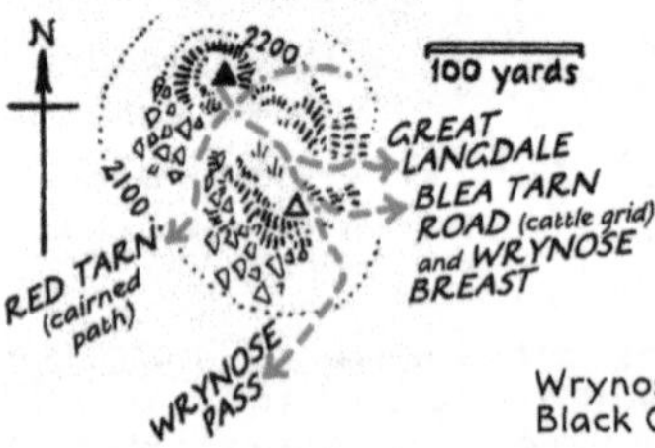
N
2200
2100
100 yards
GREAT LANGDALE
BLEA TARN ROAD (cattle grid) and WRYNOSE BREAST
RED TARN (cairned path)
WRYNOSE PASS

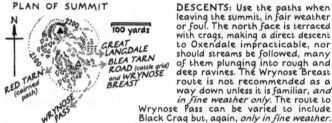

DESCENTS: Use the paths when leaving the summit, in fair weather or foul. The north face is terraced with crags, making a direct descent to Oxendale impracticable, nor should streams be followed, many of them plunging into rough and deep ravines. The Wrynose Breast route is not recommended as a way down unless it is familiar, *and in fine weather only*. The route to Wrynose Pass can be varied to include Black Crag but, again, *only in fine weather*.

RIDGE ROUTE

To COLD PIKE, 2300': 1¼ miles
SW, then W, NW, W, S and SE
Depression at 1650'
650 feet of ascent

An easy, interesting walk

Follow the path (a line of cairns) down to Red Tarn and then make use of the path to Crinkle Crags, turning left at the first stream on the plateau and crossing the bouldery slope to the prominent cairn of Cold Pike.

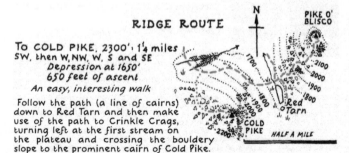

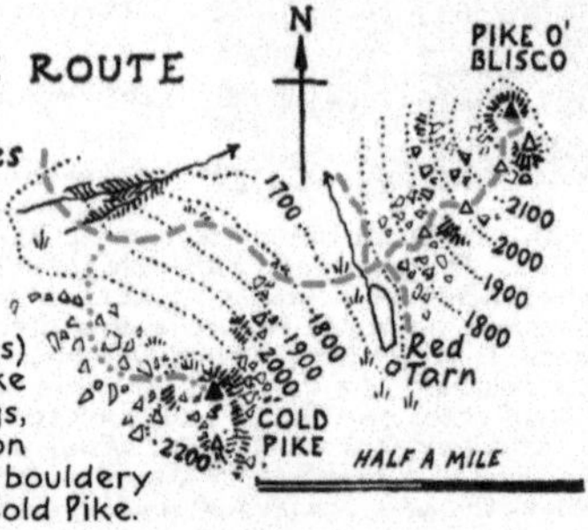
N
PIKE O' BLISCO
2100
2000
1900
1800
1700
Red Tarn
COLD PIKE
2200
HALF A MILE

THE VIEW

As the diagram suggests, most of the detail in the panorama is concentrated between north and east, and here the distant views, from Skiddaw round to the Kentmere fells, are certainly good. At close quarters, however, are Bowfell and Crinkle Crags, displaying their features to such effect that they will win most attention. Wander a few paces (not too many!) from the cairn, in the direction of Great Langdale, for a splendid prospect of that valley.

Principal Fells

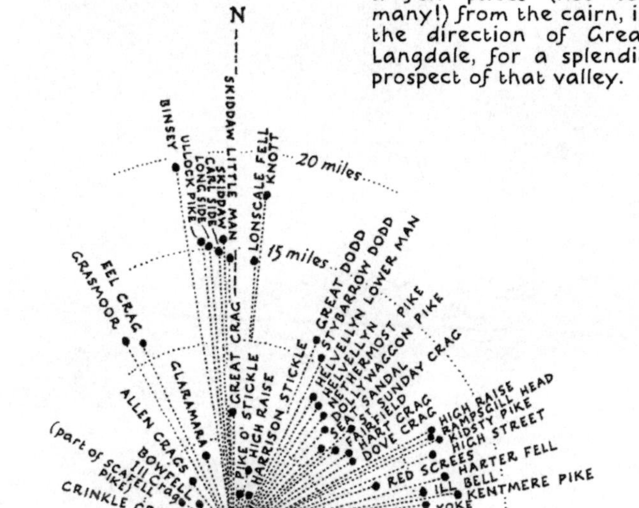
N
S
W
E
20 miles
15 miles
10 miles
5 miles
BINSEY
ULLOCK PIKE
LONG SIDE
CARL SIDE
SKIDDAW
SKIDDAW LITTLE MAN
LONSCALE FELL
KNOTT
GREAT CRAG
EEL CRAG
GRASMOOR
GLARAMARA
ALLEN CRAGS
BOWFELL
Ill Crag
(part of SCAFELL PIKE)
CRINKLE CRAGS
PIKE O' STICKLE
HIGH RAISE
HARRISON STICKLE
GREAT DODD
STYBARROW DODD
LOWER MAN
HELVELLYN
NETHERMOST PIKE
DOLLYWAGGON PIKE
SEAT SANDAL
ST SUNDAY CRAG
FAIRFIELD
HART CRAG
DOVE CRAG
HIGH RAISE
RAMPSGILL HEAD
KIDSTY PIKE
HIGH STREET
RED SCREES
HARTER FELL
ILL BELL
KENTMERE PIKE
YOKE
LOUGHRIGG
LINGMOOR FELL
WANSFELL PIKE
SALLOWS
BLACK FELL
WETHERLAM
Black Sails
SWIRL HOW
DOW CRAG
GREY FRIAR
COLD PIKE
HARTER FELL

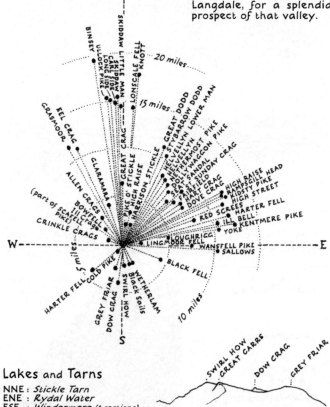

Lakes and Tarns

NNE : *Stickle Tarn*
ENE : *Rydal Water*
ESE : *Windermere (3 sections)*
SE : *Wise Een Tarn*
SE : *Esthwaite Water*
SW : *Red Tarn*

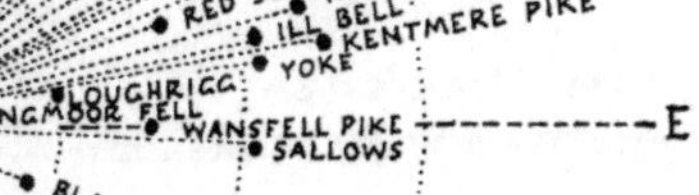
SWIRL HOW
GREAT CARRS
DOW CRAG
GREY FRIAR

looking south

Rossett Pike 2106′

OS grid ref: NY249076

from Mickleden

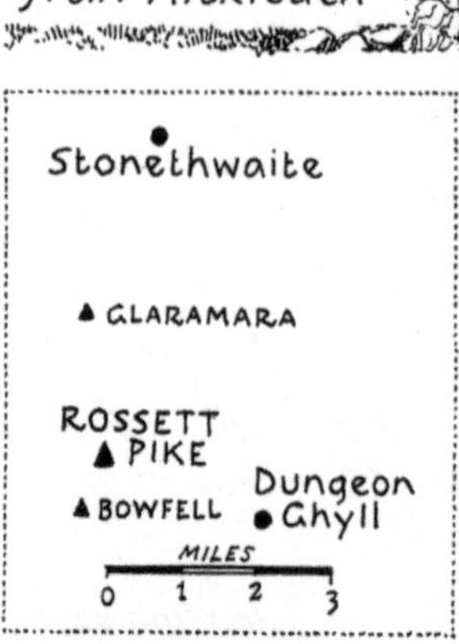
Stonethwaite
GLARAMARA
ROSSETT PIKE
BOWFELL
Dungeon Ghyll
MILES
0 1 2 3

from the top of Rossett Pass

NATURAL FEATURES

Perhaps, to be strictly correct, Rossett Pike and the fell of which it is part should be regarded as the north-east shoulder of Bowfell continuing from Hanging Knotts to Langstrath, but the sharp rise across the high saddle of Rossett Pass is so pronounced that, for present purposes, Bowfell may be considered to terminate at the Pass. It is especially convenient to regard Rossett Pike as having a separate identity because of its splendid strategical position (independent of and different in function from Bowfell's own and even more splendid position) dominating the deep glacial hollow of Mickleden and rising steeply between the two passes that provide the only routes of exit from that valley. Rossett Pass (south-west) and Stake Pass (north-east), both well known and much trodden walkers' routes, define the fell exactly. The east face, between the two diverging passes (which start from the same point at its foot), is excessively rough, but the western slopes are grassy and slope easily to Langstrath with the solitary rocky exception of Lining Crag. The crest of the fell, which carried the county boundary of Cumberland and Westmorland, is undulating and interesting.

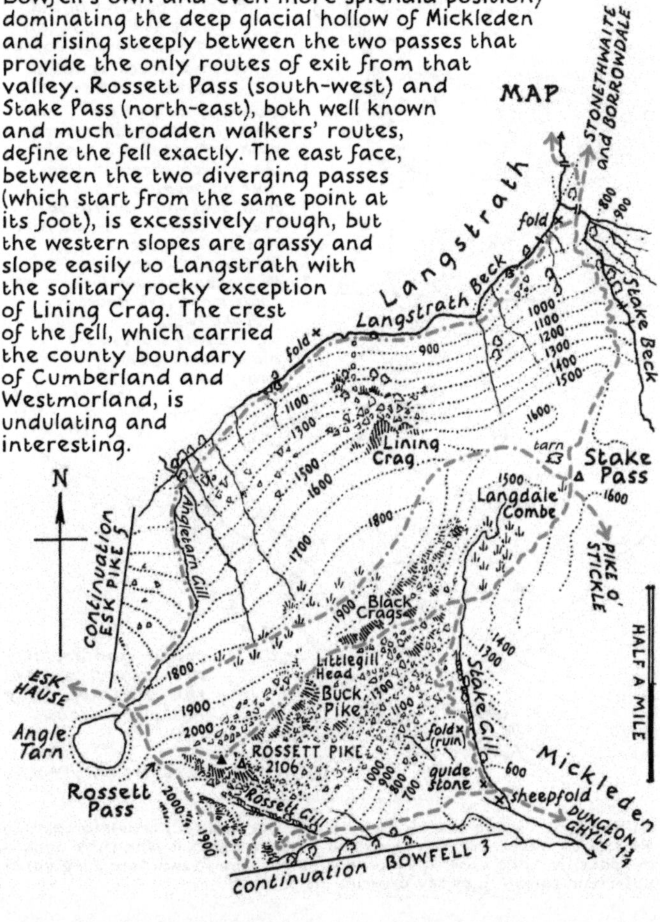
MAP
STONETHWAITE and BORROWDALE
Langstrath
Langstrath Beck
fold
Stake Beck
Lining Crag
tarn
Stake Pass
Langdale Combe
PIKE O' STICKLE
HALF A MILE
N
continuation ESK PIKE 5
Anglетarn Gill
Black Crags
Littlegill Head
Buck Pike
ESK HAUSE
Angle Tarn
ROSSETT PIKE 2106
Rossett Pass
Rossett Gill
fold (ruin)
guide stone
Stake Gill
sheepfold
Mickleden
DUNGEON GHYLL 1¾
continuation BOWFELL 3

Rossett Gill

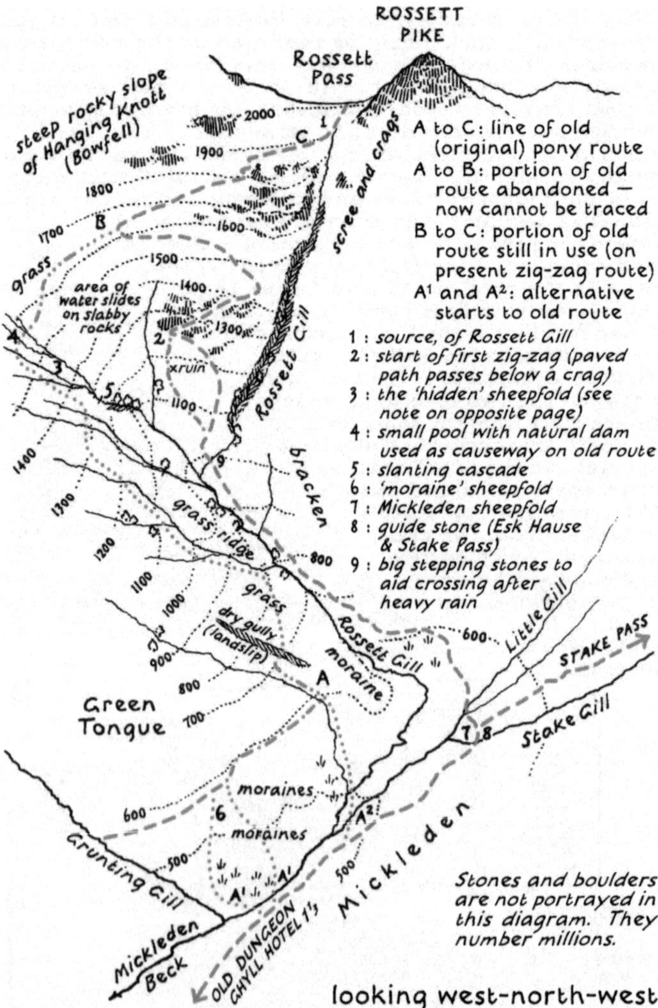
ROSSETT PIKE
Rossett Pass
steep rocky slope of Hanging Knott (Bowfell)
scree and crags
A to C: line of old (original) pony route
A to B: portion of old route abandoned — now cannot be traced
B to C: portion of old route still in use (on present zig-zag route)
A¹ and A²: alternative starts to old route
1 : source, of Rossett Gill
2 : start of first zig-zag (paved path passes below a crag)
3 : the 'hidden' sheepfold (see note on opposite page)
4 : small pool with natural dam used as causeway on old route
5 : slanting cascade
6 : 'moraine' sheepfold
7 : Mickleden sheepfold
8 : guide stone (Esk Hause & Stake Pass)
9 : big stepping stones to aid crossing after heavy rain
2000
1900
1800
1700
1600
1500
1400
1300
1100
grass
area of water slides on slabby rocks
xruin
Rossett Gill
bracken
grass ridge
800
grass
dry gully (landslip)
moraine
600
Little Gill
STAKE PASS
Stake Gill
Green Tongue
moraines
moraines
Grunting Gill
Mickleden
Mickleden Beck
OLD DUNGEON GHYLL HOTEL 1½
Stones and boulders are not portrayed in this diagram. They number millions.
looking west-north-west

NOTE : When using the old pony route the first (A¹) crossing point of Mickleden Beck near Grunting Gill may be difficult when the beck is in spate. In that case, an alternative may be found about 150 yards upstream (also A¹), or try crossing at point A².

Rossett Gill

Rossett Gill is probably the best known of Lakeland foot passes, which is not to say that it is the most popular; indeed at one time it was the least liked, due not so much to its steepness (which is more apparent than real, the gradient being nowhere in excess of 30°) but to its stoniness (a condition worsening year by year as swarming legions of booted pedestrians grind away the scanty vestiges of grass and soil). Improvements to the path have made the route very much easier, but discriminating fellwalkers may wish to revive the use of the old pony route, which makes a leisurely way round the base of Green Tongue and, keeping entirely to the slopes of Bowfell, avoids the gill altogether; its final stage is the 'zag' of the second zig-zag. The point where the old route left Mickleden is now obscure, but the streams there may easily be forded almost anywhere in normal weather. The path can barely be traced on the ground (unlike the Valley Route to Sty Head – *see Great End 7*), but the small pool with a natural dam (number 4 on the diagram) can be found and shows where the path used to go. The old route is still useful in descent (keep straight on from the bend in the big zig-zag), providing a carpet of soft grass for the feet and a solitude that contrasts well with the clatter of boots and tongues on the usual direct route.

Rossett Gill has a history, and a few evidences remain, although now almost forgotten or unknown. A knowledge of them will add some interest to the tedious climb.

The old pony route: This was originally a skilfully graded and well engineered path. It is believed to have been used for the secret transporting of goods smuggled into Ravenglass. Much of the former route seems to have been later abandoned in favour of the present double zig-zag, but they coincide in the upper stages.

The hidden sheepfold: Cleverly screened from the sight of people passing along Mickleden and Rossett Gill, and situated within the big curve of the old route, is an old sheepfold, still in good condition, used to hide sheep in the far-off days when raiders often looted the valleys.

The packwoman's grave: Neglected and forgotten, yet within very easy reach of the gill, is the grave of a woman who used to call at Langdale farms carrying a pack of articles for sale — and whose mortal remains were found and buried here over 200 years ago. A simple cross of stones laid on the ground, pointing south-east, indicates the grave; it has suffered little disturbance down the years, but because so many folk nowadays seem unable to leave things alone its precise location is not divulged here.

The packwoman's grave

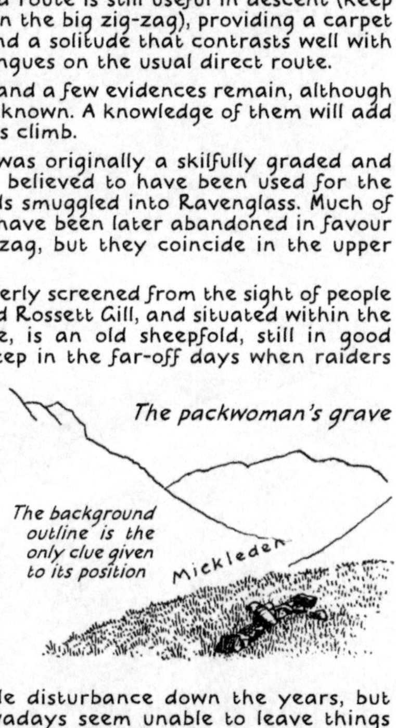
Mickleden

The background outline is the only clue given to its position

(Historical notes on this page were kindly suppied by MR. H. MOUNSEY, Skelwith.)

Rossett Pike and Rossett Gill
from the old pony route

From this viewpoint it would appear that the Pike can be reached from the top of the pass only by a steep climb. But in fact the top of the pass is further back than the illustration suggests, and a gentle grass slope there leads up to the rear of the Pike.

ASCENT FROM MICKLEDEN

1600 feet of ascent : 1½ miles from the sheepfold

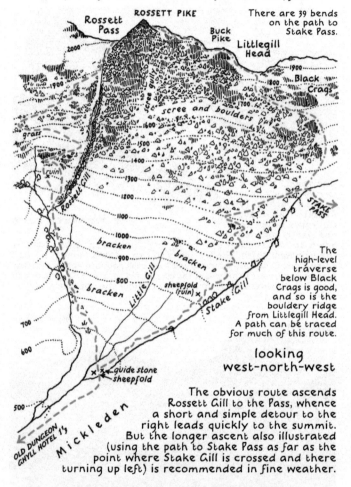

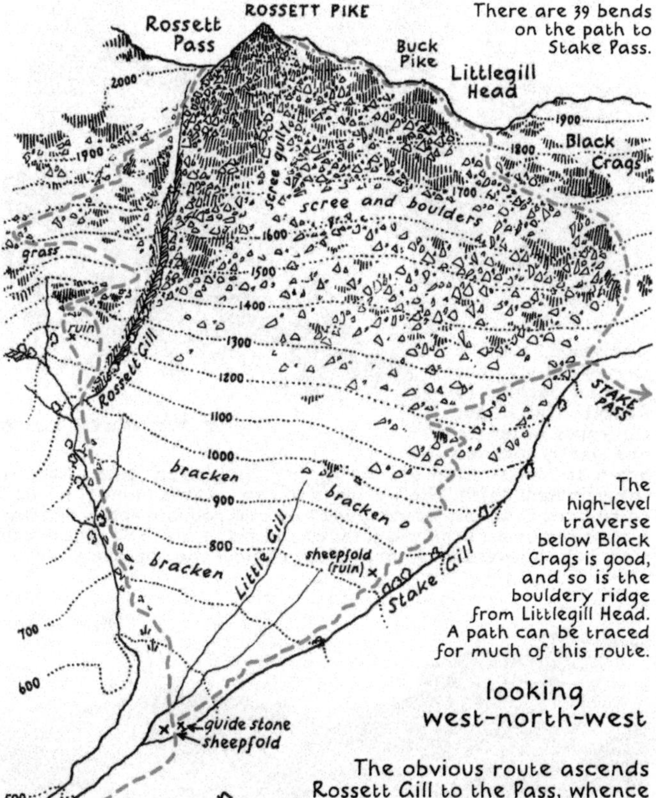
ROSSETT PIKE
Rossett Pass
Buck Pike
Littlegill Head
Black Crags
There are 39 bends on the path to Stake Pass.
2000
1900
1800
1700
1600
1500
1400
1300
1200
1100
1000
900
800
700
600
500
scree gully
scree and boulders
grass
ruin
Rossett Gill
bracken
bracken
bracken
Little Gill
sheepfold (ruin)
Stake Gill
STAKE PASS
guide stone
sheepfold
OLD DUNGEON GHYLL HOTEL 1¼
Mickleden
The high-level traverse below Black Crags is good, and so is the bouldery ridge from Littlegill Head. A path can be traced for much of this route.
looking west-north-west

The obvious route ascends Rossett Gill to the Pass, whence a short and simple detour to the right leads quickly to the summit. But the longer ascent also illustrated (using the path to Stake Pass as far as the point where Stake Gill is crossed and there turning up left) is recommended in fine weather.

ASCENT FROM STONETHWAITE

1950 feet of ascent : 4¾ miles

Rossett Pike can be climbed from Stonethwaite by way of the beautiful Langstrath valley and Stake Pass, where the route shown above can be joined. For details and a diagram, see *Bowfell 9*.

THE SUMMIT

1 2 3
1: Harrison Stickle
2: Pike o'Stickle
3: Loft Crag
4: Gimmer Crag
LANGDALE PIKES
4
Mickleden cairn

The Mickleden cairn

The summit is in the form of a stony ridge running parallel to Rossett Gill, about 120 yards in length and gently inclined down to the sudden plunge of the Mickleden face; here is the principal cairn. The west end of the ridge is higher; a small cairn here is actually overtopped by outcropping rocks nearby. A continuous escarpment fringes the ridge on the Rossett Gill side, but the west and north slopes below the top are easy.

Mickleden

THE VIEW

The view is naturally inferior to those from the greater fells close by, but it excels in an impressive aerial scene of Mickleden and in the intimate detail of Bowfell's northern cliffs, the great sloping slab of Flat Crags, unique in the district, appearing as a striking feature.

Principal Fells

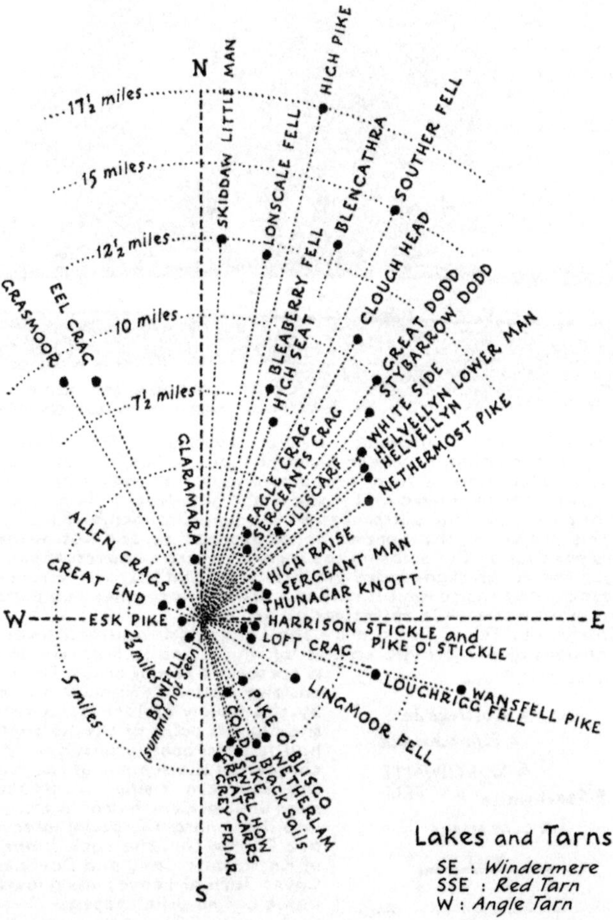
N
S
E
W
17½ miles
15 miles
12½ miles
10 miles
7½ miles
5 miles
2½ miles
SKIDDAW LITTLE MAN
HIGH PIKE
LONSCALE FELL
BLENCATHRA
SOUTHER FELL
BLEABERRY FELL
HIGH SEAT
CLOUGH HEAD
GREAT DODD
STYBARROW DODD
WHITE SIDE
HELVELLYN LOWER MAN
HELVELLYN
NETHERMOST PIKE
GRASMOOR
EEL CRAG
GLARAMARA
EAGLE CRAG
SERGEANTS CRAG
ULLSCARF
HIGH RAISE
SERGEANT MAN
THUNACAR KNOTT
ALLEN CRAGS
GREAT END
ESK PIKE
HARRISON STICKLE and PIKE O' STICKLE
LOFT CRAG
LOUGHRIGG FELL
WANSFELL PIKE
LINGMOOR FELL
BOWFELL (summit not seen)
PIKE O' BLISCO
WETHERLAM
BLACK SAILS
SWIRL HOW
GREAT CARRS
COLD PIKE
GREY FRIAR

Lakes and Tarns

SE : *Windermere*
SSE : *Red Tarn*
W : *Angle Tarn*

Rosthwaite Fell 1807'

OS grid ref: NY258125

from Stonethwaite road end

Rosthwaite Fell, shadowing the level strath of the Stonethwaite valley, is really the northern extremity of the Scafells (although seldom recognised as such) and a strong walker may start from the green pastures here and make a fine high-level walk over the fell and the adjacent Glaramara to the summit of Scafell Pike. Few do this, preferring the more orthodox approaches, and Rosthwaite Fell's pathless and undulating top is rarely visited, understandably so for the rough stony sides yield no easy and attractive routes of ascent and the summit is rather a dreary place when compared with more worthwhile objectives all around.

Rosthwaite Fell is flanked by the Langstrath and Seathwaite extensions of Borrowdale, to both of which, and to Stonethwaite, it presents a rim of crags. The top has two sections, distinctly divided by the hollow of Tarn at Leaves; the highest point of the northern half is Bessyboot (treated in this chapter as the summit of the fell), the southern rising in greater steps until, at Combe Door, it merges into Glaramara. Of special interest are Combe Gill, the rock summit of Rosthwaite Cam, and Dovenest Caves. Tarn at Leaves has a lovely name but no other appeal.

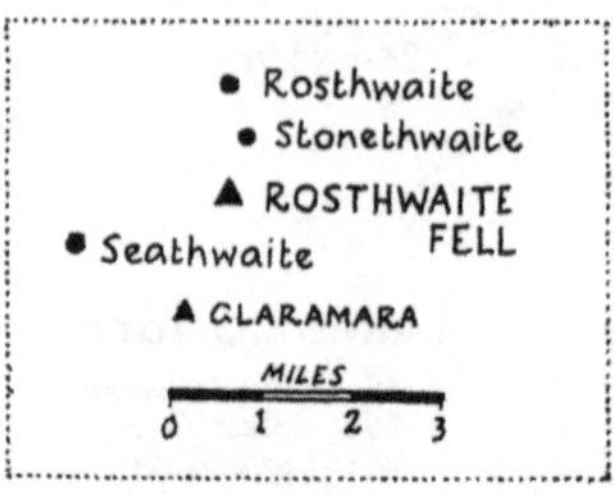

Rosthwaite
Stonethwaite
ROSTHWAITE FELL
Seathwaite
GLARAMARA
MILES
0 1 2 3

MAP

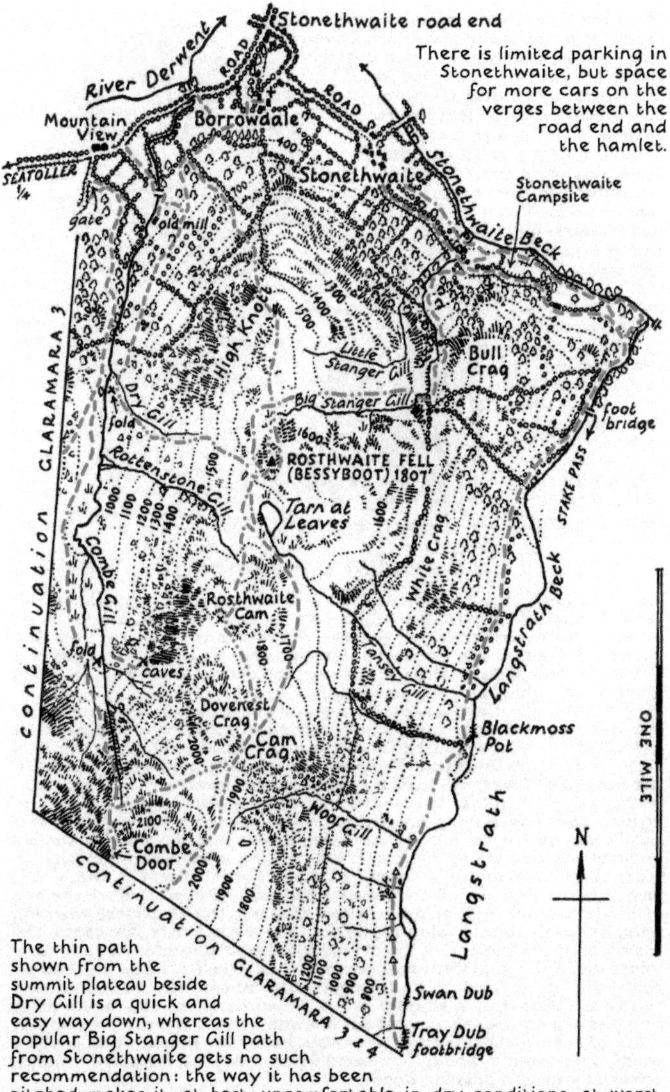
Stonethwaite road end
River Derwent
ROAD
ROAD
Mountain View
Borrowdale
SEATOLLER 1/4
Stonethwaite
Stonethwaite Campsite
Stonethwaite Beck
gate
old mill
High Knott
Little Stanger Gill
Big Stanger Gill
Bull Crag
foot bridge
Dry Gill
fold
Rottenstone Gill
ROSTHWAITE FELL (BESSYBOOT) 1807'
Tarn at Leaves
White Crag
STAKE PASS
Langstrath Beck
Combe Gill
Rosthwaite Cam
fold
caves
Tansey Gill
Dovenest Crag
Cam Crag
Blackmoss Pot
Woof Gill
Combe Door
Langstrath
Swan Dub
Tray Dub footbridge
continuation CLARAMARA 3
continuation CLARAMARA 3 & 4
ONE MILE
N
400
700
1100
1300
1400
1500
1600
1500
1000
1100
1200
1300
1400
1600
1700
1800
2000
1900
2100
2000
1900
1800
1200
1100
1000
900
800

There is limited parking in Stonethwaite, but space for more cars on the verges between the road end and the hamlet.

The thin path shown from the summit plateau beside Dry Gill is a quick and easy way down, whereas the popular Big Stanger Gill path from Stonethwaite gets no such recommendation: the way it has been pitched makes it, at best, uncomfortable in dry conditions, at worst, dangerous in the wet. Try to avoid descending by this route!

Dovenest Caves

At some time in the distant past, as the result of a natural convulsion, Dovenest Crag above Combe Gill gave a great shudder, part of the rock face breaking away and slipping downwards for a few feet before coming to rest and thus creating a cavity which today gives unusual sport: a subterranean rock climb in darkness.

The interior is out of bounds for walkers, but the place is worth a visit and gentle exploration. A path leads up scree to the bouldery entrance of South Cave. To locate the Crag, first find the sheepfold at the head of the Combe: the Crag is plainly in view here – up on the left – and is reached by a stiff climb of ten minutes.

A good idea for a wet day!

1
2
3
4
5
6
7
scree

South chimney and Cave

1 : South Chimney and Cave (usual entrance)
2 : Attic Cave (the place of emergence)
3 : North Cave
4 : The Pinnacle
5 : Central Chimney
6 : North Chimney
7 : North Gully

Caves in Lakeland

Some readers have written to ask whether there are caves in the Lake District. If they have in mind natural caves eroded by water, as in the Craven underworld of Yorkshire, the answer is NO; for the rocks of Lakeland are hard volcanic ash, granite and slate, resistant to the action of water. The softer limestone occurs in the neighbouring fringes only, chiefly to the south-east.

The natural Lakeland caves, hardly worth the name, are formed by the wedging of fallen rocks (chockstones) in gullies and clefts, or by the piling-up of boulders below crags, or, infrequently, by a slip of a rock-face, as at Dovenest. The first variety are beloved of climbers, the second of foxes, but neither will appeal to cavers.

Artificial man-made caves are plentiful, particularly in areas of copper and lead-mining operations, where tunnels, adits, levels and shafts are all to be found; more generally distributed are similar engineering devices to facilitate the shifting of stone in quarries on steep fellsides. Many of them are objects of great interest, and, if it is remembered that they were constructed manually long before the age of modern machines, of admiration too; but the strongest warning must be given to intending explorers that, except in a few cases, the mines and quarries have been unworked and abandoned for many years and their subterranean passages are derelict, often blocked by roof-falls, often flooded, and supporting timbers may be rotted and ready to collapse at a whisper. In other words, these ugly black holes and pits are not merely dangerous but damned dangerous. Sons should think of their mothers, and turn away. Husbands should think of their wives, after which gloomy contemplation many no doubt will march cheerfully in to a possible doom.

No, there is nothing in Lakeland for speleologists and cavers, unless they care to try fellwalking, *i.e.* crawling about on the surface.

ASCENT FROM STONETHWAITE
1500 feet of ascent : 1½ miles

Follow the stream to its source in a marsh where there are three options: left up a grassy gully and then following a thin path to the 'back' of Bessyboot; half-left up a broken ridge to the summit; straight on following the main path around to the left, again approaching the top from the rear.

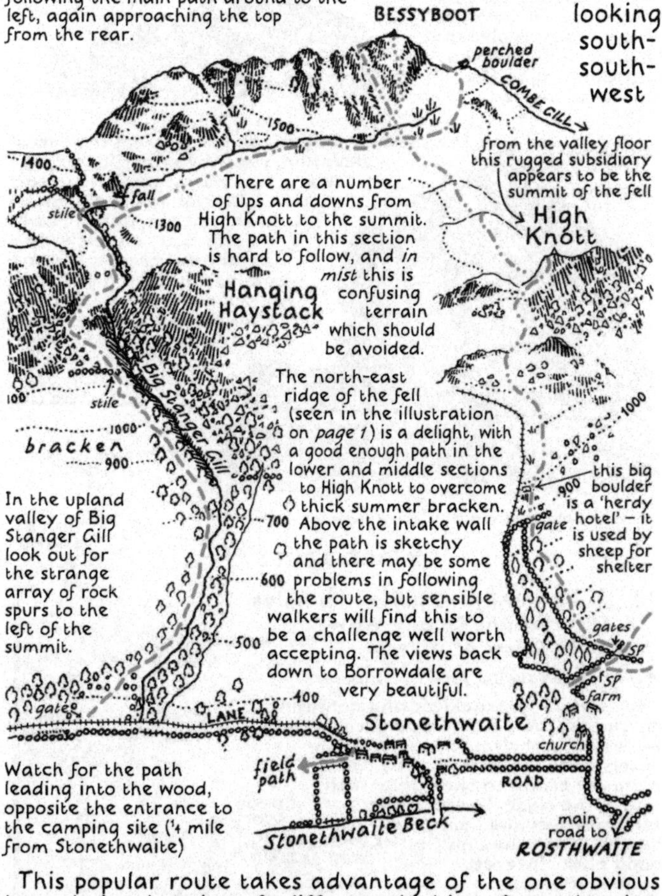
BESSYBOOT
looking south-south-west
perched boulder
COMBE GILL
1500
1400
fall
stile
1300
from the valley floor this rugged subsidiary appears to be the summit of the fell
High Knott
There are a number of ups and downs from High Knott to the summit. The path in this section is hard to follow, and *in mist* this is confusing terrain which should be avoided.
Hanging Haystack
The north-east ridge of the fell (seen in the illustration on *page 1*) is a delight, with a good enough path in the lower and middle sections to High Knott to overcome thick summer bracken. Above the intake wall the path is sketchy and there may be some problems in following the route, but sensible walkers will find this to be a challenge well worth accepting. The views back down to Borrowdale are very beautiful.
Big Stanger Gill
1100
stile
1000
bracken
900
In the upland valley of Big Stanger Gill look out for the strange array of rock spurs to the left of the summit.
700
600
500
400
1000
900
this big boulder is a 'herdy hotel' – it is used by sheep for shelter
gate
gates
SP
SP
farm
gate
LANE
Stonethwaite
church
ROAD
field path
Stonethwaite Beck
main road to ROSTHWAITE
Watch for the path leading into the wood, opposite the entrance to the camping site (¼ mile from Stonethwaite)

This popular route takes advantage of the one obvious breach in the rim of cliffs overlooking Stonethwaite, where a great notch in the skyline is formed by the deep cleft of Big Stanger Gill. The steep climb up the gill, amongst trees, is charming. The alternative, *via* the rarely climbed north-east ridge, is mountaineering on a small scale!

THE SUMMIT

Bessyboot is the most distinctive height in the northern half of the fell, and its small, neat top, easily reached through breaches in a surround of low crags, is pleasant enough, but somewhat disappointing in the matter of views.

GLARAMARA
Rosthwaite Cam
Combe Head

Rosthwaite Cam (from the south)

Arrow indicates start of easy way up.

The southern half of the fell, of greater general elevation, rises towards Glaramara; the finest of many summits in this section (although not the highest) is Rosthwaite Cam, and a really good one it is, all rock, and unassailable except for one weakness by which an agile walker may climb to touch the cairn. The summit resembles a lion (without a lamb) when seen from the approach to Combe Gill.

RIDGE ROUTE

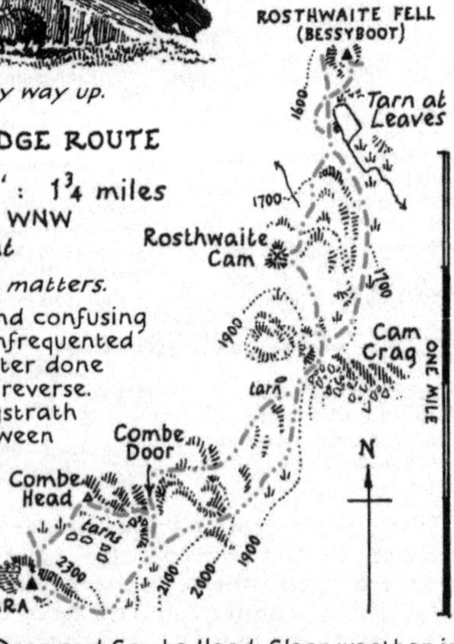
ROSTHWAITE FELL
(BESSYBOOT)
Tarn at Leaves
1600
1700
Rosthwaite Cam
1700
1900
Cam Crag
ONE MILE
tarn
Combe Door
Combe Head
N
tarns
2300
2100
2000
1900
GLARAMARA

To GLARAMARA, 2569': 1¾ miles
S, then SW and finally WNW
1000 feet of ascent

A good path would improve matters.

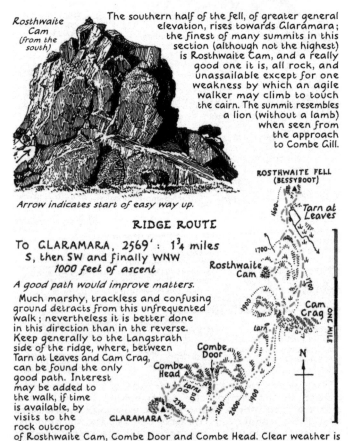

Much marshy, trackless and confusing ground detracts from this unfrequented walk; nevertheless it is better done in this direction than in the reverse. Keep generally to the Langstrath side of the ridge, where, between Tarn at Leaves and Cam Crag, can be found the only good path. Interest may be added to the walk, if time is available, by visits to the rock outcrop of Rosthwaite Cam, Combe Door and Combe Head. Clear weather is advisable for this route: *this is dangerous country in mist.*

THE VIEW

This is the view from the summit of Bessyboot. It will disappoint people who expect to look down on the villages of Borrowdale or on Stonethwaite or Langstrath, these valleys being concealed by the wide slopes around the top. The best views are obtained from mid-height during the ascent.

Principal Fells

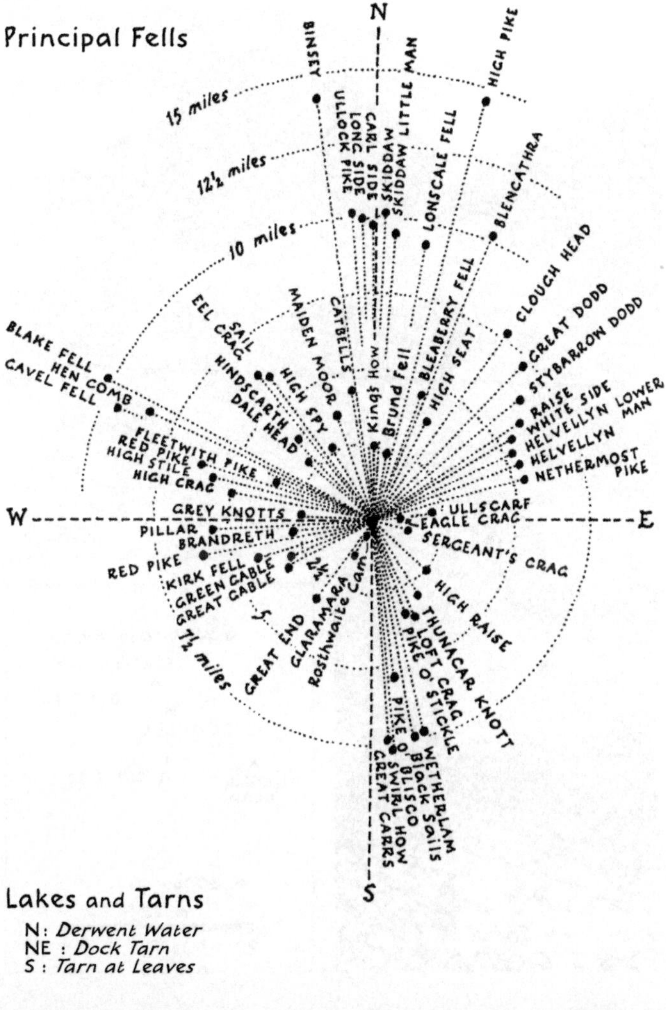
N
E
S
W
15 miles
12½ miles
10 miles
7½ miles
5
2½
BINSEY
HIGH PIKE
SKIDDAW LITTLE MAN
ULLOCK PIKE
LONG SIDE
CARL SIDE
SKIDDAW
LONSCALE FELL
BLENCATHRA
CLOUGH HEAD
GREAT DODD
STYBARROW DODD
RAISE
WHITE SIDE
HELVELLYN LOWER MAN
HELVELLYN
NETHERMOST PIKE
BLEABERRY FELL
HIGH SEAT
Brund Fell
Kings How
CATBELLS
MAIDEN MOOR
HIGH SPY
EEL CRAG
SAIL
HINDSCARTH
DALE HEAD
BLAKE FELL
HEN COMB
GAVEL FELL
FLEETWITH PIKE
RED PIKE
HIGH STILE
HIGH CRAG
GREY KNOTTS
PILLAR
BRANDRETH
RED PIKE
KIRK FELL
GREEN GABLE
GREAT GABLE
GREAT END
GLARAMARA
Rosthwaite Cam
ULLSCARF
EAGLE CRAG
SERGEANT'S CRAG
HIGH RAISE
THUNACAR KNOTT
LOFT CRAG
PIKE O' STICKLE
WETHERLAM
BLACK SAILS
PIKE O' BLISCO
SWIRL HOW
GREAT CARRS

Lakes and Tarns

N: *Derwent Water*
NE : *Dock Tarn*
S : *Tarn at Leaves*

Scafell

3162'

formerly Scawfell or Scaw Fell
(pronounced Scawfle)

OS grid ref: NY207065

Wasdale Head
SCAFELL PIKE
BOWFELL
SCAFELL
ILLGILL HEAD
SLIGHT SIDE
Boot
MILES
0 1 2 3 4

from Cam Spout

NATURAL FEATURES

When men first named the mountains, the whole of the high mass south of Sty Head was known as Scaw Fell; later, as the work of the dalesfolk took them more and more onto the heights and closer identification became necessary, they applied the name to the mountain that seemed to them the greatest, the other summits in the range, to them individually inferior, being referred to collectively as the Pikes of Scaw Fell. Many folk today, even with the added knowledge that the main Pike is not only higher but actually the highest land in the country, share the old opinion that Scaw Fell (now *Scafell*) is the superior mountain of the group.

This respect is inspired not by the huge western flank going down to Wasdale nor by the broad southern slopes ending in the Eskdale foothills but rather by the towering rampart of shadowed crags facing north and east below the summit, the greatest display of natural grandeur in the district, a spectacle of massive strength and savage wildness but without beauty, an awesome and a humbling scene. A man may stand on the lofty ridge of Mickledore, or in the green hollow beneath the precipice amongst the littered débris and boulders fallen from it, and witness the sublime architecture of buttresses and pinnacles soaring into the sky, silhouetted against racing clouds or, often, tormented by writhing mists, and, as in a great cathedral, lose all his conceit. It does a man good to realise his own insignificance in the general scheme of things, and that is his experience here.

Fuller notes on the topography are contained in the Scafell Pike chapter.

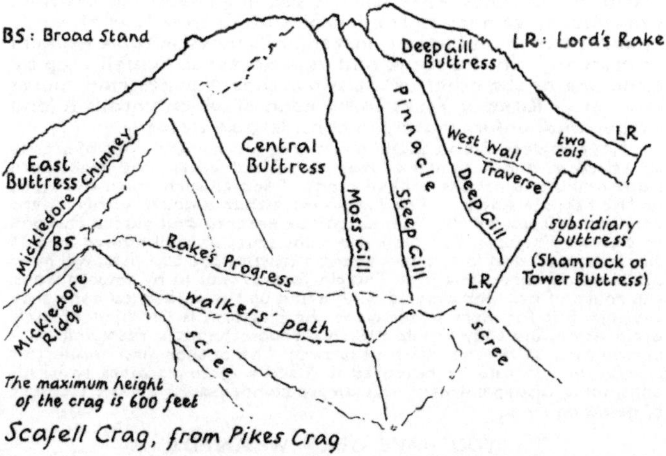
BS: Broad Stand
LR: Lord's Rake
Deep Gill Buttress
Pinnacle
West Wall Traverse
two cols
LR
East Buttress
Mickledore Chimney
Central Buttress
Moss Gill
Steep Gill
Deep Gill
subsidiary buttress (Shamrock or Tower Buttress)
BS
Rake's Progress
LR
Mickledore Ridge
Walkers' path
scree
scree
The maximum height of the crag is 600 feet

Scafell Crag, from Pikes Crag

Broad Stand
NOT FOR WALKERS
entrance

Broad Stand and Mickledore

The greatest single obstacle confronting ridge walkers on the hills of Lakeland is the notorious Broad Stand, with which every traveller from Scafell Pike to Scafell comes face to face at the far end of the Mickledore traverse. Obstacles met on other ridges can be overcome or easily by-passed; not so Broad Stand. It is an infuriating place, making a man angry with himself for his inability to climb the thirty feet of rock that bar his way to the simple rising slope beyond. From a distance it looks nothing; close at hand it still looks not much to worry about; but with the first platform underfoot, while still not seeming impossible, the next awkward movement to the left plus an uneasy fear of worse hazards above and as yet unseen, influences sensible walkers to retreat from the scene and gain access to Scafell's top by using one or the other of the two orthodox pedestrian routes (*via* Lord's Rake or Foxes Tarn), each of which entails a long detour and, unfortunately, a considerable descent.

Nevertheless, Broad Stand has a long history and a lot of stories to its name, and it should at least be visited. Where the Mickledore ridge abuts against the broken crags of Scafell turn down the scree on the Eskdale side (east) and in no more than a dozen yards a deep vertical cleft, paved with stones, can be entered and passed through to a small platform. This cleft is a tight squeeze, well named as "Fat Man's Agony", and ladies, too, whose statistics are too vital, will have an uncomfortable time in it. The platform is shut in by smooth walls, the route of exit (for experts only) being up the scratched corner on the left. But for mere pedestrians the platform is the limit of their exploration and they should return through the cleft, resolving, as is customary, to do the climb next time. The author first made this resolve in 1930 and he repeated it a score of times after that; his continuing disappointment was amply compensated by the pleasure of going on living.

YOU HAVE BEEN WARNED!

Lord's Rake

Lord's Rake is a classic route, uncomfortable underfoot but magnificent all around. It is used on the ascent of Scafell from Wasdale Head *via* Brown Tongue and on the traverse of the main ridge. The Rake is unique, but its peculiar delights and horrors have been compounded by numerous rockfalls and more are likely. *Extreme care is necessary.*

Strangers to Scafell may have some difficulty in locating the Rake, small-scale maps being unable to supply the details, but users of this book will have no such worries, of course.

The Rake starts (in ascent) as a steep, wide scree-gully or channel rising *not into* the mountain but obliquely *across* it and between the main crag and a subsidiary buttress, the top edge of which forms a parapet to the Rake. This first section is almost 100 yards in length, and ends at a perfect little col, so narrow that it can be straddled. A descent of 10 feet and a rise of 20 feet leads in 20 yards to another *col*, equally sweet, and the end of the Rake is now in sight 100 yards ahead and at the same elevation, although a steep descent to a stony amphitheatre is necessary before the exit can be reached. Here, now, is the open fell, and a rough track (left) leads to the top of Scafell.

The great thing to remember (important in mist) is that Lord's Rake has 3 ups and 2 downs, and maintains a dead-straight course throughout.

The first section calls for strenuous effort, as the assortment of buttons, bootsoles, dentures, broken pipes and other domestic articles scattered *en route* testifies. The best footing higher up is at the right side. In a place like this, where boots cannot gain a purchase on the sliding stones and polished rocks, it is common sense for walkers to take great care. The rocks are unstable. Even stalwart climbers need feel no shame at choosing to wear a helmet here and maintaining a respectful distance between themselves and others on the Rake. The yellow flower growing in crevices of the rock is the starry saxifrage.

the first section
col
subsidiary buttress
main crag
foot of Scafell Pinnacle
HOLLOW STONES

A chockstone that was wedged at the col for more than 10 years collapsed in August 2016 leaving debris on the rake.

In 2016 Lord's Rake was deemed passable *with care*. BE WARNED!

In standard of difficulty it is *much* easier than Jack's Rake on Pavey Ark, *much* harder than Rossett Gill.

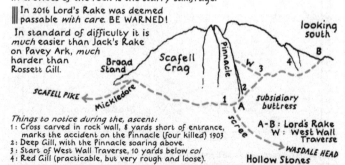

looking south
Scafell Crag
Broad Stand
Pinnacle
W
3
4
B
2
1
A
SCAFELL PIKE
Mickledore
subsidiary buttress
scree
A-B : Lord's Rake
W : West Wall Traverse
WASDALE HEAD
Hollow Stones

Things to notice during the ascent:

1: Cross carved in rock wall, 8 yards short of entrance, marks the accident on the Pinnacle (four killed) 1903
2: Deep Gill, with the Pinnacle soaring above.
3: Start of West Wall Traverse, 10 yards below *col*
4: Red Gill (practicable, but very rough and loose).

These paths are shown as good (– – –) but trodden ways here are constantly obliterated by sliding stones: the routes, however, are much-used and obvious.

MAP

Old maps show that Lingmell Gill formerly joined Lingmell Beck ¼ mile short of Wast Water. It was in 1918 when prisoners of war cut a new channel for the stream so that it debouched directly into the lake. The area was later devastated by floods (particularly by a great storm in August 1938); a concrete bridge originally built by German prisoners is choked by a mass of stones, and the stream finds its way to the lake under debris.

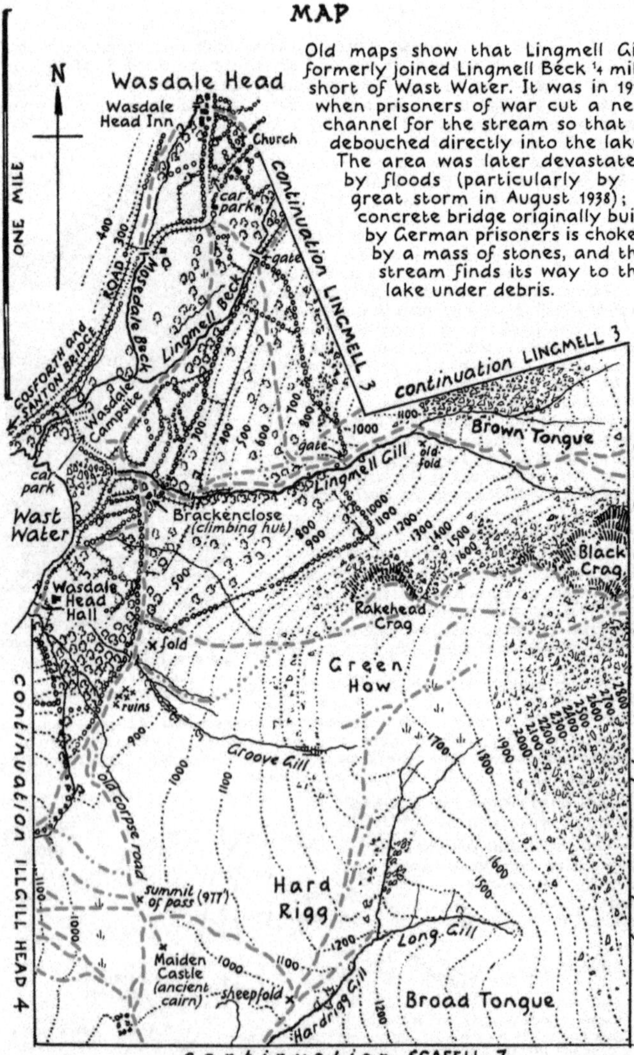

ONE MILE
N
Wasdale Head
Wasdale Head Inn
Church
car park
gate
continuation LINGMELL 3
continuation LINGMELL 3
Wasdale Beck
Lingmell Beck
ROAD
COSFORTH and SANTON BRIDGE
Wasdale Campsite
car park
Wast Water
Brackenclose (climbing hut)
Wasdale Head Hall
Lingmell Gill
gate
Brown Tongue
old fold
Black Crag
Rakehead Crag
fold
Green How
ruins
Groove Gill
old corpse road
Hard Rigg
summit of pass (977')
Maiden Castle (ancient cairn)
sheepfold
Long Gill
Hardrigg Gill
Broad Tongue
continuation ILLGILL HEAD 4
continuation on opposite page
continuation SCAFELL 7

It is worth noting that the footpath between Wasdale Head and Wasdale Campsite, which starts from the road corner just south of the car parking area, includes some stepping stones that require good balance. Also of note, there are public toilets at the parking area.

MAP

The inadequacy of maps to serve as a guide over rough and complicated ground, more especially where there are vertical elevations, is nowhere better illustrated than in the small area between Scafell and Scafell Pike. A lost and hapless wanderer standing on Mickledore ridge, trying to fit the tremendous scene around them into a half-inch space on his map, is deserving of every sympathy. So is the map-maker, furnished with many details and festooned with merging contours — and nowhere to put them; but this does not really excuse the rather nonchalant hachuring of crags on both the Ordnance Survey and Bartholomews maps, nor the omission of important paths.

The map on this page is itself little better than useless. But never mind: there is a large-scale plan of this particular area on page 14 which, while not aspiring to portray the character of the terrain, should at least be informative enough to get the afore-mentioned hapless wanderer off Mickledore and on their way safely. It is a tribute to the place that it cannot be recorded properly on a map.

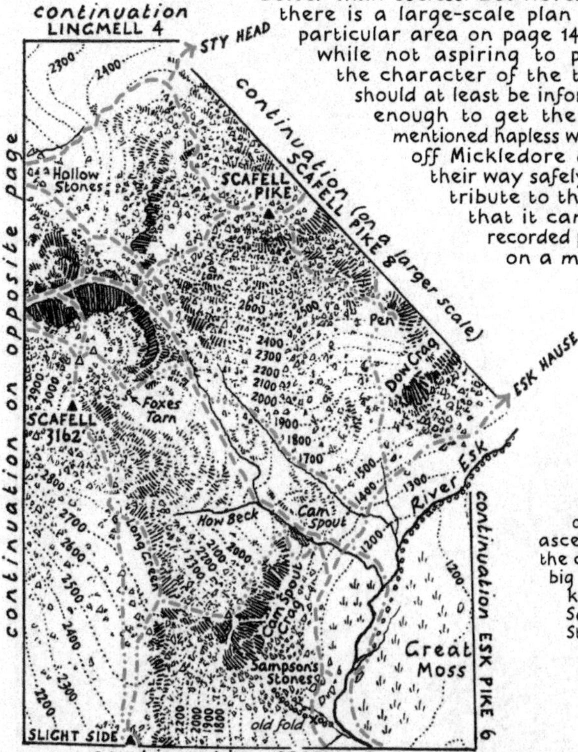
continuation LINGMELL 4
STY HEAD
continuation (on a larger scale) SCAFELL PIKE 8
continuation on opposite page
Hollow Stones
SCAFELL PIKE
Pen
Dow Crag
ESK HAUSE
Foxes Tarn
SCAFELL 3162'
How Beck
Cam Spout
River Esk
Long Green
Cam Spout Crag
Sampson's Stones
old fold
Great Moss
continuation ESK PIKE 6
SLIGHT SIDE
continuation SCAFELL 8

For the options in ascent from the cluster of big boulders known as Sampson's Stones, see *page 12.*

The western of the two paths shown above between Slight Side and Scafell is not easy to follow in ascent (from south to north) and is more often used as a quick way down for walkers bound for Eskdale — it avoids boulder fields on the Long Green ridge which slow progress in this regard.

MAP

continuation SCAFELL 5

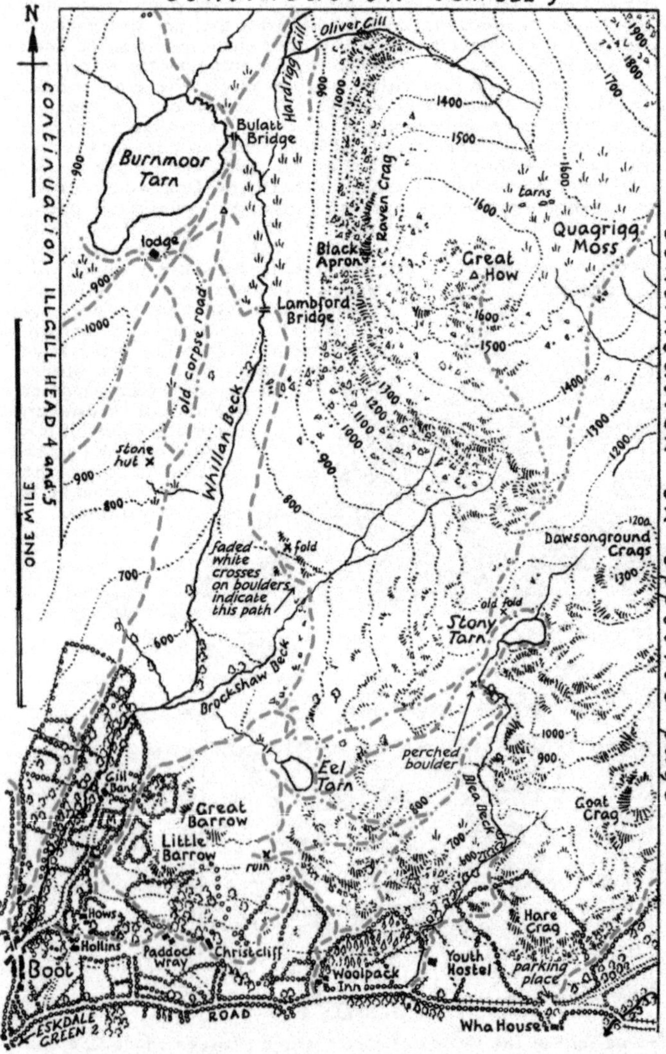
N
continuation ILLGILL HEAD 4 and 5
ONE MILE
continuation on opposite page
Oliver Gill
Hardrigg Gill
Bulatt Bridge
Burnmoor Tarn
lodge
old corpse road
Lambford Bridge
Black Apron
Raven Crag
Great How
Quagrigg Moss
tarns
Whillan Beck
stone hut
faded white crosses on boulders indicate this path
fold
Dawsonground Crags
old fold
Stony Tarn
perched boulder
Brockshaw Beck
Eel Tarn
Bleа Beck
Goat Crag
Gill Bank
Great Barrow
Little Barrow
ruin
Hows
Hollins
Boot
Paddock Wray
Christcliff
Woolpack Inn
Youth Hostel
Hare Crag
parking place
ROAD
ESKDALE GREEN 2
Wha House

The letter M near Gill Bank marks the location of a monkey puzzle tree. This incongruous Chilean native grows at a foot a year.

MAP

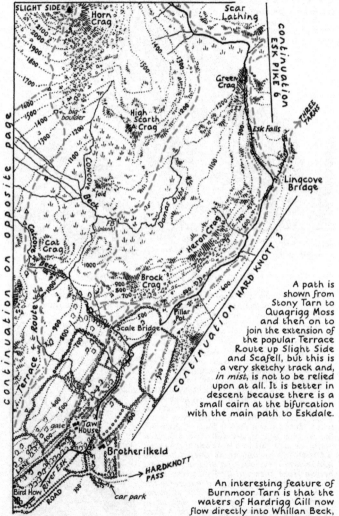

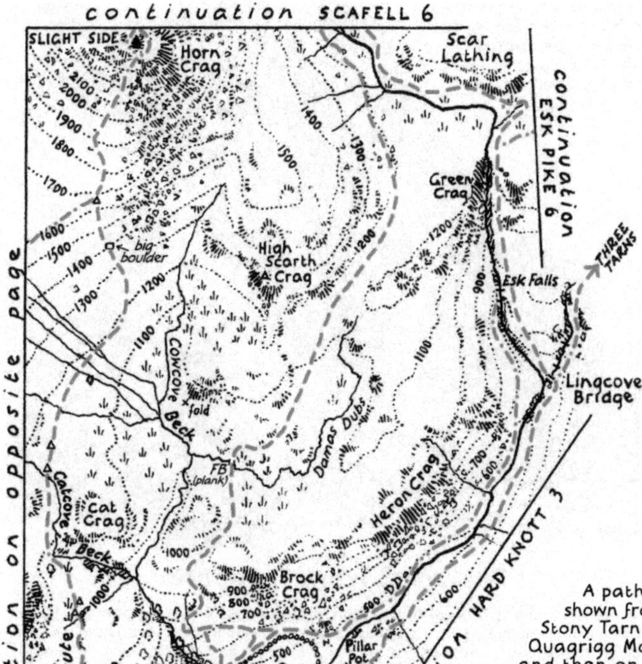
continuation SCAFELL 6
SLIGHT SIDE
Horn Crag
Scar Lathing
continuation ESK PIKE 6
2100
2000
1900
1800
1700
1600
1500
1400
1300
1200
1100
1000
900
800
700
600
500
400
300
big boulder
Green Crag
High Scarth Crag
THREE TARNS
Esk Falls
Lingcove Bridge
Cowcove Beck
fold
Damas Dubs
FB (plank)
Catcove Beck
Cat Crag
Heron Crag
Brock Crag
Pillar Pot
Scale Bridge
continuation HARD KNOTT 3
Terrace Route
continuation on opposite page
gate
Taw House
Brotherilkeld
HARDKNOTT PASS
car park
LANE
River Esk
ROAD
Bird How

A path is shown from Stony Tarn to Quagrigg Moss and then on to join the extension of the popular Terrace Route up Slight Side and Scafell, but this is a very sketchy track and, *in mist*, is not to be relied upon at all. It is better in descent because there is a small cairn at the bifurcation with the main path to Eskdale.

An interesting feature of Burnmoor Tarn is that the waters of Hardrigg Gill now flow directly into Whillan Beck, whereas in 1960 they flowed into the tarn not far from its outlet, except when there was plenty of water in the stream. It is to be expected that paths and fences will change over the years, but streams usually stay as they are.

Scafell 9

The head of Deep Gill (the top of the descent to the West Wall Traverse) with the Pinnacle (left-centre) and the Oracle (bottom right)

The West Wall Traverse

The massive crags of Scafell are split asunder by the tremendous chasm of Deep Gill, which has two vertical pitches in its lower part that put the through route out of bounds for walkers. The upper half, however, although excessively stony, can be used by all and sundry without difficulty, and is linked to Lord's Rake by a path across a grassy shelf. This is the West Wall Traverse, The rock scenery is awe-inspiring but BE WARNED! Frequent rockfalls have made access *via* Lord's Rake difficult and unstable (*see page 4*). *Extreme care is necessary!*

ASCENT: Proceed cautiously up the first section of Lord's Rake. On the left, 10 yards short of the *col*, a distinct path goes up to the grassy shelf, along which it rises to enter Deep Gill, the two pitches now being below. Steep scree then follows to the open fell at the top of the Gill. The exit is a desperate scramble up a loose and earthy wall.

DESCENT: *One glance at Deep Gill from above, will be enough to discourage most people from entering it: Those who do so should keep to the right and watch for the path turning left out of the Gill 80 yards down, where the crag on this side eases off: this path slants easily across a shelf into Lord's Rake. It is vital that this path be taken; the Gill itself, further down, drops vertically over chockstones and is entirely impracticable for walkers.*

SCAFELL PIKE
col

The start of Lord's Rake (in descent)

ASCENT FROM WASDALE HEAD

via BROWN TONGUE: *3,000 feet of ascent : 3 miles*
via GREEN HOW:
2,950 feet : 3¾ miles
(from Wasdale Head Inn)

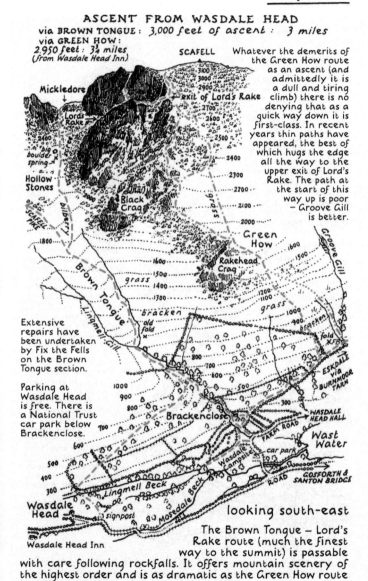

Whatever the demerits of the Green How route as an ascent (and admittedly it is a dull and tiring climb) there is no denying that as a quick way down it is first-class. In recent years thin paths have appeared, the best of which hugs the edge all the way to the upper exit of Lord's Rake. The path at the start of this way up is poor – Groove Gill is better.

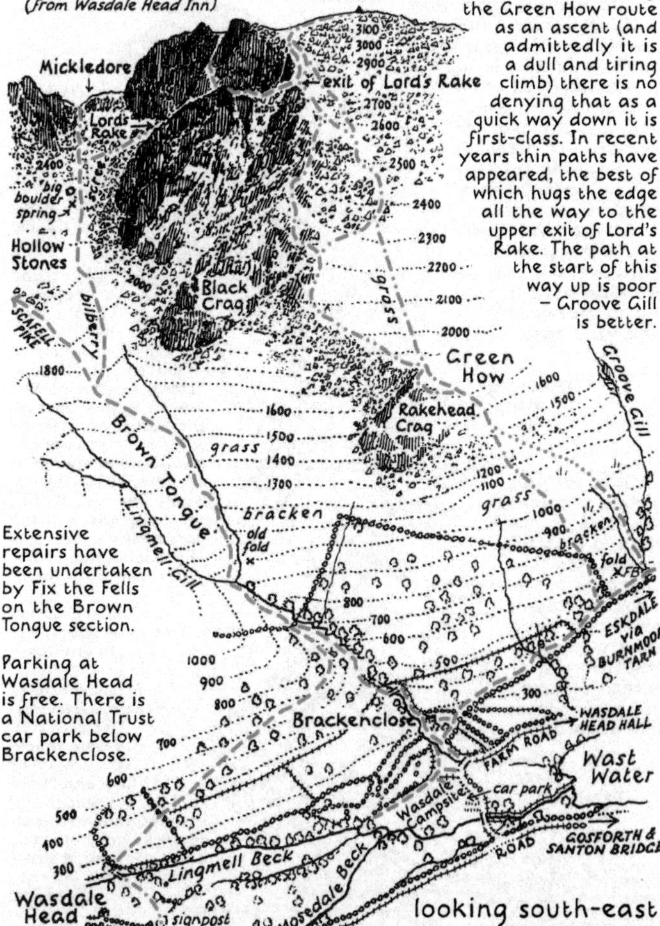
SCAFELL
3100
3000
2900
exit of Lord's Rake
Mickledore
Lord's Rake
2700
2600
2500
2400
big boulder
spring
scree
Hollow Stones
2400
2300
2200
2100
2000
Black Crag
bilberry
grass
SCAFELL PIKE
1800
Green How
1600
1500
Groove Gill
Rakehead Crag
Brown Tongue
grass
1600
1500
1400
1300
1200
1100
grass
bracken
1000
900
bracken
old fold
fold
FB
Lingmell Gill
800
700
600
ESKDALE via BURNMOOR TARN
1000
900
800
500
300
Brackenclose
WASDALE HEAD HALL
FARM ROAD
700
Wast Water
600
Wasdale Campsite
car park
500
400
300
ROAD
GOSFORTH & SANTON BRIDGE
Lingmell Beck
Mosedale Beck
Wasdale Head
signpost
Wasdale Head Inn

Extensive repairs have been undertaken by Fix the Fells on the Brown Tongue section.

Parking at Wasdale Head is free. There is a National Trust car park below Brackenclose.

looking south-east

The Brown Tongue – Lord's Rake route (much the finest way to the summit) is passable with care following rockfalls. It offers mountain scenery of the highest order and is as dramatic as the Green How route is dull. *See page 4 for details about the Lord's Rake section.*

ASCENT FROM ESKDALE

3100 feet of ascent : 6 miles from Boot

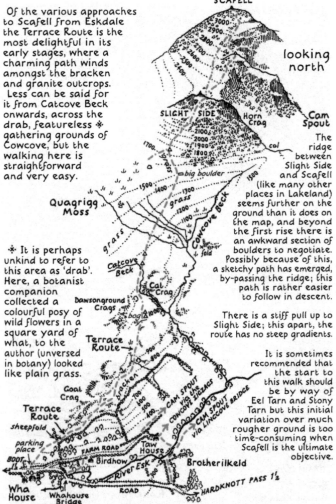

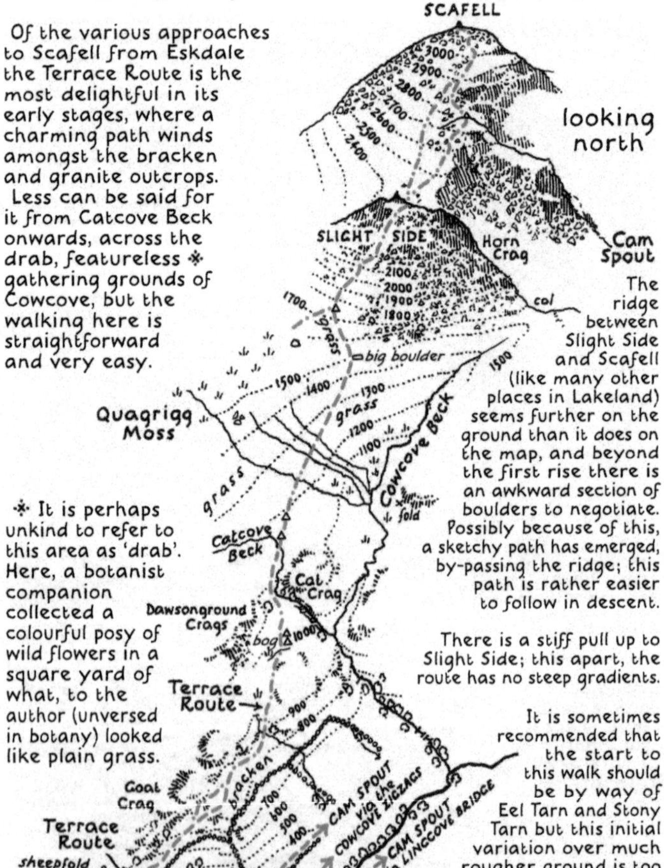
SCAFELL
looking north
3000
2900
2800
2700
2600
2500
2400
SLIGHT SIDE
Horn Crag
Cam Spout
col
2100
2000
1900
1800
1700
grass
big boulder
1500
1400
1300
1200
1100
Quagrigg Moss
Cowcove Beck
fold
Catcove Beck
Cat Crag
Dawsonground Crags
bog
1000
Terrace Route
900
800
bracken
700
600
500
400
Goat Crag
CAM SPOUT via the COWCOVE ZIGZAGS
CAM SPOUT via LINGCOVE BRIDGE
Terrace Route
sheepfold
parking place
FARM ROAD
Taw House
BOOT 1½
Birdhow
River Esk
Brotherilkeld
HARDKNOTT PASS 1½
Wha House
Whahouse Bridge
ROAD

Of the various approaches to Scafell from Eskdale the Terrace Route is the most delightful in its early stages, where a charming path winds amongst the bracken and granite outcrops. Less can be said for it from Catcove Beck onwards, across the drab, featureless * gathering grounds of Cowcove, but the walking here is straightforward and very easy.

* It is perhaps unkind to refer to this area as 'drab'. Here, a botanist companion collected a colourful posy of wild flowers in a square yard of what, to the author (unversed in botany) looked like plain grass.

The ridge between Slight Side and Scafell (like many other places in Lakeland) seems further on the ground than it does on the map, and beyond the first rise there is an awkward section of boulders to negotiate. Possibly because of this, a sketchy path has emerged, by-passing the ridge; this path is rather easier to follow in descent.

There is a stiff pull up to Slight Side; this apart, the route has no steep gradients.

It is sometimes recommended that the start to this walk should be by way of Eel Tarn and Stony Tarn but this initial variation over much rougher ground is too time-consuming when Scafell is the ultimate objective.

This is the easiest way to Scafell's top from any direction, and, in clear weather it is a splendid line of descent. Its one failing is that nothing is revealed of Scafell's magnificent crags.

ASCENT FROM ESKDALE
via CAM SPOUT
3050 feet of ascent : 7¼ miles from Boot

For a diagram and notes of the alternative routes to Cam Spout, see pages Scafell Pike 21 *and* 22.

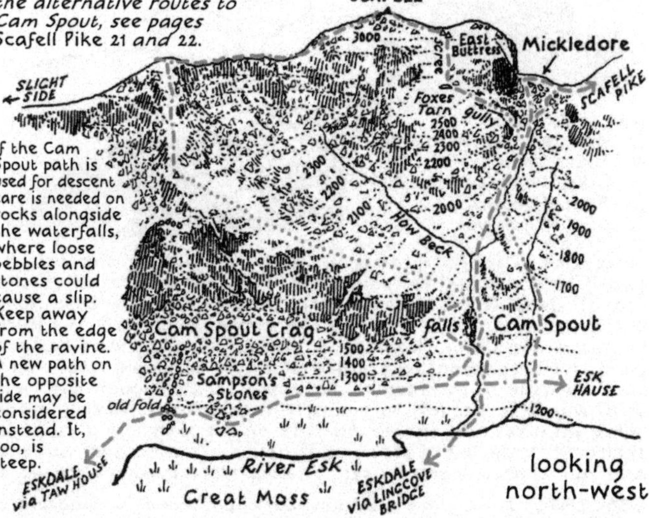
SCAFELL
3000
scree
East Buttress
Mickledore
SCAFELL PIKE
← SLIGHT SIDE
Foxes Tarn
gully
2500
2400
2300
2200
2300
2200
2100
2000
How Beck
2000
1900
1800
1700
falls
Cam Spout
Cam Spout Crag
1500
1400
1300
Sampson's Stones
old fold
ESK HAUSE
1200
River Esk
Great Moss
ESKDALE via TAW HOUSE
ESKDALE via LINGCOVE BRIDGE
looking north-west

If the Cam Spout path is used for descent care is needed on rocks alongside the waterfalls, where loose pebbles and stones could cause a slip. Keep away from the edge of the ravine. A new path on the opposite side may be considered instead. It, too, is steep.

The pathless route along the curving ridge of Cam Spout Crag is roundabout and the ridge itself is too broad to be exciting, although it narrows and becomes quite attractive near the end – a thin path begins when a cairn is reached. The one advantage of this route, of importance to people with bunions, is that it is possible to walk on grass throughout, and in fact it is the only way to the main ridge of Scafell from Cam Spout that avoids scree entirely.

Take the scrambling route to the right of the waterfalls, above which a good path goes up towards Mickledore, but before reaching the level of East Buttress and 100 yards below its nearest crags enter a stony gully going up squarely to the left; a small stream emerges from it. The gully, rough and unstable underfoot, leads directly to Foxes Tarn (which is no more than a tiny pond with a large boulder in it), whence a path on a long scree slope is climbed to the saddle above, the top then being 250 easy yards distant. This is the quickest route to the summit, avoiding the worst of the Mickledore screes, but rockfalls have rendered it more difficult in recent years.

Gluttons for punishment may, instead, continue up loose scree to the Mickledore ridge, descend the other side, and finish the climb by way of Lord's Rake (extreme caution advised here), taking half an hour longer but being rewarded by the finest scenery Scafell has to offer. *(For the perils of Lord's Rake, see page 4.)*

Three routes of ascent are shown, the longest on grass *via* Cam Spout Crag, the quickest *via* Foxes Tarn and the hardest *via* Mickledore.

THE SUMMIT

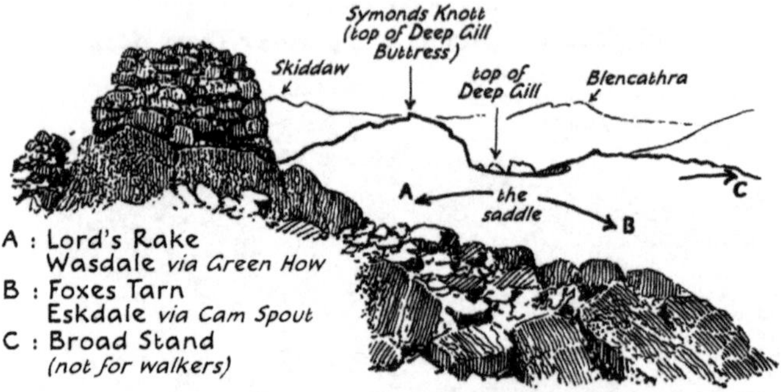
Symonds Knott (top of Deep Gill Buttress)
Skiddaw
top of Deep Gill
Blencathra
A
the saddle
B
C

A : Lord's Rake
Wasdale *via Green How*
B : Foxes Tarn
Eskdale *via Cam Spout*
C : Broad Stand
(not for walkers)

The face of Scafell Crag is the grandest sight in the district, and if only the highest point of the fell were situated on the top of Deep Gill Buttress, perched above the tremendous precipices of stone, it would be the best summit of all. As nature has arranged things, however, it lies back, away and remote from the excitement, the cairn being on a simple rise where there is little of interest at close quarters although the view southwards is enough to transfix the visitor's attention for some minutes. On the south side of the cairn is a ruinous shelter, not now more serviceable as a protection against wind and rain than the cairn itself. The top is everywhere stony.

DESCENTS: More than ordinary care is needed in choosing a route of descent. The western slope is stony, the eastern craggy, the northern precipitous. Except for Eskdale *via* Slight Side, recommended routes leave the saddle: turn left for Wasdale, right for Eskdale; go straight ahead for Deep Gill and the West Wall Traverse if the goal is Borrowdale, but rockfalls have added to the perils of the Traverse and Lord's Rake and these routes are to be used only with *great caution*.

In mist, the Slight Side route may be tried, but if lost turn right down to Hardrigg Gill and the Burnmoor path. For other destinations aim for the saddle, which is marked by a cross of stones, and follow, cautiously, the fine weather routes; see also the map on *page 14*.

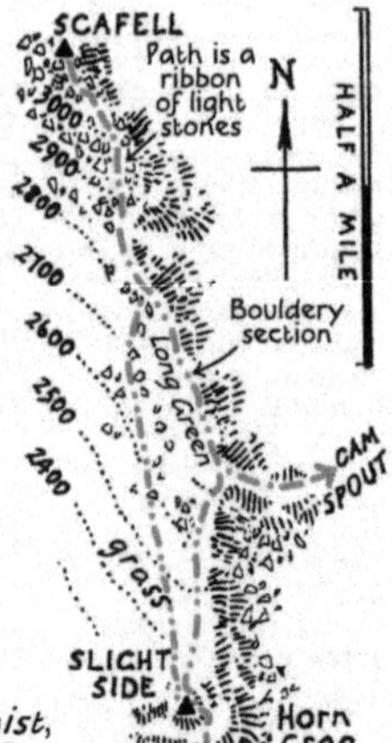
SCAFELL
Path is a ribbon of light stones
N
HALF A MILE
3000
2900
2800
2700
2600
2500
2400
Bouldery section
Long Green
CAM SPOUT
grass
SLIGHT SIDE
Horn Crag

RIDGE ROUTE

To SLIGHT SIDE, 2499′ : 1¼ miles : S

Depression at 2400′
100 feet of ascent
An easy walk, pathless on grass.

In clear weather there is no difficulty. *In mist*, remember to keep the escarpment on the left hand throughout.

RIDGE ROUTE

To SCAFELL PIKE, 3210': 1¼ miles : compass useless.
750' of ascent via Lord's Rake, 900' via Foxes Tarn.

Loins should be girded up for an hour's hard labour.

There is no bigger trap for the unwary and uninformed walker than this. Scafell Pike is clearly in view but the intervening crags cannot be seen. The natural inclination is to make a beeline for the Pike and to be deflected by the edge of the precipice down the easy slope to the right, encouraged by a good path that now appears. But this is the climbers' way to Broad Stand, which walkers cannot safely attempt. A desperate situation now arises. Just beyond the drop of Broad Stand, and tantalisingly near, is Mickledore Ridge, the easy connecting link between Scafell and the Pike. The choice is to risk a serious accident or toil all the way back and start again: not an easy decision for a walker already tired and pressed for time. The advice is to go back and start again.

From the saddle (cross of stones) three routes are available; none is easy.

1: *via* LORD'S RAKE: Rockfalls have made Lord's Rake a challenge: *see page 4 for details.* To reach it, turn left down a slope that steepens and becomes all stones. The start of the Rake is further down the fellside than will generally be expected, and it should be identified exactly *(see illustration, page 9).* Avoid the gaping entrance to Red Gill midway. On page 4 the Rake is described in ascent – it will occur to the mentally alert that if there are 3 ups and 2 downs in *ascent* there must be 3 downs and 2 ups in *descent*. From the foot of the Rake continue ahead below the crags and scramble up to Mickledore Ridge, where turn left along a good path to the Pike.

2: *via* FOXES TARN: This is also rough, and involves a greater descent and re-ascent. Turn *right* down a steepening slope to the Tarn, then *left* by the issuing stream (rough gully) to join the stony path coming up from Cam Spout for Mickledore and the Pike (right).

3: *via* THE WEST WALL TRAVERSE: This is something special but *see the notes on page 9.*

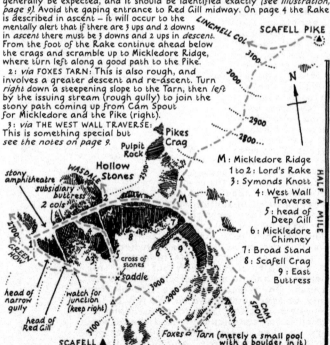

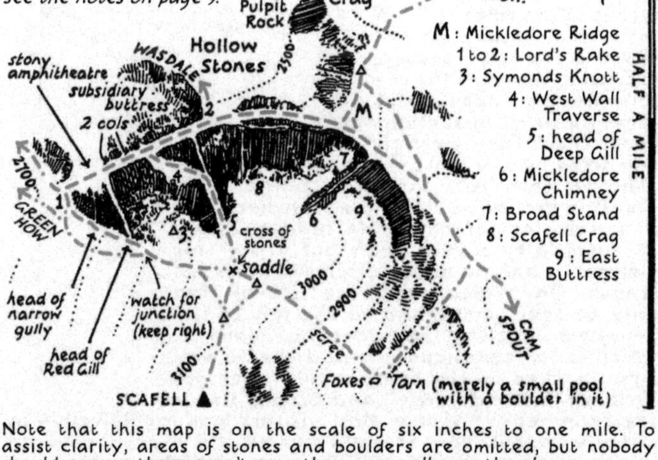
LINGMELL COL
SCAFELL PIKE
3100
3000
2900
2800
N
HALF A MILE
Pikes Crag
Pulpit Rock
Hollow Stones
WASDALE
2500
stony amphitheatre
subsidiary buttress
2 cols
2700
GREEN HOW
cross of stones
saddle
3000
2900
scree
3100
CAM SPOUT
head of narrow gully
head of Red Gill
watch for junction (keep right)
SCAFELL
Foxes Tarn (merely a small pool with a boulder in it)
M : Mickledore Ridge
1 to 2 : Lord's Rake
3 : Symonds Knott
4 : West Wall Traverse
5 : head of Deep Gill
6 : Mickledore Chimney
7 : Broad Stand
8 : Scafell Crag
9 : East Buttress

Note that this map is on the scale of six inches to one mile. To assist clarity, areas of stones and boulders are omitted, but nobody should assume there aren't any: they occur all over the place.

THE VIEW

The bulky mass of Scafell Pike, north-east, obstructs the view of a considerable slice of Lakeland, but nevertheless Scafell's top is a most excellent viewpoint and, additionally, a place for reverie, especially when reached from the north, for here there is awareness that one has come at last to the outer edge of the mountains and that, beyond, lie only declining foothills to the sea. Vaguely, in the mind of a fellwalker long past his youth, there arises a feeling of sadness, as though at this point the mountains are behind, in the past, and ahead is a commonplace world, a future in which mountains have no part, his own future. Yet this vision of low hills and green valleys, of distant sands and wide expanses of sea, is very beautiful. From Morecambe Bay to Furness and across the Duddon Estuary and Black Combe to the sand dunes of Ravenglass, and along the glorious length of Eskdale, all is smiling and serene, often when the high mountains are frowning. The bright pastures of Eskdale, won from the rough fells, have a happy quality of seeming to be in sunlight even under cloud. The view in this direction, unmarred by any scars of industry, is superb.

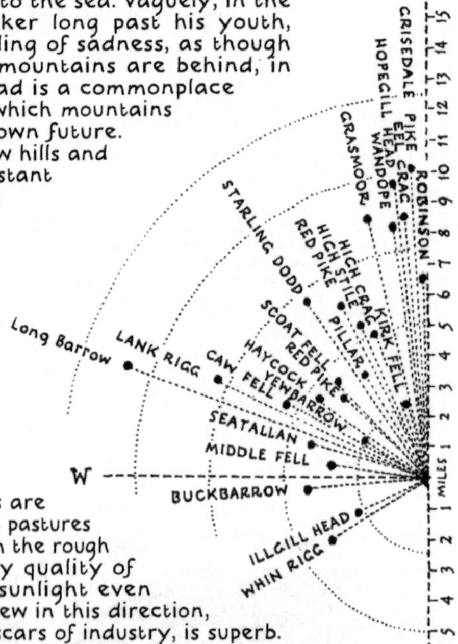
N
W
S
MILES
GRISEDALE PIKE
HOPEGILL HEAD
EEL CRAG
WANDOPE
GRASMOOR
ROBINSON
STARLING DODD
HIGH CRAG
HIGH STILE
RED PIKE
KIRK FELL
PILLAR
SCOAT FELL
RED PIKE
HAYCOCK
YEWBARROW
Long Barrow
LANK RIGG
CAW FELL
SEATALLAN
MIDDLE FELL
BUCKBARROW
ILLGILL HEAD
WHIN RIGG

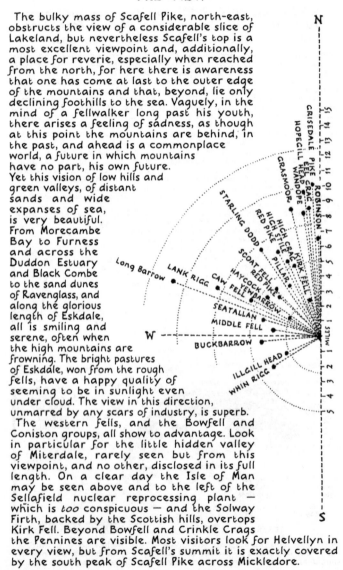

The western fells, and the Bowfell and Coniston groups, all show to advantage. Look in particular for the little hidden valley of Miterdale, rarely seen but from this viewpoint, and no other, disclosed in its full length. On a clear day the Isle of Man may be seen above and to the left of the Sellafield nuclear reprocessing plant — which is *too* conspicuous — and the Solway Firth, backed by the Scottish hills, overtops Kirk Fell. Beyond Bowfell and Crinkle Crags the Pennines are visible. Most visitors look for Helvellyn in every view, but from Scafell's summit it is exactly covered by the south peak of Scafell Pike across Mickledore.

THE VIEW

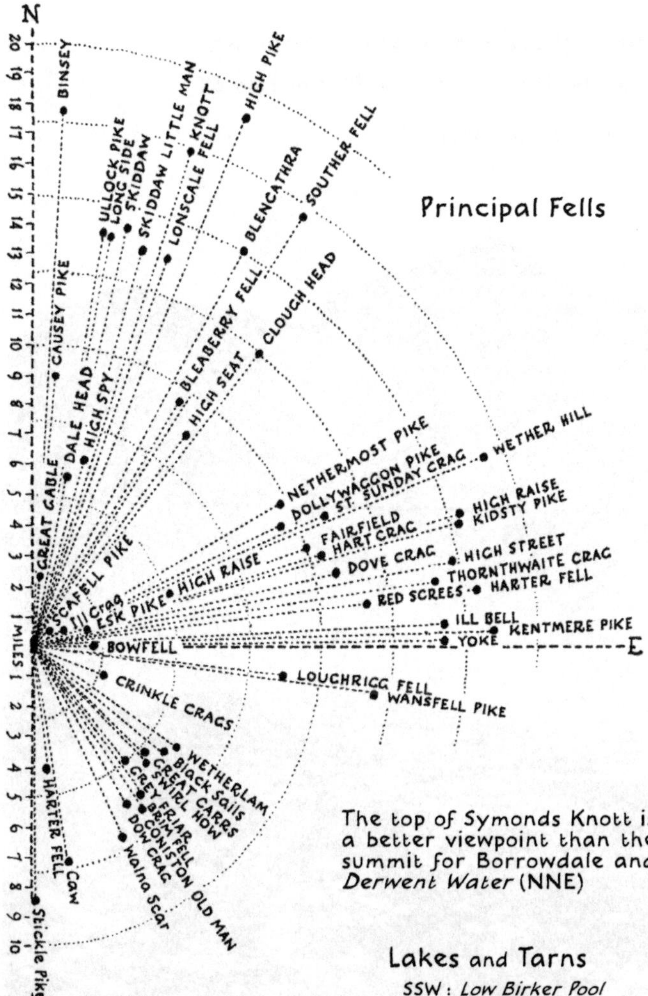

Principal Fells
N
E
S
MILES
BINSEY
ULLOCK PIKE
LONG SIDE
SKIDDAW
SKIDDAW LITTLE MAN
LONSCALE FELL
KNOTT
HIGH PIKE
BLENCATHRA
SOUTHER FELL
CAUSEY PIKE
DALE HEAD
HIGH SPY
BLEABERRY FELL
HIGH SEAT
CLOUGH HEAD
GREAT GABLE
SCAFELL PIKE
Ill Crag
ESK PIKE
HIGH RAISE
NETHERMOST PIKE
DOLLYWAGGON PIKE
ST. SUNDAY CRAG
WETHER HILL
FAIRFIELD
HART CRAG
DOVE CRAG
HIGH RAISE
KIDSTY PIKE
HIGH STREET
THORNTHWAITE CRAG
HARTER FELL
RED SCREES
ILL BELL
KENTMERE PIKE
YOKE
BOWFELL
LOUGHRIGG FELL
WANSFELL PIKE
CRINKLE CRAGS
WETHERLAM
Black Sails
GREAT CARRS
SWIRL HOW
GREY FRIAR
BRIM FELL
CONISTON OLD MAN
DOW CRAG
Walna Scar
HARTER FELL
CAW
Stickle Pike

The top of Symonds Knott is a better viewpoint than the summit for Borrowdale and *Derwent Water* (NNE)

Lakes and Tarns

SSW : *Low Birker Pool*
SSW : *Eel Tarn*
SSW : *Tarns on Great How*
SSW : *Devoke Water*
SW : *Burnmoor Tarn*
W : *Wast Water*
NW : *Low Tarn*

Scafell Pike 3210'

the highest mountain in England

formerly 'The Pikes' or 'The Pikes of Scawfell'

OS grid ref: NY215072

from Great Moss,
Upper Eskdale

Scafell Pike 2

Scafell Pike
Ill Crag
from the gorge of the Esk

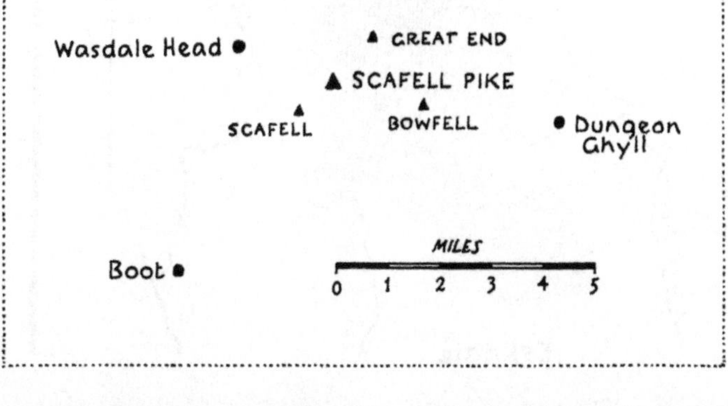
Seathwaite
GREAT GABLE
GREAT END
Wasdale Head
SCAFELL PIKE
SCAFELL
BOWFELL
Dungeon Ghyll
MILES
0 1 2 3 4 5
Boot

The Scafell Range

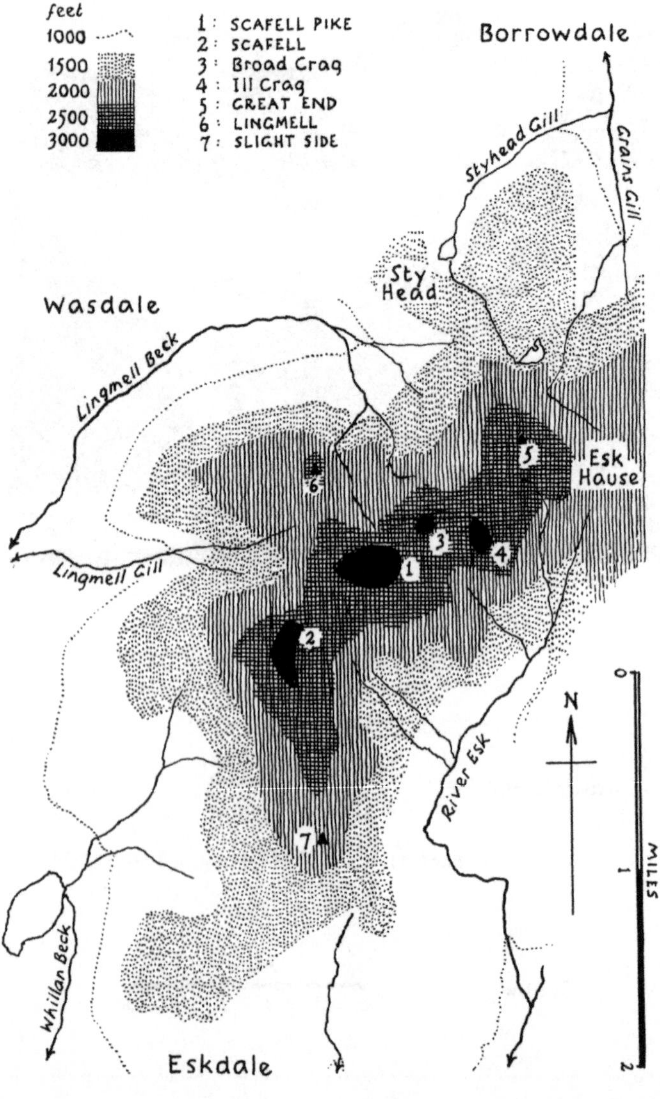
feet
1000
1500
2000
2500
3000
1 : SCAFELL PIKE
2 : SCAFELL
3 : Broad Crag
4 : Ill Crag
5 : GREAT END
6 : LINGMELL
7 : SLIGHT SIDE
Borrowdale
Styhead Gill
Grains Gill
Sty Head
Wasdale
Lingmell Beck
Esk Hause
Lingmell Gill
N
River Esk
0
1
2
MILES
Whillan Beck
Eskdale

Scafell Pike's grandest crag:
Dow Crag

Known to climbers as Esk Buttress, this 400-foot near-vertical crag rises from the fellside low down on the mountain's east flank, overlooking the River Esk.

Scafell Pike's best-known crag:
Pulpit Rock

This fine pinnacle (seen here from Mickledore) is the best feature of Pikes Crag, above Hollow Stones. Its top (easily reached from the summit-to-Mickledore path) is the best of all viewpoints for Scafell Crag.

NATURAL FEATURES

The difference between a hill and a mountain depends on *appearance*, not on *altitude* (whatever learned authorities may say to the contrary) and is thus arbitrary and a matter of personal opinion. Grass predominates on a hill, rock on a mountain. A hill is smooth, a mountain rough. In the case of Scafell Pike, opinions must agree that here is a mountain without doubt, and a mountain that is, moreover, every inch a mountain. Roughness and ruggedness are the necessary attributes, and the Pike has these in greater measure than other high ground in the country — which is just as it should be, for there is no higher ground than this.

Strictly, the name 'Scafell Pike' should be in the plural, there being three principal summits above 3000 feet, the two lesser having the distinguishing titles of Broad Crag and Ill Crag. The main Pike is, however, pre-eminent, towering over the others seemingly to a greater extent than the mere 160 feet or so by which it has superiority in altitude, and in general being a bulkier mass altogether.

The three summits rise from the main spine of an elevated ridge which keeps above 2800 feet to its abrupt termination in the cliffs of Great End, facing north to Borrowdale; lower spurs then run down to that valley. In the opposite direction, south-west, across the deep gulf of Mickledore, is the tremendous rock wall of the neighbouring and separate mountain of Scafell, which also exceeds 3000 feet: this is the parent mountain in the one sense that its name has been passed on to the Pikes. Scafell's summit ridge runs south and broadens into foothills, descending ultimately to mid-Eskdale.

continued

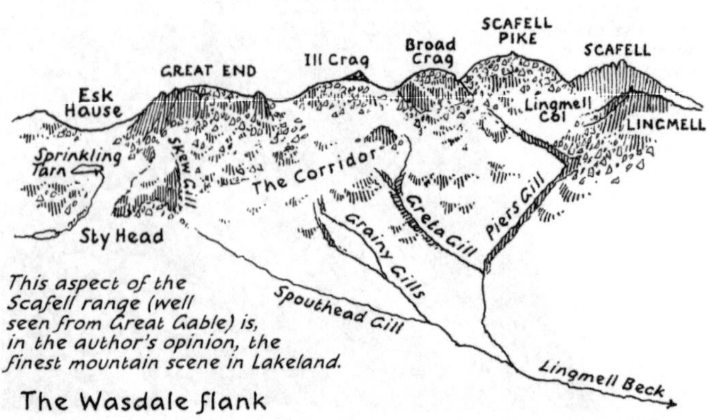
SCAFELL PIKE
Broad Crag
Ill Crag
GREAT END
SCAFELL
Esk Hause
Lingmell Col
LINGMELL
Sprinkling Tarn
Skew Gill
The Corridor
Greta Gill
Piers Gill
Grainy Gills
Sty Head
Spouthead Gill
Lingmell Beck

This aspect of the Scafell range (well seen from Great Gable) is, in the author's opinion, the finest mountain scene in Lakeland.

The Wasdale flank

NATURAL FEATURES

The flanks of the range are bounded on the west by Wasdale, and by the upper reaches of Eskdale, east. All the waters from the Pikes (and from Scafell) flow into one or other of these two valleys, ultimately to merge in the Ravenglass estuary. Thus it will be seen that Scafell Pike, despite a commanding presence, has not the same importance, geographically, as many other fells in the district. It does not stand at the head of any valley, but between valleys: it is not the hub of a wheel from which watercourses radiate; it is one of the spokes. It is inferior, in this respect, to Great Gable or Bowfell nearby, or even its own Great End.

Another interesting feature of Scafell Pike is that although it towers so mightily above Wasdale it can claim no footing in that valley, its territory tapering quickly to Brown Tongue, at the base of which it is nipped off by the widening lower slopes of Lingmell and Scafell.

Tarns are noticeably absent on the arid, stony surface of the mountain, but there is one sheet of water below the summit to the south, Broadcrag Tarn, which is small and unattractive, but, at 2725 feet, is one of the highest tarns in Lakeland.

Crags are in evidence on all sides, and big areas of the upper slopes lie devastated by a covering of piled-up boulders, a result not of disintegration but of the volcanic upheavals that laid waste to the mountain during its formation. The landscape is harsh, even savage, and has attracted to itself nothing of romance or historical legend. There is no sentiment about Scafell Pike.

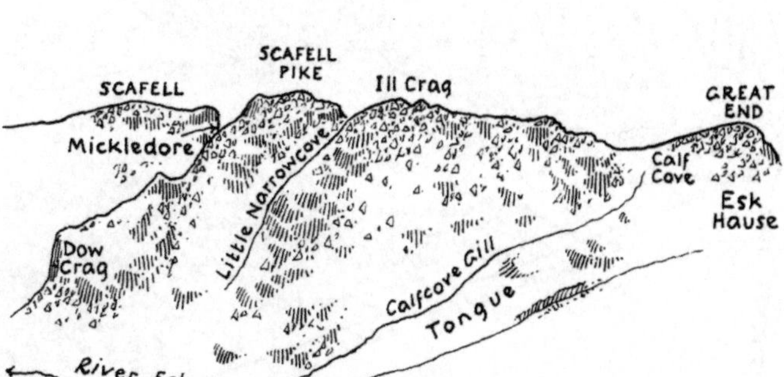
SCAFELL
SCAFELL PIKE
Ill Crag
GREAT END
Mickledore
Little Narrowcove
Calf Cove
Esk Hause
Dow Crag
Calfcove Gill
Tongue
River Esk

This view is as seen from the south ridge of Esk Pike

The Eskdale flank

MAP

ONE MILE

Note that the scale of this map is slightly greater than that generally used in the book. *All continuations shown here are on a reduced scale.*

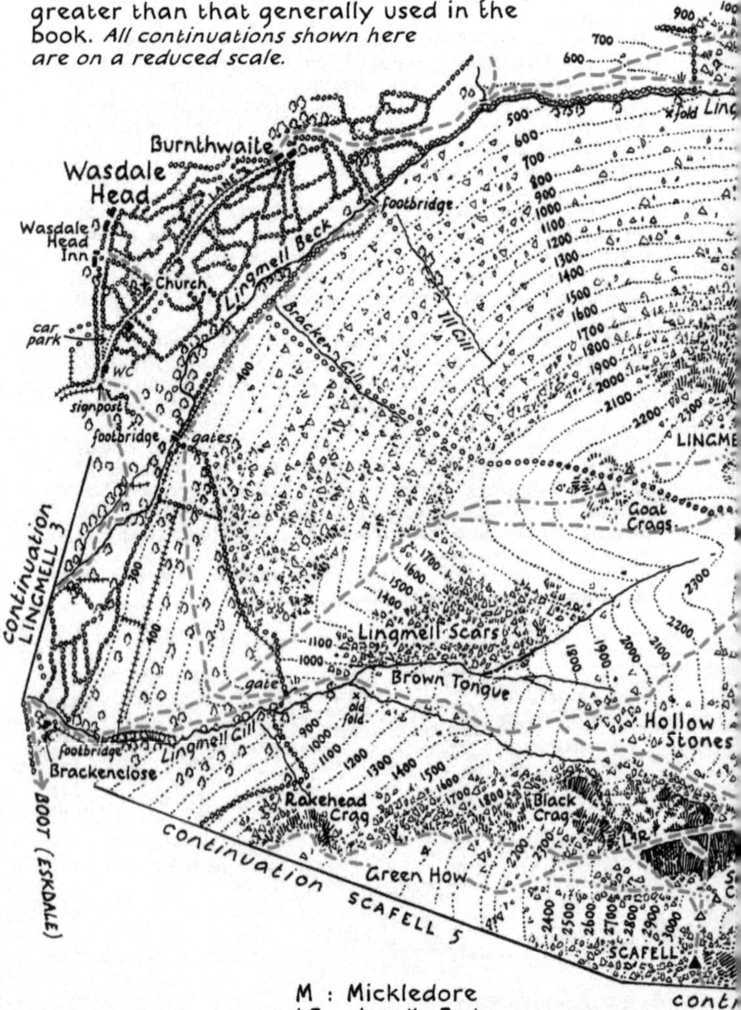
Burnthwaite
Wasdale Head
Wasdale Head Inn
LANE
Church
car park
WC
signpost
footbridge
gates
footbridge
Lingmell Beck
Bracken Gill
Ill Gill
fold
Ling
LINGME
Goat Crags
Lingmell Scars
Brown Tongue
gate
old fold
Hollow Stones
Lingmell Gill
footbridge
Brackenclose
Rakehead Crag
Black Crag
LR
Green How
SCAFELL
CONTINUATION LINGMELL 3
BOOT (ESKDALE)
CONTINUATION SCAFELL 5
cont

M : Mickledore
LR : Lord's Rake

MAP

A : to BORROWDALE
B : to GREAT LANGDALE
C : to ESKDALE (via CAM SPOUT)
Sty Head
GREAT GABLE
GABLE TRAVERSE
continuation SEATHWAITE FELL 2
Sprinkling Tarn
BORROWDALE
Spouthead Gill
Grainy Gills
The Band
Skew Gill
Corridor Route
Stand Crag
Greta Gill
Piers Gill
Ruddy Gill
continuation ALLEN CRAGS 3
Lambfoot Dub
GREAT END
Long Pike
Round How
Calf Cove
Esk Hause
tarns
Col
Broad Crag
Green Crag
Dropping Crag
Ill Crag
Tongue
Calfcove Gill
continuation ESK PIKE 5
SCAFELL PIKE 3210'
Pikes Crag
Cockly Pike
Broadcrag Tarn
Rough Crag
Little Narrowcove
Broad Crags
Pen
Dow Crag
River Esk
continuation
SCAFELL 6
N

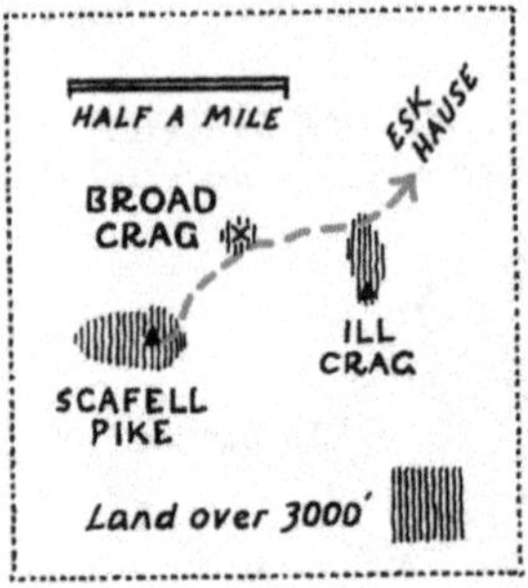
HALF A MILE
ESK HAUSE
BROAD CRAG
ILL CRAG
SCAFELL PIKE
Land over 3000'

Broad Crag, 3054'

Broad Crag is the second of the Scafell Pikes, and a worthy mountain in itself — but it has little fame, is not commonly regarded as a separate fell, and its summit is rarely visited. This latter circumstance appears strange, because the blazed highway between Esk Hause and the main Pike not only climbs over the shoulder of Broad Crag but actually passes within a hundred yards of its summit, which is not greatly elevated above the path. Yet not one person in a thousand passing along here (and thousands do!) turns aside to visit the cairn. The reason for this neglect is more obvious when on the site than it is from a mere study of the map, for the whole of the top is littered deep with piled boulders across which it is quite impossible to walk with any semblance of dignity, the detour involving a desperate and inelegant scramble and the risk of breaking a leg at every stride. Most walkers using the path encounter enough trouble underfoot without seeking more in the virgin jungle of tumbled rock all around. Broad Crag is, in fact, the roughest summit in Lakeland.

The eastern slope descends into Little Narrowcove, and is of small consequence, but the western flank is imposing. On this side the top breaks away in a semi-circle of crags, below which is a shelf traversed by the Corridor Route and bounded lower down a steepening declivity by the great gash of Piers Gill.

Only the proximity of the main Scafell Pike, overtopping the scene, robs Broad Crag of its rightful place as one of the finest of fells.

Broad Crag, and Broad Crag col (right) from the Corridor Route

Ill Crag, 3068'

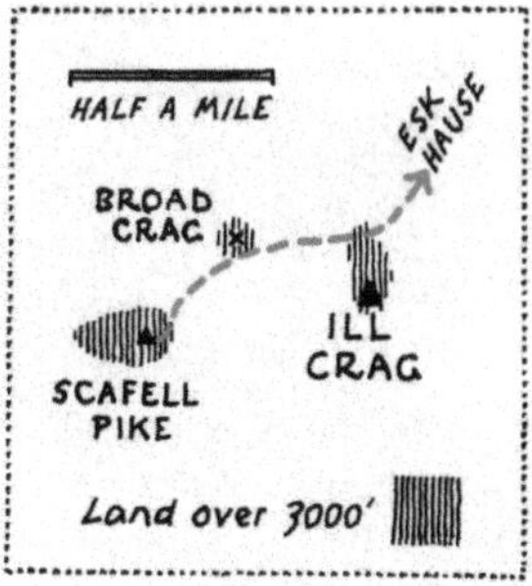
HALF A MILE
ESK HAUSE
BROAD CRAG
ILL CRAG
SCAFELL PIKE
Land over 3000'

Ill Crag is the third of the Scafell Pikes, and the most shapely, appearing as a graceful peak when viewed from upper Eskdale, which it dominates. Like Broad Crag, the summit lies off the path from Esk Hause to the main Pike but is more distant, although in this case too the shoulder of the fell is crossed at a height exceeding 3000', so that the summit is raised but little above it. The detour to the top is simple, only the final short rise being really rougher than the boulder-crossings on the path itself. Ill Crag is prominently seen from the vicinity of Esk Hause, and many wishful (and subsequently disappointed) walkers hereabouts, engaged on their first ascent of Scafell Pike will wrongly assume it to be their objective.

The western slope goes down uneventfully between Broad Crag and Great End to the Corridor Route, and the glory of the fell is its excessively steep and rough fall directly from the cairn eastwards into the wilderness of upper Eskdale: a chaotic and desolate scene set at a precipitous gradient, a frozen avalanche of crags and stones, much of it unexplored and uncharted, wild in the extreme, and offering a safe refuge for escaped convicts or an ideal depository for murdered corpses. Someday, when the regular paths become overcrowded, it may be feasible to track out an exciting and alternative route of ascent for scramblers here, but the author prefers to leave the job to someone with more energy and a lesser love of life.

Ill Crag, from the path above Esk Hause

Pulpit Rock
Pikes Crag
Mickledore Buttress
Scafell Crag
Mickledore

from Hollow Stones

Once in a while every keen fellwalker should have a pre-arranged night out amongst the mountains. Time drags and the hours of darkness can be bitterly cold, but to be on the tops at dawn is a wonderful experience and much more than recompense for the temporary discomfort.

Hollow Stones is an excellent place for a bivouac, with a wide choice of overhanging boulders for shelter, many of which have been walled-up and made draught-proof by previous occupants. Watch the rising sun flush Scafell Crag and change a black silhouette into a rosy pink castle! (This doesn't always happen. Sometimes it never stops raining.)

Not many readers, not even those who are frequent visitors to Scafell Pike, could give a caption to this picture. It is, in fact, a scene in the unfrequented hollow of Little Narrowcove, looking up towards the summit of the Pike (the top cairn is out of sight). The crags, unsuspected on the usual routes, are a great surprise. Little Narrowcove (reached from Broad Crag *col*) is a grassy basin sheltered or encircled by cliffs: a good site for a mountain camp.

ASCENTS

The ascent of Scafell Pike is the toughest proposition the 'collector' of summits is called upon to attempt, and it is the one above all others that, as a patriot, he cannot omit. The difficulties are due more to roughness of the ground than to altitude, and to the remoteness of the summit from frequented valleys. From all bases except Wasdale Head the climb is long and arduous, and progress is slow: this is a full-day expedition, and the appropriate preparations should be made. Paths are good, but only in the sense that they are distinct; they are abominably stony, even bouldery — which is no great impediment when ascending but mitigates against quick descent. Ample time should be allowed for getting off the mountain.

In winter especially, when conditions can be Arctic, it is important to select a fine clear day, to start early, and keep moving; reserve three hours of daylight for the return journey. If under deep snow the mountain is better left alone altogether, for progress would then be laborious, and even dangerous across the concealed boulders, with a greater chance of death from exposure than of early rescue if an accident were to occur.

Scafell Pike may be ascended most easily from Wasdale Head, less conveniently from Borrowdale or Great Langdale or Eskdale. But all routes are alike in grandeur of scenery.

from WASDALE HEAD:

The usual route from Wasdale Head, *via* Brown Tongue, is the shortest way to the top from any inhabited place but also the dullest unless the opportunity is taken to visit Mickledore by a deviation from the trodden path, which may then be used throughout for descent. But consider the Corridor Route or Piers Gill to add variety to the walk.

3 hours up, 2 down

from BORROWDALE:

The ascent from Borrowdale is pre-eminent, because not only is the scenery excellent throughout but there is the advantage of two interesting and well-contrasted routes, so that one may be used in ascent and the other in descent, the whole round, in settled weather, being perhaps the finest mountain walk in the district. *From Seathwaite — 3½ hours up, 2½ down*

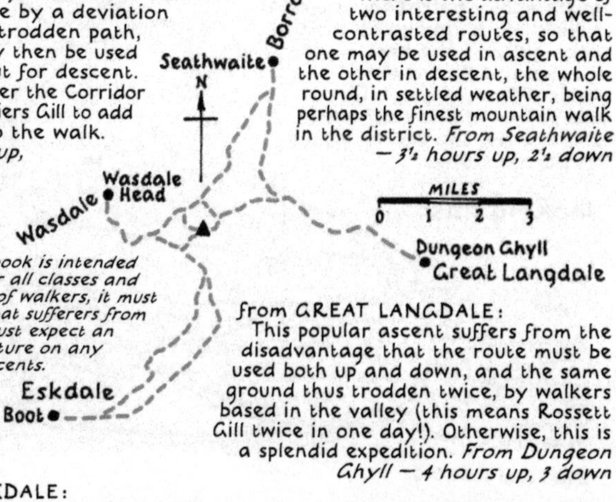
Borrowdale
Seathwaite
N
Wasdale Head
Wasdale
MILES
0 1 2 3
Dungeon Ghyll
Great Langdale
Eskdale
Boot

Since this book is intended to cater for all classes and conditions of walkers, it must be added that sufferers from bad feet must expect an orgy of torture on any of these ascents.

from GREAT LANGDALE:

This popular ascent suffers from the disadvantage that the route must be used both up and down, and the same ground thus trodden twice, by walkers based in the valley (this means Rossett Gill twice in one day!). Otherwise, this is a splendid expedition. *From Dungeon Ghyll — 4 hours up, 3 down*

from ESKDALE:

This is the best line of approach to the mountain: from the south its grandest and most rugged aspect is seen. Variations of route may be adopted, but time is a great enemy: the walk is lengthy (a feature most noticed when returning). *From Boot — 4½ hours up, 3½ down*

ASCENT FROM WASDALE HEAD
via BROWN TONGUE

3,000 feet of ascent
3½ miles
(from Wasdale Head Inn)

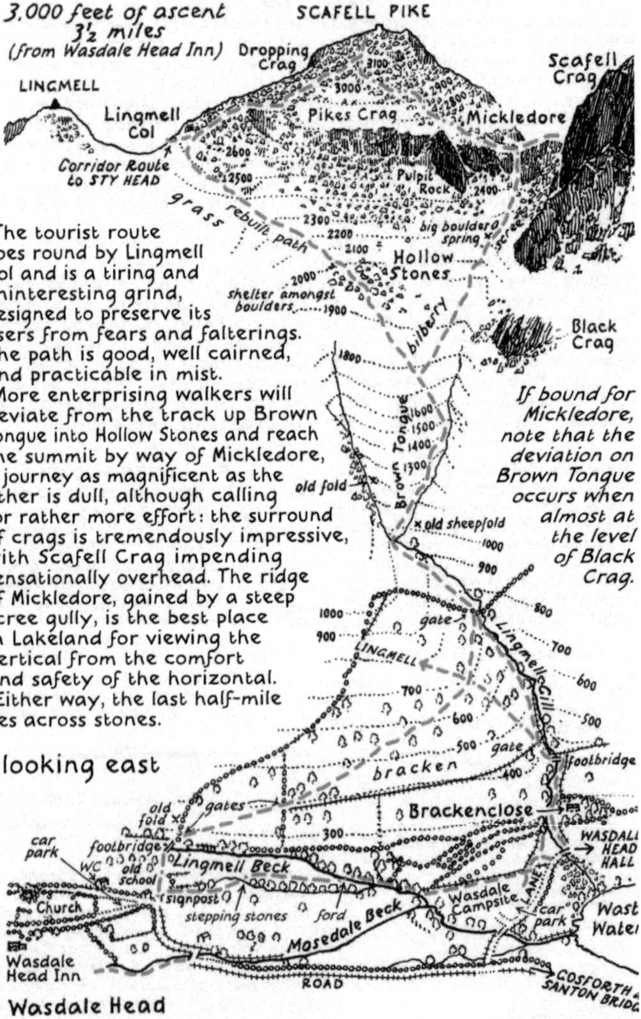
SCAFELL PIKE
Dropping Crag
Scafell Crag
LINGMELL
Lingmell Col
Pikes Crag
Mickledore
Corridor Route to STY HEAD
Pulpit Rock
grass
rebuilt path
big boulder
spring
scree
Hollow Stones
shelter amongst boulders
bilberry
Black Crag
Brown Tongue
old fold
old sheepfold
gate
LINGMELL
Lingmell Gill
bracken
gate
footbridge
gates
old fold
Brackenclose
WASDALE HEAD HALL
car park
footbridge
WC
old school
Lingmell Beck
Church
signpost
stepping stones
ford
Mosedale Beck
Wasdale Campsite
LANE
car park
Wast Water
Wasdale Head Inn
ROAD
GOSFORTH & SANTON BRIDGE

The tourist route goes round by Lingmell Col and is a tiring and uninteresting grind, designed to preserve its users from fears and falterings. The path is good, well cairned, and practicable in mist.

More enterprising walkers will deviate from the track up Brown Tongue into Hollow Stones and reach the summit by way of Mickledore, a journey as magnificent as the other is dull, although calling for rather more effort: the surround of crags is tremendously impressive, with Scafell Crag impending sensationally overhead. The ridge of Mickledore, gained by a steep scree gully, is the best place in Lakeland for viewing the vertical from the comfort and safety of the horizontal.

Either way, the last half-mile lies across stones.

If bound for Mickledore, note that the deviation on Brown Tongue occurs when almost at the level of Black Crag.

looking east

Wasdale Head

The shortest, the most direct and, consequently, the busiest ascent route up Scafell Pike. This is not a route for lovers of solitude.

ASCENT FROM WASDALE HEAD
via PIERS GILL

3,000 feet of ascent
3¾ miles
(from Wasdale Head Inn)

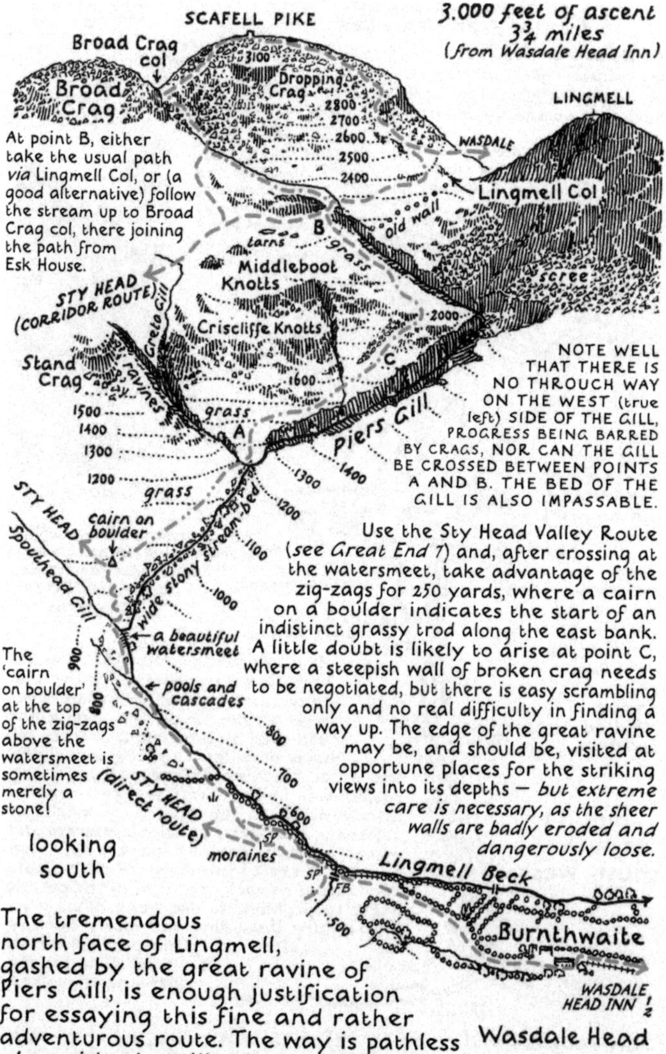

SCAFELL PIKE
Broad Crag col
Broad Crag
3100
Dropping Crag
2800
2700
2600
2500
2400
LINGMELL
WASDALE
Lingmell Col
old wall
B
tarns
grass
Middleboot Knotts
scree
STY HEAD (CORRIDOR ROUTE)
Greta Gill
2000
Criscliffe Knotts
Stand Crag
ravines
C
1600
1500
1400
1300
1200
grass
A
Piers Gill
1300
1400
1200
grass
STY HEAD
cairn on boulder
Spouthead Gill
1100
wide stony stream-bed
1000
900
a beautiful watersmeet
pools and cascades
800
800
700
600
STY HEAD (direct route)
SP
moraines
looking south
Lingmell Beck
SP
FB
500
Burnthwaite
WASDALE HEAD INN ½
Wasdale Head

At point B, either take the usual path *via* Lingmell Col, or (a good alternative) follow the stream up to Broad Crag col, there joining the path from Esk House.

NOTE WELL THAT THERE IS NO THROUGH WAY ON THE WEST (true left) SIDE OF THE GILL, PROGRESS BEING BARRED BY CRAGS, NOR CAN THE GILL BE CROSSED BETWEEN POINTS A AND B. THE BED OF THE GILL IS ALSO IMPASSABLE.

Use the Sty Head Valley Route (*see Great End 7*) and, after crossing at the watersmeet, take advantage of the zig-zags for 250 yards, where a cairn on a boulder indicates the start of an indistinct grassy trod along the east bank. A little doubt is likely to arise at point C, where a steepish wall of broken crag needs to be negotiated, but there is easy scrambling only and no real difficulty in finding a way up. The edge of the great ravine may be, and should be, visited at opportune places for the striking views into its depths — *but extreme care is necessary, as the sheer walls are badly eroded and dangerously loose.*

The 'cairn on boulder' at the top of the zig-zags above the watersmeet is sometimes merely a stone!

The tremendous north face of Lingmell, gashed by the great ravine of Piers Gill, is enough justification for essaying this fine and rather adventurous route. The way is pathless alongside the gill; clear weather is advisable for ascent and essential for descent by this route.

ASCENT FROM BORROWDALE
via STY HEAD

3,000 feet of ascent
6 miles from Seatoller

Having duly arrived at Styhead Tarn (so proving the reliability of the diagram thus far) refer now (with confidence) to the foot of the next page for the continuation of the route.

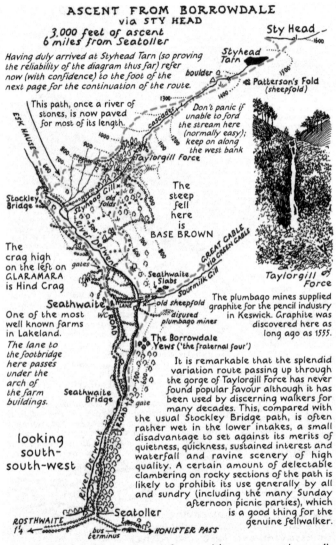

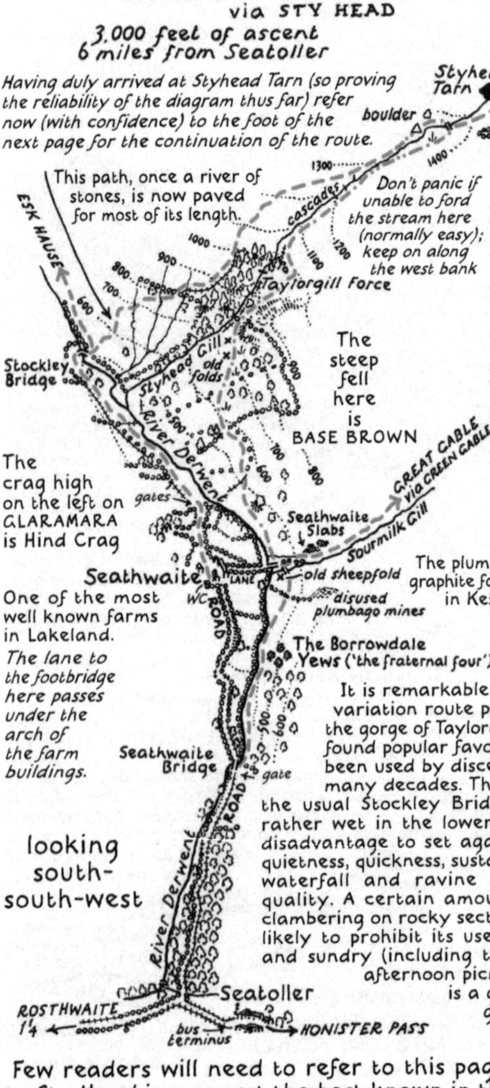
Sty Head
1600
Styhead Tarn
boulder
1500
Patterson's Fold (sheepfold)
1400
1300
This path, once a river of stones, is now paved for most of its length.
ESK HAUSE
cascades
Don't panic if unable to ford the stream here (normally easy); keep on along the west bank
1000
1100
1200
900
800
700
600
Taylorgill Force
The steep fell here is BASE BROWN
Stockley Bridge
Styhead Gill
old folds
500
River Derwent
700
600
800
GREAT CABLE via GREEN GABLE
The crag high on the left on GLARAMARA is Hind Crag
gates
Seathwaite Slabs
Sourmilk Gill
Seathwaite
LANE
old sheepfold
WC
ROAD
disused plumbago mines
One of the most well known farms in Lakeland.
The Borrowdale Yews ('the fraternal four')
The lane to the footbridge here passes under the arch of the farm buildings.
500
600
Seathwaite Bridge
gate
ROAD
looking south-south-west
River Derwent
Seatoller
ROSTHWAITE 1¼
bus terminus
HONISTER PASS

Taylorgill Force

The plumbago mines supplied graphite for the pencil industry in Keswick. Graphite was discovered here as long ago as 1555.

It is remarkable that the splendid variation route passing up through the gorge of Taylorgill Force has never found popular favour although it has been used by discerning walkers for many decades. This, compared with the usual Stockley Bridge path, is often rather wet in the lower intakes, a small disadvantage to set against its merits of quietness, quickness, sustained interest and waterfall and ravine scenery of high quality. A certain amount of delectable clambering on rocky sections of the path is likely to prohibit its use generally by all and sundry (including the many Sunday afternoon picnic parties), which is a good thing for the genuine fellwalker.

Few readers will need to refer to this page, as the walk to Sty Head is amongst the best known in the district, this being evidenced by the severe wear and tear of the path.

ASCENT FROM BORROWDALE
via STY HEAD

continued

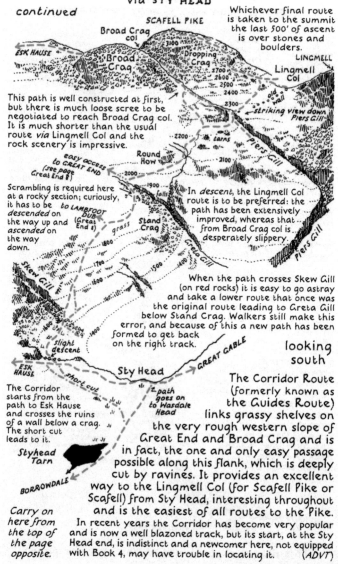

Whichever final route is taken to the summit the last 500' of ascent is over stones and boulders.

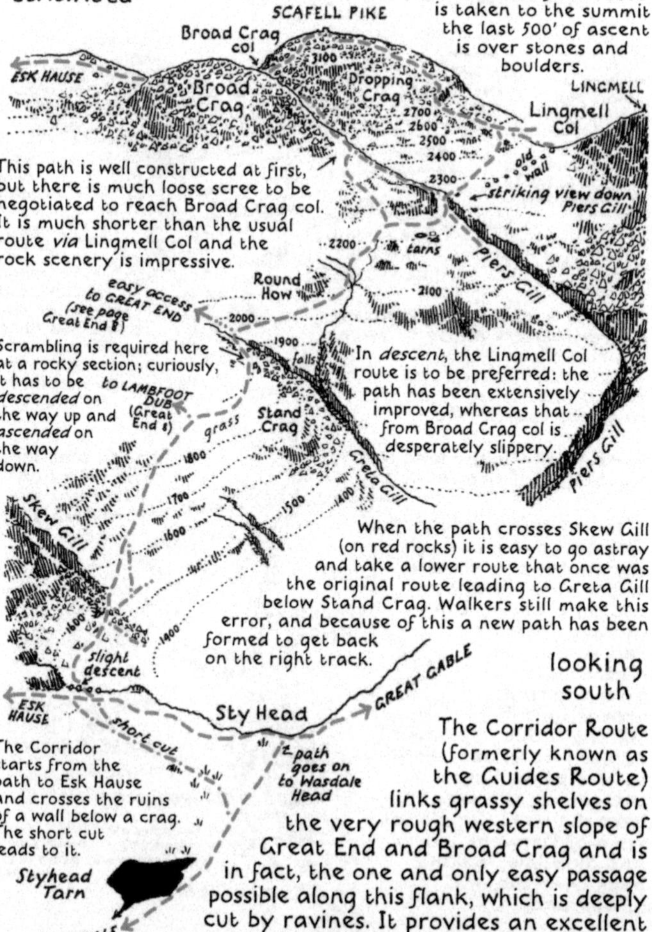
SCAFELL PIKE
Broad Crag col
ESK HAUSE
Broad Crag
3100
Dropping Crag
2700
2600
2500
2400
2300
2200
2100
2000
1900
1800
1700
1600
1500
1400
LINGMELL
Lingmell Col
old wall
striking view down Piers Gill
tarns
Piers Gill
Round How
easy access to GREAT END (see page Great End 8)
falls
to LAMBFOOT DUB (Great End 8)
Stand Crag
grass
Greta Gill
Skew Gill
slight descent
ESK HAUSE
Sty Head
GREAT GABLE
short cut
path goes on to Wasdale Head
Styhead Tarn
BORROWDALE

This path is well constructed at first, but there is much loose scree to be negotiated to reach Broad Crag col. It is much shorter than the usual route *via* Lingmell Col and the rock scenery is impressive.

Scrambling is required here at a rocky section; curiously, it has to be *descended* on the way up and *ascended* on the way down.

In *descent*, the Lingmell Col route is to be preferred: the path has been extensively improved, whereas that from Broad Crag col is desperately slippery.

When the path crosses Skew Gill (on red rocks) it is easy to go astray and take a lower route that once was the original route leading to Greta Gill below Stand Crag. Walkers still make this error, and because of this a new path has been formed to get back on the right track.

looking south

The Corridor starts from the path to Esk Hause and crosses the ruins of a wall below a crag. The short cut leads to it.

The Corridor Route (formerly known as the Guides Route) links grassy shelves on the very rough western slope of Great End and Broad Crag and is in fact, the one and only easy passage possible along this flank, which is deeply cut by ravines. It provides an excellent way to the Lingmell Col (for Scafell Pike or Scafell) from Sty Head, interesting throughout and is the easiest of all routes to the Pike.

Carry on here from the top of the page opposite.

In recent years the Corridor has become very popular and is now a well blazoned track, but its start, at the Sty Head end, is indistinct and a newcomer here, not equipped with Book 4, may have trouble in locating it. *(ADVT)*

ASCENT FROM BORROWDALE
via ESK HAUSE
3,200 feet of ascent : 5½ miles from Seatoller

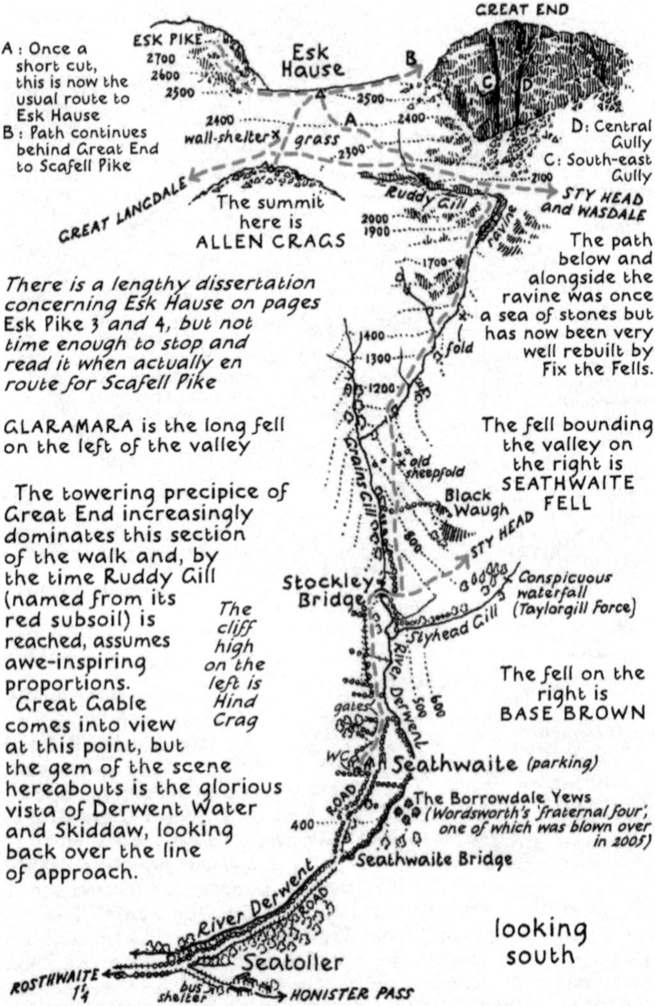
GREAT END
ESK PIKE
2700
2600
2500
Esk Hause
B
C
D
2500
2400
A
2400
wall-shelter
grass
2300
GREAT LANGDALE
The summit here is ALLEN CRAGS
Ruddy Gill
2100
STY HEAD and WASDALE
2000
1900
ravine
1700
fold
1400
1300
1200
Grains Gill
old sheepfold
Black Waugh
STY HEAD
800
Stockley Bridge
Conspicuous waterfall (Taylorgill Force)
Styhead Gill
River Derwent
500
600
gates
WC
Seathwaite (parking)
The Borrowdale Yews (Wordsworth's 'fraternal four', one of which was blown over in 2005)
ROAD
400
Seathwaite Bridge
River Derwent
ROAD
Seatoller
ROSTHWAITE 1¼
bus shelter
HONISTER PASS
looking south

A : Once a short cut, this is now the usual route to Esk Hause

B : Path continues behind Great End to Scafell Pike

D: Central Gully

C: South-east Gully

The path below and alongside the ravine was once a sea of stones but has now been very well rebuilt by Fix the Fells.

There is a lengthy dissertation concerning Esk Hause on pages Esk Pike 3 *and* 4, *but not time enough to stop and read it when actually en route for Scafell Pike*

GLARAMARA is the long fell on the left of the valley

The fell bounding the valley on the right is SEATHWAITE FELL

The towering precipice of Great End increasingly dominates this section of the walk and, by the time Ruddy Gill (named from its red subsoil) is reached, assumes awe-inspiring proportions.
Great Gable comes into view at this point, but the gem of the scene hereabouts is the glorious vista of Derwent Water and Skiddaw, looking back over the line of approach.

The cliff high on the left is Hind Crag

The fell on the right is BASE BROWN

This diagram continues on the opposite page

ASCENT FROM BORROWDALE
via ESK HAUSE

continued

This diagram is on a larger scale than that on the opposite page.

Ill Crag is prominently in view from the section of path between Esk House and Calf Cove. It is the highest thing in sight, and wishful thinkers will assume it to be the summit — until the Pike itself is finally revealed, indisputably higher and still far distant across a waste of stones.

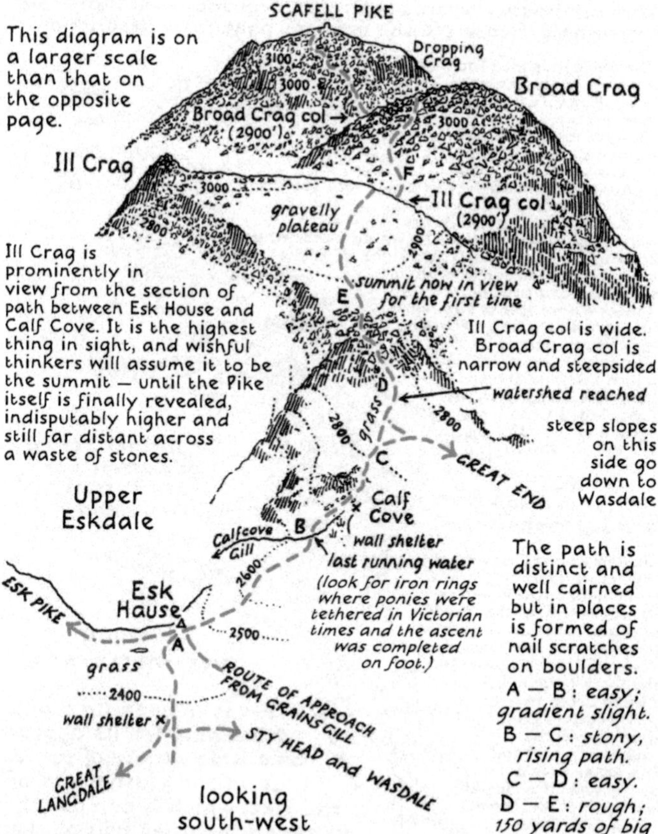
SCAFELL PIKE
Dropping Crag
Broad Crag
3100
3000
Broad Crag col →
(2900')
3000
Ill Crag
3000
F
← Ill Crag col
(2900')
gravelly plateau
2900
2800
summit now in view for the first time
E
Ill Crag col is wide. Broad Crag col is narrow and steepsided
D
watershed reached
grass
2800
2800
steep slopes on this side go down to Wasdale
C
GREAT END
Upper Eskdale
Calf Cove
B
Calfcove Gill
wall shelter
last running water
(look for iron rings where ponies were tethered in Victorian times and the ascent was completed on foot.)
2600
ESK PIKE
Esk Hause
A
2500
grass
2400
wall shelter
ROUTE OF APPROACH FROM GRAINS GILL
STY HEAD and WASDALE
GREAT LANGDALE
looking south-west

The path is distinct and well cairned but in places is formed of nail scratches on boulders.

A — B : *easy; gradient slight.*

B — C : *stony, rising path.*

C — D : *easy.*

D — E : *rough; 150 yards of big stones to cross.*

E — F : *easy.*

F onwards : *excessively rough — inescapable boulders, stones and scree.*

Of the many routes of approach to Scafell Pike, this, from Borrowdale *via* Esk Hause, is the finest. The transition from the quiet beauty of the valley pastures and woods to the rugged wildness of the mountain-top is complete, but comes gradually as height is gained and after passing through varied scenery both nearby and distant, that sustains interest throughout the long march.

ASCENT FROM GREAT LANGDALE

***3,400 feet of ascent : $5\frac{1}{2}$ miles** (from Old Dungeon Ghyll Hotel)*

From Esk House onwards the route coincides with that from Borrowdale. Please see the previous page for a description.

The walk falls into four distinct and well contrasted sections:

1 : *to Mickleden Sheepfold* — easy, level walking. Gimmer Crag and Pike o' Stickle high on the right and the Band rising on the left.

2 : *Rossett Gill* — gradual climbing. Bowfell's crags well seen on left, Rossett Pike on right.

3 : *Rossett Pass to Esk House* — undulating grass shelf with two descents where streams flow to Langstrath, right. Esk Pike is on the left, Great End ahead and Allen Crags right.

4 : *Esk Hause to the summit* — easy gradients, but becoming very rough across a lofty plateau; two more descents before the final steep, stony rise, Great End, right, Broad Crag, right, and Ill Crag, left, are by-passed.

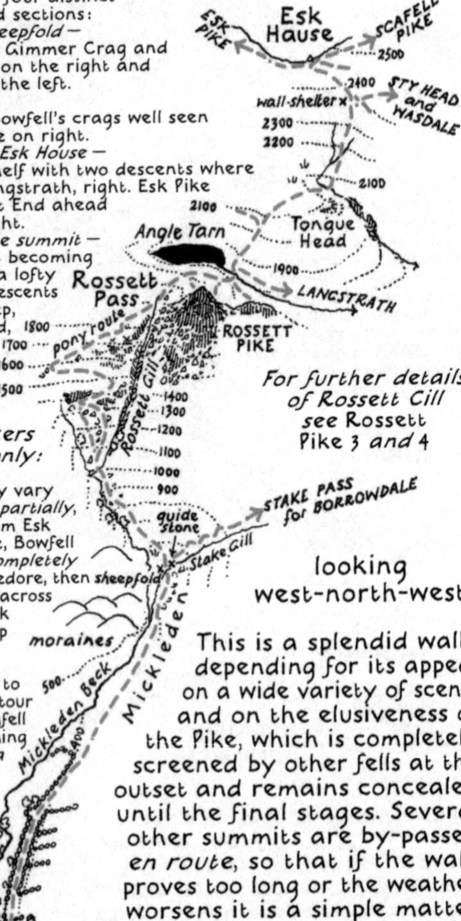
Esk Hause
ESK PIKE
SCAFELL PIKE
2500
2400
STY HEAD and WASDALE
wall-shelter x
2300
2200
2100
2100
Tongue Head
Angle Tarn
1900
LANGSTRATH
Rossett Pass
ROSSETT PIKE
pony route
1800
1700
1600
1500
Rossett Gill
1400
1300
1200
1100
1000
900
guide stone
STAKE PASS for BORROWDALE
Stake Gill
sheepfold
Mickleden
moraines
500
Mickleden Beck
400
WALL END
Old Dungeon Ghyll Hotel (car park)
looking west-north-west

For further details of Rossett Gill see Rossett Pike 3 *and* 4

NOTE
for strong walkers and supermen only:

Strong walkers may vary the return journey, *partially*, by coming back (from Esk Hause) over Esk Pike, Bowfell and the Band; or *completely* by going on to Mickledore, then down to Cam Spout, across the south ridge of Esk Pike to Green Hole, up to Three Tarns and down the Band.

Supermen can add to this latter walk a detour to the summit of Scafell *via* Lord's Rake, coming off to Cam Spout *via* Foxes Tarn: this involves 5000 feet of climbing in one day, all of it rough.

This is a splendid walk, depending for its appeal on a wide variety of scene, and on the elusiveness of the Pike, which is completely screened by other fells at the outset and remains concealed until the final stages. Several other summits are by-passed *en route*, so that if the walk proves too long or the weather worsens it is a simple matter to change plans in favour of a nearer 'top'. The route suffers from the disadvantage that it cannot be varied, by the average walker, if the return is to be made to Langdale.

Two views on the walk from Esk Hause to the summit

Many hearts have sunk into many boots as this scene unfolds. Here, on the shoulder of Ill Crag, the summit comes into sight, at last; not almost within reach as confidently expected by walkers who feel they have already done quite enough to deserve success, but still a rough half-mile distant, with two considerable descents (*Ill Crag col and Broad Crag col*) and much climbing yet to be faced before the goal is reached.

Bowfell
Crinkle Crags

Looking down into Little Narrowcove and Eskdale, with Ill Crag on the left, from Broad Crag col

ASCENT FROM ESKDALE
3100 feet of ascent : $7\frac{1}{2}$ miles from Boot

continued on following page

Wet and bedraggled pedestrians can rejoice at the prospect of shelter upon reaching Sampson's Stones (huge boulders) but should go no further if bad weather persists.

Do not follow the sketchy path along the west bank of the Esk (except for the purpose of visiting Esk Falls): it enters a gorge below Green Crag from which escape is difficult.

The path from Brotherilkeld (pronounced locally *Butterilket*) via Lingcove Bridge has too many distractions and temptations to halt and provides a final problem in crossing Great Moss dryshod.

✻ At the crossing of the small stream (which unexpectedly flows to the left) the path becomes indistinct on wet ground, but there is no risk of going astray if it is remembered that the path follows the boundary between the marsh on the right and dry land on the left. This is a beautiful spot, cut off from civilisation and surrounded by mountains, with bog myrtle and cotton grass growing near by.

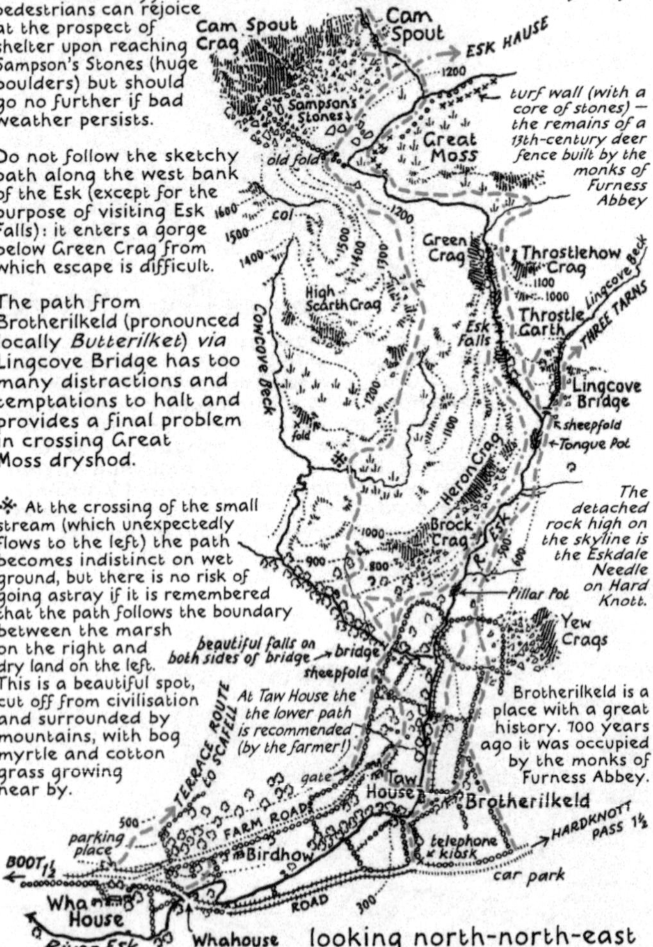

Cam Spout Crag
Cam Spout
ESK HAUSE
1200
Sampson's Stones
old fold
Great Moss
col
1600
1500
1400
1200
1500
1400
1700
Green Crag
Throstlehow Crag
1100
1000
Lingcove Beck
THREE TARNS
High Scarth Crag
Cowcove Beck
Esk Falls
Throstle Garth
Lingcove Bridge
sheepfold
Tongue Pot
fold
1200
1100
Heron Crag
Brock Crag
ESK
1000
900
800
700
600
Pillar Pot
Yew Crags
beautiful falls on both sides of bridge
bridge
sheepfold
At Taw House the the lower path is recommended (by the farmer!)
TERRACE ROUTE TO SCAFELL
gate
Taw House
Brotherilkeld
FARM ROAD
500
parking place
Birdhow
telephone kiosk
HARDKNOTT PASS 1½
BOOT 1½
car park
Wha House
ROAD
300
River Esk
Whahouse Bridge

turf wall (with a core of stones) — the remains of a 13th-century deer fence built by the monks of Furness Abbey

The detached rock high on the skyline is the Eskdale Needle on Hard Knott.

Brotherilkeld is a place with a great history. 700 years ago it was occupied by the monks of Furness Abbey.

looking north-north-east

There is no time for dawdling when bound for Scafell Pike, and the fine high-level approach by way of Taw House and the Cowcove zig-zags is recommended as the quickest route to Cam Spout. Here the serious climbing starts.

ASCENT FROM ESKDALE

Is there time enough to go on from Cam Spout? 3 hours is not too much to allow for the rest of the climb and return to this point via *Mickledore, nearer 4* via *Little Narrowcove and Pen.*

continued

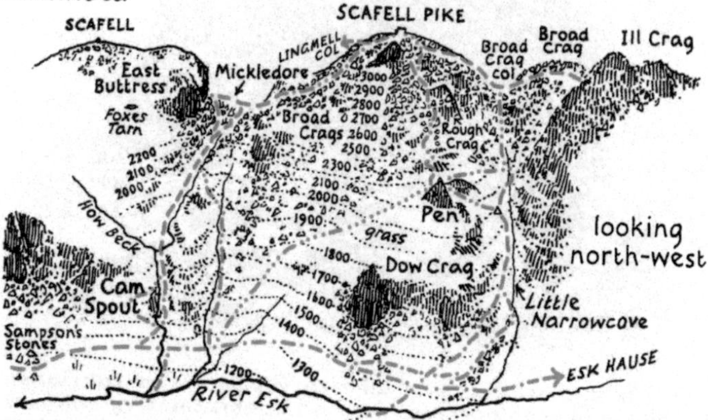
SCAFELL
SCAFELL PIKE
LINGMELL COL
Broad Crag col
Broad Crag
Ill Crag
East Buttress
Mickledore
Foxes Tarn
3000
2900
2800
2700
2600
2500
Broad Crags
Rough Crag
2200
2100
2000
How Beck
2300
2100
2000
1900
Pen
grass
looking north-west
1800
Dow Crag
1700
Cam Spout
1600
1500
1400
Little Narrowcove
Sampson's Stones
1200
1300
River Esk
ESK HAUSE

via MICKLEDORE

The usual route from Cam Spout goes up steeply by the waterfalls and proceeds thereafter on a good path, becoming a river of stones, to the ridge of Mickledore, where a track climbs across boulders to the summit. The rock-scenery on the last stages of the struggle to Mickledore is good, Scafell East Buttress being extremely impressive, but conditions underfoot are abominable. *This route can be done in mist.*

via LITTLE NARROWCOVE and BROAD CRAG COL

A secluded but circuitous and no less rough alternative is offered by Little Narrowcove, reached by passing below the imposing buttress of Dow Crag and completely dominated by the tremendous cliff of Ill Crag. Instead of following the bouldery beck up from valley, take a thin grassy path that heads for a gully on the skyline – this is easier.

via PEN

The author originally wrote: *It seems remarkable that England's highest mountain has no direct path to its summit on this, its finest side. It is not merely steepness that has kept walkers away from it, but rather the unavoidable, inescapable shawl of boulders covering the final 500 feet, where progress is not only painfully slow but carries a risk of displacing stones that have never before been trodden and may be balanced precariously and easily disturbed. There is no fun in pioneering routes over such rough terrain, which is safest left in virgin state.*

In recent years a direct route to the summit has been developed by walkers starting from the subsidiary peak of Pen. There are two ways of reaching Pen: a very steep grassy trudge from the valley floor not far from Cam Spout, or, far better from Little Narrowcove; at a small cairn a direct route is possible by following a gully, although it is recommended to climb higher into the hanging valley to enjoy the view illustrated on *page 11* before turning left. From Pen, a thin track heads for the Pike where low crags appear to bar the way, but there is one breach: look for a stony path 40′ above the rocks – below this scramble up left then right to reach the path. From here, the route zig-zags through the crags and boulders with a final steep scree climb to the summit. A visit to the pointed top of Rough Crag is recommended. *Clear weather is essential for this route.*

THE SUMMIT

This is it: the Mecca of all weary pilgrims in Lakeland; the place of many ceremonies and celebrations, of bonfires and birthday parties; the ultimate; the supreme; the one objective above all others; the highest ground in England; the top of Scafell Pike.

It is a magnet, not because of its beauty for this is not a place of beauty, not because of the exhilaration of the climb for there is no exhilaration in toiling upwards over endless stones, not because of its view for although this is good there are others belter. It is a magnet simply because it is the highest ground in England.

There is a huge cairn that from afar looks like a hotel: a well built circular edifice with steps leading up to its flat top from the west. Set into the vertical nine-foot north wall of the cairn is a tablet commemorating the gift of the summit to the nation. A few yards distant, to the west, is a triangulation column of the Ordnance Survey; a visitor in doubt and seeking confirmation of his whereabouts should consult the number on the front plate of the column: if it is anything other than S.1537 he has good cause for doubt — heaven knows where his erring steps have led him, but it is certainly not to the summit of Scafell Pike.

The surrounding area is barren, a tumbled wilderness of stones of all shapes and sizes, but it is not true, as has oft been written and may be thought, that the top is entirely devoid of vegetation; there is, indeed, a patch of grass on the south side of the cairn sufficient to provide a couch for a few hundredweights of exhausted flesh.

Yet this rough and desolate summit is, after all, just as it should be, and none of us would really want it different. A smooth green promenade here would be wrong. This is the summit of England, and it is fitting that it should be sturdy and rugged and strong.

THE SUMMIT

DESCENTS: It is an exaggeration to describe walkers' routes across the top of Scafell Pike as *paths*, because they make an uneasy pavement of angular boulders that are too unyielding ever to be trodden into subjection; nevertheless the routes are quite distinct, the particular boulders selected for their feet by the pioneers having, in the past century or so, become so extensively scratched by bootnails that they now appear as white ribbons across the grey waste of stones. Thus there is no difficulty in following them, even in mist.

The only place in descent where a walker might go astray is in going down by the Wasdale Head path to join the Corridor Route for Sty Head, the bifurcation above Lingmell Col being surprisingly vague: in mist a walker might find himself well down Brown Tongue before discovering his error. It is actually safer for a stranger seeking the Corridor Route, particularly in mist, to use the Esk Hause path as far as the first col, at this point turning off *left* down into a hollow; a stream rises here and is a certain guide to the Corridor, which is reached exactly and unmistakably at the head of Piers Gill.

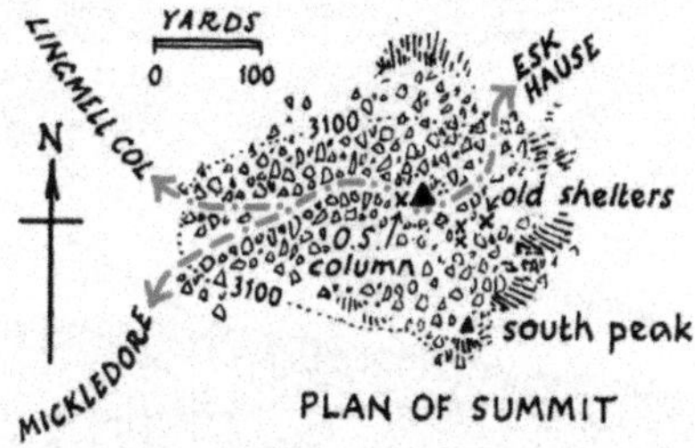
YARDS
0
100
LINGMELL COL
N
ESK HAUSE
3100
old shelters
O.S.
column
3100
south peak
MICKLEDORE

PLAN OF SUMMIT

Soliloquy.......

In summertime the cairn often becomes overrun with tourists, and a seeker after solitary contemplation may then be recommended to go across to the south peak, where, after enjoying the splendid view of Eskdale, he can observe the visitors to the summit from this distance. He may find himself wondering what impulse had driven these good folk to leave the comforts of the valley and make the weary ascent to this inhospitable place.

Why does a man climb mountains? Why has he forced his tired and sweating body up here when he might instead have been sitting at his ease in a deckchair at the seaside, looking at girls in bikinis, or fast asleep, or sucking ice cream, according to his fancy. On the face of it the thing doesn't make sense.

Yet more and more people are turning to the hills; they find something in these wild places that can be found nowhere else. It may be solace for some, satisfaction for others: the joy of exercising muscles that modern ways of living have cramped, perhaps; or a balm for jangled nerves in the solitude and silence of the peaks; or escape from the clamour and tumult of everyday existence. It may have something to do with a man's subconscious search for beauty, growing keener as so much in the world grows uglier. It may be a need to readjust his sights, to get out of his own narrow groove and climb above it to see wider horizons and truer perspectives. In a few cases, it may even be a curiosity inspired by awainwright's Pictorial Guides. Or it may be and for most walkers it will be, quite simply, a deep love of the hills, a love that has grown over the years, whatever motive first took them there: a feeling that these hills are friends, tried and trusted friends, always there when needed.

It is a question every man must answer for himself.

THE VIEW

(with distances in miles)

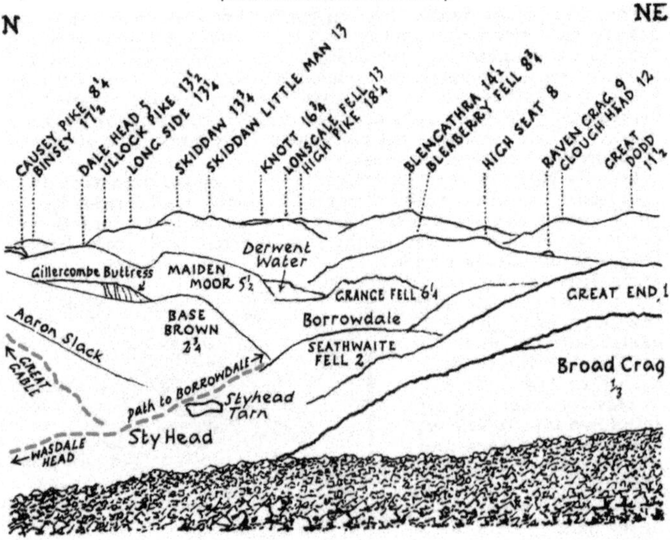
N
NE
CAUSEY PIKE 8¼
BINSEY 17½
DALE HEAD 5
ULLOCK PIKE 13½
LONG SIDE 13¼
SKIDDAW 13¾
SKIDDAW LITTLE MAN 13
KNOTT 16¾
LONSCALE FELL 13
HIGH PIKE 18¼
BLENCATHRA 14½
BLEABERRY FELL 8¾
HIGH SEAT 8
RAVEN CRAG 9
CLOUGH HEAD 12
GREAT DODD 11½
Derwent Water
Gillercombe Buttress
MAIDEN MOOR 5½
GRANGE FELL 6¼
GREAT END 1
BASE BROWN 2¾
Borrowdale
Aaron Slack
GREAT GABLE
SEATHWAITE FELL 2
Broad Crag ⅓
path to BORROWDALE
Styhead Tarn
Sty Head
WASDALE HEAD

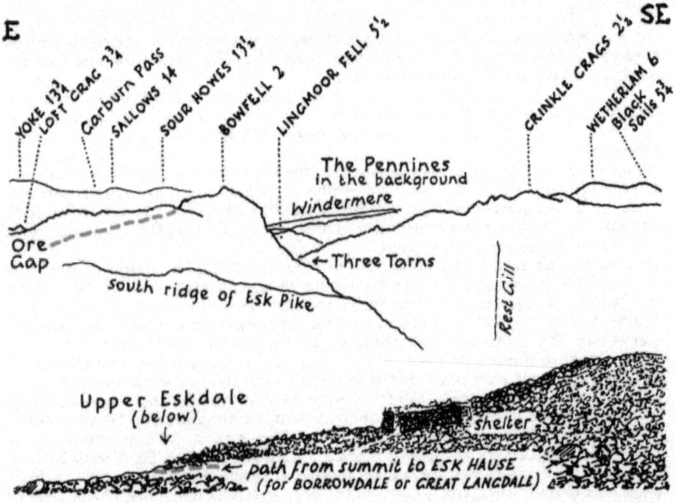
E
SE
YOKE 13¾
LOFT CRAG 3¾
Carburn Pass
SALLOWS 14
SOUR HOWES 13½
BOWFELL 2
LINGMOOR FELL 5½
CRINKLE CRAGS 2½
WETHERLAM 6
Black Sails 5¾
The Pennines in the background
Windermere
Ore Gap
Three Tarns
south ridge of Esk Pike
Rest Gill
Upper Eskdale (below)
shelter
path from summit to ESK HAUSE (for BORROWDALE or GREAT LANGDALE)

THE VIEW

NE E

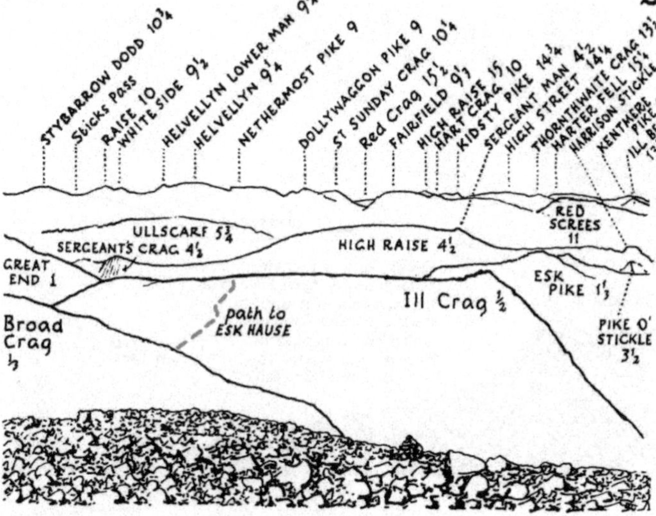
STYBARROW DODD 10¼
Sticks Pass
RAISE 10
WHITE SIDE 9½
HELVELLYN LOWER MAN 9¼
HELVELLYN 9¼
NETHERMOST PIKE 9
DOLLYWAGGON PIKE 9
ST SUNDAY CRAG 10¼
Red Crag 15½
FAIRFIELD 9⅓
HIGH RAISE 15
HART CRAG 10
KIDSTY PIKE 14¾
SERGEANT MAN 4½
HIGH STREET 14¼
THORNTHWAITE CRAG 13½
HARTER FELL 15¼
HARRISON STICKLE 4
KENTMERE PIKE 15¼
ILL BELL 13¾
ULLSCARF 5¾
SERGEANT'S CRAG 4½
HIGH RAISE 4½
RED SCREES 11
GREAT END 1
ESK PIKE 1⅓
Ill Crag ½
path to ESK HAUSE
Broad Crag ⅓
PIKE O' STICKLE 3½

SE S

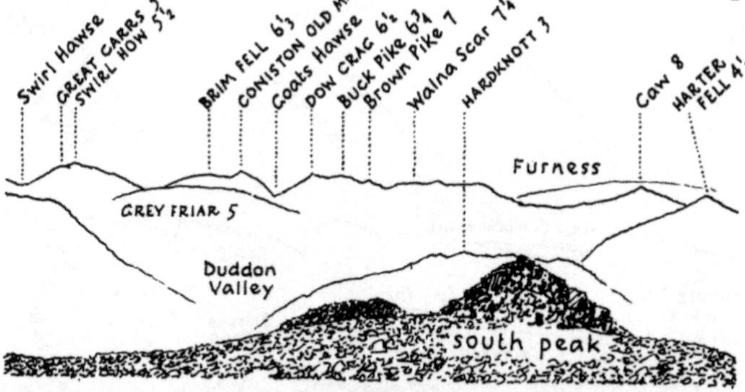
Swirl Hawse
GREAT CARRS 5¼
SWIRL HOW 5½
BRIM FELL 6⅓
CONISTON OLD MAN 7
Goats Hawse
DOW CRAG 6½
Buck Pike 6¾
Brown Pike 7
Walna Scar 7¼
HARDKNOTT 3
Caw 8
HARTER FELL 4½
Furness
GREY FRIAR 5
Duddon Valley
south peak

This being the highest ground in England the view is the most extensive, although not appreciably more so than those seen from many nearby fells. There is much interesting detail in every direction, and no denying the superiority of altitude, for all else is below eye-level, with old favourites like Great Gable and Bowfell seeming, if not humbled, less proud than they usually do (Scafell, across Mickledore, often *looks* of equal or greater height). Despite the wide variety of landscape, however, this is not the most pleasing of summit views, none of the valleys or lakes in view being seen really well.

THE VIEW

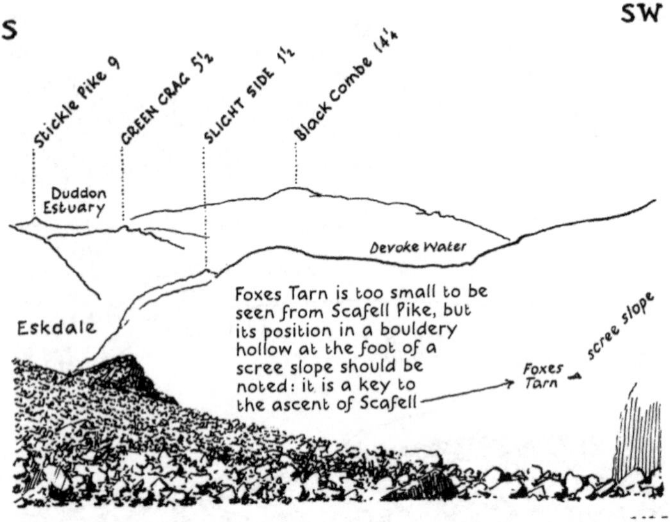
S
SW
Stickle Pike 9
GREEN CRAG 5½
SLIGHT SIDE 1½
Black Combe 14¼
Duddon Estuary
Devoke Water
Eskdale
Foxes Tarn is too small to be seen from Scafell Pike, but its position in a bouldery hollow at the foot of a scree slope should be noted: it is a key to the ascent of Scafell
Foxes Tarn
scree slope

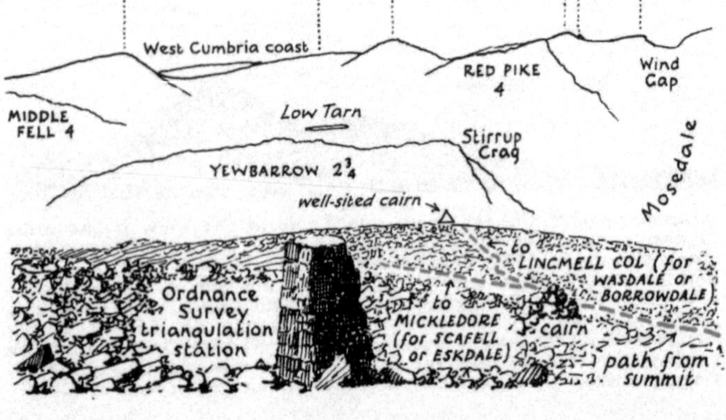
W
NW
SEATALLAN 4¾
CAW FELL 6
HAYCOCK 5
SCOAT FELL 4⅓
STEEPLE 4½
Black Crag 4
West Cumbria coast
RED PIKE 4
Wind Gap
MIDDLE FELL 4
Low Tarn
Stirrup Crag
YEWBARROW 2¾
Mosedale
well-sited cairn
Ordnance Survey triangulation station
to MICKLEDORE (for SCAFELL or ESKDALE)
to LINGMELL COL (for WASDALE or BORROWDALE)
cairn
path from summit

THE VIEW

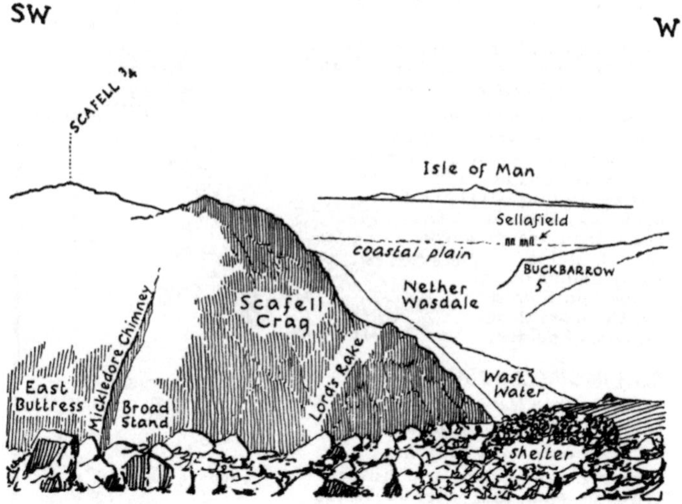
SW
W
SCAFELL 3/4
Isle of Man
Sellafield
coastal plain
BUCKBARROW 5
Nether Wasdale
Scafell Crag
Mickledore Chimney
East Buttress
Broad Stand
Lord's Rake
Wast Water
shelter

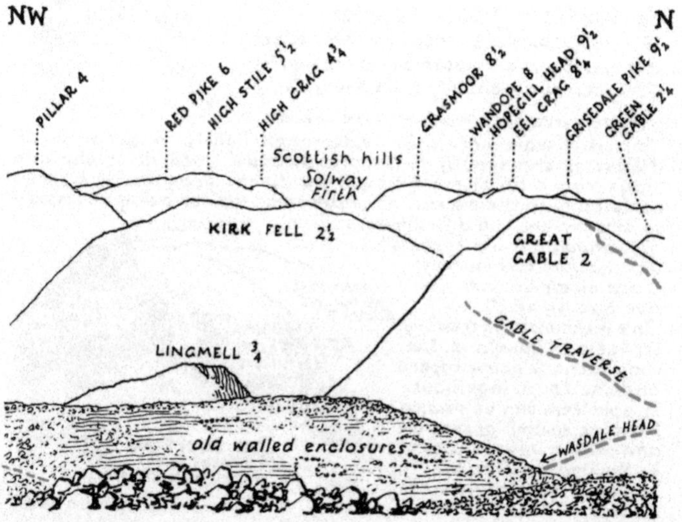
NW
N
PILLAR 4
RED PIKE 6
HIGH STILE 5½
HIGH CRAG 4¾
CRASMOOR 8½
WANDOPE 8
HOPEGILL HEAD 9½
EEL CRAG 8¼
GRISEDALE PIKE 9½
GREEN GABLE 2¼
Scottish hills
Solway Firth
KIRK FELL 2½
GREAT GABLE 2
GABLE TRAVERSE
LINGMELL ¾
old walled enclosures
WASDALE HEAD

RIDGE ROUTES

To GREAT END, 2984′ : 1⅓ miles
NE, then N

Three depressions (Broad Crag col, 2900′, Ill Crag col, 2900′, Calf Cove col, 2830′)

350 feet of ascent

Rough ground; slow progress.

This route makes use of the popular path to Esk Hause, much trodden but never smoothed, this being left when easier ground is reached above Calf Cove. Great End End is then straight ahead ahead, and is easily gained up a good path on a gentle grass slope between boulders.

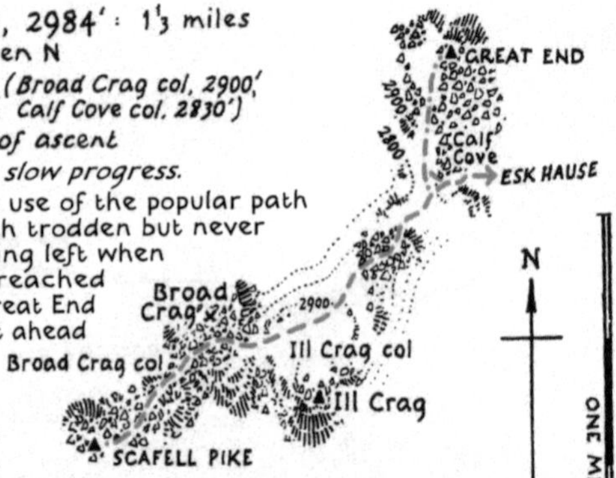
GREAT END
2900
2800
Calf Cove
ESK HAUSE
N
Broad Crag
2900
Ill Crag col
Broad Crag col
Ill Crag
SCAFELL PIKE
ONE MILE

To LINGMELL, 2649′ : ⅞ mile : NNW

Depression (Lingmell Col) at 2370′

280 feet of ascent

An easy walk to a fine top.

Use the well pitched and distinct Wasdale path and when it swings away to the left go on ahead across the grassy col and straight up the other side to the summit cairn.

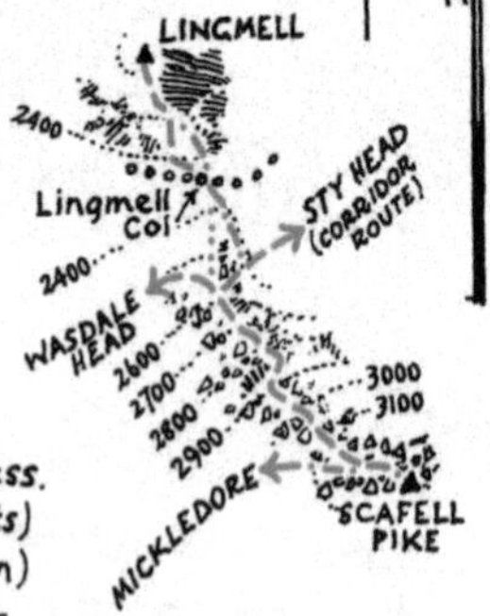
LINGMELL
2400
Lingmell Col
STY HEAD (CORRIDOR ROUTE)
2400
WASDALE HEAD
2600
2700
2800
2900
3000
3100
MICKLEDORE
SCAFELL PIKE

To SCAFELL, 3162′ : 1¼ miles
SW to Mickledore; then compass useless.

Many depressions (especially of the spirits)

700 feet of ascent (850 via Foxes Tarn)

Medals have been won for lesser deeds.

This is a walk not to be undertaken lightly, and not at all if time is short or if limbs are already tired. It is the one ridge route on these hills where direct progress is barred completely to the walker, a considerable detour being necessary to circumvent the difficulties.

(If Langdale is the evening's destination, this journey is too much for the average walker.)

This is the most interesting traverse in Lakeland, the rock scenery being superb and the route ingenious. The problem can be studied from the summit of the Pike and on the initial descent to Mickledore. *(See the diagram but also further details on Scafell 4.)*

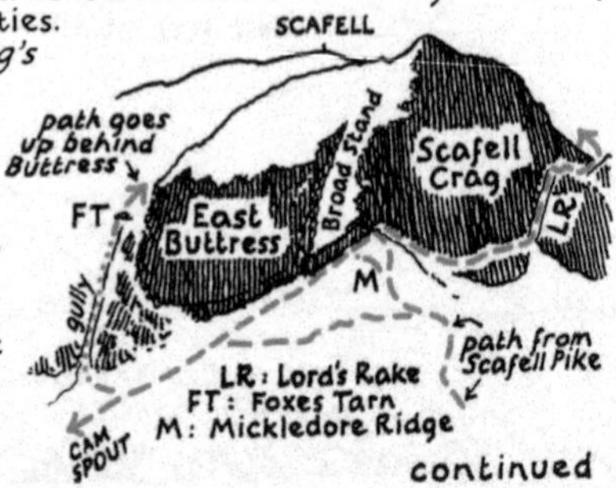
SCAFELL
path goes up behind Buttress
FT
East Buttress
Broad Stand
Scafell Crag
LR
gully
M
path from Scafell Pike
LR : Lord's Rake
FT : Foxes Tarn
M : Mickledore Ridge
CAM SPOUT

continued

RIDGE ROUTES

To SCAFELL (continued)

On the way down to Mickeldore it appears that the route must continue up the narrow slope directly beyond it, *but this is Broad Stand:* no way here. A choice must be made between the two pedestrian routes *via* Lord's Rake or Foxes Tarn. For Foxes Tarn, descend left (scree) from the near end of Mickeldore Ridge to join the main path for Cam Spout but leave this 150 yards lower and enter and ascend a gully on the right to a small pond: this is Foxes Tarn. Steep scree, right, leads up to the top. For Lord's Rake, go to the far end of Mickeldore Ridge and (after agreeing that Broad Stand is impossible) slither to the right down scree to a path that runs below the crags to the foot of Lord's Rake *(now see Scafell 4 and 9 for details).*

And the best of luck...

Lord's Rake
(top of first section)

Lord's Rake as seen *from Mickledore*

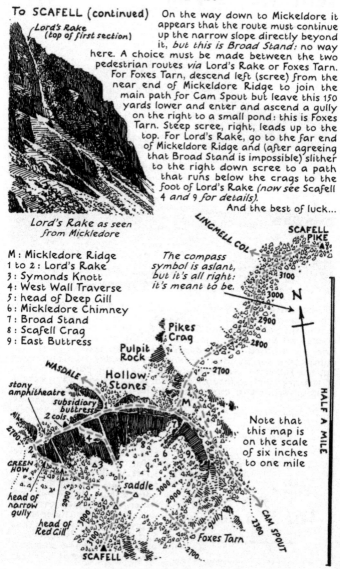

M : Mickledore Ridge
1 to 2 : Lord's Rake
3 : Symonds Knott
4 : West Wall Traverse
5 : head of Deep Gill
6 : Mickledore Chimney
7 : Broad Stand
8 : Scafell Crag
9 : East Buttress

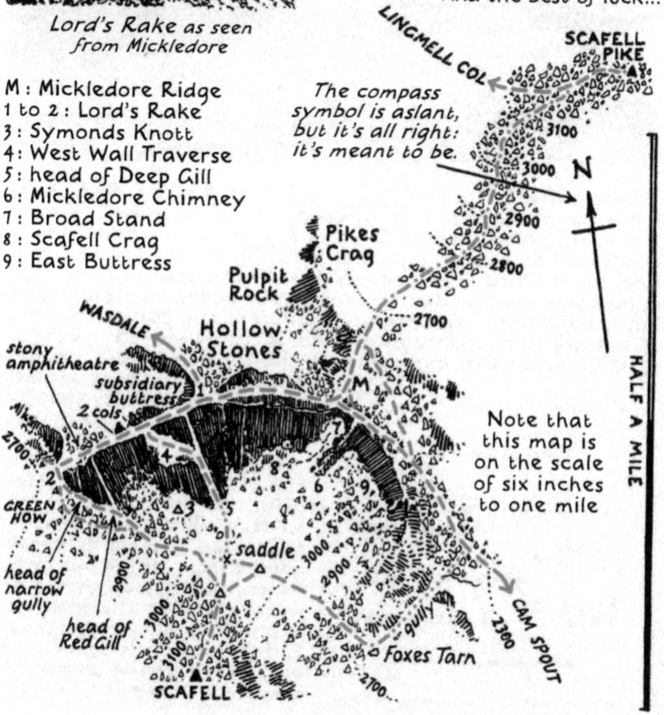
LINGMELL COL
SCAFELL PIKE
The compass symbol is aslant, but it's all right: it's meant to be.
3100
3000
N
2900
2800
Pikes Crag
Pulpit Rock
2700
WASDALE
Hollow Stones
stony amphitheatre
subsidiary buttress
2 cols
M
1
2
3
4
5
6
7
8
9
2700
GREEN HOW
saddle
3000
2900
head of narrow gully
head of Red Gill
2900
3000
3100
SCAFELL
gully
Foxes Tarn
2700
2300
CAM SPOUT
HALF A MILE
Note that this map is on the scale of six inches to one mile

Seathwaite Fell 1970'

OS grid ref: NY229102

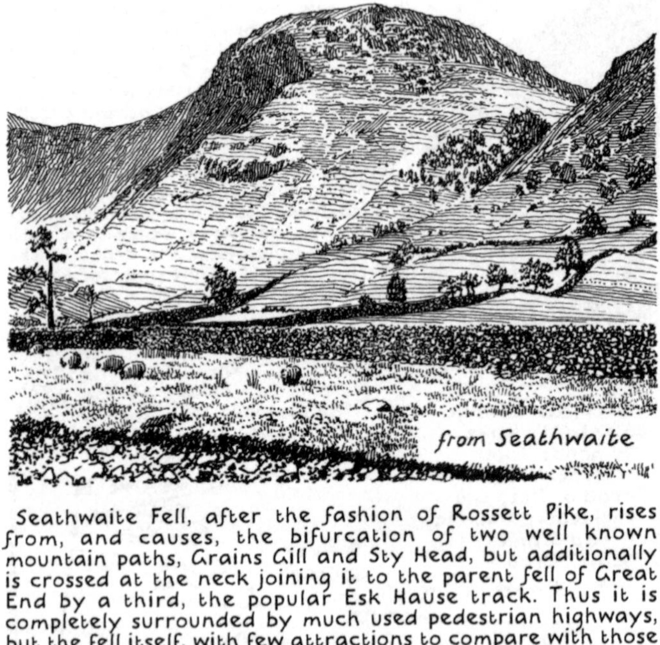

from Seathwaite

Seathwaite Fell, after the fashion of Rossett Pike, rises from, and causes, the bifurcation of two well known mountain paths, Grains Gill and Sty Head, but additionally is crossed at the neck joining it to the parent fell of Great End by a third, the popular Esk Hause track. Thus it is completely surrounded by much used pedestrian highways, but the fell itself, with few attractions to compare with those of the greater mountains around, is rarely visited – except, of course, by the custodian of the infamous rain gauges which record, to its shame, that the fell and its vicinity has much the heaviest rainfall in the country.

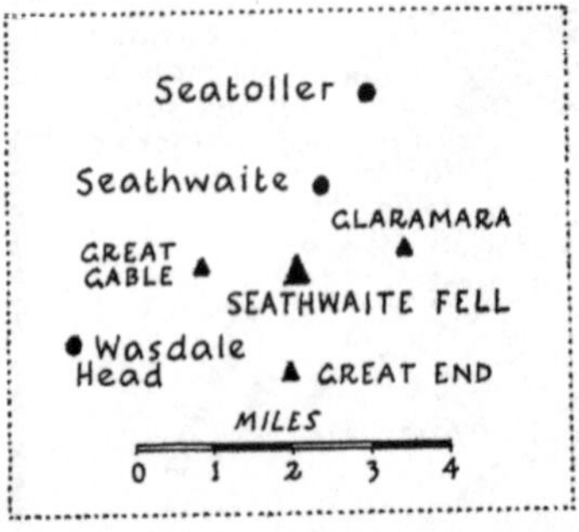
Seatoller
Seathwaite
GLARAMARA
GREAT GABLE
SEATHWAITE FELL
Wasdale Head
GREAT END
MILES
0 1 2 3 4

Steep, rough slopes and a rim of crags on three sides offer no encouragement to stray from the beaten paths, but the top is easily gained from Sprinkling Tarn, which, with lesser sheets of water, provide the interest of a wide, undulating plateau. Sprinkling Tarn is commonly accredited as the source of the River Derwent.

MAP

Stockley Bridge

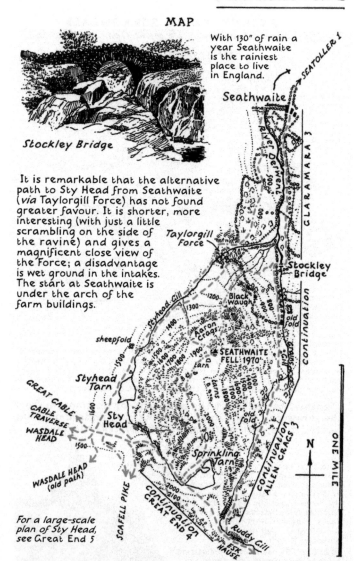

With 130" of rain a year Seathwaite is the rainiest place to live in England.

It is remarkable that the alternative path to Sty Head from Seathwaite (*via* Taylorgill Force) has not found greater favour. It is shorter, more interesting (with just a little scrambling on the side of the ravine) and gives a magnificent close view of the Force; a disadvantage is wet ground in the intakes. The start at Seathwaite is under the arch of the farm buildings.

SEATOLLER 1
Seathwaite
River Derwent
500
600
CLARAMARA 3
Taylorgill Force
Stockley Bridge
Black Waugh
1200
1300
800
900
old fold
Continuation
Styhead Gill
1400
Aaron Crags
sheepfold
1500
1600
1700
1800
1900
SEATHWAITE FELL 1970'
tarn
tarns
Grains Gill
Styhead Tarn
GREAT GABLE
GABLE TRAVERSE
WASDALE HEAD
Sty Head
2000
old fold
CONTINUATION ALLEN CRAGS 3
N
ONE MILE
WASDALE HEAD (old path)
Sprinkling Tarn
SCAFELL PIKE
CONTINUATION GREAT END 4
2100
Ruddy Gill
ESK HAUSE

For a large-scale plan of Sty Head, see Great End 5

The highest point of the fell is 300 yards north-west of a tarn in a rocky basin north of Sprinkling Tarn. This point is not considered to be the summit, however, which is on a rocky outcrop overlooking Seathwaite.

ASCENT FROM BORROWDALE

1550 feet of ascent : 1¾ miles from Seathwaite

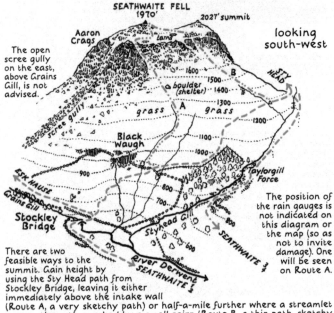

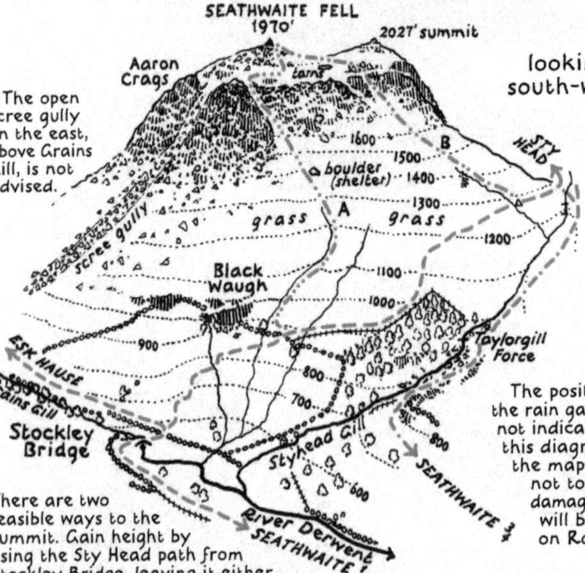
SEATHWAITE FELL
1970'
2027' summit
Aaron Crags
tarns
looking south-west
1600
B
STY HEAD
1500
boulder (shelter)
1400
1300
A
grass
grass
scree gully
1200
Black Waugh
1100
1000
Taylorgill Force
ESK HAUSE
900
800
700
Grains Gill
Stockley Bridge
Styhead Gill
800
600
SEATHWAITE ¾
River Derwent
SEATHWAITE ½

The open scree gully on the east, above Grains Gill, is not advised.

The position of the rain gauges is not indicated on this diagram or the map (so as not to invite damage). One will be seen on Route A.

There are two feasible ways to the summit. Gain height by using the Sty Head path from Stockley Bridge, leaving it either immediately above the intake wall (Route A, a very sketchy path) or half-a-mile further where a streamlet crosses the path, marked by a small cairn (Route B, a thin path, sketchy in places). In each case aim for a grassy gully ahead. The top of the rock tower on the left of Route A affords a startling view of Grains Gill. Route A becomes very steep in the gully; Route B is easier.

Seathwaite Fell is not the most popular destination from the farmstead of the same name but is a rewarding ascent nevertheless, with a summit worthy of exploration.

THE SUMMIT

The 2000' contour occurs in a few places on the map of Seathwaite Fell, but the small areas of ground so enclosed are not nearly as prominent or distinctive as the shapelier pyramid at the north end of the top plateau, where a cairn at 1970', buttressed by blistered rocks, is generally regarded as the summit of the fell although obviously it isn't.

DESCENTS: Use Route B for getting down to Borrowdale most easily. Route A is tricky to find from above and, *in mist*, should not be sought.

THE VIEW

The diagram indicates the view from the distinctive summit at 1970', the usually accepted 'top' but not quite the highest point of the fell. Northwards the scene is excellent: there is no better place for viewing the Seathwaite valley. Less beautiful, but more impressive, is the close surround of much higher mountains. Seathwaite Fell is such a lowly member of this group that it is a surprise to see a considerable mileage of the ridge of the Helvellyn Dodds occupying the skyline.

From the next and higher cairn, 300 yards south-west, a vista of Wasdale Head is seen. Additional summits in the view are YEWBARROW, BOWFELL and ULLOCK PIKE. A portion of *Styhead Tarn* is also visible.

From the highest part of the fell, 500 yards to the north of Sprinkling Tarn, the view includes SEATALLAN, RED PIKE in Mosedale, CARL SIDE and LONG SIDE. A small corner of *Sprinkling Tarn* can be seen, but Styhead Tarn is now concealed from sight.

Principal Fells

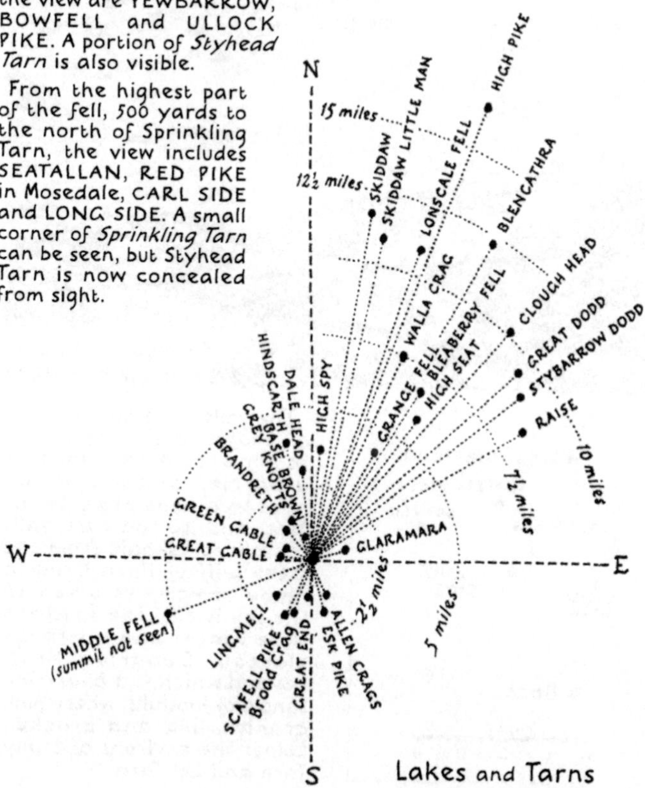
N
S
E
W
15 miles
12½ miles
10 miles
7½ miles
5 miles
2½ miles
HIGH PIKE
SKIDDAW LITTLE MAN
LONSCALE FELL
SKIDDAW
BLENCATHRA
CLOUGH HEAD
GREAT DODD
STYBARROW DODD
RAISE
WALLA CRAG
BLEABERRY FELL
HIGH SEAT
GRANGE FELL
HIGH SPY
DALE HEAD
HINDSCARTH
BASE BROWN
GREY KNOTTS
BRANDRETH
GREEN GABLE
GREAT GABLE
GLARAMARA
MIDDLE FELL
(summit not seen)
LINGMELL
SCAFELL PIKE
Broad Crag
GREAT END
ESK PIKE
ALLEN CRAGS

Lakes and Tarns

NNE: *Derwent Water* and many small tarns on the broad top of the fell.

Slight Side

2499′

OS grid ref: NY210050

from Catcove Beck

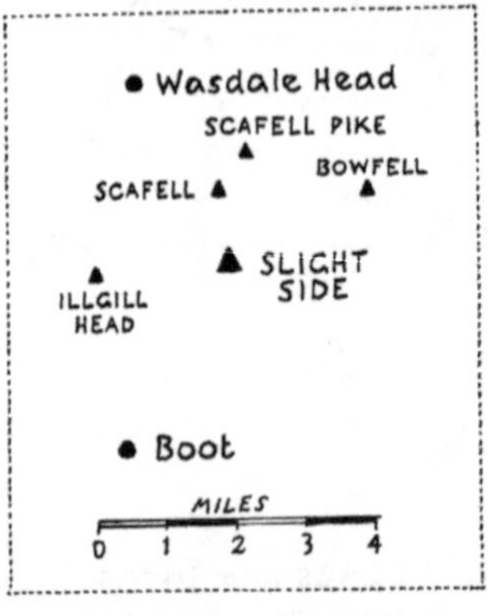

Wasdale Head
SCAFELL PIKE
BOWFELL
SCAFELL
SLIGHT SIDE
ILLGILL HEAD
Boot
MILES
0 1 2 3 4

The mile-long south ridge of Scafell descends loftily to an abrupt terminus at a barrier of rock, which rises to a neat peak, Slight Side, and, to the east, falls sharply to Eskdale from the steep cliff of Horn Crag (a name sometimes given to the fell itself). The southern slope widens into a strange plateau, Quagrigg Moss, beyond which is a charming tangle of foothills, where pink granite, ling and bracken colour the environs of Stony Tarn and Eel Tarn.

The official altitude of Slight Side is a tribute to the meticulous care of the Ordnance Survey. But if Nelson had been in charge of the surveying party, and been a mountaineer too, surely he would have recorded 2500!

MAP

At this late stage in the book's preparation space is becoming terribly short and cannot be spared for repetition of information already given. As the map of Scafell includes the whole, area of Slight Side, would readers mind referring to pages Scafell 5-8?

ASCENT FROM ESKDALE

2350 feet of ascent : 4¾ miles from Boot

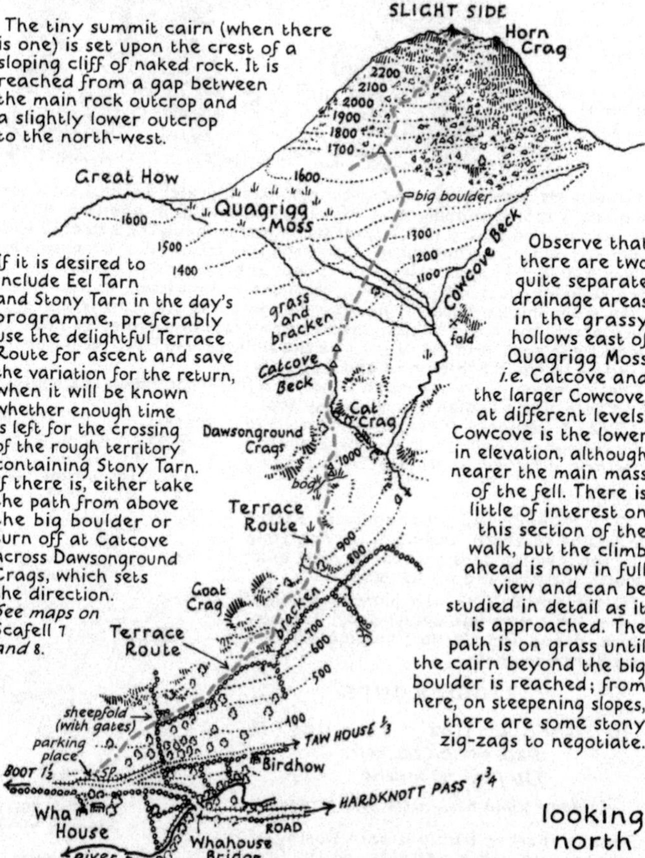

SLIGHT SIDE
Horn Crag
2200
2100
2000
1900
1800
1700
Great How
1600
Quagrigg Moss
big boulder
Cowcove Beck
1600
1500
1400
1300
1200
1100
grass and bracken
fold
Catcove Beck
Cat Crag
Dawsonground Crags
1000
bog
Terrace Route
900
800
Goat Crag
bracken
700
600
500
Terrace Route
sheepfold (with gates)
parking place
400
TAW HOUSE ⅓
Birdhow
BOOT 1½
HARDKNOTT PASS 1¾
Wha House
ROAD
Whahouse Bridge
River Esk
looking north

The tiny summit cairn (when there is one) is set upon the crest of a sloping cliff of naked rock. It is reached from a gap between the main rock outcrop and a slightly lower outcrop to the north-west.

If it is desired to include Eel Tarn and Stony Tarn in the day's programme, preferably use the delightful Terrace Route for ascent and save the variation for the return, when it will be known whether enough time is left for the crossing of the rough territory containing Stony Tarn. If there is, either take the path from above the big boulder or turn off at Catcove across Dawsonground Crags, which sets the direction. *See maps on* Scafell 7 *and* 8.

Observe that there are two quite separate drainage areas in the grassy hollows east of Quagrigg Moss *i.e.* Catcove and the larger Cowcove, at different levels. Cowcove is the lower in elevation, although nearer the main mass of the fell. There is little of interest on this section of the walk, but the climb ahead is now in full view and can be studied in detail as it is approached. The path is on grass until the cairn beyond the big boulder is reached; from here, on steepening slopes, there are some stony zig-zags to negotiate.

A walk of three parts: a delightful approach along the attractive Terrace Route, a grassy tramp from Cat Crag, and then a steepening climb beyond the big boulder.

THE SUMMIT

The cairn shown in the illustration comes and goes, most probably because the stones find it difficult to adhere to the smooth summit rocks.

Scafell
Ill Crag
Esk Hause

Fellwalkers, having climbed their mountain, prefer to find that the summit is rocky, shapely and well defined; and if, in addition, it can be attained only by a rough final scramble, so much the better. Slight Side has all these qualifications, and the further merit of an excellent view. A defect in its architecture is that the lofty ridge continuing to Scafell behind it is but little lower than the summit itself, so that when seen from this direction it has less significance. Still, this is a grand airy perch, the cairn being poised on the crest of a sweep of slabs of good clean rock, and many must be the walkers who have set out from Eskdale to climb Scafell and given up here.

Considered only as a summit, and not as a fell, Slight Side is the neatest and best of the Scafell group's many tops.

NOTE: A memorial 170 yards north-east of the summit marks where a Hurricane aircraft crashed in 1941 killing its two Polish aircrew.

DESCENTS:

TO ESKDALE: The usual route of ascent should be reversed, and no other way from the top is worth considering. For most of its length the path is easy to follow.

TO WASDALE: from the plateau north of the summit turn left (west) down a grassy slope, Broad Tongue, to Hardrigg Gill and the Burnmoor path.

RIDGE ROUTE

To SCAFELL, 3162': 1¼ miles : N

Depression at 2400'

750 feet of ascent

An easy climb with little of interest.

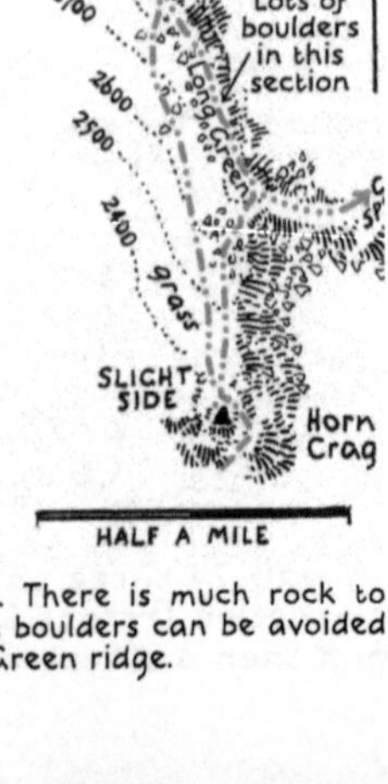
SCAFELL
N
Path is a ribbon of light stones
3000
2900
2800
2700
Lots of boulders in this section
Long Green
2600
2500
2400
grass
SLIGHT SIDE
Horn Crag
HALF A MILE

Initially there is barely a path worthy of the name but one materialises on the first steep rise. By keeping to the edge of the continuous escarpment on the right there are good views that relieve the dull ascent. There is much rock to negotiate on the way up, but the worst of the boulders can be avoided by a sketchy path that stays left of the Long Green ridge.

THE VIEW

Slight Side's unique situation, at the point where the high mountains of the Scafell range sweep majestically down in foothills to green valleys and the silver sea, gives it a rare distinction as a viewpoint for the coastal area of Lakeland. The prospect seawards is in fact even better than it is from the parent Scafell although much inferior in other directions — but it must be stated in Slight Side's favour that the unlovely sprawl of the Sellafield complex is concealed by Illgill Head. As a geography lesson in mountain structure, on the formation and flow of rivers and valleys and the winning of land by man from nature, the picture here simply presented is excellent. There is historical significance in the scene, too, for this is the land the Romans knew, and, before them, the primitive Britons of the Bronze Age.

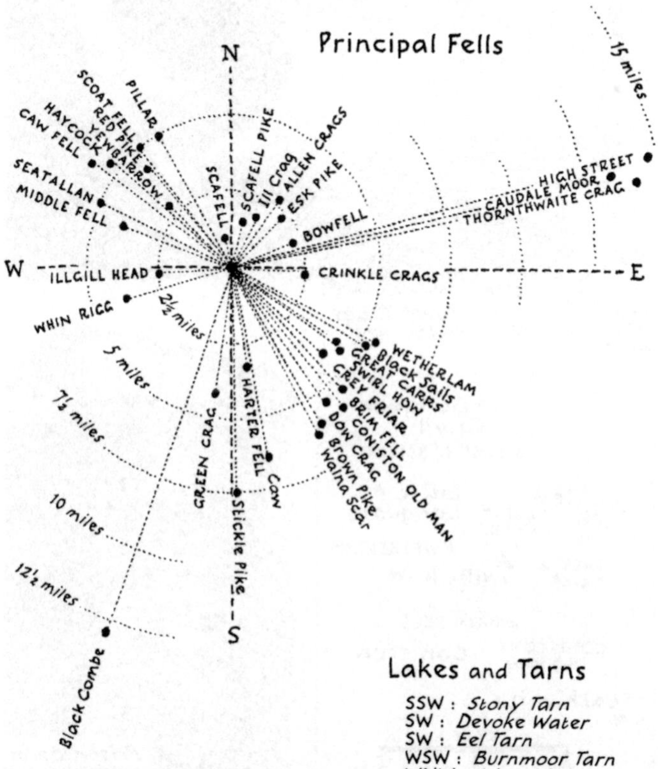
Principal Fells
N
S
E
W
15 miles
HIGH STREET
CAUDALE MOOR
THORNTHWAITE CRAG
SCOAT FELL
PILLAR
RED PIKE
HAYCOCK
YEWBARROW
CAW FELL
SEATALLAN
MIDDLE FELL
SCAFELL
SCAFELL PIKE
Ill Crag
ALLEN CRAGS
ESK PIKE
BOWFELL
ILLGILL HEAD
CRINKLE CRAGS
WHIN RIGG
2½ miles
5 miles
7½ miles
10 miles
12½ miles
WETHERLAM
Black Sails
GREAT CARRS
SWIRL HOW
GREY FRIAR
BRIM FELL
CONISTON OLD MAN
DOW CRAG
Brown Pike
Walna Scar
HARTER FELL
GREEN CRAG
Caw
Stickle Pike
Black Combe

Lakes and Tarns

SSW : *Stony Tarn*
SW : *Devoke Water*
SW : *Eel Tarn*
WSW : *Burnmoor Tarn*
WNW : *Wast Water*

Swirl How 2630′

OS grid ref: NY273006

from Rough Crags
(Great Carrs on the right)

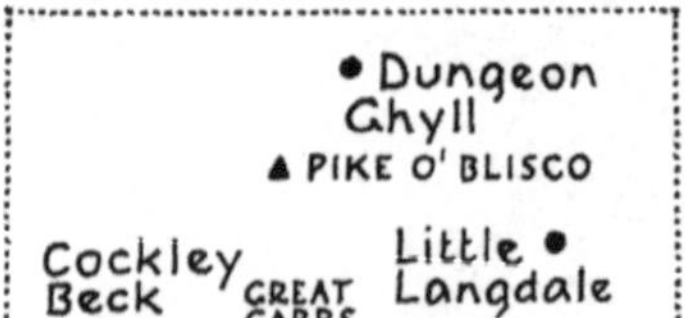
Dungeon Ghyll
PIKE O' BLISCO
Cockley Beck
Little Langdale
GREAT CARRS
WETHERLAM
GREY FRIAR
SWIRL HOW
BRIM FELL
CONISTON OLD MAN
Coniston
Seathwaite
MILES
0 1 2 3 4

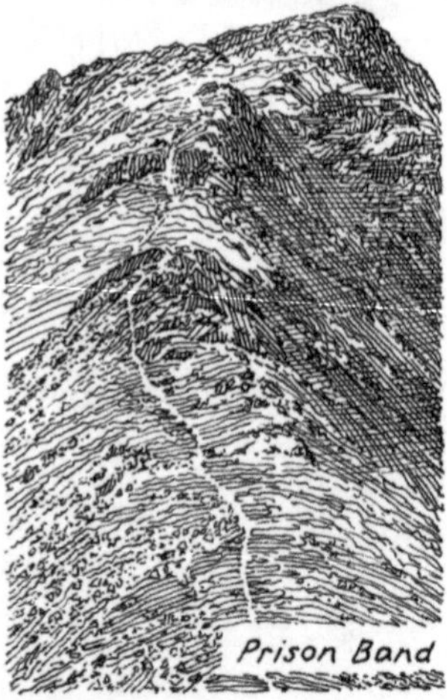

Prison Band

NATURAL FEATURES

Swirl How, although not quite the highest of the Coniston Fells, is the geographical centre of the group, radiating splendid ridges from a peaked summit to the four points of the compass. It is never seen really conspicuously in distant views, being crowded by surrounding fells; nevertheless its appearance is good, especially in profile, for the long southern plateau breaks sharply at the actual summit into a steep and craggy declivity. The area of Swirl How is not extensive, the ridges quickly merging into other fells on all four sides, but worthy of mention is the subsidiary height of Great How Crags on the southern plateau, a pillar of rock rising from the deep hollow of Levers Water and seeming from some viewpoints to be a separate summit.

The geographical supremacy of Swirl How is well illustrated by the direction of flow of its streams, which join the Duddon and the Brathay and Coniston Water (a distinction not shared by any other fell in the group) whereas those of the Old Man, which is slightly higher and popularly but wrongly regarded as the principal fell in the area, feed Coniston Water only. If only Swirl How asserted itself a little more and overtopped its satellites by a few hundred feet it would rank with the noblest fells in Lakeland, its 'build-up' being topographically excellent.

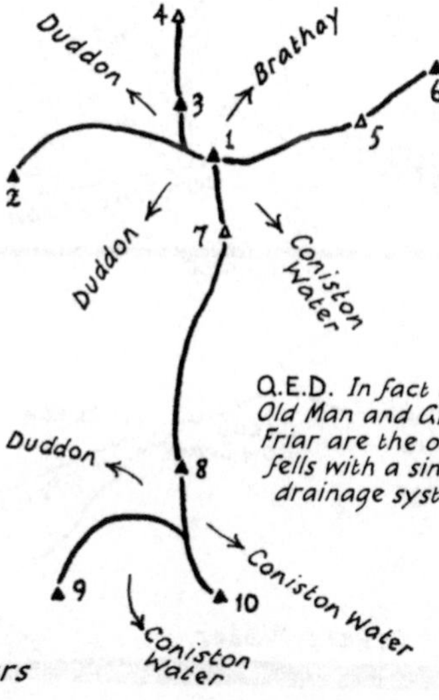
Duddon
4
Brathay
6
3
1
5
2
7
Duddon
Coniston Water
Duddon
8
9
10
Coniston Water
Coniston Water

1 : SWIRL HOW
2 : GREY FRIAR
3 : GREAT CARRS
4 : Little Carrs
5 : Black Sails
6 : WETHERLAM
7 : Great How Crags
8 : BRIM FELL
9 : DOW CRAG
10 : CONISTON OLD MAN

Q.E.D. *In fact the Old Man and Grey Friar are the only fells with a single drainage system*

The main ridges, and direction of flow of waters

MAP

Swirl Hawse......

Swirl Hawse is a true mountain pass, a neat and narrow defile with a small summit marked by a big cairn. An unusual feature is that there is no stream descending from it into Greenburn, the beck there coming down from the much higher depression of Broad Slack. The main path from Swirl Hawse to Levers Water does not follow the valley, but crosses the lower slopes of the Black Sails ridge.

The western of the two paths between Swirl Hawse and Levers Water is a recent alternative that is particularly good in descent. It can be wet in places during periods of rain.

Levers Water is used as a water supply for people living in the Coniston area.

Greenburn Reservoir
Greenburn Beck
High Keld Gill
Low Keld Gill
1300
x Sheepfold
1600
1700
1800
continuation GREAT CARRS 3
continuation WETHERLAM 3
WETHERLAM
GREAT CARRS
Broad Slack
1900
2000
2100
2200
Swirl Hawse
Fairfield
continuation GREY FRIAR 4
2400
SWIRL HOW 2630'
Prison Band
continuation WETHERLAM 3 & 5
Great How Crags
Swirl Hawse Beck
Little How Crags
Erin Crag
Brock How
Tarn Head Beck
Levers Hawse
Seathwaite Tarn
Levers Water
1400
continuation BRIM FELL 2
CONISTON
ONE MILE

looking north-west from Levers Water

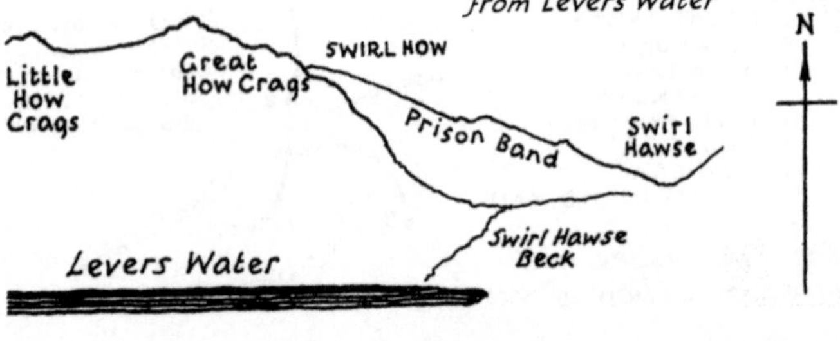

N
Little How Crags
Great How Crags
SWIRL HOW
Prison Band
Swirl Hawse
Swirl Hawse Beck
Levers Water

ASCENT FROM CONISTON

2450 feet of ascent : 3½ miles

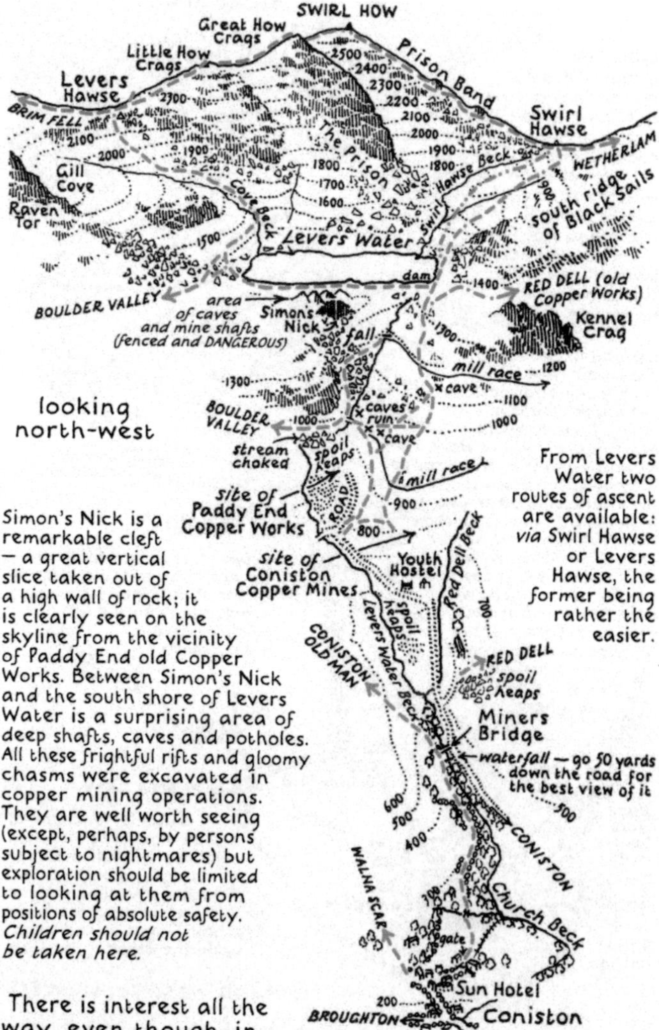
SWIRL HOW
Great How Crags
Little How Crags
Levers Hawse
BRIM FELL
Prison Band
Swirl Hawse
WETHERLAM
The Prison
Swirl Hawse Beck
south ridge of Black Sails
Gill Cove
Raven Tor
Cove Beck
Levers Water
dam
BOULDER VALLEY
area of caves and mine shafts (fenced and DANGEROUS)
Simon's Nick
fall
RED DELL (old Copper Works)
Kennel Crag
mill race
cave
caves
ruin
BOULDER VALLEY
stream choked
spoil heaps
site of Paddy End Copper Works
ROAD
site of Coniston Copper Mines
Youth Hostel
Red Dell Beck
CONISTON OLD MAN
Levers Water Beck
RED DELL
spoil heaps
Miners Bridge
waterfall — go 50 yards down the road for the best view of it
CONISTON
WALNA SCAR
Church Beck
gate
Sun Hotel
BROUGHTON
Coniston

looking north-west

Simon's Nick is a remarkable cleft — a great vertical slice taken out of a high wall of rock; it is clearly seen on the skyline from the vicinity of Paddy End old Copper Works. Between Simon's Nick and the south shore of Levers Water is a surprising area of deep shafts, caves and potholes. All these frightful rifts and gloomy chasms were excavated in copper mining operations. They are well worth seeing (except, perhaps, by persons subject to nightmares) but exploration should be limited to looking at them from positions of absolute safety. *Children should not be taken here.*

From Levers Water two routes of ascent are available: *via* Swirl Hawse or Levers Hawse, the former being rather the easier.

There is interest all the way, even though, in places, the interest is in things desolate and derelict. A most excellent expedition.

ASCENT FROM LITTLE LANGDALE
2400 feet of ascent : 4 miles

Swirl How is concealed by Wetherlam during much of the walk up Greenburn, which is dominated by the rocky front of Great Carrs. Note well (and especially *in mist*) that Greenburn Beck comes down from Broad Slack and not from the main depression, Swirl Hawse. The slopes below the Hawse are dry.

Beyond Greenburn Reservoir waste no time looking for paths but climb up above the valley floor to avoid marshy ground and work forwards and then leftwards up easy bouldery slopes to the Hawse. An interesting alternative from the old works is to follow the neglected path to the Long Crag level, which is located by a spoil heap and can be investigated with care. 150 yards above entrance turn right across rough ground. There is only a very sketchy path here.

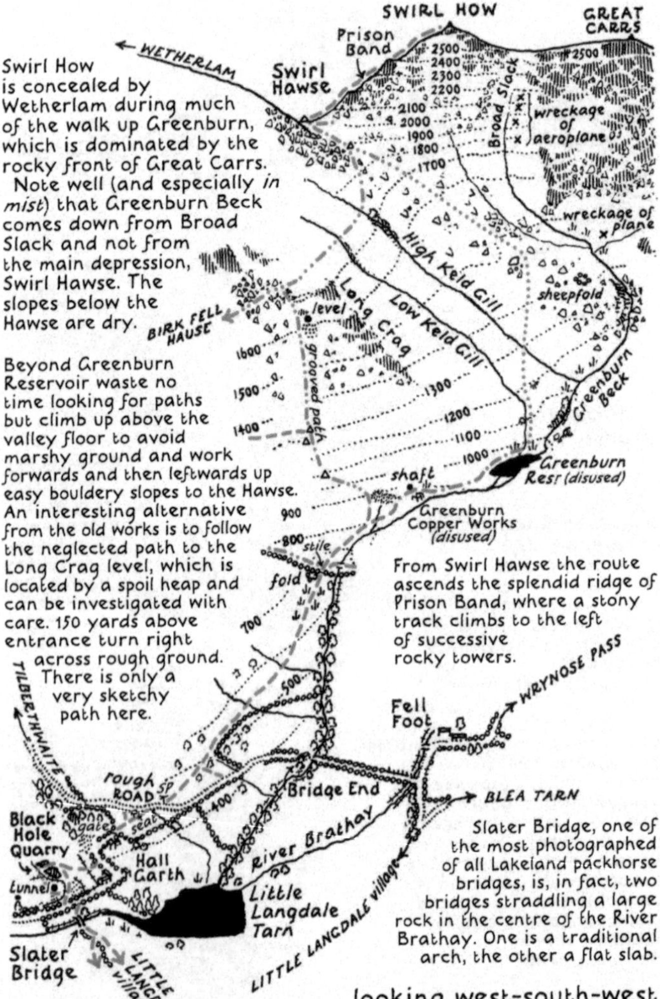
SWIRL HOW
GREAT CARRS
Prison Band
Swirl Hawse
WETHERLAM
2500
2400
2300
2200
2100
2000
1900
1800
1700
1600
1500
1400
1300
1200
1100
1000
900
800
700
500
400
Broad Slack
wreckage of aeroplane
wreckage of plane
High Keld Gill
Low Keld Gill
Long Crag
level
grooved path
BIRK FELL HAUSE
sheepfold
Greenburn Beck
Greenburn Resr (disused)
shaft
Greenburn Copper Works (disused)
stile
fold
Fell Foot
WRYNOSE PASS
BLEA TARN
Bridge End
River Brathay
rough ROAD
SP
seat
gate
Black Hole Quarry
Hall Garth
tunnel
Little Langdale Tarn
Slater Bridge
LITTLE LANGDALE village
TILBERTHWAITE

From Swirl Hawse the route ascends the splendid ridge of Prison Band, where a stony track climbs to the left of successive rocky towers.

Slater Bridge, one of the most photographed of all Lakeland packhorse bridges, is, in fact, two bridges straddling a large rock in the centre of the River Brathay. One is a traditional arch, the other a flat slab.

looking west-south-west

Greenburn is the only line of approach that does not pass over other summits. This interesting valley offers a simple walk and the final section above Swirl Hawse is excellent.

THE SUMMIT

The cairn is splendidly sited at the extreme end of the long and level summit-plateau, just at the point where the northern slope falls away abruptly; perhaps it is not quite on the highest ground which appears to be a few yards west. The cairn is well built, with convex sides, like those on Brim Fell and Coniston Old Man.

DESCENTS: TO CONISTON: Swirl Hawse is a better way off the fell than Levers Hawse, which initially is steep and stony and requires care, but, *especially in mist*, go straight down to Levers Water from Swirl Hawse.

TO LITTLE LANGDALE: The finest route of descent lies over Great Carrs and Wet Side Edge, but if Greenburn is preferred descend thereto by the easy slope from Swirl Hawse, not *via* Broad Slack. No trouble need be expected on either route in mist.

RIDGE ROUTES

SWIRL HOW
N
HALF A MILE
2600
2500
2400
2300
Great How Crags
Little How Crags
Levers Hawse
2200
2300
2400
2500
cairns
BRIM FELL
2600

TO BRIM FELL, 2611′: 1½ miles: S, SW and S
Depression (Levers Hawse) at 2240′
380 feet of ascent

Aim south across the plateau along a good path that follows the ridge down to Levers Hawse. It continues up the easy slopes of Brim Fell marked by cairns. *In mist* keep to the right of the escarpment.

TO WETHERLAM, 2502′: 1¼ miles
ENE, NE, ENE and E
Depression (Swirl Hawse) at 2020′
500 feet of ascent

Go down Prison Band by the track, cross the Hawse, and bear left up the opposite slope. The first summit on the right is Black Sails, not to be mistaken for Wetherlam.

WETHERLAM
2100
Red Dell Head
Black Sails
2443′
2100
Swirl Hawse
2300
Prison Band
SWIRL HOW

TO GREAT CARRS, 2575′: ⅓ mile: W, NW and N
Depression at 2500′ · 75 feet of ascent

A simple seven-minute stroll around the head of Greenburn. The memorial is a moving spot.

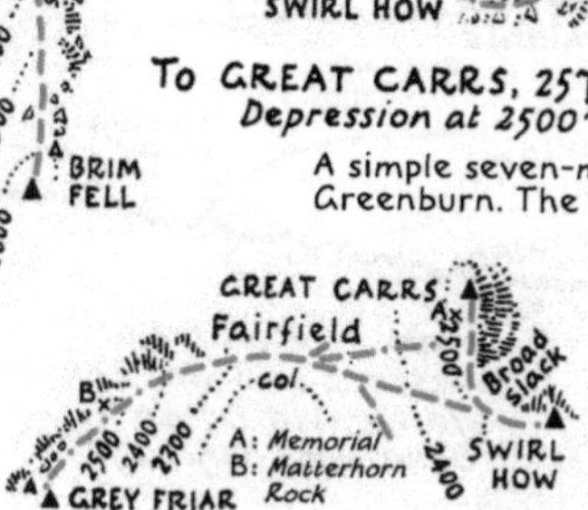
GREAT CARRS
A
2500
Fairfield
Broad Slack
col
B
2500
2400
2300
A: Memorial
B: Matterhorn Rock
2400
SWIRL HOW
GREY FRIAR

TO GREY FRIAR, 2536′
1 mile: WNW, W and SW.
Depression at 2275′
270 feet of ascent

Steeper climbing follows an easy descent on a clear path. Look out for the Matterhorn Rock on the summit plateau.

Grey Friar is not recommended *in mist*.

THE VIEW

(with distances in miles)

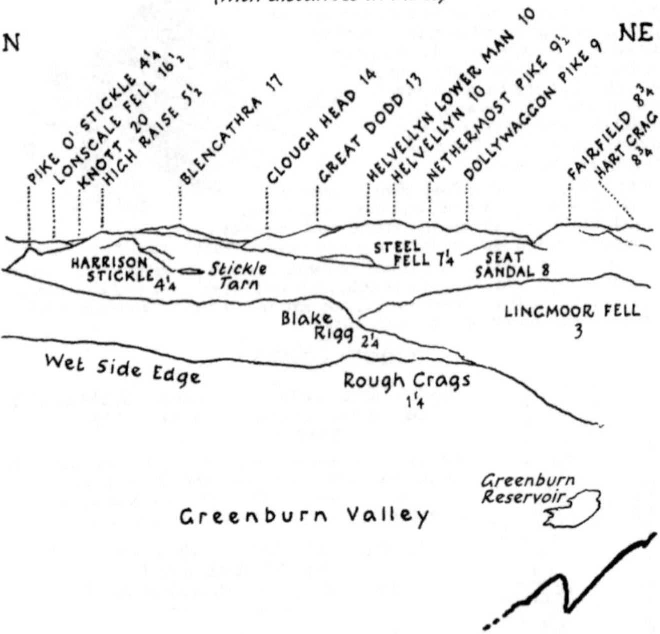
N
NE
PIKE O' STICKLE 4¼
LONSCALE FELL 16½
KNOTT 20
HIGH RAISE 5½
BLENCATHRA 17
CLOUGH HEAD 14
GREAT DODD 13
HELVELLYN LOWER MAN 10
HELVELLYN 10
NETHERMOST PIKE 9½
DOLLYWAGGON PIKE 9
FAIRFIELD 8¾
HART CRAG 8¾
HARRISON STICKLE 4¼
Stickle Tarn
STEEL FELL 7¼
SEAT SANDAL 8
LINGMOOR FELL 3
Blake Rigg 2¼
Wet Side Edge
Rough Crags 1¼
Greenburn Valley
Greenburn Reservoir

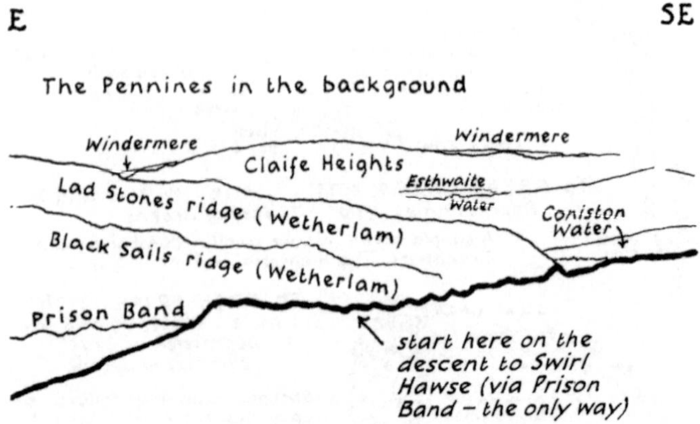
E
SE
The Pennines in the background
Windermere
Windermere
Claife Heights
Esthwaite Water
Lad Stones ridge (Wetherlam)
Coniston Water
Black Sails ridge (Wetherlam)
Prison Band
start here on the descent to Swirl Hawse (via Prison Band – the only way)

THE VIEW

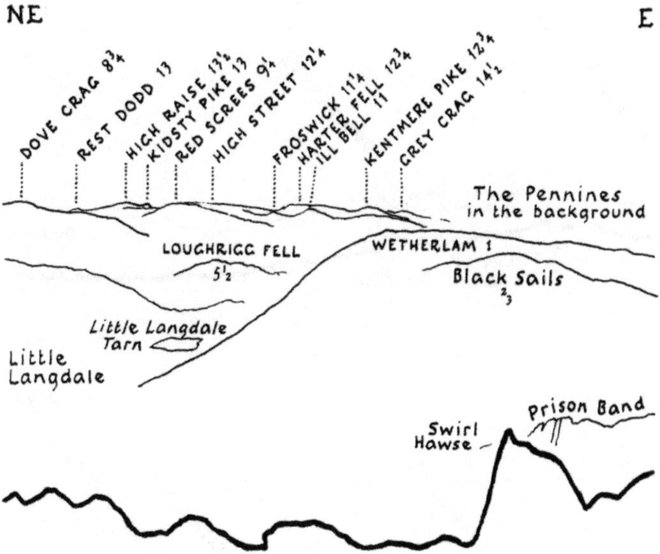
NE
E
DOVE CRAG 8¾
REST DODD 13
HIGH RAISE 13½
KIDSTY PIKE 13
RED SCREES 9¼
HIGH STREET 12¼
FROSWICK 11¼
HARTER FELL 12¾
ILL BELL 11
KENTMERE PIKE 12¾
GREY CRAG 14½
The Pennines
in the background
LOUGHRIGG FELL
5½
WETHERLAM 1
Black Sails
⅔
Little Langdale
Tarn
Little
Langdale
Swirl
Hawse
Prison Band

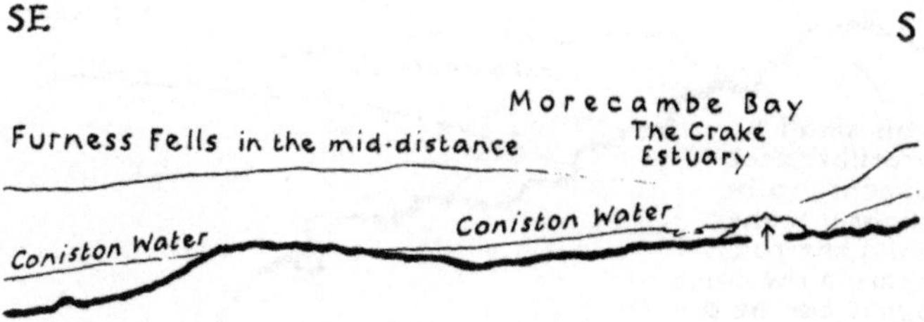
SE
S
Morecambe Bay
Furness Fells in the mid-distance
The Crake
Estuary
Coniston Water
Coniston Water

The thick line marks the visible boundaries
of the summit from the cairn

THE VIEW

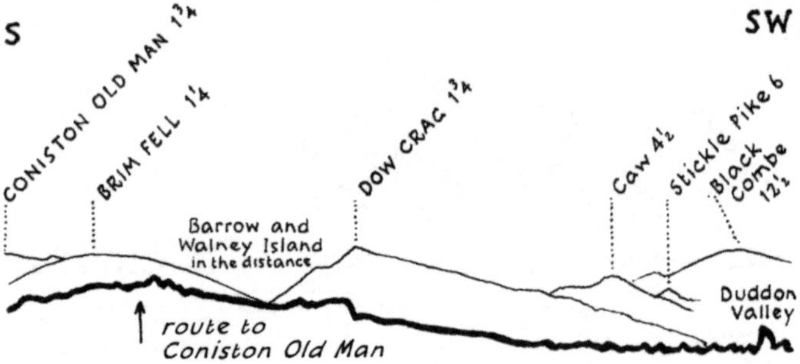
S
SW
CONISTON OLD MAN 1¾
BRIM FELL 1¼
DOW CRAG 1¾
Caw 4½
Stickle Pike 6
Black Combe 12½
Barrow and Walney Island in the distance
Duddon Valley
route to Coniston Old Man

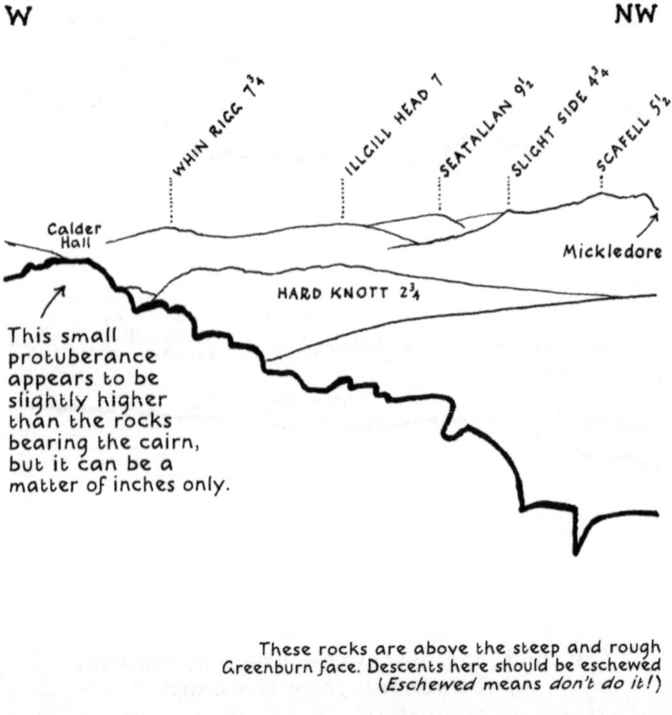
W
NW
WHIN RIGG 7¾
ILLGILL HEAD 7
SEATALLAN 9½
SLIGHT SIDE 4¾
SCAFELL 5½
Calder Hall
Mickledore
HARD KNOTT 2¾
This small protuberance appears to be slightly higher than the rocks bearing the cairn, but it can be a matter of inches only.
These rocks are above the steep and rough Greenburn face. Descents here should be eschewed (*Eschewed* means *don't do it!*)

THE VIEW

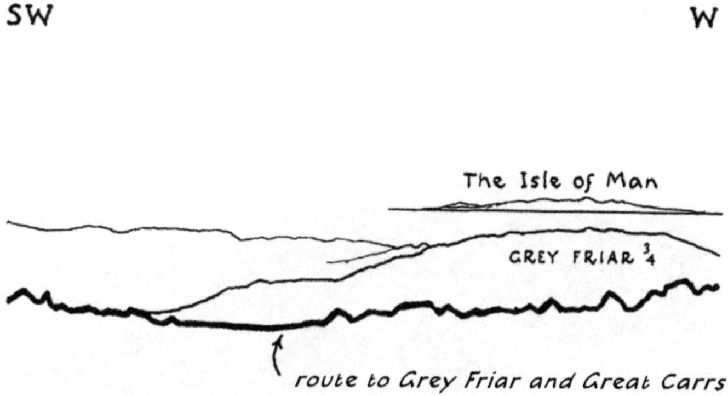
SW
W
The Isle of Man
GREY FRIAR ¾
route to Grey Friar and Great Carrs

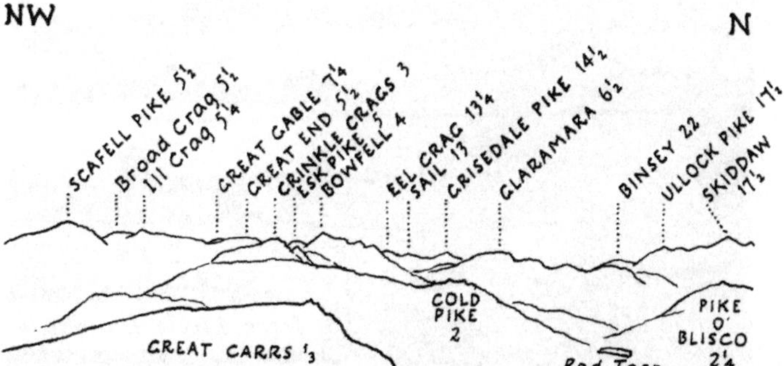
NW
N
SCAFELL PIKE 5½
Broad Crag 5½
Ill Crag 5¼
GREAT GABLE 7¼
GREAT END 5½
CRINKLE CRAGS 3
ESK PIKE 5
BOWFELL 4
EEL CRAG 13¼
SAIL 13
GRISEDALE PIKE 14½
GLARAMARA 6½
BINSEY 22
ULLOCK PIKE 17½
SKIDDAW 17½
COLD PIKE 2
PIKE O' BLISCO 2¼
GREAT CARRS ⅓
Red Tarn
Little Carrs ⅔

Some walkers seem to experience a fierce joy in the sight of the Isle of Man in a view; others find greater pleasure in the sight of a first primrose in springtime. For the benefit of the former, the Isle of Man is shown in this diagram: it is visible from many Lakeland tops in good conditions, but from Swirl How its location can be determined particularly quickly for it appears exactly above the long flat top of Grey Friar nearby. The odds against seeing it on any given day are 50 to 1. At dusk or during night-bivouacs on the tops its position can be fixed in clear weather by the regular beams of its shore lighthouses. *But oh! the delights of that first primrose.......*

Wetherlam

2502′

OS grid ref: NY288011

from Little Langdale

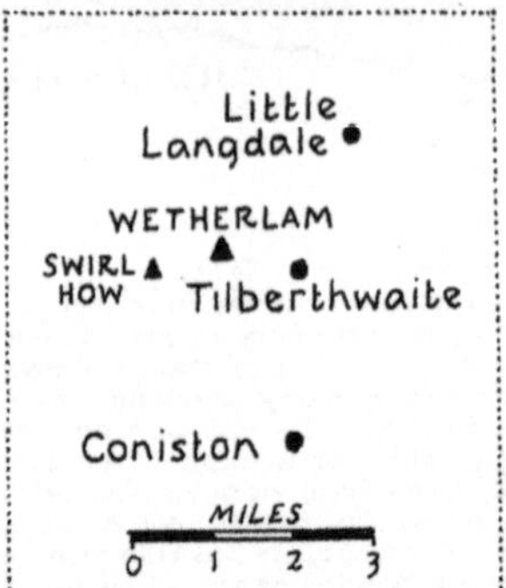
Little Langdale
WETHERLAM
SWIRL HOW
Tilberthwaite
Coniston
MILES
0 1 2 3

from Great Carrs

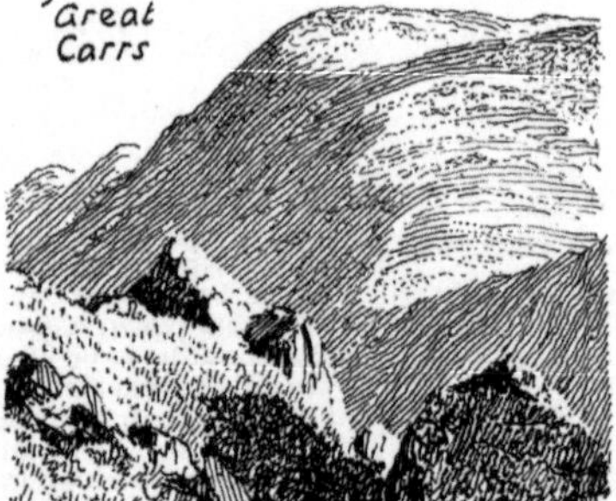

NATURAL FEATURES

Wetherlam features prominently in Brathay views like a giant whale surfacing above waves of lesser hills; the long rising line of the back springs from the fields of Coniston to a maximum height at the tip of the head, from which the blunt nose curves steeply down into Little Langdale. The outline is simple, but deceptive, for the rising ridge coming up from the south is one only (and not the best) of three parallel ridges that give this fell a strong individuality. Quite apart from an unusual shape of structure, however, and in addition to its merit both as a climb and as a viewpoint, Wetherlam has one great claim deserving of close attention.

Ingleborough, which is in view thirty miles away, is often and with much justification considered to be the most interesting mountain in England because of its potentialities to the explorer on, in and under the ground. But Wetherlam, too, is pierced and pitted with holes — caves, tunnels, shafts and excavations — in not less profusion, although, unlike Ingleborough's, all are man-made. These are the levels and shafts and workings of a dead industry — copper mining — and of a living industry — quarrying — that between them, over the centuries, have made Wetherlam the most-industrialised of Lakeland mountains. This fine hill, however is too vast and sturdy to be disfigured and weakened by man's feeble scratchings of its surface, and remains today, as of old, a compelling presence to which walkers in Brathay will oft turn their eager steps.

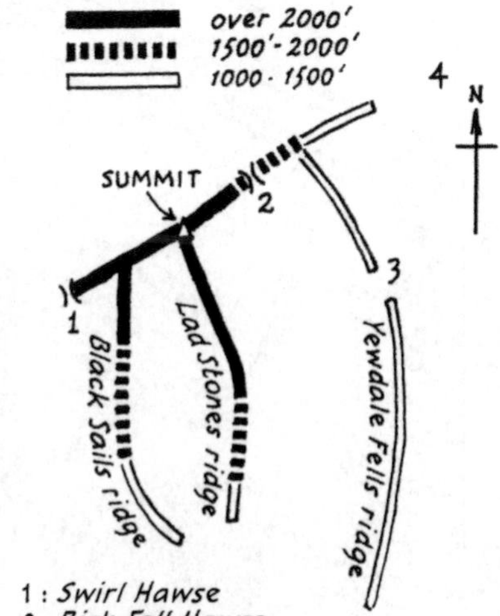
over 2000'
1500'-2000'
1000-1500'
4
N
SUMMIT
2
3
1
Black Sails ridge
Lad Stones ridge
Yewdale Fells ridge
1 : Swirl Hawse
2 : Birk Fell Hawse
3 : Tilberthwaite Gill
4 : Little Langdale
5 : Coniston
5

The plan of the main ridges

MAP

On this and the next three pages, levels and shafts of old mine and quarry workings are indicated *only* in locations where they may be noticed on usual walking routes, in order to relieve the maps of overmuch detail. A simplified diagram on page 7 gives the positions of the various workings.

The square mile of territory between Tilberthwaite Gill and the Brathay *(see map on opposite page)* is scenically one of the loveliest in Lakeland (in spite of the quarries) and surely one of the most interesting (because of the quarries). The valley road is a favourite of visitors, but they generally have little knowledge of the many fascinating places concealed by the screen of trees. Here, in the quarries, it can be seen that Lakeland's beauty is not merely skin deep, that it goes down below the surface in veins of rich and colourful stone. Here, too, can be admired (indeed, cannot but be admired) the ingenious devices and engineering feats of the old quarrymen of pre-machine days in their efforts to win from the craggy fellside this further precious bounty of an over-generous Nature.

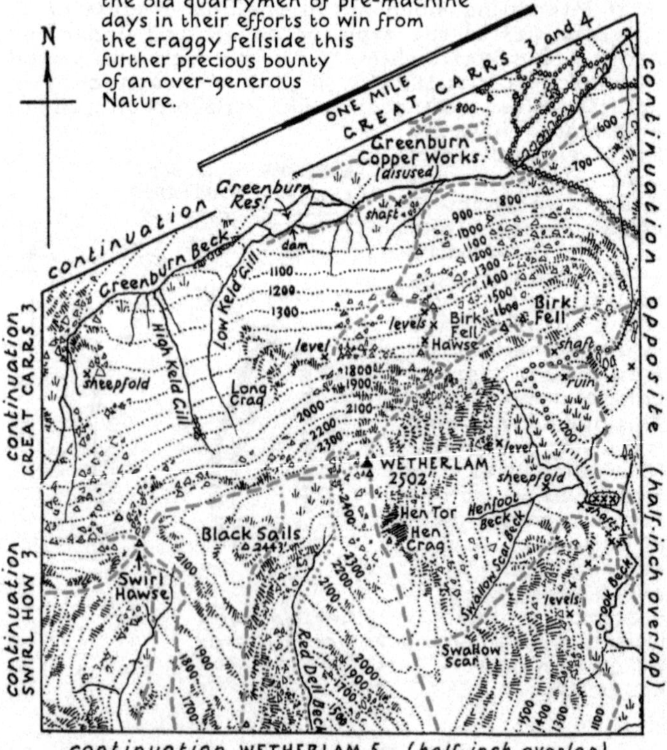
N
ONE MILE
continuation GREAT CARRS 3 and 4
continuation
continuation GREAT CARRS 3
continuation SWIRL HOW 3
continuation opposite (half-inch overlap)
Greenburn Copper Works (disused)
Greenburn Res!
dam
shaft
Greenburn Beck
Low Keld Gill
High Keld Gill
sheepfold
Long Crag
level
levels
Birk Fell Hawse
Birk Fell
shaft
ruin
level
WETHERLAM 2502'
sheepfold
Hen Tor
Hen Crag
Henfoot Beck
Swallow Scar Beck
shafts
levels
Crook Beck
Swallow Scar
Black Sails 2443'
Swirl Hawse
Red Dell Beck
800
600
700
900
1000
1100
1200
1300
1400
1500
1600
1800
1900
2000
2100
2200
2300
2400
1700

continuation WETHERLAM 5 (half-inch overlap)

MAP

Little Langdale Tarn is situated in a marshy area of the valley and has no public access. The tarn and the surrounding area were designated as a Site of Special Scientific Interest in 1965. The area around the tarn is managed by the National Trust.

Greenburn Reservoir was built in the 19th century as part of mining operations in the area. A storm in the winter of 1979–80 caused the dam to burst, reducing its size.

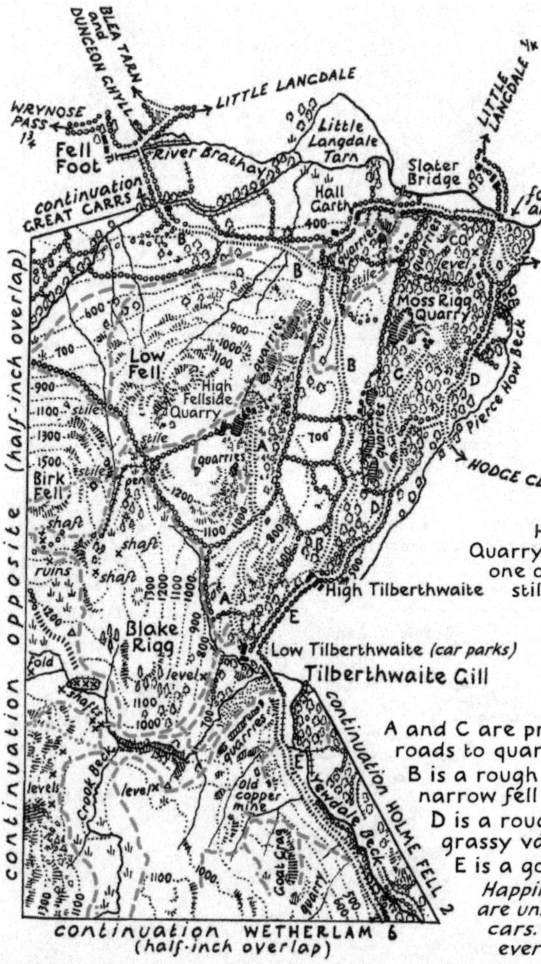
BLEA TARN and DUNGEON GHYLL
LITTLE LANGDALE
LITTLE LANGDALE
WRYNOSE PASS 1¾
Fell Foot
River Brathay
Little Langdale Tarn
Slater Bridge
footbridge and ford
Hall Garth
continuation GREAT CARRS 4
HIGH PARK ½
quarries
CQ
level
stile
Moss Rigg Quarry
Low Fell
High Fellside Quarry
Pierce How Beck
HODGE CLOSE ¼
Birk Fell
pen
shaft
ruins
High Tilberthwaite
Blake Rigg
Low Tilberthwaite (car parks)
Tilberthwaite Gill
fold
shafts
levels
Crook Beck
Old copper mine
Goat Crag
Yewdale Beck
quarry
continuation HOLME FELL 2
continuation opposite (half-inch overlap)
continuation WETHERLAM 6 (half-inch overlap)

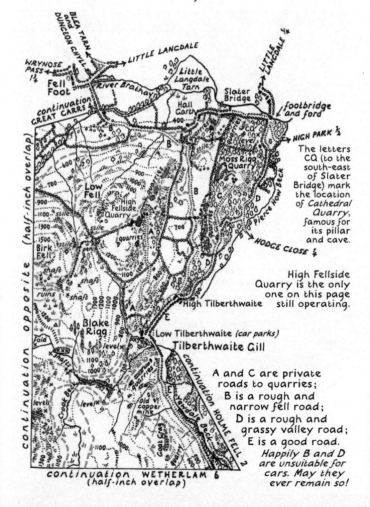

The letters CQ (to the south-east of Slater Bridge) mark the location of *Cathedral Quarry*, famous for its pillar and cave.

High Fellside Quarry is the only one on this page still operating.

A and C are private roads to quarries;
B is a rough and narrow fell road;
D is a rough and grassy valley road;
E is a good road.

Happily B and D are unsuitable for cars. May they ever remain so!

Wetherlam 5

MAP

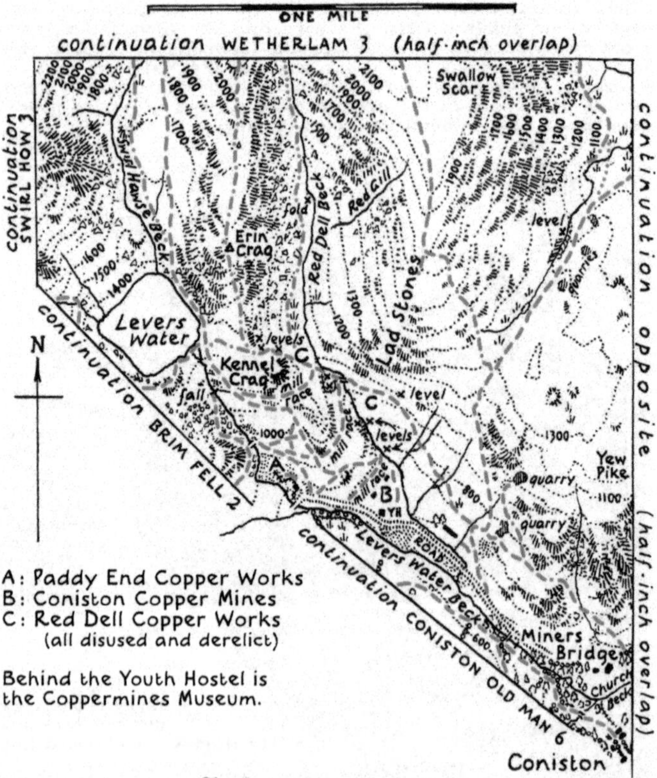
ONE MILE
continuation WETHERLAM 3 (half·inch overlap)
continuation SWIRL HOW 3
continuation opposite (half·inch overlap)
continuation BRIM FELL 2
continuation CONISTON OLD MAN 6
N
Swallow Scar
Swirl Hawse Beck
Erin Crag
Red Dell Beck
Red Gill
fold
Lad Stones
Levers Water
Kennel Crag
levels
level
mill race
fall
race
A
B
C
YH
ROAD
Levers Water Beck
quarries
quarry
Yew Pike
Miners Bridge
Church Beck
Coniston

A: Paddy End Copper Works
B: Coniston Copper Mines
C: Red Dell Copper Works
(all disused and derelict)

Behind the Youth Hostel is the Coppermines Museum.

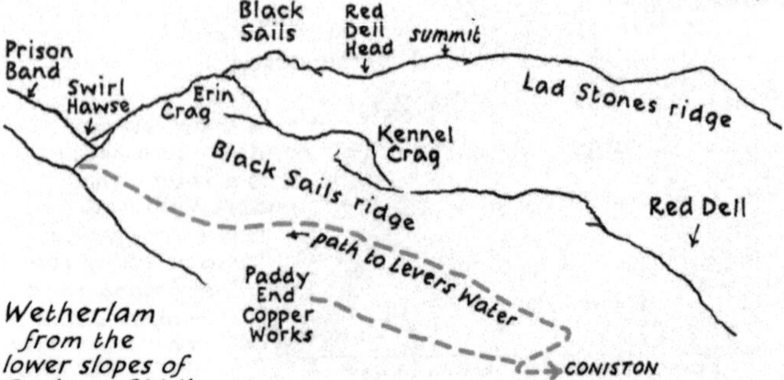
Prison Band
Swirl Hawse
Erin Crag
Black Sails
Red Dell Head
summit
Lad Stones ridge
Kennel Crag
Black Sails ridge
Red Dell
path to Levers Water
Paddy End Copper Works
CONISTON

Wetherlam from the lower slopes of Coniston Old Man

MAP

continuation WETHERLAM 4
(half-inch overlap)
continuation opposite (half-inch overlap)
continuation HOLME FELL 2
AMBLESIDE 6
Crook Beck
Goat Crag
quarry
level
quarries
Yewdale Fells
White Gill
stile
Low Yewdale
Rigg Head
Yew Pike
Mouldry Bank Beck
Yewdale Beck
ROAD
Y.H.
Church Beck
Museum
HAWKSHEAD
HAWKSHEAD 4
WALNA SCAR
Church
Coniston
TORVER 2½
1300
1200
1100
1000
900
800
700
600
500
400
300

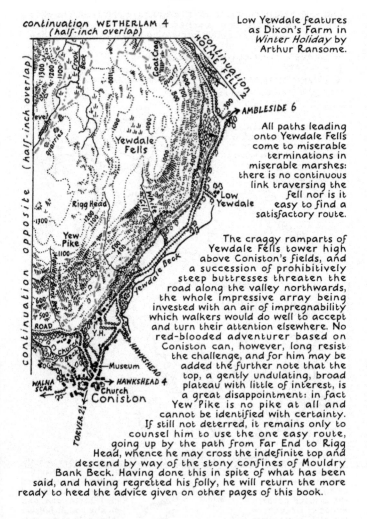

Low Yewdale features as Dixon's Farm in *Winter Holiday* by Arthur Ransome.

All paths leading onto Yewdale Fells come to miserable terminations in miserable marshes: there is no continuous link traversing the fell nor is it easy to find a satisfactory route.

The craggy ramparts of Yewdale Fells tower high above Coniston's fields, and a succession of prohibitively steep buttresses threaten the road along the valley northwards, the whole impressive array being invested with an air of impregnability which walkers would do well to accept and turn their attention elsewhere. No red-blooded adventurer based on Coniston can, however, long resist the challenge, and for him may be added the further note that the top, a gently undulating, broad plateau with little of interest, is a great disappointment: in fact Yew Pike is no pike at all and cannot be identified with certainty. If still not deterred, it remains only to counsel him to use the one easy route, going up by the path from Far End to Rigg Head, whence he may cross the indefinite top and descend by way of the stony confines of Mouldry Bank Beck. Having done this in spite of what has been said, and having regretted his folly, he will return the more ready to heed the advice given on other pages of this book.

A miners' path not well known but strongly recommended for its unusual appeal is that rising by the old quarries above the cottages in Coppermines Valley and continuing to the head of Tilberthwaite Gill; a good alternative to the usual walk by road.

Wetherlam's Hundred Holes —

The sole object of this map is to indicate the locations of the various caves, shafts and quarries, and detail has been omitted other than that helpful in the fascinating pastime of finding them.

- o : CAVES, TUNNELS and LEVELS
- ● : SHAFTS
- ◍ : OPEN QUARRIES

('Open' means 'open to the sky,' not 'open for business'.)

Caves and shafts within open quarries are omitted

Caves and shafts often occur in clusters. Where for this reason space is insufficient to indicate them separately on this map, they are shown thus: ∞ CAVES ♣ SHAFTS and such a symbol may represent any number from three to six.

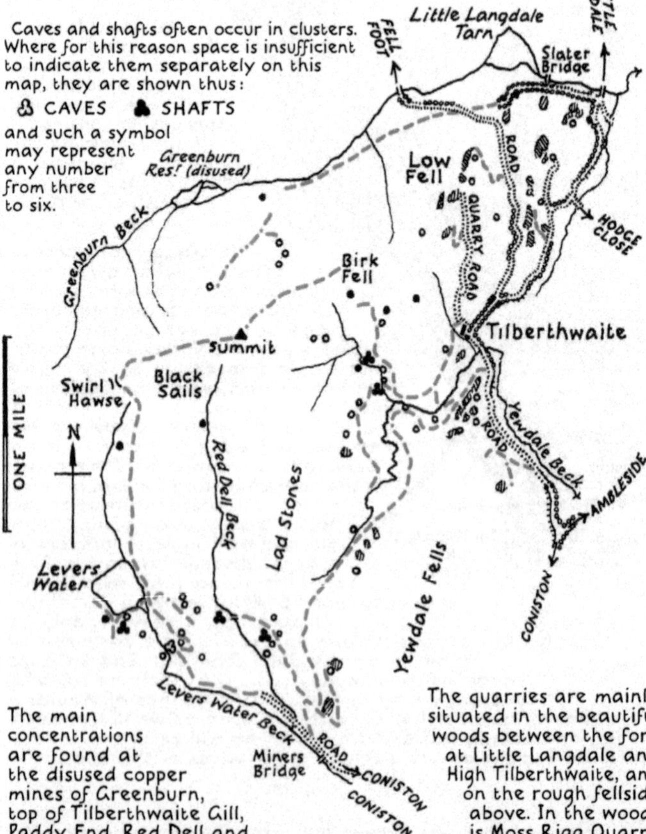

Little Langdale Tarn
FELL FOOT
LITTLE LANGDALE
Slater Bridge
Greenburn Res.r (disused)
Low Fell
ROAD
QUARRY ROAD
HODGE CLOSE
Greenburn Beck
Birk Fell
Tilberthwaite
Summit
Swirl Hawse
Black Sails
ONE MILE
N
Red Dell Beck
Lad Stones
ROAD
Yewdale Beck
AMBLESIDE
Yewdale Fells
CONISTON
Levers Water
Levers Water Beck
Miners Bridge
ROAD
CONISTON
CONISTON

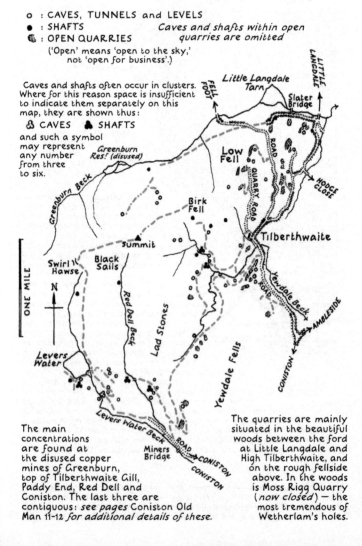

The main concentrations are found at the disused copper mines of Greenburn, top of Tilberthwaite Gill, Paddy End, Red Dell and Coniston. The last three are contiguous: *see pages* Coniston Old Man 11-12 *for additional details of these.*

The quarries are mainly situated in the beautiful woods between the ford at Little Langdale and High Tilberthwaite, and on the rough fellside above. In the woods is Moss Rigg Quarry (*now closed*) — the most tremendous of Wetherlam's holes.

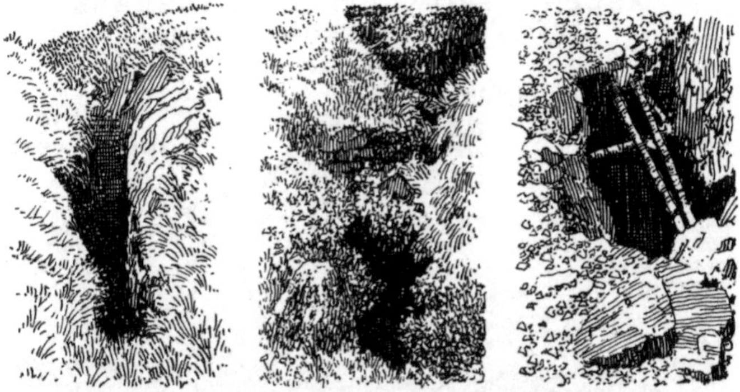

Typical copper-mine shafts

A quarry cave

A copper level

Be content to find the openings, and do not be tempted to enter them. *Roof-falls, flooded passages and rotted timber supports make them DANGEROUS. The shafts (protected by fences) are particularly so.* Keep children away, and do not frighten sheep in the vicinity. It really is a matter for surprise that these fearful death-traps are not half-choked with the mingled remains of too-intrepid explorers, sheep, foxes, dogs, and women whose husbands have tired of them.

The Great Arch, Black Hole Quarry

This disused quarry near Slater Bridge has features common to many hereabouts: the arch, the ravine entrance, the deep shaft from which a tunnel connects with the open fellside.

ASCENT FROM LITTLE LANGDALE
2250 feet of ascent : 3 miles

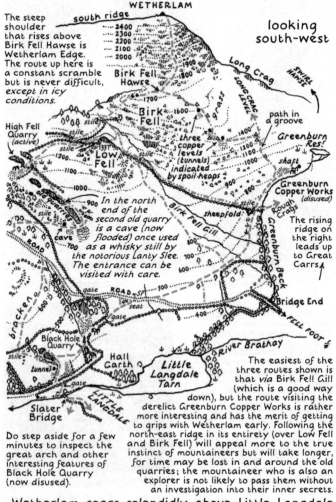

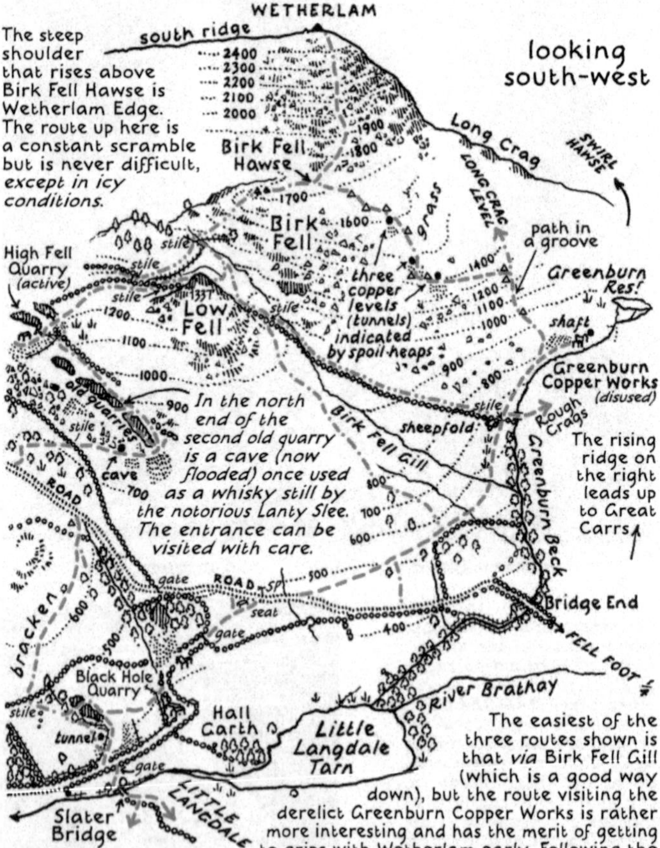
WETHERLAM
south ridge
The steep shoulder that rises above Birk Fell Hawse is Wetherlam Edge. The route up here is a constant scramble but is never difficult, *except in icy conditions.*
looking south-west
2400
2300
2200
2100
2000
1900
1800
1700
1600
1400
1200
1100
1000
900
800
700
600
500
400
Birk Fell Hawse
Long Crag
SWIRL HAWSE
LONG CRAG LEVEL
grass
Birk Fell
path in a groove
Greenburn Res^r
High Fell Quarry (active)
stile
1337
Low Fell
three copper levels (tunnels) indicated by spoil-heaps
shaft
Greenburn Copper Works (disused)
old quarries
In the north end of the second old quarry is a cave (now flooded) once used as a whisky still by the notorious Lanty Slee. The entrance can be visited with care.
Birk Fell Gill
sheepfold
Rough Crags
The rising ridge on the right leads up to Great Carrs
Greenburn Beck
cave
ROAD
bracken
gate
seat
Bridge End
FELL FOOT
Black Hole Quarry
Hall Garth
Little Langdale Tarn
River Brathay
tunnel
Slater Bridge
LITTLE LANGDALE

The easiest of the three routes shown is that *via* Birk Fell Gill (which is a good way down), but the route visiting the derelict Greenburn Copper Works is rather more interesting and has the merit of getting to grips with Wetherlam early. Following the north-east ridge in its entirety (over Low Fell and Birk Fell) will appeal more to the true instinct of mountaineers but will take longer, for time may be lost in and around the old quarries; the mountaineer who is also an explorer is not likely to pass them without an investigation into their inner secrets.

Do step aside for a few minutes to inspect the great arch and other interesting features of Black Hole Quarry (now disused).

Wetherlam soars splendidly above Little Langdale behind an enticing foreground, and here are three ways of tackling what looks like a daunting climb but which is, in fact, far easier than it looks.

ASCENT FROM TILBERTHWAITE

via Steel Edge

2100 feet of ascent : 2 miles

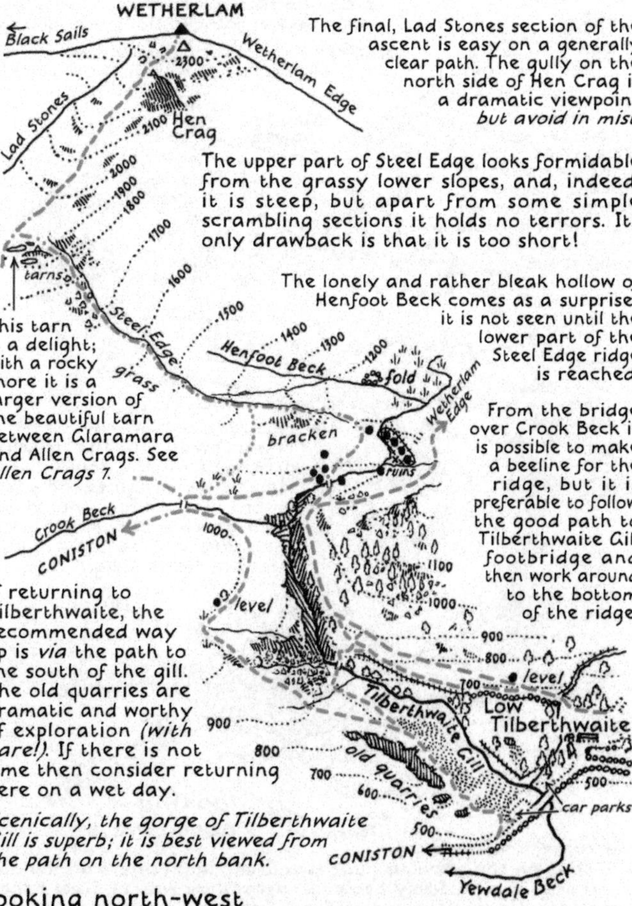
WETHERLAM
Black Sails
Wetherlam Edge
2300
Lad Stones
2100 Hen Crag
2000
1900
1800
1700
tarns
1600
1500
Steel Edge
1400
1300
1200
Henfoot Beck
fold
grass
Wetherlam Edge
bracken
ruins
Crook Beck
CONISTON
1000
1100
level
1000
900
800
level
700
Low Tilberthwaite
Tilberthwaite Gill
900
800
700
old quarries
600
500
car parks
500
CONISTON
Yewdale Beck

The final, Lad Stones section of the ascent is easy on a generally clear path. The gully on the north side of Hen Crag is a dramatic viewpoint *but avoid in mist.*

The upper part of Steel Edge looks formidable from the grassy lower slopes, and, indeed, it is steep, but apart from some simple scrambling sections it holds no terrors. Its only drawback is that it is too short!

The lonely and rather bleak hollow of Henfoot Beck comes as a surprise; it is not seen until the lower part of the Steel Edge ridge is reached.

This tarn is a delight; with a rocky shore it is a larger version of the beautiful tarn between Glaramara and Allen Crags. See *Allen Crags 7.*

From the bridge over Crook Beck it is possible to make a beeline for the ridge, but it is preferable to follow the good path to Tilberthwaite Gill footbridge and then work around to the bottom of the ridge.

If returning to Tilberthwaite, the recommended way up is *via* the path to the south of the gill. The old quarries are dramatic and worthy of exploration *(with care!)*. If there is not time then consider returning here on a wet day.

Scenically, the gorge of Tilberthwaite Gill is superb; it is best viewed from the path on the north bank.

looking north-west

The ascent of Wetherlam by way of Steel Edge – a shapely and prominent spur at right-angles to the Lad Stones ridge – is deservedly popular. Coupled with a descent *via* Wetherlam Edge, this is a round trip of the very highest order. Tilberthwaite has good parking.

ASCENT FROM TILBERTHWAITE
via Wetherlam Edge
2100 feet of ascent : 2 miles

WETHERLAM
levels: horizontal underground passages with cave entrances. Many are flooded.
shafts: vertical rifts, usually with narrow slit openings. Deep. Frightful places!
Wetherlam Edge
Birk Fell Hawse
Birk Fell
Gradients are easy as far as the Hawse, with the steepest section up Wetherlam Edge; this is a constant scramble but with no difficulties.
2400
2300
2200
2100
2000
1900
1800
1700
1600
1500
1400
1300
1200
1100
1000
900
800
700
600
500
fenced shaft
Hawk Rigg
ruin
levels
Dry Cove Moss
– very wet; almost a tarn
Henfoot Beck
fold
shafts and levels (old copper mines)
ruins
Blake Rigg
Tilberthwaite Gill is usually ascended on the south bank but the well engineered path on the north bank should be used on this occasion to its terminus at the old copper mines at Hawk Rigg.
level
ROAD
QUARRIES
Low Tilberthwaite
Tilberthwaite Gill
quarry
old quarries
car parks
LITTLE LANGDALE
Don't come this way down in the dark!
CONISTON
Yewdale Beck
looking north-west

This route, combined with that on the previous page (*via* Steel Edge) offers a splendid round trip. It is probably better to ascend by way of Steel Edge; in reverse, finding the top of Steel Edge can be difficult.

This splendid climb in attractive and contrasting scenery is given added interest by short detours of inspection to the many old copper workings, which should be approached with caution, although the shafts are invariably protected by fences.

ASCENT FROM CONISTON

2450 feet of ascent : 3¾ miles

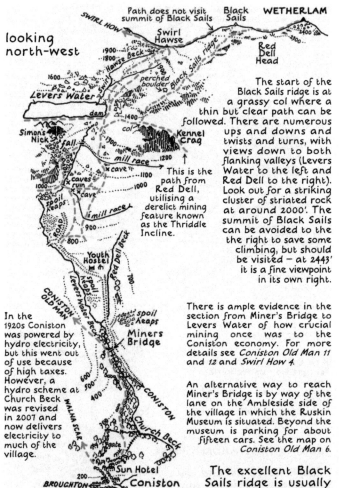

looking north-west

Path does not visit summit of Black Sails
Black Sails
WETHERLAM
SWIRL HOW
Swirl Hawse
2400
2300
Red Dell Head
1900
1800
Swirl Hawse Beck
1900
perched boulder
Black Sails ridge
1600
Levers Water
dam
1400
col
Kennel Crag
Simon's Nick
fall
1300
mill race
1200
cave
1100
caves
ruin
1000
1000
cave
spoil heaps
mill race
ROAD
900
800
Youth Hostel
Red Dell Beck
spoil heaps
700
Levers Water Beck
CONISTON OLD MAN
spoil heaps
Miners Bridge
600
500
400
CONISTON
WALNA SCAR
Church Beck
gate
Sun Hotel
200
BROUGHTON
Coniston
This is the path from Red Dell, utilising a derelict mining feature known as the Thriddle Incline.

The start of the Black Sails ridge is at a grassy col where a thin but clear path can be followed. There are numerous ups and downs and twists and turns, with views down to both flanking valleys (Levers Water to the left and Red Dell to the right). Look out for a striking cluster of striated rock at around 2000'. The summit of Black Sails can be avoided to the the right to save some climbing, but should be visited – at 2443' it is a fine viewpoint in its own right.

There is ample evidence in the section from Miner's Bridge to Levers Water of how crucial mining once was to the Coniston economy. For more details see *Coniston Old Man 11* and *12* and *Swirl How 4*.

An alternative way to reach Miner's Bridge is by way of the lane on the Ambleside side of the village in which the Ruskin Museum is situated. Beyond the museum is parking for about fifteen cars. See the map on *Coniston Old Man 6*.

In the 1920s Coniston was powered by hydro electricity, but this went out of use because of high taxes. However, a hydro scheme at Church Beck was revised in 2007 and now delivers electricity to much of the village.

The excellent Black Sails ridge is usually climbed from the Red Dell side (*see next page*), but this approach is just as good, with a wealth of derelict industrial heritage on the way that adds interest to the climb. The Swirl Hawse alternative is dull by comparison but better in descent.

ASCENT FROM CONISTON

2350 feet of ascent : 3½ miles

The secondary ridge from Kennel Crag to Black Sails is a good alternative to Red Dell Beck as a way up, the key being the Thriddle Incline beyond Red Dell Beck.

Black Sails
WETHERLAM
gully
2300
2200
2100
2000
1900
1800
grass terrace
old working (flooded shaft)
Black Sails Ridge (see page 12)
cascades
Red Gill
tarns
Lad Stones
Kennel Crag
col
caves (old levels)
sheepfold
1700
1600
1500
1200
tarn
1400
TILBERTHWAITE
mill race
fenced potholes
cave (quarry)
hut
1300
1200
Red Dell Copper Works
cave in ravine (Cobbler Hole)
1100
tower
mill race
water pipe
bracken
wide grass path
900
1000
quarries
site of Coniston Copper Mines
Youth Hostel
Red Dell Beck
700
800
quarry
Levers Water Beck
row of five cottages (originally ten)
CONISTON OLD MAN
spoil heaps
600
waterfalls in rocky gorge
Miners Bridge
waterfall
ROAD
CONISTON
500
WALNA SCAR
400
Church Beck
Sun Hotel
300
Black Bull Hotel
BROUGHTON
Coniston

Beyond the tarns the ridge steepens but gradients are never severe.

If descending by the Lad Stones ridge do not persevere to its craggy extremity but slant down left to join the grass path coming from Tilberthwaite.

All quarries and mines shown on the diagram are DISUSED, DERELICT, *DANGEROUS!*

waterfall – walk 50 yards down the road for the best view of it

Red Dell offers the only feasible way up Wetherlam that doesn't involve a ridge walk; from Red Dell Head, the depression to the right of Black Sails, it is only a short walk to the summit.

looking north-north-west

Preferably, ascend by the deeply enclosed and bouldery valley of Red Dell, where the old copper works add an interest to dreary surroundings and the gradients are easy, and descend by the pleasant and generally dry ridge of Lad Stones, which has excellent views.

THE SUMMIT

The summit is gently domed on three sides, with steepening curves to north and east, the fourth (south) being a level ridge. There is much rock about, weathered to an ashen-grey colour but, when broken, revealing the tinges of brown characteristic of the spoil-heaps of the copper mines on the lower slopes. The highest point is occupied by a low mound of stones. Although the summit is much trodden it bears little imprint of paths.

DESCENTS: Considering the popularity of the fell as a climb it is remarkable that there are not good paths linking summit and valley, but there are not, and in fact the selection of a way across the foothills, especially to Little Langdale, is not simple.

TO LITTLE LANGDALE: Go down Wetherlam Edge, keeping slightly to the left at first, on grass, and looking for the insufficient cairns. A stony track materialises and descends roughly to Birk Fell Hawse; a turn down the pathless slope to the left here (into Greenburn) is the simplest and quickest route to take. The direct ridge route beyond the Hawse goes on over Birk Fell and Low Fell, and is interesting (if there is ample time for trial and error), *but is unsuitable in mist.*

TO TILBERTHWAITE: From the col between the two summits of Birk Fell take a path going down to the right and passing a fenced shaft. The path crosses a broken wall and joins the wide grassy mines-path seen in front: this descends easily to the valley.

TO CONISTON: Go along the gradual south ridge (Lad Stones) for a full mile on a thin but generally clear path until easier ground on the left permits a descent to a path going down to the Coppermines Valley. The south ridge, if persisted in too far, will lead to difficulties above Red Dell Copper Works.

In mist, the absence of clear paths in the immediate vicinity of the summit makes the top confusing. If quite unable to take bearings, it is useful to know that the lower cairn, 20 yards away, is *south* of the main cairn, and a tiny rocky pool (which dries up in drought) a few paces distant is to the *west*. The start of the route down the convex slope to Birk Fell Hawse is not easy to locate: hunt around for cairns (they are insufficient at first but become profuse). The south ridge presents no difficulties, but the ridge running south from Black Sails is best left alone.

THE VIEW

Wetherlam thrusts well forward, away from the main bulk of the Coniston fells, and thus provides a view free from near obstruction, unlike the others in the group. It rises, moreover, immediately above the deep valley of Little Langdale, so that the mountain scene beyond is given unusual height. The picture is everywhere good, but best of all is the lovely countryside of Brathay, seen in all its glory as from an aeroplane, and revealing a large array of sparkling waters. In the far distance, across Windermere, is the long line of the Pennines. To the south is the estuary of the Kent, and, to the horizon, Morecambe Bay. This is a view that, more than most, benefits by sunlight and dappled shadows.

Principal Fells

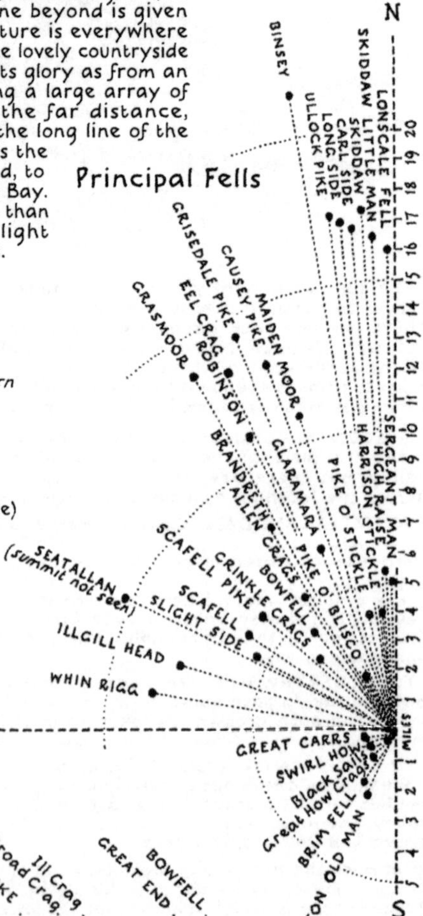
N
BINSEY
SKIDDAW
LONSCALE FELL
SKIDDAW LITTLE MAN
CARL SIDE
LONG SIDE
ULLOCK PIKE
GRISEDALE PIKE
CAUSEY PIKE
MAIDEN MOOR
EEL CRAG
GRASMOOR
ROBINSON
GLARAMARA
BRANDRETH
ALLEN CRAGS
PIKE O' STICKLE
HARRISON STICKLE
HIGH RAISE
SERGEANT MAN
PIKE O' BLISCO
BOWFELL
CRINKLE CRAGS
SCAFELL PIKE
SCAFELL
SLIGHT SIDE
SEATALLAN (summit not seen)
ILLGILL HEAD
WHIN RIGG
W
MILES
GREAT CARRS
SWIRL HOW
Black Sails
Great How Crags
BRIM FELL
CONISTON OLD MAN
S

Lakes and Tarns

N : *Stickle Tarn*
N : *Blea Tarn*
NE : *Little Langdale Tarn*
NE : *Elter Water*
E : Windermere (head)
E : *Blelham Tarn*
ESE : *Tarn Hows*
ESE : *Wise Een Tarn*
SE : *Esthwaite Water*
SE : *Windermere* (middle)
S : *Coniston Water*
S : *Beacon Tarn*
S : *Torver Reservoir*
SSW : *Low Water*
NW : *Red Tarn*

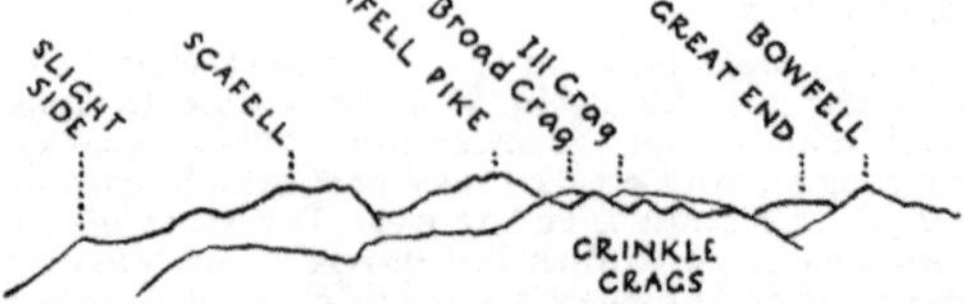
SLIGHT SIDE
SCAFELL
SCAFELL PIKE
Broad Crag
Ill Crag
GREAT END
BOWFELL
CRINKLE CRAGS

looking north-west

THE VIEW

N
E
S
MILES
1 2 3 4 5 6 7 8 9 10 11 12 13 14 15 16 17 18 19 20
1 2 3 4 5
KNOTT
BLENCATHRA
CLOUGH HEAD
GREAT DODD
HELVELLYN LOWER MAN
HELVELLYN
NETHERMOST PIKE
DOLLYWAGGON PIKE
SEAT SANDAL
STEEL FELL
HELM CRAG
SILVER HOW
FAIRFIELD
GREAT RIGG
HART CRAG
DOVE CRAG
REST DODD
HIGH RAISE
RED SCREES
HIGH STREET
THORNTHWAITE CRAG
MARDALE ILL BELL
FROSWICK
HARTER FELL
ILL BELL
KENTMERE PIKE
TARN CRAG
GREY CRAG
YOKE
LOUGHRIGG FELL
WANSFELL PIKE
SALLOWS
SOUR HOWES
BLACK FELL
HOLME FELL

Lanty Slee's Cave
(page 9)

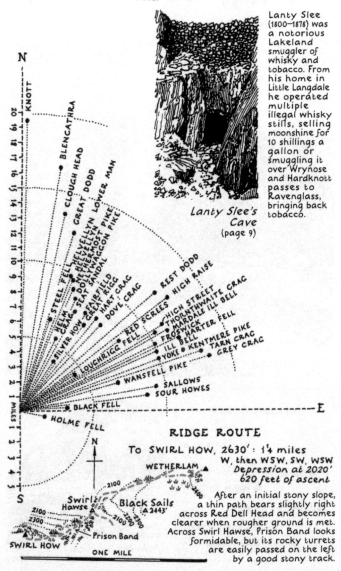

Lanty Slee (1800–1878) was a notorious Lakeland smuggler of whisky and tobacco. From his home in Little Langdale he operated multiple illegal whisky stills, selling moonshine for 10 shillings a gallon or smuggling it over Wrynose and Hardknott passes to Ravenglass, bringing back tobacco.

RIDGE ROUTE

To SWIRL HOW, 2630′ : 1¼ miles

W, then WSW, SW, WSW
Depression at 2020′
620 feet of ascent

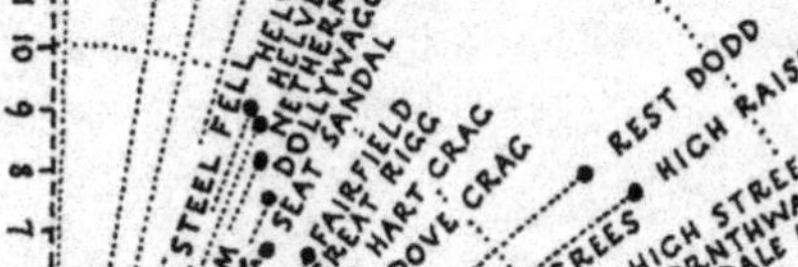
N
WETHERLAM
2100
2400
Swirl Hawse
Black Sails
2443′
2100
2200
2300
2100
2300
Prison Band
SWIRL HOW
ONE MILE

After an initial stony slope, a thin path bears slightly right across Red Dell Head and becomes clearer when rougher ground is met. Across Swirl Hawse, Prison Band looks formidable, but its rocky turrets are easily passed on the left by a good stony track.

Whin Rigg

1755'

OS grid ref: NY152034

from Strands

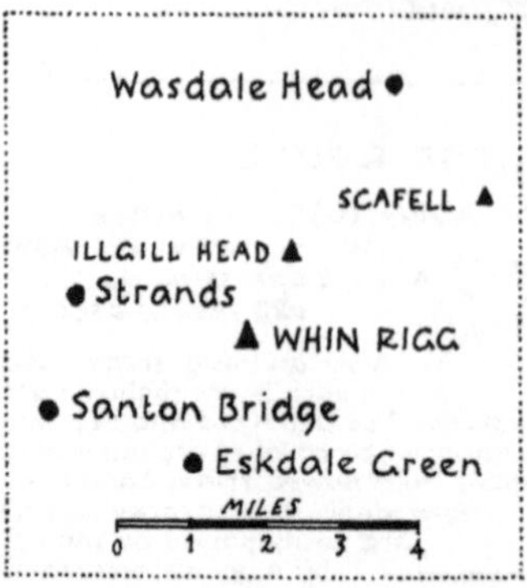
Wasdale Head
SCAFELL
ILLGILL HEAD
Strands
WHIN RIGG
Santon Bridge
Eskdale Green
MILES
0
1
2
3
4

from the north-east
(on the approach from Illgill Head)

NATURAL FEATURES

No mountain in Lakeland, not even Great Gable nor Blencathra nor the Langdale Pikes, can show a grander front than Whin Rigg, modest in elevation though the latter is, and so little known that most visitors to the district will not have heard the name. Wastwater Screes, of course, is a place familiar to many; Whin Rigg is the southern terminus of the shattered ridge above Wast Water, beyond the screes, where the great grey cliffs have resisted erosion and rise in gigantic towers over the foot of the lake to culminate finally in a small shapely summit, a proud eyrie indeed. This savage scene is tempered and given a rare beauty by the blending of dark waters and rich woodlands that form the base of every view of the soaring buttresses — but there is no denying the steepness and severity of its precipices and chasms. This is one fellside that walkers can write off at a glance as having no access for them.

The opposite flank, to the east, is, in a contrast absolute, gently graded and everywhere grassy; it descends dully to the narrow branch-valley of Miterdale, a lovely and almost secret fold of the hills, unspoiled, serene.

The southern ridge of the fell declines to the long grassy shoulder of Irton Fell and the rocky Irton Pike, now largely under timber; beyond is a pleasant countryside watered by the Esk and the Irt, both of them fed by Whin Rigg, and then, to the far horizon, is the sea.

It is along this ridge that walkers may find a simple way to the summit and so look down on the lake from the cairn, and, by going a little further, between the vertical walls of the tremendous gullies. This is dramatic scenery, quite unique, and with an abiding impression of grandeur that makes the ascent of Whin Rigg a walk to be remembered and thought about often.

Whin Rigg 3

MAP

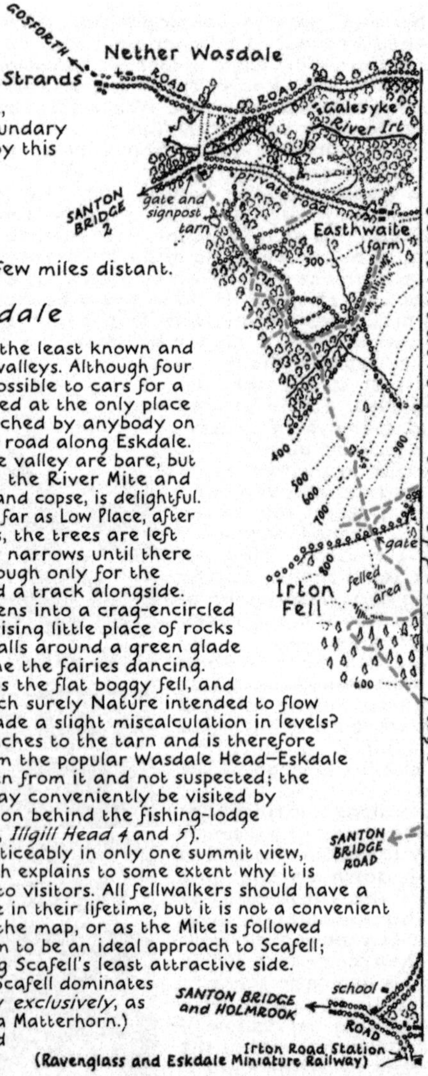
GOSFORTH
Nether Wasdale
Strands
ROAD
ROAD
Galesyke
River Irt
private road
SANTON BRIDGE 2
gate and signpost
tarn
Easthwaite (farm)
300
400
500
600
700
800
900
gate
Irton Fell
felled area
600
SANTON BRIDGE ROAD
SANTON BRIDGE and HOLMROOK
school
ROAD
Irton Road Station (Ravenglass and Eskdale Miniature Railway)
continuation on opposite page

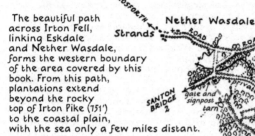

The beautiful path across Irton Fell, linking Eskdale and Nether Wasdale, forms the western boundary of the area covered by this book. From this path, plantations extend beyond the rocky top of Irton Pike (751') to the coastal plain, with the sea only a few miles distant.

Miterdale

Miterdale is perhaps the least known and quietest of Lakeland's valleys. Although four miles in length, and possible to cars for a mile, it is not signposted at the only place whence it may be reached by anybody on wheels from the main road along Eskdale.

The fells enclosing the valley are bare, but its floor, threaded by the River Mite and adorned by woodland and copse, is delightful. The scene is pastoral as far as Low Place, after which, a mile onwards, the trees are left behind and the valley narrows until there is accommodation enough only for the bed of the stream and a track alongside. But at its head it widens into a crag-encircled amphitheatre, a surprising little place of rocks and trees and waterfalls around a green glade where one can imagine the fairies dancing. Immediately beyond is the flat boggy fell, and Burnmoor Tarn — which surely Nature intended to flow into Miterdale and made a slight miscalculation in levels?

Miterdale almost reaches to the tarn and is therefore quickly accessible from the popular Wasdale Head–Eskdale path although not seen from it and not suspected; the unique valley-head may conveniently be visited by a short detour, going on behind the fishing-lodge for five minutes. (Map, *Illgill Head 4* and *5*).

Miterdale features noticeably in only one summit view, that from Scafell, which explains to some extent why it is not generally known to visitors. All fellwalkers should have a look at this valley once in their lifetime, but it is not a convenient route to the hills. On the map, or as the Mite is followed upstream, it would seem to be an ideal approach to Scafell; but it is not, this being Scafell's least attractive side. (It is remarkable how Scafell dominates the head of the valley *exclusively*, as if it were solitary like a Matterhorn.) Nor is Miterdale a good place to start the ascents of Whin Rigg or Illgill Head, which border the valley, the facing slopes being easy, if bracken and swamps can be avoided, but very tedious.

MAP

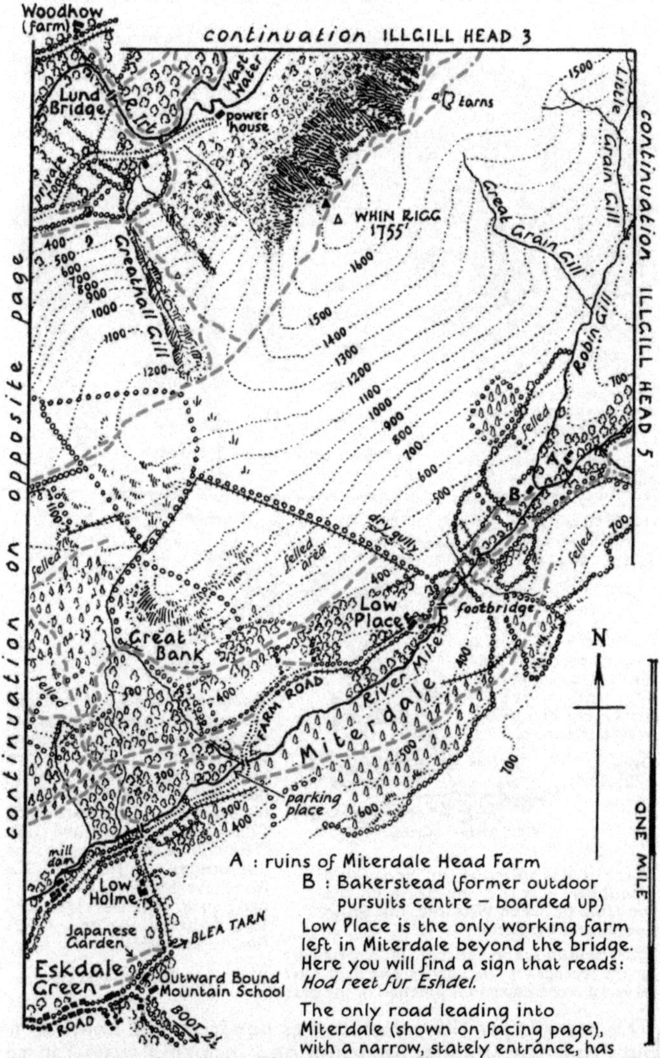
continuation ILLGILL HEAD 3
continuation ILLGILL HEAD 5
continuation on opposite page
Woodhow (farm)
Lund Bridge
R. Irt
Wast Water
power house
private road
tarns
WHIN RIGG 1755'
Little Grain Gill
Great Grain Gill
Robin Gill
Greathall Gill
felled
felled area
dry gully
Low Place
footbridge
Great Bank
FARM ROAD
River Mite
Miterdale
parking place
A
B
N
ONE MILE
mill dam
Low Holme
Japanese Garden
BLEA TARN
Eskdale Green
Outward Bound Mountain School
ROAD
BOOT 2½

A : ruins of Miterdale Head Farm

B : Bakerstead (former outdoor pursuits centre – boarded up)

Low Place is the only working farm left in Miterdale beyond the bridge. Here you will find a sign that reads: *Hod reet fur Eshdel.*

The only road leading into Miterdale (shown on facing page), with a narrow, stately entrance, has the appearance of a private drive, the happy effect being that the valley remains undisturbed. The lane beside the Outward Bound school is not suitable for vehicles, but is perfect for walkers. There is parking nearby.

ASCENT FROM NETHER WASDALE

1600 feet of ascent : 2 miles from Woodhow farm

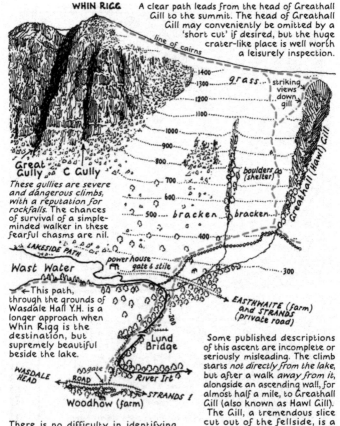

A clear path leads from the head of Greathall Gill to the summit. The head of Greathall Gill may conveniently be omitted by a 'short cut' if desired, but the huge crater-like place is well worth a leisurely inspection.

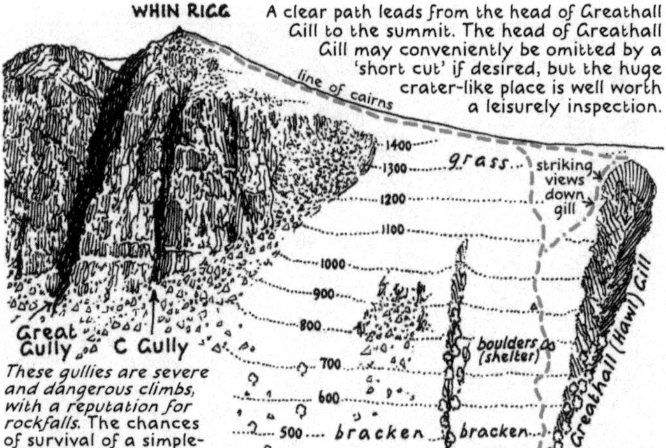
WHIN RIGG
line of cairns
1400
1300
grass
striking views down gill
1200
1100
1000
900
800
Great Gully
C Gully
boulders (shelter)
Greathall (Hawl) Gill
700
600
500
bracken
bracken
400
LAKESIDE PATH
power house
gate & stile
Wast Water
300
EASTHWAITE (farm) and STRANDS (private road)
200
Lund Bridge
WASDALE HEAD
gate
ROAD
River Irt
STRANDS
Woodhow (farm)

These gullies are severe and dangerous climbs, with a reputation for rockfalls. The chances of survival of a simple-minded walker in these fearful chasms are nil.

←This path, through the grounds of Wasdale Hall Y.H. is a longer approach when Whin Rigg is the destination, but supremely beautiful beside the lake.

Some published descriptions of this ascent are incomplete or seriously misleading. The climb starts *not directly from the lake*, but after a walk *away from it*, alongside an ascending wall, for almost half a mile, to Greathall Gill (also known as Hawl Gill).

The Gill, a tremendous slice cut out of the fellside, is a favourite hunting ground of geologists. Take the right fork to see the ravine or the left fork to save time.

There is no difficulty in identifying Woodhow: it is the only farm on the roadside between Wasdale Hall Youth Hostel and Strands.

Lund Bridge is too substantial a structure for the footpath it now carries, and must have served a more important function in the past.

looking east

The reward for this climb comes not from the doing of it but from the unique, beautiful and inspiring situation to which it leads: the top of the towering crags and gullies of the Screes, a scene without a counterpart elsewhere.

ASCENT FROM ESKDALE GREEN

1650 feet of ascent : 3½ miles

The ridge is an easy ascent with the highlight, at the midway point, passing the head of the remarkable, crater-like Greathall Gill.

When the ridge wall is reached leave the path to Nether Wasdale and follow a path, right, by the far side of the wall.

A unique and ingenious signpost

Probably the work of a forest employee, this signpost is no longer to be found.

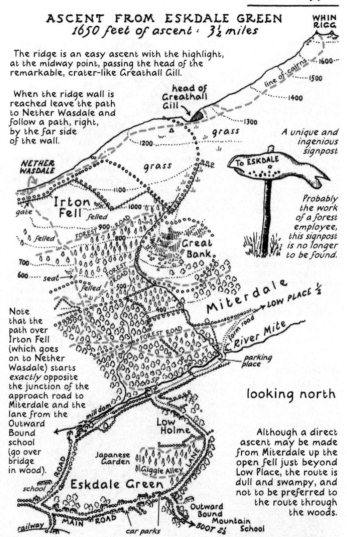

Note that the path over Irton Fell (which goes on to Nether Wasdale) starts *exactly* opposite the junction of the approach road to Miterdale and the lane from the Outward Bound school (go over bridge in wood).

Although a direct ascent may be made from Miterdale up the open fell just beyond Low Place, the route is dull and swampy, and not to be preferred to the route through the woods.

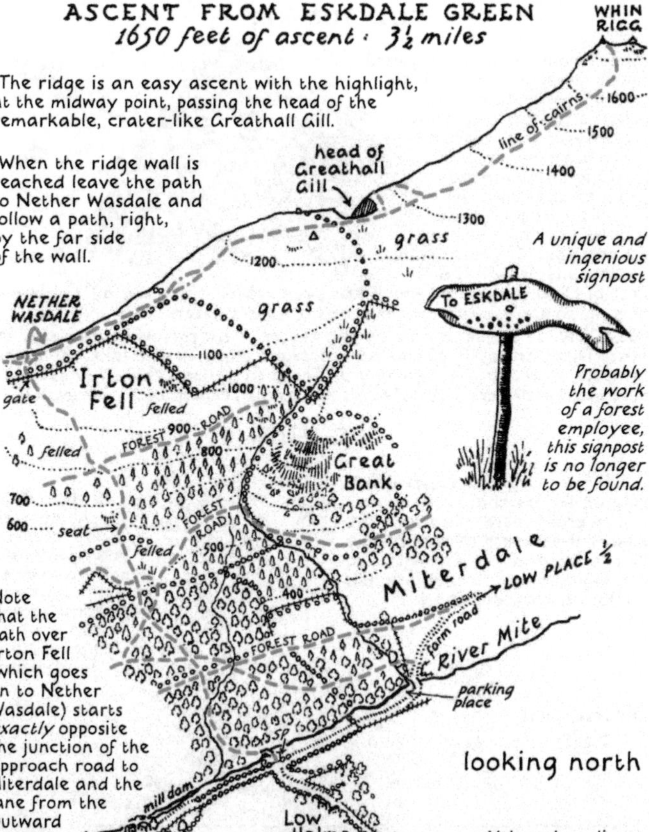
WHIN RIGG
1600
1500
line of cairns
1400
head of Greathall Gill
1300
grass
1200
NETHER WASDALE
grass
TO ESKDALE
1100
Irton Fell
gate
1000
felled
FOREST ROAD
900
felled
800
Great Bank
700
600
seat
FOREST ROAD
felled
500
Miterdale
LOW PLACE ½
400
farm road
River Mite
FOREST ROAD
parking place
SP
looking north
mill dam
Low Holme
Japanese Garden
Giggle Alley
LANE
ROAD
school
Eskdale Green
railway
MAIN ROAD
car parks
Outward Bound Mountain School
BOOT 2½

The way shown makes use of the pleasant Irton Fell path to gain the ridge, and gives lovely views seawards across the lower valleys of the Irt and Esk.

THE SUMMIT

ILLGILL HEAD

The cairn is so delicately poised above the cliffs that a single stride from one side to the other is sufficient to bring Wast Water into view, and a dramatic moment this is, a highlight indeed. In other directions the summit is simple; there is a second cairn on the Eskdale edge. The ridge path, grassy, passes within a few feet of the main cairn, which has been rebuilt since the author drew this illustration and now serves as a wind shelter.

DESCENTS: Descend *only* by the routes of ascent, which are safe in mist. There is *positively* no way straight down to the lake. *Don't be tempted into the wide opening of Great Gully: this fearful chasm has seventeen near-vertical pitches (as well as the remains of an aeroplane).*

THE VIEW

This is a splendid viewpoint, relying for its charm mainly on the strong contrast between the pastoral softness of the valleys of the Irt and the Esk with the sea beyond, and the sombre hills enclosing Wasdale Head.

As Whin Rigg is the nearest of the Southern Fells to Sellafield (only seven miles away) the nuclear reprocessing plant is seen in all its glory — if glory is the word.

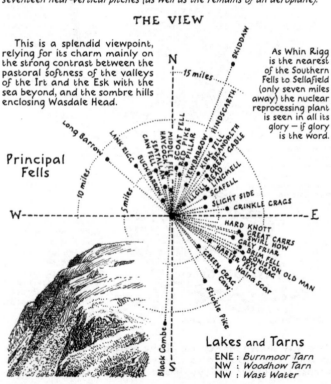

Principal Fells

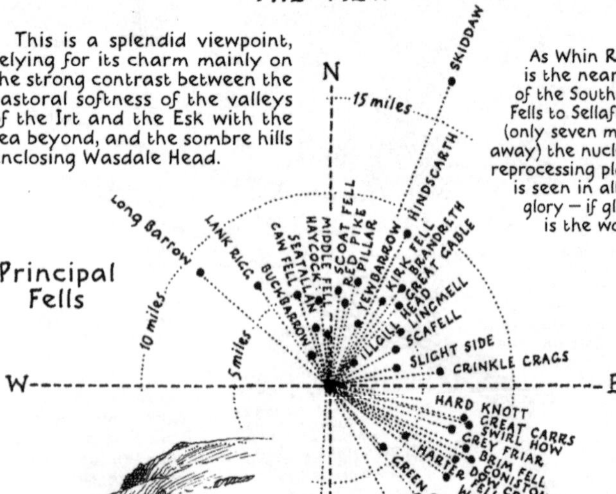
N
S
E
W
15 miles
10 miles
5 miles
SKIDDAW
HINDSCARTH
Long Barrow
LANK RIGG
CAW FELL
HAYCOCK
MIDDLE FELL
SCOAT FELL
RED PIKE
PILLAR
SEATALLAN
BUCKBARROW
YEWBARROW
KIRK FELL
BRANDRETH
GREAT GABLE
ILLGILL HEAD
LINGMELL
SCAFELL
SLIGHT SIDE
CRINKLE CRAGS
HARD KNOTT
GREAT CARRS
SWIRL HOW
GREY FRIAR
BRIM FELL
CONISTON OLD MAN
HARTER FELL
DOW CRAG
Walna Scar
GREEN CRAG
CAW
Stickle Pike
Black Combe

Lakes and Tarns

ENE : *Burnmoor Tarn*
NW : *Woodhow Tarn*
NW : *Wast Water*

RIDGE ROUTE

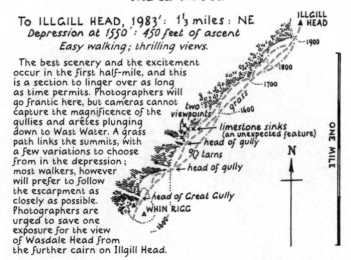

To ILLGILL HEAD, 1983′: 1⅓ miles: NE

Depression at 1550′: 450 feet of ascent

Easy walking; thrilling views.

ILLGILL HEAD
1900
1800
1700
grass
1600
two viewpoints
limestone sinks (an unexpected feature)
head of gully
tarns
head of gully
head of Great Gully
WHIN RIGG
1600
N
ONE MILE

The best scenery and the excitement occur in the first half-mile, and this is a section to linger over as long as time permits. Photographers will go frantic here, but cameras cannot capture the magnificence of the gullies and arêtes plunging down to Wast Water. A grass path links the summits, with a few variations to choose from in the depression; most walkers, however will prefer to follow the escarpment as closely as possible. Photographers are urged to save one exposure for the view of Wasdale Head from the further cairn on Illgill Head.

The two viewpoints indicated on the diagram (as seen from the north-east, i.e. the Illgill Head side)

That on the left forms a small peak on the brink of the escarpment, and is a prominent object on the ridge walk. The other is a narrow arête (Broken Rib) going down from the ridge. Both places are easily visited.

Wastwater Screes and Gullies

Here is the finest example of the natural ravages of weather, the whole fellside being in a state of decay. The disintegration of the crags has produced many grotesque formations, firm

sections of rock remaining like fangs amidst the crumbled debris. (Note the dark tower isolated in scree, 2 inches from the left edge of the drawing). Climbing on these freak pinnacles and spires is unsafe. Whin Rigg is the summit on the extreme right.

Some Personal notes in conclusion

I have said my farewells to Mickledore and Esk Hause and Bowfell and all the other grand places described in this book, with the same 'hollow' feeling one has when taking leave of friends knowing that it may be for the last time. For the next few years I shall be engaged elsewhere, to the north and west, and although I shall be straining my eyes to see these old favourites from afar, I shall not be visiting them during this period; and perhaps never again.

There has been a clamour for Book Four ever since the first in the series appeared, and there is no doubt at all that the region of the Southern Fells has priority in the minds of most lovers of the Lake District, and especially those whose joy it is to walk upon the mountains. I agree, without saying a word to detract from the merits of other areas. All Lakeland is exquisitely beautiful; the Southern Fells just happen to be a bit of heaven fallen upon the earth.

The past two years, spent preparing the book, have been a grand experience — in spite of countless ascents of Rossett Gill (which, incidentally, seems to get easier if you keep on doing it). Fortune smiled on me hugely during the months I had set aside for the Scafells — day after day of magnificent weather, with visibility so amazingly good that one simply got used to seeing the Scottish hills and the Isle of Man permanently on the horizon. I had feared delays on the Scafells by unsuitable conditions or even normal weather, but this never happened. Many glorious mountain days, followed by happy evenings in Wasdale and Eskdale — that was the pattern for the summer of 1959.

It has taken me over 300 pages to describe the fells in this area, and I need say no more about them; but I must emphasise the supreme beauty of the approaches along the valleys — every yard of the way to the tops, and every minute of every day, is utter joy. But a special word for Eskdale: this is walkers' territory par excellence, and as traffic in other valleys increases, it is likely to become the last stronghold for travellers on foot. This lovely valley is quiet and unfrequented. I rarely met anybody when climbing out of Eskdale but, on reaching the watershed, found the ridges alive with folk who had come up from Borrowdale and Langdale.

Great Langdale is a growing problem. This used to be a walkers' valley too, and one of the best. Nowadays walkers are beginning to feel out of place. Coaches, cars, caravans, motor-bikes and tents throng the valley. One cannot complain about people who want to see the scenery but some of the characters infesting the place at weekends have eyes only for mischief. These slovenly layabouts, of both sexes, cause endless damage and trouble, and it behoves all respectable visitors (still in the majority) to help the police and farmers to preserve order. Poor Langdale! How green was my valley!

I finished the Langdale tops in 1958 but had occasion to return in the spring of 1959. Glancing up from the valley to the cairn on Pike o' Blisco (as I always do) I was dismayed to notice that it had been mutilated. I went up to see and found that the tall column of stones had been beheaded, the top part having been demolished, apparently by human agency. Are the wreckers getting up on the tops, too?..... If all readers who visit this summit will replace one stone firmly, please, the cairn may in time again look as it does in the Pike o' Blisco chapter.

I ought to mention that I am aware that the Duddon Valley is also properly known as Dunnerdale, a name I haven't used in the book, preferring the former; just as I never refer to Blencathra by its better-known modern name of Saddleback. It's a matter of personal choice. I like the Duddon Valley and Blencathra. I don't like Dunnerdale and Saddleback.

Several letters, and even petitions, from Great Gable enthusiasts have been sent in asking me to do Book Seven next after Book Four, and Book Five last. What a frightfully untidy suggestion! It springs from a generally accepted view, of course, that there is nothing "back o' Skidda" worth exploring. I want to go and find out. There is a big tract of lonely fells here, wild and desolate; but this is immortal ground, the John Peel country, and I rely further on a centuries-old saying that "Caldbeck Fells are worth all England else". A land rich with promise, surely!

On this occasion I intend to make an excuse for defects in penmanship. I am going to lay the blame fairly and squarely on the head of Cindy, a Sealyham puppy with roving eyes, introduced to the household some time ago. Cindy has shown absolutely no sympathy whatever with my efforts to write a classic — a fearful waste of time when I might otherwise be tickling her tummy or throwing her ball or having a tug-of-war with an old stocking. Her persistent pokings and tuggings at critical moments of concentration must have resulted in inferior work, for which I am sorry. But it's Cindy's fault, not mine.

AW

Christmas
1959.

STARTING POINTS

CHAPEL STILE
Lingmoor Fell 7

CONISTON ROAD (A593)
Black Fell 3

CONISTON
Brim Fell 3
Coniston Old Man 7, 8
Dow Crag 8
Swirl How 4
Wetherlam 12, 13

DRUNKEN DUCK INN
Black Fell 3

DUDDON VALLEY
(incl. BIRKS BRIDGE, COCKLEY BECK BRIDGE, GRASSGUARDS and SEATHWAITE)
Crinkle Crags 9
Dow Crag 9
Grey Friar 6
Harter Fell 5

DUNGEON GHYLL
(incl. MICKLEDEN)
Bowfell 5–6, 7
Crinkle Crags 5, 6, 7
Esk Pike 10
Great End 10
Lingmoor Fell 5
Pike o' Blisco 5, 6
Rossett Pike 6
Scafell Pike 19

ELTERWATER
Lingmoor Fell 7

ESKDALE
(incl. BOOT, BROTHERILKELD, ESKDALE GREEN, TAW HOUSE, WHA HOUSE and WOOLPACK INN)
Bowfell 8
Crinkle Crags 8
Esk Pike 7
Green Crag 3
Harter Fell 6
Scafell 11–12
Scafell Pike 21–22
Slight Side 2
Whin Rigg 6

HARDKNOTT PASS
Hard Knott 5
Harter Fell 7

HODGE CLOSE
Holme Fell 3

HOLME GROUND
Holme Fell 3

LITTLE LANGDALE
Great Carrs 5
Lingmoor Fell 8
Pike o' Blisco 7
Swirl How 5
Wetherlam 9

NETHER WASDALE
Whin Rigg 5

OXEN FELL
Holme Fell 3

ROSTHWAITE
Glaramara 5

SEATHWAITE/SEATOLLER
Allen Crags 4
Esk Pike 9
Glaramara 5
Great End 6
Great End 9
Scafell Pike 15–16, 17–18
Seathwaite Fell 3

SKELWITH BRIDGE
Black Fell 3

STONETHWAITE
(incl. LANGSTRATH)
Bowfell 9
Glaramara 6
Rosthwaite Fell 4

SUNNY BROW
Black Fell 3

TARN HOWS
Black Fell 3

TILBERTHWAITE
Wetherlam 10, 11

TORVER
Coniston Old Man 9
Dow Crag 7

WASDALE HEAD
Bowfell 6
Esk Pike 8
Great End 6, 8
Illgill Head 6
Lingmell 5, 6
Scafell 10
Scafell Pike 13, 14

WRYNOSE BOTTOM
Cold Pike 2
Grey Friar 7

WRYNOSE PASS
Cold Pike 2
Crinkle Crags 10
Great Carrs 5
Grey Friar 7
Pike o' Blisco 8

YEW TREE FARM
Holme Fell 3